CW00739338

The **Guardian**
Political Almanac
1993/4

David McKie

Fourth Estate ● London

First published in Great Britain by
Fourth Estate Limited
289 Westbourne Grove
London W11 2QA

Copyright © 1993 Guardian Newspapers Ltd
A catalogue record for this book is available from the British Library

ISBN 1-85702-157-6

All rights reserved. No part of this publication may be reproduced
transmitted or stored in a retrieval system, in any form or by any means,
without permission in writing from Fourth Estate Limited

Designed and produced: by Gary Phillips with Jane and Rik Gadsby and Dan
Bindman, The Guardian, London
Editor: Clive Graham-Ranger
Researcher: Dan Bindman
Picture research: Georgina Fagelson.
Photographs: Katz Pictures, Syndication International, Guzelian Photography, Peter
Grant, Frank Martin, Kenneth Saunders, Sportsphoto, Enterprise News and Pictures,
Graham Turner, Associated Press, Don McPhee, E Hamilton West, Network, Universal
Pictorial Press
Acknowledgements for their assistance Simon Beavis, Owen Bowcott, Alex
Brummer, Duncan Campbell, Malcolm Dean, James Erlichman, David Fairhall, John
Gittings, Keith Harper, Georgina Henry, Victor Keegan, Helen Martin and staff of the
Guardian Library, James Meikle, Rebecca Smithers, Jo Swain, John Vidal

Printed in Great Britain by Cambridge University Press

CONTENTS

For E C B SMITH

From the Marquis of Salisbury to John Major

PREFACE

This book is modelled on the Guardian Guide to the General Election 1992. The purpose is the same: to assemble under one roof as much information as possible about the political year just ended and the political year to come. As in that model of reference books, Wisden, we have sought to season the facts and figures with argument, entertainment and, I hope, some wit and good writing.

The mixture is intended to change year by year. This edition is still coloured by the last election: subsequent ones will reflect the imminence of the next one. We have not, for instance, included an account of the recommendations of the boundary commissioners for altering parliamentary constituencies because past experience suggests that almost three-quarters of their recommendations for change will later be varied.

David McKie

July 30 1993

INTRODUCTION

John Biffen

It has been a period of momentous change. After an unexpected election victory the fortunes of the Government have fallen like Lucifer. In the light of the Newbury and Christchurch results no Tory seat is safe in a by-election, and the county council elections in May strongly suggest that Labour and Liberal voters are learning the attractions of tactical voting. This more than anything else puts a shadow over John Major's further victory in 1996. These ministerial misfortunes have been compounded by reluctant Cabinet departures, David Mellor in disgrace and Norman Lamont in acrimony.

And yet must it all end in Tory tears? At long last the Maastricht treaty has been ratified. The alliance of conviction and convenience between Tory sceptics and Labour will soon pass into memory and eventually folklore. The furore over political funding and the activities of Asil Nadir will do likewise — but the televised clash of Colonel Michael Mates and Madam Speaker must surely last for all time.

It is economic recovery on which the Government now depends. At last there are tangible signs that departure from the Exchange Rate Mechanism has led to some recovery following the fall in exchange and domestic interest rates. Both John Smith and Gordon Brown have been effective in arguing Labour's economic case, but the going may get more difficult.

The Government needs time, above all, to enable the economic recovery to be translated into political convalescence. To this end all of Westminster's oratory will matter little alongside the no-confidence debate decision of nine Ulster Unionist MPs to support the Government. That simple act — at a stroke — doubled the Government's majority. "Nothing was asked, nothing was offered, nothing was given." Truly an Irish bargain.

The Guardian Political Almanac is an excellent guide to a political year that can reasonably be interpreted as both a Shakespearian drama and a Byzantine court. Twenty six sections cover the main areas of activity. They are succinct and well-researched and are much more than a compendium of events.

Will Hutton predictably makes a lively interpretation of economic events and the chapter on Maastricht is a model of restrained and fair analysis. And for those who, in these dark days, weary of Wisden, there are all those Westminster statistics.

July 30 1993

Lest we forget: Baroness Thatcher may have become one of them, but the spectre of her policies continued to loom over the party she ruled with an iron grip

LINGERING LEGACY OF
THE IRON LADY

Hugo Young

The night before Norman Lamont was fired from the Treasury, May 26 1993, I called on a minister few people have heard of. A cerebral fellow, he was not among those summoned to the cameras to slag off John Major's encircling enemies, though his time will come. Even before the little earthquake next day, the Government was in its usual many-sided chaos, but he made a sanguine remark. "We all know what we are about," he said. "Everyone in the Government knows what the central project is, and there's no argument about it."

Immured in a great department beyond the limelight, he sounded out of touch. But distance, I later saw, has something to offer the truth. It helps isolate the nature of Major's problem. This is not, essentially, about high ideas but low politics. It is not about his purposes but his methods. Seen from his seat, this may be a comfort. It exposes the hysterical, and therefore perhaps disposable, quality of the battles surrounding him. But it also shapes the deeper menace he confronts.

What most people in the Government know they care about has a simple, though universally rejected, name. Their project is the pursuit of Thatcherism by other means. The old Thatcherites repudiate this because their heroine has gone, the Majorites because it suits them to call the 1990s a new age. Norman Tebbit would disdain to grace anything now happening with the Thatcher name. Major himself insists he has moved beyond it, and the speeches of allies such as David Hunt, the employment secretary, are sometimes put to service by headline writers wishing to say that Thatcherism is dead. But the inheritance of the lady has a continuing existence, in two vital dimensions. It is what binds modern Conservatives' ideology. At the same time, it incapacitates their politics.

Look at the Major Government's programme and see where it comes from. Its salient measures have a clear origin. Its 1993 Act bashing trade union power is the seventh since 1980. Privatising British Rail, with a promise of the Post Office to follow, continues Thatcherism's most distinctive invention. Imposing central state power in school classrooms is something that began more than five years ago. Everything happening in the NHS was foreshadowed then as well. The contracting out of public service, which will soon give "Whitehall" the same anachronistic status as "Fleet Street", accelerates relentlessly from a slow start in the Thatcher era.

This was iconoclastic stuff. It created the environment in which similar assaults on sacred cows can proceed with credibility. Before the Thatcher age, it would have been impossible to conduct the kind of debate about welfare cuts now under way. By comparison with such seismic shifts in the landscape of the plausible, Major's distinctive contributions are forgettably meagre: a council tax that almost reinvents the rates, and a citizen's charter that most people regard as a joke.

Nor is the economic policy counter-Thatcherite either. Low income tax is still god, low inflation still the holy grail, and a balanced budget the target, however remote now, to which other policies are supposed to bend. There has been difficulty in keeping the economy under control, but that was part of Thatcherism as well. The large point is that on all these big policies there is no big argument. The orthodoxy prevails, above all in the Cabinet. Lamont's supplanting by Kenneth Clarke had no impact on that. Clarke, like Lamont, is a functionary of Thatcherism in its pragmatic phase.

Even over Europe the Thatcher link prevailed. It was Major's ultra-Thatcherite line that earned him such acclaim after the Maastricht summit. He had the foresight to do what she had neglected to contemplate during negotiation of the Single European Act: see what the treaty meant and exclude Britain from the parts the Tory party would not wear. His Europeanism grew directly out of the decade in which the prime minister, while pushing Britain further in, educated the British people to believe in all the nightmares about Europe that Major was subsequently forced to take account of.

His performance at Maastricht, therefore, was, by universal agreement, critical. He himself thought it the high point of his pre-election premiership. And he won the election.

This personal triumph, against the apparent odds, seemed to confirm the wisdom of his selection: which lay, to put it precisely, in the political talents he personally brought to making Thatcherism electable. On the Thatcher agenda, with a few exceptions, every minister and candidate agreed. And now, behind this faintly improbable figure, their trick had worked.

So what went wrong? The answer lies in the contradictions that have finally got the better of the party and their leader. It has less to do with what he wants than what he is. It makes for the unavoidable conclusion that the very reason Major was chosen, his political persona and skills, turns out to be the weakness that may be his undoing. This is where the political frailty of the Thatcher legacy becomes as prominent as its ideological strength.

Part of this is hardly Major's fault. There's not much he can do about the rancour of the dispossessed. The last election returned, in some cases for the fourth time, MPs bitter at not having jobs and with few ties of loyalty to a leader whom, in their ignorance, they had put in power. Mistaking the importance of substance over style, they had thought him as crudely Thatcherite as they were, and couldn't forgive him their own misjudgment. A cohort of reckless enemies formed, many viciously disappointed ex-ministers among them, and the first Danish referendum on Maastricht, in June 1992, gave them a cause that obliterated any gratitude they may have felt when Major got them elected just two months before. The acrid Euro-argument, originally designed to be short and sharp, continues to course through the party and bedevil such periods of relative calm Major momentarily enjoys.

Two other factors overlaid the Thatcherist accord, of which he once seemed such an acceptable exponent. First, the recession lingered on, wrecking economic confidence and making liars of every minister who got elected by promising it was over. Second, the parliamentary majority, standing at 20 rather than 100, radically shifted the terms of political trade. Together these constraints redoubled the premium on a talent for sheer politics: the heavyweight wisdom needed to secure popular consent for unpopular measures, and make the right choices.

What goes to make up this wisdom in autumn 1993 depends on what you think is happening. The common illusion is that this is a post-Thatcherite world. But if what is happening is in fact the pursuit of Thatcherism, there is a problem. The old iconoclasm has lost its iconoclastic leader. It is pursued, instead, by a man whose main desire is to be liked as Consensus Man, and who faces problems, from the need for welfare cuts to the smell of corruption — another Thatcherite bequest — wafting around Tory party finances, to which his qualities are not well matched. His predicament reminds us that Thatcher, for all her screaming weaknesses, was often an effective low politician, whose style matched her project. Equally, it cannot help making Tories look again at what happened when Major was elected to succeed her — and what might happen if the experience was repeated.

In the 1990 field were two politicians of superior stature, and neither of them was Major. If Conservative MPs had understood how well the orthodoxy was established — why it is that ministers, despite everything, still think they know what they are about — maybe their choice would have fallen to one of the men who were always less likely to be knocked about as an unimprovable lightweight than was Major throughout 1993. But Douglas Hurd and Michael Heseltine were unelectable. They had the weight, they couldn't have unmade the orthodoxy, they were stronger leaders for the politics of the 1990s. But the Thatcher factor meant they didn't have a chance.

As a result, the greatest deficiency of Thatcherism stands exposed: the generation of weak politicians it produced. The leaders of this generation turned out to be Major and Lamont. Lamont's resignation speech, pinning blame on everyone except himself but most of all on the man who decided he was expendable, was a cameo of the times. Speaking one after the other, these one-time close associates performed a grisly pas de deux, each trying vainly to shake off the other's deadly embrace.

The truth is that Lamont was an over-promoted chancellor. He was the best Major could afford to have, given the circumstances of his election. Even Major knew as much. If Chris Patten had held Bath, Lamont would have been offered alternative accommodation and this particular crisis might not have happened. His policies were not indefensible, even his remaining in the ERM. But he was judged a man who could not be believed in. City, party and press ridiculed his judgment, private as well as public. Acceptable to the keepers of the Thatcherite flame, his survival was less a measure of their power than of the pitifully thin talent at their disposal after 15 years in control of the party.

Major has a similar provenance. A larger man than Lamont, he did, inextinguishably, win an election. The British people saw something in him, even if the Tories don't: a point he often alluded to as his personal poll-rating dipped below 20 per cent during the summer. But one thing he shrinks from being is bloody tough.

Lauded as the 1990s' natural successor to the woman of the 1980s, he seems, by contrast, the wrong man at the wrong time. He owed his election to a delusion: that the age of Thatcherism was over. In fact, for want of anything better, Thatcherism lives: and for its survival needs a leader possessed of raw strength and cruel skills, to match the massive problems these unbroken years have given rise to.

Never was the absence of such commodities more clear than at the moment the curtain came down on the limp partnership. It was as if Major wanted to maximise our insight into each partner's problems, but especially his own. Instead of a wide reshuffle, disposing of two or three other ministers who were plainly below par, his performance called attention to the self-mutilation inherent in sacking the one minister whose record called in question his own. Lamont's replacement then sealed the effect of his departure. In Kenneth Clarke it brought to the Treasury a man who personifies better than any other politician the paradoxical requirements of the mid-1990s: a reformed wet, who was a key player in the eviction of Mrs Thatcher, but honed his profile and proved his talent for ministerial brutality to the satisfaction of a sceptical constituency on the other wing of the party.

Moving towards autumn, Major faced the real season of political conflict. Maastricht continues to leak its poison. But the budget and public spending will provoke the fiercest combat. The same disputes between colleagues and worries in the party that have assailed every leader in every time and country have to be mediated and settled. With the deficit at £50 billion, the assault on public services will need a rigour to delight the severest Thatcherites, even though tax rises beckon as well.

Such a choice, however, is exactly what government is about. We are not living with Labour ministers canvassing the alternative merits of a command economy, or Tory factions disputing the importance of M3. I return to my cerebral informant. All ministers agree the central project, whichever side of the Maastricht barricades they come from. They will fight for their own budgets. There will be anguish about the fate of many sets of losers. But the onward effort is about objectives no Tory disputes: reducing government, cutting the public sector, targeting public services, keeping inflation down, trying to lower taxes.

These are political tasks of a very conventional kind. They have nothing to do with ideology. They do not ask the questions the more paranoid Tories continue to push about Europe. So in a way, Major's task should be easier than it sounds every time he turns on the television news. This is nothing like the Thatcher period, circa 1981, when every other minister would come out of a

Cabinet meeting and tell one the lady was a lunatic bent on bringing Britain to the brink of civil war.

On the other hand, it makes Major deeply vulnerable. The reason he was chosen no longer holds. The defence of Thatcherism no longer rests in his exclusive hands. On the contrary, it is suspected by many Conservatives of different stripes that he may be incapable of doing it, and sustaining their hegemony. If all can agree that this is the task, many may begin to understand that it is better done by a man with a larger mind, a broader bottom and a cold unfeeling soul.●

Sara Dale was put out on the street by her landlord, Norman Lamont, but he hung on grimly to No 11 until he was reshuffled out of the Treasury and on to the back benches

BALANCING ABOVE THE ABYSS

Will Hutton

By the summer of 1993 the prospects for the British economy looked more promising than for some time — even though the starting point was scarcely satisfactory and the continuing structural problems were immense. Inflation at 1.2 per cent was near a 30-year low; unemployment, at 2.91 million, had begun to fall much sooner than in previous economic cycles, and had fallen for five consecutive months; and manufacturing was growing at an annual rate of some 6 per cent — having recovered around half of the output lost during the recession. Devaluation, cheap money and a large budget deficit were proving once again their durability as economic stimulants. The emerging consensus was that overall output would grow at close to 2 per cent in 1993, probably accelerating into 1994.

Yet the legacy of the 1980s continued to dog the recovery. Consumption, private and public, was still far too high as a proportion of national output; and that had created an industrial base that serviced an unsustainable level of domestic spending rather than international markets. Manufacturing, at 19 per cent of GDP, had shrunk further and farther than in other industrialised countries — and this was reflected in an escalating balance of payments deficit. Britain has shopping malls and offices aplenty; but too few significant companies with a commanding market share in domestic and foreign markets.

For although exports rose strongly, powered by the products from new factories built by overseas investors, imports rose even faster. With free movement of capital in a world capital market, the conventional orthodoxy was that the resulting balance of payments deficit did not matter as a constraint upon economic growth, since it could be comfortably financed. Yet after six years of deficits and no prospect of balance in the foreseeable future, such optimism could prove misplaced. And were foreigners to lose their confidence in sterling assets, there would be a collapse both in sterling and in the price of the bonds, shares and assets they held.

Yet it was difficult to see how the transfer of resources into economic activity that competed both in overseas markets and at home against imports was going to be achieved without further depreciation of the exchange rate — or without a sustained period of low interest rates to stimulate investment. Equally, businesses needed to see the prospect of reasonable levels of demand both at home and abroad before they were ready to undertake risky investment. And with key European markets still in the depths of recession, and the scope for EC governments to stimulate recovery constrained by their commitment to the ERM and the Maastricht treaty, it was not clear how rapid any improvement in the European market might be.

Paradoxically the struggle to give some semblance of balance to the recovery was actually being helped by some of the by-products of the 1980s' boom. Such was Britain's overhang of debt and disillusion that one of the long wayward trends in the British economy, excessive consumption, was at last under assault. British recoveries have nearly all been driven largely by consumer spending. And consumption had indeed risen over the 12 months to mid-1993. But so unusually had exports — and investment was flattening out sooner, with manufacturing investment rising earlier and faster than after the last two recessions. This promised, in short, to be one of the more balanced UK recoveries.

In particular, the housing market, which had destabilised the economy throughout the 1970s and 1980s, was more subdued and likely to stay that way. As a result, the feel-good effect of rising house prices on consumer confidence, and the direct withdrawal of equity from the housing market to support spending, promised to be less than in the 1980s. That opened up the prospect of the Government being able to keep interest rates down without re-igniting either inflation or the housing market.

Although prices for quality houses had firmed in premium districts, the mass of the housing market remained trapped in negative equity, excessive mortgages and lost confidence. Indeed, one analysis of the market argued that the overhang of unsold houses was now so great that even if mortgage demand returned to the boom levels of the 1980s, prices would slip until 1995 — with a still worse performance if confidence remained weak.

So a depressed housing market, combined with extraordinary growth in productivity (up 8.7 per cent over the three months to the end of May compared with the previous three) and falling unit labour costs (down 3.6 per cent on the same basis) to make the inflationary impact of devaluation much less than had been feared even six months before. And world inflation, as much an influence on British price increases as any domestic cost pressure, was even more depressed — with the oil price in real terms back to the levels of the early 1970s.

So consumers were cautious and looking for bargains; and inflation was held at bay. The Great British Consumer and the Great British Inflation had — temporarily at least — ceased to haunt the economic feast. The emerging economic opportunity was thus considerable. If European markets were weak the recovery in North America was becoming better established, and Asia was turning. Even in Europe there was evidence that Germany was over the worst. As long as sterling remained competitive, the upward trend in exports looked likely to continue.

With no exchange or capital controls, the only way any rise in sterling could be headed off was by further reductions in interest rates; but as long as the housing market and consumption remained depressed, such cuts would not necessarily trigger the inflation the Government feared. Even when, as seemed likely, underlying inflation (retail price inflation less housing costs) surpassed the Government's absurd upper 4 per cent target ceiling, the Government seemed likely to remain relaxed, confident that it would not go much higher. Interest rates of 5 per cent, even of 4 per cent, looked within grasp as sterling rose.

Thus, wholly accidentally, Britain found itself confronting a period of cheap money, spare capacity, a turning world economy and a competitive exchange rate — and all with inflationary dangers the lowest for a generation. Equally, with government borrowing highly sensitive to changes in the growth rate, the higher-than-expected rate of output bred hope that the public sector borrowing requirement might not after all reach the feared £50 billion in 1993/94 — and might very well fall to £40 billion or lower in 1994/95.

If short-term economic statistics alone were the determinant of political fortunes, John Major's Conservatives would have had every right to boast about recovery. Unhappily, though, the underlying structure of the British economy remained as anti-production and pro-consumption as ever. The strategic task from now on had to be to capitalise on the new, benign conjuncture so that the switch of resources into exports and investment could continue — with any further rise in consumption remaining subdued.

To make that work the Conservative party would have to attack the interests of its own constituency and embrace the interests of producers as much as consumers and the service sector. Already in his final budget (March 1993) Norman Lamont found himself announcing tax increases that would ultimately yield some £10 billion a year. During the public spending round in the autumn of 1992 he sought to boost investment by borrowing Labour's idea of temporarily increasing capital allowances. This was a trend that his successor, Kenneth Clarke, looked destined to follow.

Unlike Messrs Maudling, Barber and Lawson, Clarke did not have the option of launching a consumer boom via tax cuts and a relaxation of credit controls, though that course might have unleashed a rise in house prices, warming hearts throughout the Conservatives' 200 seats in the Home Counties. But there were no credit controls left to relax, and taxes were destined to rise rather than fall.

The warning signals were lighting up even as ministers hailed the recovery. Some companies which insisted on pay freezes a year before were rewarding their workforces with increases well above inflation. And a financial system racked by bad debts and its traditional aversion to supporting long-term production and investment threatened to force producers to exploit their competitive advantage by raising prices rather than output.

The banking system remained fixated by property lending, while the workforces in those sectors of the economy sheltered from international competition were looking to restore their lost earning power now the recession was over. The structures which had ensured that every British recovery since the war was biased to inflation and consumption rather than production remained securely in place — and blessed by the doctrine of deregulation, tax cuts and non-intervention. And the size of the balance of payments deficit was a constant reminder of the gaping hole that existed in many areas of Britain's productive capacity.

The task was to construct international comparative advantage and create a self-sustaining manufacturing sector of small and medium-sized firms. But for that, the Government would have to build on its change of heart, intervening purposefully in the economy and creating new institutions and structures. Banking, training, research and development, export promotion — all needed change and revitalisation.

Thus the next few years are especially difficult to predict. The optimists point to subdued inflation and the hope that excessive consumer debt will allow the Government to lower interest rates much further and for longer than ever before — so stimulating investment and keeping sterling competitive. The pessimists say that little structural in the British economy has changed, and if the upturn does prove to be enduring, it will sooner or later re-ignite inflation and consumption. After all, low interest rates have always triggered rises in house prices. It may take longer for the housing market to respond — but sooner or later it will. And Britain will enter another destabilising upturn.

From the Government's point of view, recovery may produce less political relief than it supposes. It can hardly claim credit for events whose foundations it resolutely opposed, especially now that it has to reverse what it stands for to sustain it. Tax increases, depressing consumption, moving resources to exports and investment require determination and imply austerity. Can Major's Conservative party deliver its own transformation without irretrievable splits? On that, the direction of politics over the next few years hangs.●

WHAT'S IN STORE FOR '94?

Michael White

On the face of it 1994 held out better prospects for the long-suffering and dis-appointed British people than at any time since the economy first faltered in 1989, then stumbled over the edge into recession during the Kuwait-dominated summer of 1990.

By general consent the Great Deflation had been a grim chapter. Factories had closed in seemingly endless succession. Swathes of businesses, the fruit of the supply-side revolution of the 1980s, had gone bust. Every high street had boarded-up shops, every shopping centre jobless and aimless teenagers.

Houses, most Britons' favourite one-way bet, lost their value and were unsaleable or repossessed. People spoke of something called "negative equity". Above all, *hope* had been dashed — along with the self-confidence of the southern middle classes who had, for once, taken their share of the beating . . .

It remained to be seen whether the beneficiaries of recovery would include the man who had headed the Queen's government throughout the hangover that followed the Thatcher-Lawson binge. By the time MPs headed for the hills and beaches after the most disastrous post-election session in recent memory at the end of July, it was not clear to some old hands whether John Major would last another parliament, another year — or be gone by September.

The extent of public bitterness and disaffection was shown by the Government's successive by-election humiliations in prosperous Newbury and Christchurch, compounded by a more-than-usually painful thrashing in the summer's Test series against Australia. True, Jonathan Foster had done unexpectedly well at a rain-free Wimbledon and had not England's sportsmen been defeated by the United States at football once before — 40 years earlier? But the reserves of national self-esteem were lower at this stage in the cycle, just as the trade deficit was higher.

The case for the ministerial optimists was best put by the likes of the irrepressible new chancellor, Kenneth Clarke and — before his heart attack in June — by Michael Heseltine, who had been re-shaping the Department of Trade and Industry into his own version of a sophisticated support system for British industry in the competitive 1990s.

"The fundamentals of the economy are in much better shape than they were after the 1981 recession," he would tell listeners. "We have a far more entrepreneurial culture, many more small businesses, far more disposable income in the hands of the risk-takers." Unlike his predecessor, the gloomily

Nordic Norman Lamont, Clarke also sounded like a man who still got eight hours sleep.

Though ministers were cautious after spotting premature green shoots in 1991-92, the statistics seemed to bear their optimism out. In the wake of the enforced devaluation of sterling in September 1992, exports rose 15 per cent by volume, manufacturing productivity at an annualised rate of 10.5 per cent, output on the same basis at a rate of 6 per cent. Low interest rates were not threatened by renewed inflation. Above all, unemployment started falling far quicker than past experience predicted. Export-led growth without over-heating! It was the long-sought holy grail — if they could pull it off.

But for Major, pottering around Downing Street and through Huntingdon before his summer holiday in Portugal, the calendar remained full of dates with red circles round them — red for danger. A touch optimistically, conventional wisdom argued that he would be safe until after the European Community's five-yearly elections for the Strasbourg parliament in June 1994 — or at the very least until the local elections on May 5.

The Tories had taken a beating in the recent local elections, almost to the point where the pendulum could scarcely swing much further. "My activists won't care if the Euro-candidate goes down the pan. They will mind losing more councillors. In which case they'll either blame Major or my big mouth," one Euro-rebel observed. As for the Strasbourg contest, 1989 had been an informal referendum on late Thatcherism which turned a Tory lead of 60 seats to Labour's 17 in 1984, into a 45-32 seat win for Neil Kinnock, with 40.1 to 34.7 per cent of the vote. With the Maastricht trauma behind him, the Tory Euro-sceptics finally, if belatedly, forced to heel and Lady Thatcher's referendum plea trampled in the dust, Major should have looked far better placed than she had been in 1989. At the head of a reunited party, he could exploit the voters' gut anti-federalism combined with its feeling that "the heart of Europe" was the safest place — like Whoopi Goldberg hiding in a nunnery — in which to indulge these feelings.

But Maastricht had left the prime minister's party brutally divided. Loyalists wanted retribution meted out to the 23 hardcore rebels who had defied the three line whip to put the social chapter (briefly) into limbo on July 22. Major and, most forcefully, Douglas Hurd, wanted conciliation. So did leading rebels like Bill Cash, who confidently expected to be fending off pro-social chapter litigation in the courts and creeping federalist directives from the Brussels Commission —the reverse of Lord Rees-Mogg's mid-summer bid to have British ratification declared unconstitutional.

Cash and his allies also wanted to make sure that the informal links between Tory MEPs and the pan-EC European Peoples' Party did not produce a flagrantly federalist Euro-manifesto. All in all there was plenty of scope for continuous guerrilla warfare, with domination of the party conference in Blackpool on October 5-8 the immediate prize.

In 1992 it had taken all Hurd's authority to contain a Tebbit-led insurgency from the floor. This year the platform faced the added distraction of the imminent publication of the Thatcher memoirs, expected to be as self-justificatory as any since Napoleon's. Even now not every Tory was convinced she was writing from Elba rather than St Helena.

Major's allies clung to the hope that John Smith's conference problems, one member one vote (OMOV) and proportional representation (PR), would prove worse. It was no longer a hope to be relied on. Smith had endured a turbulent first year, disappointing to many. But he had not yet lost control of his agenda, nor fallen out with potential Liberal Democrat allies. He had not embraced them either.

The Tory fight over Maastricht had also encouraged the habits as well as organisational skills of factionalism. Scarcely was the vote of confidence won by 339 to 299 with the help of Jim Molyneaux's official Ulster Unionist Party (UUP) than some senior Tories began fretting over right-wing economic populists — not all of them the same anti-Maastricht rebels.

They threatened to adopt similar tactics to force the Treasury to cut public spending rather than raise taxes in its efforts to contain the projected £50 billion public deficit. It was the backdrop for the first unified tax-and-spend budget scheduled for November 30, a Lamont innovation borrowed from Smith and inherited by Clarke.

Here again the omens looked brighter for ministers as they braced themselves for the year ahead. If the recovery was stronger, then tax receipts would be more buoyant and social security payments lower than feared. Clarke and his deputy, Michael Portillo, ambitious men whose ambitions were compatible on grounds of age if not ideology, had set a tough 1993-94 spending round: to stay within limits prescribed the previous year.

All summer long kite-flying exercises had been under way to test what the voters would stand, everything from old favourites like "hotel charges" for staying in hospital, season tickets for prescriptions and an end to mortgage tax relief to new heresies such as broadening the Vat base to include food, children's clothing, books and newspapers.

Though he made boisterously disrespectful noises about the pound rejoining the ERM, the new chancellor also kept his options open on the greatest Thatcherite heresy of all: raising direct taxes, perhaps as a temporary expedient. In any case, direct taxes were due to rise under Lamont's poison pill budget in March 1993: higher national insurance contributions and lower allowances amounted to the same thing.

Another kite suggested that broadening the Vat base could reopen another politically popular option: cancelling the second half of Lamont's imposition of Vat on domestic heat and fuel bills, the first 8.5 per cent tranche of which was due to go on bills from April 1, just in time to annoy voters before the local elections.

Whatever he did would take place against a background of strategic reviews in major Whitehall spending departments; Home Office, Defence, Education and Social Security having been singled out first by Portillo. His ally, Peter Lilley, meanwhile wrestled with Smith's Commission on Social Justice to control the debate on the cost of the welfare state: universalism v targeting, private v public and the growing EC-wide burden of an ageing population: Europe as Bournemouth, as one wit put it.

For Major there was opportunity in all of this. Yet his unsure handling of the past year's controversies and his lack of a clear ideological message to the faithful helped demoralise a party spoiled by a decade of glory.

With Lamont gone, there were no reshuffles left which would make much difference to a flagging cabinet — except the Big One. Plenty of MPs felt that if party chairman, Norman Fowler, and chief whip, Richard Ryder, both trusted intimates, told him the game was up, Major — unlike Heath or Thatcher — would quit rather than be pushed.

What would do it? Who could say? Heseltine's famous formula in the years of exile, that he could "foresee no circumstances" in which he would challenge Margaret Thatcher, perfectly illustrated the unpredictable nature of politics in an era where most institutions of the state seemed to be tottering at one moment or another: monarchy and BBC, Lloyd's and the Grand National, the Treasury, the Stock Exchange's new computer . . . were they symptoms of systemic crisis or of turbulent renewal?

As the coal crisis showed, anything could trigger a final bust-up for Major, whose best card was the lack of a clear, consensual successor, which Clarke was not. More trouble in former Yugoslavia? Rail or coal privatisation folly? The law and order issue, no longer a Tory monopoly thanks to Tony Blair and the Sheehy report's yuppie views on police management? Hydra-headed Europe, or Ireland?

The latter also highlighted Major's dilemma. In buying off the nine UUP votes with hints, chats and promises he might have doubled his de facto majority from 18 to 36 rather than merely doing a shrewd day's work. Old hands such as John Biffen seemed to think so at the time. But the price of an "Orange-Con Pact", heir to Callaghan's Lib-Lab-Orange version, might be the destabilising of Northern Ireland — angering Washington as well as Dublin and Brussels.

As with the EC-US tensions over Bosnia, Somalia and Russia, there was no telling where it all might end in the new world of post cold-war uncertainty that had grown up since 1989.

At home a much darker scenario hovered, almost unmentionable in polite society, but one which could threaten and, one day, overthrow the cosy assumptions of the political elites and time-honoured calculations eroded by relative economic decline and the collapse of old certainties. Violent crime in the street, vigilantism in rural villages, dwindling faith in justice and large armies of young men, unwilling or unable to work to support the children they fathered: these were just some of the troubling symptoms.

There was still much evidence of Orwell's stoic, gentler England in the lives of most citizens, and some grounds for careful optimism. But without hope it did not require a visionary to see where those sort of trends might end. With Thatcher gone, it was hard to see who could face down a British le Pen, or worse, if things did not improve. Certainly not nice, pragmatic John Major. If he needed luck, so did the country.●

VIEWS FROM THE GALLERY

Andrew Rawnsley

Tiller girl takes the helm

Betty Boothroyd was "dragged" to the Chair in the traditional way which dates back to the days when the job was as fraught with peril as being chairman of British Rail or manager of the England football team. But for the first time in seven centuries the drag act was not also a reference to the Speaker's taste in dress. The House of Commons had elected a 155th Speaker who, like every predecessor wore blonde curls and black stockings but, unlike any of them, was a woman.

As the first Madam Speaker was pushed towards her new hot seat, she was immediately confronted with her first test in maintaining the etiquette of Erskine May. MPs, new and old, supporters and opponents, stood and burst out clapping. Five years training as deputy Speaker told her to put a stop to this breach with decorum instantly. Five seconds as Miss Speaker told her to enjoy the moment.

"Order! Order!" she eventually cried, another pretty show of mock reluctance. Show, of course, it was. Just about everybody reminded us that there had not been a contest for the job since 1951. The usual cocktail of excitement on the first parliamentary day after a general election was laced with an extra upper. There was squashing room only as in crowded MPs, the returned jostling with the retreaded scrumming with the untested. New faces sat in familiar places. Old faces sat in unfamiliar places. Sir Edward Heath, at last experiencing fatherhood at the age of 75, hugely enjoyed presiding over the Commons. His tails waggled and his shoulders belly-heaved with such satisfied pleasure that for a moment you thought Ted might even decide to nominate himself for Speaker.

Black Rod arrived to begin the ritual by summoning MPs to the Lords, which prompted the next and equally traditional part of the ancient ceremony: an intervention from Dennis Skinner, re-elected without opposition as Mr Heckler. "If you stay here long enough," Heckler barked at Rod, "you'll get nominated for Speaker."

Black Rod grabbed Father Ted and led MPs off in a bridal procession to the Lords. John Major gave Neil Kinnock a pat on the back. After Kinnock, and after his job, walked John Smith and Bryan Gould in jovial conversation, to show the world that they were the best of friends. But when they arrived back in the Commons, Margaret Beckett came and sat between them on the Labour front bench, breaking up this beautiful rivalry.

Heath then explained the rules for electing the Speaker, which were almost as complicated and confused as those for electing the leader of the Labour Party. But the rules for those making speeches turned out to be surprisingly simple. The first rule was that it was mandatory for the candidates' sponsors to alternate glowing tributes with constant references to what a desperately awful life it was being Speaker.

"The loneliest job in parliament," said Sir Michael Neubert, who wanted the honour for Peter Brooke. The Speaker had to control both mutinous back-benchers and overweening front benchers.

The terrible powers of Charles I now resided in the hands of Citizen John, warned Tony Benn, who wanted Boothroyd as his protector. All reminded us that nine previous occupants of the Chair had died violently. Innocent observers, unacquainted with parliamentary ritual, might have wondered why anybody should want a job which combined the danger of bungee-jumping with the tedium of train-spotting.

And the second rule was that the contenders should pretend that they really did not want it at all. The former Northern Ireland secretary compared himself to the King of the Matabele who had addressed Queen Victoria with the words: "We are but as the lice on the edge of Your Majesty's blanket." The former Tiller Girl also humbled herself, but to more effect. "I have been a deputy Speaker, but I have always at heart been a backbencher"— reminding the majority of voters she was one of them.

She did not want the Chair as an exercise in positive discrimination for women or a consolation prize for the Labour party. "Elect me for what I am, not for what I was born." And they did.

Having broken seven centuries of precedent by her election, she promised to "preserve and cherish the traditions of the House". As if to prove it, her first act in the Chair was to take a bogus point of order from Tony Banks, re-electing himself as Mr Jester. He was anxious to explain that he had intended to vote for her, but got himself locked out of the division lobbies and was desperate for Madam Speaker's forgiveness.

When he next seeks to catch her all-powerful eye, he will know whether he has got it.

April 28, 1992

The Lady is for ermine

In the House of Lords yesterday afternoon they at last made a Lady out of Margaret Thatcher. She paraded into the mock-Gothic slap and tickle of the Upper House dressed in scarlet, gold braid and black cap, the pelts of several small animals hanging from her shoulders, like a cross between Little Red Riding Hood and the wolf. In poop-deck hats, Lord Boyd-Carpenter, her first ministerial boss, and Lord Joseph, her ideological guru, marched fore and aft, like two tugs guiding an old liner to its final harbour.

The shore was crowded. The Lords has not been as packed since . . . well, since the last debate on grouse shooting. Around the throne there was standing room only — although this may just have been a wise precaution when she came to look for a seat. On the red leather benches there was walking stick room only.

Sir Denis gazed from above as she knelt to present her writ of patent to the Lord Chancellor; a moment to gaze around the spray-on gold leaf and old master wallpaper of this plushest of retirement homes. The Lords may be proof that there is life after political death, but it is still only a half-life. Staring out at her were the whitened hair and wizened features of political ghosties, ghoulies and ministers she made go bump in the night.

As that all too familiar voice intoned the Loyal Oath, a little shiver went up the old wet spine of Lord Pym, withdrawing his tortoise-like head into his shoulders.

The clerk read out the Patent. "Elizabeth II, by the grace of God . . ." Lord Callaghan was descending into a deep sulk, clearly thinking that they were letting in anybody these days. ". . . Advance, create and prefer our trusty and well-beloved counsellor Margaret Hilda Thatcher . . ." Lord Whitelaw gently rolled those weary oyster eyes at what she might do to their sleepy, exquisitely well-mannered club where noblesse was still oblige. ". . . To the state, degree, title and honour of Baroness Thatcher of Kesteven."

Lord Hailsham seemed to enjoy a private joke. As a commoner, she might have behaved like a duchess; as a peer, she would be a mere baroness. The clerk unrolled more parchment containing the writ of summons. "Whereas our parliament, for arduous and urgent affairs concerning us, the state and the defence of the United Kingdom . . ." (this was composed before the Maastricht treaty) ". . . is now met at our city of Westminster, we command you . . ." (she clutched her repeat-action handbag to her side) ". . . that considering the difficulty of the said affairs and dangers impending, you may be personally present at our aforesaid parliament to treat and give your counsel." Try stopping her.

The Wrought Iron Peer rose and bowed. The Lord Chancellor doffed his tricorn. Her sponsors doffed back. Once. Twice. Thrice. She strode up the Chamber to shake hands with the Woolsack, departing to a loud and ironic cheer from those peers who knew what was coming next. When she returned disrobed, to take a corner seat downwind of the Government front bench, it was just in time to hear the Lords putting her in her place. They had organised a discussion on whether there should be a referendum on Maastricht, taking a great deal of time and pleasure in saying how much they opposed one. "A device," said one earl, curling his lip at the new Baroness Thatcher, "of very recent and foreign origin."

She may now be one of them, but Her Upstairs had been instantly reminded that the Lords were never one of us.

July 1, 1992

Fruits of the earth turn sour in Gummer's Eden

In the beginning God created the heaven and the earth. And some years later, in an idle moment, God said: let there be John Selwyn Gummer.

And God gave to Gummer dominion over the fish of the sea and the fowl of the air, and in co-ordination with his EC partners, over the Common Agriculture Policy, the set-aside scheme, the potato quota and the banana tariff, over the wine lakes and the butter mountains which soared unto the very heavens themselves.

And God, in his infinite wisdom, sanctified Gummer and lavished upon him the fruits of the earth. God gave to him a six-bedroom manor house with original Victorian features and extremely pleasant views of the Suffolk country.

And God attached to the house an attractive two-acre garden. And the Lord God took him into the Garden of Gummer to dress it and keep it. And there went up a mist from the earth and watered the face of the ground. And in the Garden of Gummer, the Lord God created a pond. And God saw this was good. But the minister reckoned there was still some room for improvement.

Now, the serpent was the most subtle of beasts which the Lord God had made. And he sayeth to the Gummer: the EC farm ministers are hithering here for an agricultural show and that pond is in a bit of an sorry state. And hark ye, Hillsdown Holdings, verily a big meat company, will pay £2,600 to dredge and clean it.

And Gummer sayeth unto the serpent: but should a Minister of the Crown accept money from a meat company? And the serpent sayeth: there is nothing to feel guilty about. You need not even declareth the payment unto the Register of Members' Interests.

And Gummer also gazed upon his barn and the fencing around the Garden of Gummer. And he had £17,000-worth of labour done to them. For the serpent sayeth to him: the work is necessary for the security of the Garden of Gummer, and all who liveth and breatheth in it, and the money should come from ministry funds.

And the work was done. And Gummer saw that it was good. But some time later the payments leaked. And now the eyes of all the world were opened unto what Gummer had done. And the wrath of the Select Committee on Members' Interests descended upon his head. And every creeping thing that doth crawl across the face of Westminster crieth out at question time: "What about the pond?"

And Gummer pressed on trying to answer a question about EC fraud. Quoth he: "There is a great deal to be done in this field." And they crieth out again: "But what about in the barn?"

And then came a man by the name of Dennis Skinner, known as the Beast. Now, Skinner was a rough and hairy man with a voice like the crack of doom. And the Beast belloweth at the Gummer: "Thou art accursed. Upon thy belly shalt thee go. And dust shalt thou eat all the days of your life" — or words to that general effect.

And the Beast suggesteth that there were plans to use taxpayers' money to turn the Garden of Gummer into a fish farm and an horse racing stud. And Gummer heard the voice of Skinner and was sore afraid. He squeaketh: "I doubt if the House wants an answer to that!" And the Labour multitude crieth out: "Yes we do! Oh yes we do!"

And now Gummer turneth a little pink and hideth his face upon the front bench. But repenteth he not. For verily is it said that it is easier for a camel to pass through the eye of a meat hygiene inspector than it is to get an admission of a mistake out of a cabinet minister.

February 26, 1992

Norman's lament

Dark, furtive and saturnine, Norman Lamont has always exuded the air of a Neapolitan mobster. Never more so than yesterday as the Cabinet's former bag-man broke his silence to turn devastating state's evidence against John Major.

As he spilled the worms in juicy, wriggling detail, the ex-chancellor did not sing quite like a canary. This was a stool pigeon returning as a carrion crow. Hell hath no fury like a chucked chancellor, especially when he is also a dumped chum. But the performance was the more damaging for being elegantly and sometimes wittily dressed in a tone pretending to be more informed by sorrow than anger. The barbs were the more damning for being presented not as the venom of an embittered enemy but the concern of a disappointed friend.

He detained MPs for a while attempting to establish his own alibis for the extortions and rackets visited on the country over the last two years. Entry into the ERM? Not me who took us in, guv. The recession? Economy was broke when I was given it, guv. Black Wednesday? Have to confess, I had my doubts. Only following orders, guv. Each sentence of the 20-minute speech made another Wednesday ever blacker for a motionless Major. The corpse of his late chancellor had leapt out of the grave to read a glowing testimonial to the deceased. It went on to dig a hole under the prime minister's own feet.

Turning an ironic smile towards the prime minister and his new chancellor, he wished Major and Clarke every happiness together, in the style of a man cheerfully waving a married couple off on their honeymoon — only because he knows the car is heading over a cliff. It reminded the Commons that while there may be honour among thieves, the commodity is rarer among Tories. The ex-chancellor revealed that he had carefully kept some documentary evidence. He read with relish the billet doux Major had popped through the letter box on the night of Black Wednesday saying that he wasn't planning to resign "and I should not do so either". That raised a great opposition laugh.

Madam Speaker had ritually reminded MPs that resignation speeches are "heard in silence, without interruption", no doubt in the certain expectation that the ruling would be ignored. Wincing Ooohs from the Tory benches were accompanied by gleeful Aaaahs from the Opposition. The loudest of both came when the former chancellor observed: "We give the impression of being in office, but not in power."

In delivery and impact, it was more reminiscent of Nigel Lawson's bitter farewell to Margaret Thatcher than Geoffrey Howe's mortal adieu.

The speech which was most disastrous for Major was not the stinging contempt of Lamont or the searing scorn of John Smith. The performance which had loyalist Tory MPs staring at their socks, and finally closing their eyes in prayer that it would quickly come to an end, was the speech delivered by the prime minister. Closer comes the day when the Tory party's hit men approach Major with an offer he can't refuse.

June 10, 1993

Maastricht: from dead heat to dead beat

The division bells began to toll at 10pm. As MPs massed and milled around the Chamber, surging and swilling towards the lobbies, we finally understood why John Major had risked so much in opposition to the social chapter.

In no other European legislative factory but the Commons would it be permissible for the management to carry on like this. Every employee, however sick, lame or unwilling, dragged into the lobbies, cramming and jostling together in the most insanitary conditions in the middle of the night.

And, after all the danger to political life and limb, absolutely nothing was resolved. As the divisions were called, passageways heaved with bodies. Tory loyalists made one last-ditch assault on Tory rebels, twisting arms, bending ears. The biggest of all the Government heavies, Nicholas Soames, pinned one of the most diehard Euro-phobes, Nicholas Winterton, against a wall. Geoffrey Dickens made a one-man road block of himself, jovially throwing himself in front of opposition MPs heading for their lobby. Stone-faced Ulster Unionists trooped towards the Government lobby through a forest of accusing Labour fingers.

No corridor was clear, no exit was unblocked. God knows what would have happened if a minister, realising that his government was on the brink of humiliating defeat, had resorted to yelling "Fire!" The chapter's health and safety provisions would surely have outlawed a chief executive — however gravely endangered his business — wheeling through the lobbies ministers recovering from heart attacks and violent bouts of gastro-enteritis. Though by the end of the night, Michael Heseltine was probably not the only member of the Cabinet to have had a cardiac tremor, and John Patten must have been far from alone among ministers in urgently requiring the lavatory. As for the noise levels generated by last night's scenes, they surely broke every conceivable Brussels directive on decibel harmonisation.

It was utter bedlam in the final moments. Through the heaving crowds of MPs you could spot the Government whips, scurrying to the front bench with advance information of the first vote. The poker faces of the whips were more impossible than ever to decipher. They did not look terribly cheerful. Nor did they look totally struck down. There was only one explanation, and the tellers pushed their way through the heaving throng of MPs to share it with everyone. "The Ayes to the Right, 317!" yelled the Government whip. "The Noes to the Left, 317!" Six hundred and fifty mouths let out a huge gasp. Some strong men looked as though they might faint. "The numbers being equal. . ." (intoned Madam Speaker, about the only cool head left in the place) ". . .in accordance with precedent. . . " (though, off-hand, even the longest toothed veterans of historic parliamentary occasions could not remember a precedent) ". . .I cast my vote with the Noes."

A dead heat in the first vote, the Government knew it now faced being dead beat in the second vote. The Government chief whip, Richard Ryder, led his team on ever more frantic patrols of the door to the Aye lobby. Like bouncers outside desperate night clubs, the Tory whips were chucking them in. In vain. This time the result was clear to all long before the whips had muscled their way through the crowd to announce the numbers. A deafening roar from the Labour benches, complemented by hand-clapping and cries of "Resign!", erupted before the Opposition whip took the place on the Government side allotted to a division's winners. The tension was momentarily broken when a Labour voice cried: "You win some, you lose some!" When he had heard he had lost by eight, Major rose to the despatch box with a small piece of paper trembling in his hand. Even the grey had drained from his face as the prime minister announced that he would be coming back to the House in the morning with a confidence motion. The bells will toll again. Nobody need ask for whom.●

July 22, 1993

Commons' stars, clockwise from top left: Speaker Betty Boothroyd, Kenneth Clarke, Tony Blair, James Cran, Geoff Hoon

OUR FAMOUS FIVE

Simon Hoggart

TONY BLAIR
Providing problems for
senior ministers

Tony Blair was one of the few Opposition speakers to to have anything
which could remotely be called a
good 12 months. John Smith had, to
put it politely, a mixed parliamentary
year with lacklustre, slow-footed performances at Question Time twice a
week. The lugubrious Gordon Brown
produced a host of policies, yet failed
to capture the public mood, even at
the height of anxiety about the state of
the economy.

Blair, however, made a real
impact, taking on the Conservatives
on what has traditionally been one of
their strongest issues: law and order.
Admittedly he was kicking at an open
goal; after 14 years the Conservatives
were hardly in a position to blame
Labour for the rise in the crime rate
and the consequent public distress.
Predictably they tried to blame
"trendy" education, lack of religion
and even television. Blair performed a
delicate tightrope act in which he
managed to blame unemployment,
social conditions and lack of support
for the police (who cheered him from
the same conference at which they
had jeered the then home secretary,
Kenneth Clarke) without falling into
the trap of appearing "soft" on crime.

Blair's mild and thoughtful tone,
which articulates the operation of a
tough legal mind, provided more
problems for senior ministers than
any other front- bencher, with the
possible exception of George Robertson. Not surprisingly, when Labour
MPs mutter darkly that the time has
come to "skip a generation", they
don't mean trading up to Denis
Healey, but to Tony Blair.

BETTY BOOTHROYD
Respect for her is
undiminished by one failure

Betty Boothroyd became in less than a
year quite the most popular Speaker
of modern times. To be fair, all Speakers become popular early on and
often remain so, since MPs, like
schoolchildren, deep down prefer the
smack of firm discipline.

And discipline them she does. Her
cry of "order, orrrderrr!" would chill a
basilisk. When trouble looms, she
generally starts by adopting a genteel,
even gentrified voice; the vowels, if
not strangled, are at least having trouble breathing. As things get worse, her
natural voice re-asserts itself. As one
Labour MP said: "You half expect her
to shout 'If I don't get some hush in
this bar, I'll put the towel back on the
pumps'." The image of a lovable but
irascible barmaid is heightened by her

habitual cry of "Time's Up" at the end of Questions. MPs love it.

But this bold and confident display conceals an acute mind and a politician of considerable honesty. The Maastricht debate has offered the opportunity for appalling behind-the-scenes cock-ups, with the interests of Government, Opposition and back-bench members often in a three-way conflict. Given that the Bill implies a host of constitutional changes, there were few precedents to guide her. Yet Betty (as she is universally known) gave firm, well-argued rulings that were accepted by all sides, and enhanced rather than threatened her authority.

Her darkest half hour came with the Michael Mates speech when the sacked minister ploughed on through a speech which appeared to break the House's own rules on prejudice, in spite of innumerable interruptions from the Chair and — at one point — an unambiguous instruction to sit down. Mates clearly won that bout, but such is the respect Betty commands that her position was quite undiminished by this failure.

KENNETH CLARKE
Major's performance is dreary by comparison

Kenneth Clarke has come to occupy what ought to be a formal position, with its own car and driver: Next Leader of the Conservative party. The person who occupies this post rarely if ever becomes the next leader: it has been held at various times by the likes of Rab Butler, Reggie Maudling, Willie Whitelaw, Francis Pym, Michael Heseltine and Norman Tebbit. It was never occupied by John Major or Margaret Thatcher.

Yet at this stage it is hard to see who could defeat him. Clarke's parliamentary performances have been as robust as ever, serving largely to heighten the sense that Major's have been feeble and dreary. On the day in June when Norman Lamont made his devastating resignation speech — "they are in office but not in power" — when John Smith followed with a coruscating personal assault on Major, who replied with a speech that was flat, nervous and depressing for the troops behind him, the party was saved only by a bravura performance by Clarke, both savage and insouciant. Typically, he then retired to the Stranger's Bar, most plebeian of all the Commons watering holes, to drink to his own success in pints of bitter.

Part of Clarke's success is that he evidently has the famous "hinterland", the interests that are as important as politics and which provide the essential independence of spirit a successful MP needs. In his case the hinterland is made up of a host of varied interests: sport, bird-watching, pub life, even archaeological digs, which he visits with his wife Gillian. He is able to break all the rules by virtually announcing that he wants to become prime minister because, in the end, he won't mind too much if he isn't.

However, that hasn't prevented some deft footwork. After a semi-public row with Tebbit in which Clarke admitted to not having read the Maastricht treaty, and saying of the Euro-rebels that "more sense has been spoken in Waco, Texas, than on the floor of the House of Commons", he wisely promised not to return Britain to the hated ERM within the life of this Parliament. The right has grudgingly decided that he might just do, after all.

JAMES CRAN
Managing the Tory
Euro-rebels' every move

There is little doubt about the MPs who dominated this parliamentary year: the Conservative rebels who fought the Maastricht Bill inch by inch and line by line through to the rout of their own government in the social chapter vote at the end of July. Critics — who constantly misjudged their skill, their determination and most important of all, their sincerity — accused them of playing party games. To driven figures such as Bill Cash, Nicholas and Ann Winterton, Richard Shepherd (who made the best of their speeches), Teddy Taylor or the powerful Peter Tapsell (a convert to the rebel cause midway through the Bill) no issue could have been more serious or more critical. They were not playing games; on the contrary, they believed they were fighting to save the nation.

At the very heart of the operation, speaking little but managing every move, was James Cran, the MP for Beverley, Yorkshire, who along with his friend Christopher Gill of Ludlow was the unofficial whip of the rebel forces, and constantly more persuasive — to judge by his results — than the official whips or the prime minister.

The world outside heard little from Cran. He entered the Commons in 1987, after an uneasy spell with the Confederation of British Industry, first as director for the Northern region, then for the West Midlands. He is unambiguously on the right of the party: a confrontational Thatcherite (though with no great taste, it is said, for Thatcher herself) who found the CBI "a pretty soggy bunch" and did not try to hide it.

There was no point in using against him the whips' traditional double whammy of inducements coupled with threats — though some of his colleagues believe Cran would some day like a job in government. When the whips move in on you, as he told the Yorkshire Post in a rare interview, "naturally you kick them back. I'm afraid none of them seems to understand this".

He was born in 1944, the son of a gamekeeper. He is a north-east Scot and a graduate of Aberdeen University and Tory Central Office. He came close to getting elected in Gordon (West Aberdeenshire) in 1983 and was then selected for Beverley. Seeing his skills at work, ministers must have wondered whether it might not have been better to (as John Major said, quoting Lyndon Johnson) have him inside the tent pissing out instead of outside pissing in.

On the other hand, Cran is no team player. As with Cash, Shepherd, the Wintertons and many other rebels, the cause of forcing back the integrationism of Brussels has come to transcend all others for him. As the argument moves beyond Maastricht, Cran will be there to badger the Government every step of the way.

GEOFF HOON
Best of the new boys

By common consent at Westminster, the 1992 Labour intake is one of the best for years, with much of the talent on the Tony Blair-Gordon Brown modernising wing of the party. Some, like John Denham from Southampton, are reconstructed Trotskyists. (Roger Berry of Kingswood, though still on the left of the party, is described in Andrew Roth's Parliamentary Profiles as "a former admirer of Ken Livingstone".)

Predictions of the best and worst of new intakes are highly unreliable — almost nobody would have picked Margaret Thatcher out from the 1959 crop of Tories. But one who has consistently impressed in the last year is the member for Ashfield, Geoff Hoon. Hoon is the third Labour member for this seat since 1966. The first was David Marquand, the Gaitskellite son of a former Labour cabinet minister who might as well have worn a hat band labelled "Hampstead intellectual". The second was Frank Haynes, the sort of elemental working class figure now largely gone from the Commons. He had the highest decibel count in the building.

Hoon represented another sudden change to the model of the New Labour Coming Man, the Nigel Barton of his day. He combines underprivileged origins (his father is a railwayman) with a fast track performance through Nottingham High School (which also gave us chancellor Kenneth Clarke) and Cambridge to a law lectureship at Leeds and a seat in the European Parliament at the age of 30.

Hoon, who was 40 in January 1993, is one of three Labour MPs who since 1992 have had seats in both assemblies. This will end with the 1994 European elections; Labour opposes the dual mandate, so he will not be able to stand again for Strasbourg. However, his time in Europe served him well in a year dominated by Maastricht. With Stephen Byers (Wallsend), Hoon drafted the amendment on the social chapter which brought the Government to a humbling defeat on July 22 and pushed John Major's premiership to the brink.

He also delivered some of the best speeches in the Maastricht debate (including, weirdly, one which had a three-week break in the middle, since the House adjourned soon after he started speaking and did not return to the topic for the best part of a month).

Above all, speaking as someone who knew both ends of the operation, he made the most telling case for the democratisation of Europe by changing the European Parliament *and* the Westminster Parliament. That speech, on a theme which ought to dominate the European debate over the next four years, tipped the balance for him in this Almanac, nudging him ahead of several other contenders from among the new boys.●

PAYING THE PIPER WHO HAS ALL THE WRONG TUNES

David McKie

The Conservative victory against the odds in April 1992 was seen above all as a triumph for John Major. But it could equally be said to have vindicated the judgment of party chairman Chris Patten, who had consistently argued that the opinion polls must be wrong. Patten's direction of the campaign had been bitterly attacked in Conservative newspapers, as well as by those on the Thatcherite wing of the party, who had never had much time for him. His decision to cut back on press advertising, for which he would have been pilloried had the Conservatives lost — fed Fleet Street discontent even further.

But that saving looked even more prudent as the Conservatives emerged from the election with a thumping deficit and an overdraft reported in mid-1993 to have reached £19 million. The new Central Office team put most of the blame on the stewardship of Kenneth Baker, who left Central Office on the fall of Margaret Thatcher, but Baker argued that most of the problems pre-dated his arrival.

Patten's successor at Central Office was Sir Norman Fowler, who had left the Cabinet in January 1990 saying he wanted to spend more time with his family. Fowler promised a fundamental review of the party's organisation and structure. Some of the old guard left, including the party Treasurer, Lord Beaverbrook, who had serious financial problems of his own. A chief executive was installed with the title of director general: this job went to Paul Judge, a former executive in the food industry now running an organisation called Food for Britain.

While Fowler struggled to keep down Central Office bills, controversy raged about where the money which had paid for the 1992 campaign had come from. The issue came to a head in June 1993 with the flight to Cyprus of Asil Nadir, the entrepreneur who built the Polly Peck empire, facing charges of fraud after investigations by the Serious Fraud Office. Nadir had given £440,000 to Conservative party funds, money that opposition parties alleged was effectively stolen and ought to be repaid. A second fugitive businessman, Octav Botnar, claimed from Switzerland to have given the party £90,000. Other foreign millionaires known to have been benefactors included the Greek shipping magnate John Latsis, who as Labour liked to point out had championed the regime of the Greek colonels.

But the source of other donations remained a mystery. The Conservatives had funds of £27 million in election year. The party's accounts failed to disclose the source of some £19 million. Some of it could be traced through the published accounts of companies that had made donations, but the provenance of around £14 million remained a secret — and the Conservatives intended to keep it that way.

Even before the Nadir disclosures the absence of any obligation for parties to disclose their sources of income had become a contentious issue, taken up by the Commons select committee on home affairs — some members of which at a hearing on June 22 tried vainly to tempt Fowler to share the secret with them. The Commons debated the issue on the same day. Labour demanded that all political parties should be required to publish fully audited accounts, disclosing the source of all large donations, and that donations from foreign governments and individuals should be disbarred. They also drew attention to the apparent correlation between money given by captains of industry to Conservative party funds and subsequent knighthoods and peerages.

The Conservatives asserted that the principle of voluntary funding under-pinned the strength of democratic political parties. They defended the right of people and organisations to give money to whomever they wished without hav-ing the facts blazoned across the newspapers. And they condemned the Labour party for allowing the unions to dictate party policy in return for substantial funding through affiliation. The Liberal Democrats, who had no big battalions to call on, and financed their election campaigns for a fraction of what the Conser-vatives and Labour spent, called for openness and a top limit on donations. Few uglier debates, it was widely agreed, had taken place in the Commons since the election.

Fowler was also under pressure from a ginger group of Conservative activists calling themselves the Party Reform Steering Committee to democratise the Con-servative party. They called for the replacement of the party executive by a body half of whose members would be elected by postal ballot. Although when Fowler took on the chairmanship he promised to look at the case for democrati-sation, no concessions were made and the argument deteriorated to a point where both sides took legal advice.

A more serious grassroots discontent sprang from the party's poll ratings, from the sense that issues such as pit closures and testing in schools had not been competently handled, and from apprehension about closer integration in Europe. These were already clearly apparent at the party conference in Brighton in October 1992, when Lord Tebbit was wildly cheered by about one-third of the hall for a speech that denounced the Maastricht treaty and opposed re-entry to ERM. The mood at the grassroots was still further soured by the party's disas-trous performance in the county council elections in May 1993 — the same day which saw them lose the Newbury by-election. Many Conservative councillors felt they had lost their seats not through any fault of their own but because Major and colleagues had lost the trust of the country. The disaffection of local parties was illustrated by the way some responded to pressure from the national party leadership to get tough with those Tory MPs who were impeding the pro-cess of the Maastricht Bill. Some MPs, such as Nicholas Budgen in Wolverhamp-ton SW, were put under pressure, but elsewhere parties endorsed the stands their dissident members had taken. ●

INSPIRATION NOT INTELLECT IS THE KEY

Patrick Wintour

N eil Kinnock once said: "nothing, but nothing can prepare anyone for the pressures of being leader of the Labour party". It is a judgment that John Smith, after a year of success and failures in equal and unexpected measure, probably now accepts with fervour.

Elected by an overwhelming 90.9 per cent majority of his shell-shocked party last June, Smith was known as the man prone to play the longest of long games. His impressive Social Justice Commission, established in December 1992, is unlikely to produce a final report until the autumn of 1994. The party will then probably take a further year to propose its tax plans. Similarly, detailed policies for economic recovery, education, health and crime will not start to emerge from the Labour policy-making factory at least until 1994.

In his first year as leader, Smith confined himself to limited targets — largely matters of unfinished business left over from the previous administration. The agenda of unfinished business left by Kinnock centred on the completion of the party's modernisation programme and on the resolution of its three-year-old debate on electoral reform. Both issues had been referred to internal party committees before Smith took on the leadership, but he faced the demanding task of managing their crucial final stages. In so doing, he showed himself to be a much more relaxed and consensual leader than Kinnock. As a matter of personality, as much as of deliberate policy, Smith left the committees to their own devices. Kinnock, chastised by some for authoritarianism, believed that to give the party an inch meant the party taking a mile. Smith, chastised by others for enervation, believed the party was now mature enough to allow the leader to loosen the reins.

In the case of electoral reform, Labour's working party on electoral systems, chaired since its inception in December 1990 by Professor Raymond Plant, Professor of Politics at Southampton University, committed itself readily to electoral reform for the European elections, but found itself badly divided on whether to support abandonment of first-past-the-post for the Commons. To many Labour MPs, especially from the north, such a decision would have been a historic betrayal and would guarantee that Labour never governed alone again. To others, support for PR would symbolise a new pluralistic approach to democratic politics in which a culture of co-operation with other political parties would flourish.

By the slimmest of margins, the 16-strong committee eventually supported the principle of reforming the voting system for general elections, but then baulked at backing a fully proportional system. Plant, previously an agnostic, came personally down in support of PR. But Smith, a proponent of broad constitutional change, did not. He said he remained sceptical of the need for electoral reform, especially if the power of state was to be circumscribed by a Bill of Rights, as he proposed.

Instead, he suggested a referendum on the subject when Labour came to power. The decision was denounced as dangerously half-hearted by the Liberal Democrats, but for Smith it appeared to have done the intended trick of defusing the issue inside his party.

He had, however, conspicuously less success in handling the much more explosive issue of links with the unions. During his election campaign, Smith had said that he wanted Labour parliamentary candidates to be elected by one member, one vote and that the Labour leader should be elected with half the votes going to MPs and the remainder to constituency parties. But in Labour's Byzantine constitutional affairs, the devil is in the detail, and Smith, new to party management, only sketched out his thoughts. Much was still up for grabs.

Over the autumn and winter of 1992-93, relations between the unions and the party were allowed to sour. Many in the unions, not just the general secretaries, became convinced that they were being made the scapegoats for Labour's fourth election defeat and suspected a long-standing conspiracy from within the modernisers' camp to oust them from the party step by step. Once reliable allies, like John Edmonds, leader of the GMB general workers union, Smith's own sponsoring union, began to defend the place of the unions in the party. They had modernised and resented being described as part of a cloth cap past that had made Labour unelectable.

They were willing to reform radically the way they cast their votes inside the Labour party, but they would not have their votes taken away altogether. They had created Labour and the party still needed the unions to broaden its diminishing membership. "No Say, No Pay" became their watchword.

Increasingly, they blamed the party's so-called modernisers — Tony Blair, Gordon Brown and their back-bench friend Peter Mandelson — for harbouring plans to turn Labour into a fully-fledged social democratic organisation. The union counter-attack was fuelled by a growing irritation with the indifferent performance of some of the new-look Labour front bench. The Government was in turmoil, but the media attention focused exclusively on the turmoil inside the Tory party. The Labour attack in the Commons was passing with little notice.

As shadow chancellor, Brown attracted special criticism from the left for not setting out a distinctive policy during the ERM crisis last October. Fearful of being accused of advocating, or even causing, devaluation, Brown was reluctant to press the case for a realignment. Nor, with the Public Sector Borrowing Requirement set to reach £50 billion, would he press the case for a large-scale borrowing programme.

By late spring, union conference after union conference had rejected Smith's plans and the leader looked to be facing inevitable defeat at his party conference in the autumn. Even in the constituencies, the tide of support for OMOV seemed to be ebbing. Smith looked at the bleak arithmetic and sought a compromise. Union political levy payers who signed a statement of support for Labour would, after all, be entitled to vote in leadership elections. However, on parliamentary candidates, Smith held his ground. Only full party members would be entitled to vote, although the membership fee would be cut to make it easier for trades unionists to be recruited. Smith's opponents in the bigger unions, including the GMB and the TGWU, did not quickly embrace the new package, leaving the outcome highly dependent on some of the middle-ranking unions changing their stance.

If it could not be said as he began his second year that he had failed in any of his self-appointed tasks, neither could it be said that he had set the Thames alight. The Labour party had got what it was always offered by John Smith — a steady, intelligent and trustworthy competence with little of the excitements of his predecessor. Inside parliament, especially in set-piece debates, his intellect had flourished. But as a party campaigner, able to address and inspire his troops in the country with the outlines of a new political agenda, he had so far failed. Given the troops' demoralisation, it was a failure he needed to rectify soon.●

Reborn?: despite huge by-election victories at Newbury and Christchurch, Paddy Ashdown's LibDems were still open to the charge of being little more than a painless vehicle for protest

WINNING THE BATTLES, BUT NOT THE WAR

Patrick Wintour

The Liberal Democrats are like one of those weighted rubber toys: the harder you hit it, the harder it bounces back. In the general election, Paddy Ashdown's party saw its vote drop nationwide by 4.8 per cent overall on its 1987 performance. The decline was registered in every single region. It was the second election in a row in which the party's overall vote had fallen, leaving the party with only 20 seats. Ashdown's carefully prepared war games in the event of a hung parliament, including the demand for four seats at the Cabinet table, proved to be nothing more than that — games. Every by-election gain trumpeted in the previous parliament — from Eastbourne to Ribble Valley — had been lost. The prospect remained for Ashdown of another five years living on his wits to attract attention for Britain's third political force.

That likelihood left Ashdown exhausted and disheartened. He had led the party for more than four years through the difficult merger talks with the SDP and the disastrous European election performances of 1989, and had overseen a painful party reorganisation. He, more than any other political leader, dominated his party. Yet he had received no reward.

The demoralisation deepened when it became clear that Labour had survived its fourth defeat with astonishing equanimity. Before the election, Ashdown had spoken of his party becoming the gathering force for radical forces in the event of a fourth Conservative victory. No such gathering occurred.

Ashdown tried to nudge the process by setting out his terms for Left realignment at a speech in Chard, Somerset, on May 9. It revealed his determination to find a route to power for his party. It was no good the Liberal Democrats simply acting as a test-bed for political ideas or holding to a strong local government base, he said. A means not just to express but to organise the anti-Conservative majority in the country had to be found.

He ruled out pacts, but suggested the forces ranged on the Left should attempt a more inclusive, pluralistic dialogue. With many in his own party, particularly at grassroots local government level, deeply suspicious of Labour, he could not proffer more without risking a revolt at party conference. Besides, he personally doubted the momentum behind the modernisation movement inside the Labour party. In particular, a Labour commitment to proportional representation, the sine qua non of realignment for him, seemed as far away as ever. Later in the year, his party's decision to vote with the Government in the

November Maastricht paving debate, so saving John Major from a possible general election, created new tensions between Labour and the Liberal Democrats.

Ashdown threw himself into the moral and military quagmire of Bosnia, seeing the conflict at first hand in July and August and repeatedly urging Major to send troops to stop the fighting. He was soon judged to be having a "good civil war", leaving the Labour party looking flat-footed and disengaged. Raising the conflict on 12 occasions at prime minister's questions, Ashdown seemed to have more to say on Bosnia than on any domestic subject, but he said it well.

It was a high-risk strategy and one that gained him little but jeers in the Commons, where his reputation for sanctimony grew apace. But Ashdown was also quietly reinventing himself. It might have been a clever route for the leader of any third party to adopt, but increasingly Ashdown presented himself as the anti-politician politician. New means of communication with the public fascinated him. Bill Clinton's electronic town hall meetings were one model, direct TV democracy another. It was a theme that dovetailed well with his private visits at the start of 1993 to live and work with "ordinary people". If a single theme emerged from these six months of travels, each lasting two to three days a week, it was the disenchantment, disrespect and pure cynicism of the public with the geriatric political process at Westminster. The disenchantment had spread throughout Western Europe, he said.

Increasingly he sounded like a British edition of Ross Perot or the Lombard League, a new kind of leader willing to challenge the gridlock of the Whitehall system not only over the budget deficit, but also the self-interest and corruption of the political establishment.

The evolution of this New Ashdown reached its zenith with a speech to the pressure group Charter 88 in July 1993 in which he advocated regular policy referendums, unelected Cabinet members and hypothecated, or earmarked, taxes to strengthen the link between paying income tax and welfare services. And more importantly for Ashdown, the intellectual fizz began to draw electoral reward. May 6 1993 was the most successful night in the party's five-year history. In the Newbury by-election, the Conservatives' 12,000 majority was overturned by a 28 per cent swing, prompting the dismissal of the chancellor, Norman Lamont. In the local elections, the party gained 400 seats, leaving it with control or influence over 30 per cent of local authorities.

On July 9, the Gallup 9,000 poll for the Daily Telegraph put the party in second place for the first time since 1985 with 26.5 per cent of the vote, two points ahead of the Conservatives. More importantly, the vote appeared for the first time to be concentrating geographically — the key to a breakthrough under the first-past-the-post system. A MORI poll for the Times showed that in the three months to the end of June, the Liberal Democrats had 45 per cent of the vote in the south west, up from 29 per cent in the previous quarter. A swathe of Tory seats in Cornwall, Somerset, Dorset and Devon appeared vulnerable.

The party's resurgence threatened to be a bubble that would burst, as it had on many previous occasions. Ashdown remained vulnerable to the charge of opportunism, and his party to the charge of being little more than a painless vehicle for protest. Some of its zanier ideas, on controlling pollution for instance, or on mortgage tax relief, risked coming back to haunt it when the middle-class studied the implications for the price of their petrol or taxes. It seemed that the closer to a share of power the Liberal Democrats came, the sharper this scrutiny would become. The toughest times for Ashdown were still to come.●

POLICY

This section of the Almanac provides a record of events, planned and unplanned, from the 1992 election onwards, across the whole range of political activity from inflation, taxation and deregulation to Bosnia, Belfast, and the Bomb

CONTENTS

Text by David McKie.
Tables compiled by David McKie and Dan Bindman.

THE BEST FUTURE FOR BRITAIN

THE CONSERVATIVE MANIFESTO 1992

Survival: John Major's threat to the Tory Euro-rebels over the Maastricht Bill seemed to be 'vote for me, because if there's an election, I'm so unpopular you'll all lose your seats'

ONE
ECONOMIC MANAGEMENT

If the past had been any guide, John Major would have been doomed. Few British governments had sought re-election against such a daunting array of hostile economic indicators as that which faced the Conservatives in April 1992. The green shoots of economic spring which his chancellor, Norman Lamont, claimed to have spotted when he spoke to the Conservative party conference of 1991 now looked to have been a mirage.

Unemployment in March 1992, the month when the election was announced, stood at 2,648 million (9.4 per cent). Business bankruptcies and house repossessions were running at record levels. Indicators of business confidence told much the same story. The Public Sector Borrowing Requirement (PSBR) had been swollen by the costs of recession — more spent on social security benefits, less revenue flowing in from taxation.

That was to be expected. What was much less predictable was the accumulating deficit on the balance of trade. There was a deficit of £2.9 billion on the first quarter of 1992: the deficit on the year would be just under £12 billion. Usually in recession the balance of trade improved, since people had less to spend on imported goods, and manufacturers, starved of home markets, had an extra incentive to sell abroad. There was no such consolation from the figures this time.

Why were the green shoots taking so long to show? Could the problem be the election itself? People would not go out and spend, ministers argued, while the threat of a Labour government still hung over them. "Thursday is essential for recovery," Major declared two days before polling day. "It is the remaining ingredient to ensure a return to growth and prosperity."

But clearly there were other constraints on expansion. One was the level of interest rates, which appeared to reflect less the needs of the economy than the obligations forced on the government by membership of the ERM — the Exchange Rate Mechanism of the European Monetary System.

The decision to take Britain into the ERM was announced on October 8 1990. One powerful attraction was its perceived potential for helping achieve the supreme priority of government economic policy, under Major as under Thatcher: the conquest of inflation. That process, it was always accepted, might have deleterious consequences elsewhere in the economy. "If it isn't hurting, it isn't working," Major had said of the Government's anti-inflation policy when he took over as chancellor. Unemployment, his successor at the Treasury Norman Lamont told the Commons on May 16, 1992, was "a price worth paying" for success against inflation.

In the early days, the figures seemed to indicate that the policy was working as planned. Inflation sharply subsided, from 10.9 per cent in the month of entry to 3.7 per cent a year later.

But Britain had entered at a parity (DM2.95) which even at the start looked hard to defend. Our membership came more and more to be seen as a brake on recovery. For its own reasons Germany had to keep its interest rates high; and while German rates remained high, the cost of borrowing here could not be cut further. Interest rates fell from 15 per cent on the eve of British entry to 10 per cent in the month after the election: but there, despite the clamour of industry and the opposition parties, they stuck.

So recession persisted. Getting rid of the threat of a Labour government did not seem to have done the trick. In the opening months of the new Major government, things looked worse, not better. Uncertainties caused by events elsewhere in Europe, especially the Danish and French referendums on the Maastricht treaty, compounded the chancellor's problems. The strains of keeping the pound at the chosen parity became, in the end, unsustainable. On September 16 an irresistible run on the pound forced Lamont to abandon his previous strategy and take Britain out of the ERM, letting the pound float down to a more sustainable level. At the time this day was tagged Black Wednesday, though opponents of

ERM were later to call it White Wednesday: the day when Britain resumed control of its own economic destiny. The cost of Lamont's doomed attempt to defend the pound and the policy was later assessed at £5 billion (Treasury faces £5 billion loss for Black Wednesday/Ruth Kelly/ Guardian February 27 1993).

It was later to be argued that an agreed realignment within the ERM, easing the strains on the pound, was there for the taking had Lamont only gone for it. A Guardian reconstruction of events at the Bath summit of September 4-6, (Britain spurned ERM deal/Economic, Financial and Foreign Staff/Guardian, November 30 1992), said Lamont had resisted German pressure for Britain to join an ERM realignment even though some senior British and European officials had accepted the need for a sterling devaluation of between 5-10 per cent. As chairman of the meeting, Lamont had kept the issue out of discussions.

But Opposition criticism was muted. Both Labour and the Liberal Democrats were strongly committed to continuing British membership of the ERM. Indeed, Labour had cited ERM membership as one guarantee that there would not be runaway inflation under a Labour government, as there had been in 1974-76 before an incomes policy was brought in to stop it. In the Commons on July 2, John Smith, then shadow chancellor, had seemed to favour an agreed realignment. To overcome the difficulties caused by Germany's problems with reunification, he said, the Community ought to consider not just a co-ordinated programme of interest rate cuts but an upward revaluation of the

RATES OF CHANGE IN GDP
Rates of change in GDP constant factor cost average estimate

1971	1.7	1979	2.8	1987	4.6
1972	2.8	1980	-2.0	1988	4.5
1973	7.4	1981	-1.1	1989	2.1
1974	-1.5	1982	1.7	1990	0.6
1975	-0.8	1983	3.7	1991	-2.4
1976	2.6	1984	2.0	1992	-0.6
1977	2.6	1985	4.0		
1978	2.9	1986	3.8		

Source: CSO Blue Book

HOW SPENDING POWER GREW
1. Rates of change of Personal Disposable Income at constant prices
2. per capita at constant prices

	1	2
1979	5.8	5.7
1980	1.5	1.4
1981	-0.7	-0.7
1982	-0.5	-0.4
1983	2.6	2.6
1984	3.5	3.3
1985	3.3	3.1
1986	4.1	3.8
1987	3.5	3.2
1988	6.0	5.8
1989	4.5	4.2
1990	2.5	2.2
1991	-0.5	-0.7
1992	2.6	

Source: CSO Blue Book

mark against all other currencies. But at a meeting of the parliamentary party on September 10, six days before Black Wednesday, Smith's successor as shadow chancellor, Gordon Brown, fought off attempts by Bryan Gould, Michael Meacher and David Blunkett to commit the party to devaluation and realignment. "Our policy is not one of devaluation, nor is it one of revaluation and realignment," he said. "One of the things the Germans may wish to propose is whether a realignment of currencies will bring interest rates down. There is no guarantee that would happen, and it is not our policy."

Unthinkable though they had claimed it to be only a few days before, Britain's exit from the ERM was soon being portrayed by ministers as a change to Britain's advantage. The chancellor, it was reported, had been singing in his bath. From now on, he told his party conference, he would be pursuing a policy on ERM which was "right for Britain" — which seemed to some an admission that the previous policy had not been. Interest rates tumbled: from 12 per cent (at one stage, Lamont had even threatened 15) on Black Wednesday to 10 per cent next day, 9 per cent on September 22 and 8 per cent on October 16.

Now at last there was a decided smell of recovery. The mood of the Conservative party conference in October was overwhelmingly hostile to ERM, and insistent that there should be no early return — if indeed there was to be any return at all. The climate became more expansionary. Inflation, though still a priority, was not the overwhelming priority it had been before. At the party conference,

the Trade and Industry secretary Michael Heseltine pledged himself to intervene before breakfast, before lunch, before tea and before dinner in the interests of British industry. In television appearances on the night of October 20, the prime minister signalled the change of course. "A strategy for growth is what we need; a strategy for growth is what we are going to have," he told ITN. Scattered signs of recovery — a better-than-feared Christmas in the high streets, a stirring of the property market in the spring, some return of business confidence — began to suggest that recovery was tentatively under way.

On conventional definitions — two successive quarters of negative growth are, for purely arbitrary reasons, taken as meaning recession — Britain emerged from recession with the publication on April 26 of the figures for GDP (Gross Domestic Product), the main indicator of the nation's economic activity, for the first three months of the year. They were up by 0.2 per cent. The recession had lasted eight quarters, against seven in 1980-81, though the fall in output was smaller this time. Unemployment fell in February and again in March and April, though the figures were disputed. March figures for manufacturing output showed an increase of 2.5 per cent over two months. The April survey of the Institute of Directors showed the highest level of business confidence for four years. And inflation as measured by the retail price index fell to 1.3 per cent — the lowest figure since February 1964 — in April.

But the underlying trend of inflation looked higher, and over all this progress there loomed what came to

THE GROWTH LEAGUE TABLE
GDP per head, current prices and purchasing power parities US$

1971		1981		1991	
1. Switzerland	5,522	1. US	13,191	1. US	22,204
2. US	5,288	2. Switzerland	12,770	2. Switzerland	21,747
3. Luxembourg	4,063	3. Canada	11,356	3. Luxembourg	21,372
4. Sweden	4,009	4. Germany	10,621	4. Germany	19,500
5. Germany	3,958	5. Iceland	10,239	5. Canada	19,178
6. Canada	3,936	6. France	10,232	6. Japan	19,107
7. Netherlands	3,842	7. Luxembourg	10,115	7. France	18,227
8. France	3,832	8. Sweden	9,965	8. Denmark	17,621
9. Australia	3,803	9. Australia	9,649	9. Belgium	17,454
10. Denmark	3,766	10. Netherlands	9,595	10. Austria	17,280
11. New Zealand	3,764	11. Austria	9,479	11. Iceland	17,237
12. UK	**3,486**	12. Belgium	9,399	12. Norway	16,904
13. Belgium	3,428	13. Denmark	9,338	13. Italy	16,896
14. Austria	3,317	14. Italy	9,182	14. Sweden	16,729
15. Italy	3,156	15. Norway	9,133	15. Netherlands	16,530
16. Iceland	3,113	16. N. Zealand	8,945	16. Australia	16,085
17. Finland	3,092	17. Japan	8,900	17. Finland	15,997
18. Japan	3,048	18. Finland	8,892	**18. UK**	**15,720**
19. Norway	2,947	**19. UK**	**8,607**	19. N. Zealand	13,883
20. Spain	2,449	20. Spain	6,316	20. Spain	12,719
21. Ireland	1,884	21. Ireland	5,490	21. Ireland	11,507
22. Portugal	1,658	22. Portugal	4,749	22. Portugal	9,191
23. Greece	1,623	23. Greece	4,631	23. Greece	7,775
24. Turkey	670	24. Turkey	1,785	24. Turkey	3,491

Source: OECD National Accounts Statistics

CONSUMER CREDIT OUTSTANDING AT END OF YEAR (£ BN)

82	83	84	85	86	87	88	89	90	91
16.0	18.9	22.3	26.1	30.1	36.2	42.5	48.4	52.6	53.6

Source: Social Trends

be known as the twin deficits: the PSBR and trade. In late spring and early summer, the papers were full of leaks and forecasts about cuts in social security spending. Because of changes which followed the establishment of the EC single market, trade figures were harder than usual to get, but those that did appear, for the non-EC balance of trade, were not encouraging. Jubilation over signs of recovery was muted by such evidence. Opinion polls plotted continuing discontent. And in the City and industry, one thing which conspicuously failed to recover was the reputation of the chancellor.

He survived Black Wednesday: he was ready, he later said, to resign, but Major was against it. But he could not re-establish himself. Some of his troubles had nothing to do with his economic direction. On moving to 11 Downing Street, he let his Notting Hill flat to a women described as a sex therapist. He had her evicted. Part of the cost of this operation was found to have been paid by the taxpayer, Treasury officials having decided that since the hassle involved affected his job as chancellor, some part of the cost of his legal fees was properly ascribable to public funds. He was late with his Access card payment, which led to a curious dispute about whether or not he had purchased cheap champagne and cigarettes at a Paddington off-licence. What hurt him even more were repeated unguarded asides which seemed to suggest an insouciance about the human suffering inflicted by the recession — not least on a lot of former Conservative voters who had never really tasted recession before. Asked at the Newbury by-election if he had any regrets,

he quoted Edith Piaf: "Je ne regrette rien". It became his epitaph.

Party managers blamed Lamont for the Conservatives' wretched performance at Newbury. Backbenchers complained that, even if he wasn't guilty as charged, his retention as chancellor was impeding both economic and political recovery. On May 27 he was summoned to Downing Street and told he would have to go. He refused a transfer to environment.

Angered by what he saw as injustice and ingratitude, he declined to write the formal letter of resignation traditional on these occasions, and took his revenge in a resignation statement to the Commons on June 9. In this he disclosed that he had considered suspending British membership of the ERM well before it had occurred, but Major had been against it. He had favoured the establishment of an independent central bank, particularly as a barrier to short-term manipulation of interest rates for political purposes; but Major hadn't been ready for that either. He saw short-term thinking as the besetting vice of Major's government and added bitterly that the government was in office, but not in power.

Lamont blamed the depths of the recession not on the ERM but on the boom of 1988-89 — when Nigel Lawson was chancellor and Major, MPs remembered, was chief secretary. Since the war, he mordantly noted, there had been only two chancellors (the other was Selwyn Lloyd) who had succeeded in getting inflation down below 2 per cent. Both had been sacked.

Within days the new chancellor was enmeshed in disputes about how

THE COST OF LIVING

Retail price index monthly from 1983

	Jan	Feb	Mar	Apr	May	Jun	Jul	Aug	Sep	Oct	Nov	Dec
83	4.9	5.3	4.6	4.0	3.7	3.7	4.2	4.6	5.1	5.0	4.8	5.3
84	5.1	5.1	5.2	5.2	5.1	5.1	4.5	5.0	4.7	5.0	4.9	4.6
85	5.0	5.4	6.1	6.9	7.0	7.0	6.9	6.2	5.9	5.4	5.5	5.7
86	5.5	5.1	4.2	3.0	2.8	2.5	2.4	2.4	3.0	3.0	3.5	3.7
87	3.9	3.9	4.0	4.2	4.1	4.2	4.4	4.4	4.2	4.5	4.1	3.7
88	3.3	3.3	3.5	3.9	4.2	4.6	4.8	5.7	5.9	6.4	6.4	6.8
89	7.5	7.8	7.9	8.0	8.3	8.3	8.2	7.3	7.6	7.3	7.7	7.7
90	7.7	7.5	8.1	9.4	9.7	9.8	9.8	10.6	10.9	10.9	9.7	9.3
91	9.0	8.9	8.2	6.4	5.8	5.8	5.5	4.7	4.1	3.7	4.3	4.5
92	4.1	4.1	4.0	4.3	4.3	3.9	3.7	3.6	3.6	3.6	3.0	2.6
93	1.7	1.8	1.9	1.3	1.3	1.2						

Source: Economic Trends

PURCHASING POWER OF THE POUND

	What your 1979 £ would have been worth	what your 1992 £ would have been worth
1980	85p	£2.07
1981	76p	£1.85
1982	70p	£1.7
1983	66p	£1.61
1984	63p	£1.54
1985	60p	£1.46
1986	58p	£1.41
1987	56p	£1.37
1988	53p	£1.29
1989	49p	£1.20
1990	45p	£1.10
1991	42p	£1.02
1992	41p	£1.00

Source: recalculated from Economic Trends

to bring the PSBR down — whether by raising taxes, against the grain of Conservative party thinking and the manifesto which had carried it to victory only a year before, or by cuts in public spending, which would need to be savage and might still further reduce its levels of popularity — already the worst since opinion polling began.

Within weeks of Lamont's departure, however, events appeared to vindicate him. June and July produced an exceptional run of good economic indicators. Inflation, at 1.2 per cent, was down to its lowest level since February 1964: there had not been a lower figure since July 1963. Unemployment was down for the fifth successive month; manufacturing output — up 1.8 per cent in May — at its best since 1990; and retail sales up 1.3 per cent in June, bringing hopes that life was at last being restored to the high streets. Manufacturers' unit costs were falling at a rate of almost 3 per cent a year, helped by a fall in average earnings to 3.75 per cent in May. The increase in manufacturing productivity, 10.5 per cent in May, was the best since 1980. There was even modest good news on the twin deficits, with public borrowing figures edging down enough to feed hopes that the dreaded £50 billion might not be reached, and a surge in exports cutting back the deficit on the balance of trade to its lowest point for two years.

In the Commons on July 15, Lamont sardonically congratulated his successor on getting such good results so quickly. The implication was clear: these were Norman's own achievements, and he wasn't getting the credit. Others, though, thought the apparent upturn owed rather more to George Soros, the financier whose manoeuvres had done so much to force the government out of the ERM on Black Wednesday.

But whatever the attribution, it was uplifting news for John Major's beleaguered government. The country, said David Hunt, the employment secretary, in a radio interview on July 22, was now "full of optimism". If it was, the result of the Christchurch by-election a week later suggested the tide had yet to wash over Dorset. Still, as ministers told themselves as they set off for their summer holidays - give it time, and it will. ●

ANNUAL INCREASE IN PRICES

	1989	1990	1991	1992	12 months to April 1993
US	4.8	5.4	4.2	3.0	3.2
Japan	2.3	3.1	3.3	1.7	0.9
France	3.6	3.4	3.2	2.4	1.4
Germany	2.8	2.7	3.5	4.0	2.8
Italy	6.6	6.1	6.5	5.3	2.1
UK	7.8	9.5	5.9	3.7	1.3
Canada	5.0	4.8	5.6	1.5	1.8

Source: OECD Economic Outlook

GROUP OF SEVEN UNEMPLOYMENT RATES
(% by ILO/OECD guidelines)

	1989	1990	1991	1992
US	5.2	5.5	6.7	7.4
Japan	2.3	2.1	2.1	2.2
France	9.4	8.9	9.5	10.2
Germany*	5.5	6.2	6.7	7.7
Italy	10.9	11.1	11.0	10.7
UK	7.1	5.9	8.3	10.1
Canada	7.5	8.1	10.3	11.3

* W Germany until 1990, unified Germany thereafter

Source: OECD Economic Outlook

WHAT GOVERNMENTS SPEND
Total outlays of government spending as % of GDP

	1988	1989	1990	1991	1992
US	32.5	32.4	33.3	34.2	35.4
Japan	31.6	30.9	31.7	31.4	32.2
France	50.0	44.1	49.8	50.6	52.0
Germany	46.3	44.8	45.2	48.7	44.4
Italy	50.3	51.3	53.2	53.6	53.2
UK	38.0	37.6	39.9	40.8	44.1
Canada	42.5	43.2	45.9	48.8	49.7

Source: OECD Economic Outlook

ECONOMIC GROWTH
Growth of real GNP/GDP

	1989	1990	1991	1992
US	2.5	0.8	-1.2	2.1
Japan	4.7	4.8	4.0	1.3
France	4.3	2.5	0.7	1.3
Germany	3.4	5.1	3.7	2.0
Italy	2.9	2.1	1.3	0.9
UK	2.1	0.5	-2.2	-0.6
Canada	2.3	-0.5	-1.7	0.9

Source: OECD Economic Outlook

POUND, DOLLAR AND MARK
First Monday of each month since Britain entered ERM

1990	$	DM
November	1.8735	2.935
December	1.944	2.945
1991		
January	1.9335	2.9125
February	1.9765	2.9
March	1.898	2.9175
April	1.739	2.965
May	1.695	2.96
June	1.699	2.955
July	1.619	2.9375
August	1.685	2.94
September	1.8855	2.9438
October	1.739	2.915
November	1.7495	2.905
December	1.765	2.87
1992		
January	1.8465	2.855
February	1.79	2.8775
March	1.757	2.8775

	$	DM
April	1.7435	2.835
May	1.785	2.93
June	1.829	2.94
July	1.904	2.9
August	1.92	2.8425
September	1.9955	2.8
Black Wednesday September 16		
October	1.7815	2.5175
November	1.5315	2.4037
December	1.5335	2.4272
1993		
January	1.5029	2.4571
February	1.4535	2.3787
March	1.4408	2.3747
April	1.5215	2.4272
May	1.5727	2.4720
June	1.5208	2.4645
July	1.5115	2.5635

INTEREST RATES
Changes in interest rates from British entry into ERM, October 8 1990

1990	October 8	14.0	(down from 15.0)
1991	February 12	13.5	
	February 27	13.0	
	March 22	12.5	
	April 12	12.0	
	May 24	11.5	
	July 12	11.0	
	September 4	10.5	
1992	May 5	10.0	
	September 16	*12.0	
	September 18	10.0	
	September 22	9.0	
	October 16	8.0	
	November 13	7.0	
1993	January 26	**6.0	

*Black Wednesday. Interest rates were raised to 12 per cent. A further increase to 15 per cent was announced but later rescinded. ** the lowest rate since 1977.

THE ROAD TO BLACK WEDNESDAY

June 2: Danish referendum narrowly rejects Maastricht treaty, raising doubts about progress towards monetary union. **3:** French government decides to hold referendum on Maastricht. **4:** Italian long-term interest rates harden. **19:** Pro-Maastricht vote in Irish referendum does little to lift prevailing uncertainty.

July 10: Lamont speech to European Policy Forum rules out every option other than keeping the pound in the ERM. To leave the ERM and cut interest rates, he says, would be "the cut and run option" leading to a run on the pound. "The credibility of our anti-inflation strategy would be in tatters.. we would have surrendered." **16:** Bundesbank raises the discount rate by 0.75 points to 8.75 per cent; Italy raises discount rate by the same margin to 13.75 per cent. **16-30:** France and Germany discuss possible ERM realignment. Britain signals willingness to consider it.

August 4: Italy cuts discount and advance rates by 0.5 points. **25:** Opinion polls in France suggest Government may lose on Maastricht referendum.. **26-27:** Realignment discussed at meeting of G7 group of leading industrial countries. **28:** Joint EMS statement rules out devaluation.

September 3: Government takes out 10 billion Ecu loan to add to foreign reserves. Sterling rises sharply. **4:** Heavy selling pressure on lira: discount rates up by 1.75 per cent. **5:** EC finance ministers hold summit meeting at Bath. **10:** Major tells Scottish CBI there will be no retreat; he will stand up to the speculators. **16:** Intense pressure on pound throughout morning. Interest rates put up from 10 to 12 per cent, but this fails to stop the slide. Further rise on the following day, to 15 per cent, is announced. But in early evening, this defence is abandoned. chancellor says Britain will suspend its membership of ERM. The increase to 15 per cent is abandoned. **17:** Bank rate comes down to 10 per cent.

TWO
TAXATION & PUBLIC SPENDING

It was one of the proudest claims of the Thatcher years that in 1986 the Government liquidated the Public Sector Borrowing Requirement — the gap between what the government raises in taxes and what it spends. At the time it was claimed that the bad old days would never be back. But the 1991-93 recession disposed of that. The forecasts made in the Budget of 1992 were grim enough — deficits of £28 billion in 1992-93 and of £32 billion in the following year. But the out-turn was very much worse: £35 billion for 1992-93, a projected £50 billion for 1993-94.

How much of this was due to recession and how much to other, "structural", factors was a matter of dispute. John Major told Welsh Conservatives on June 11 1993 that roughly 70 per cent of the deficit seemed to be cyclical — brought on by recession. But that still left a structural element of 30 per cent, or roughly £15 billion of the projected £50 billion total.

Clearly the recession had a lot to do with it. Recessions cut revenue (because tax receipts from people and companies drop) and boost social security spending. On average, it was estimated, an unemployed person cost the state £8,000 a year. Sickness and invalidity benefit claims also burgeoned amid complaints that some who ought to have been drawing unemployment benefit (and would thus appear on the unemployment register) had been redefined and were drawing these benefits instead.

Some believed that as growth resumed the PSBR would dwindle to manageable levels. Others dissented. Other inexorable forces — especially demographic changes which were pushing up the number of people dependent on the state, while the number of those in work and able to pay for them shrank — would ensure the growth of claims on public money even after recession.

The summer public spending round — the process by which bids submitted by ministers are reduced to a point which the Treasury thinks it can carry — threatened to be even tougher in 1993 than in previous years. But the chief secretary to the Treasury, Michael Portillo, was also charged with looking beyond that process, by examining how insatiable demand and insufficient supply could be reconciled.

There were two obvious courses. The first was to cut public spending. And through the spring and summer, there was agonised speculation, sometimes backed up by leaked information, as to where Portillo was planning to look for savings. Would he cut or abolish child benefit? Reduce the numbers who qualified for invalidity benefit, or subject those who drew it to tax? Would he try to introduce "hotel charges" in the health service, requiring patients to contribute to the cost of their stays in hospital? Would prescription charges be imposed on some at present exempt? Would students (or their parents) have to pay tuition fees?

The Conservative right, militantly opposed to tax cuts, grew impatient with the Government's reluctance to take the axe to what it saw as areas of spending extravagance. In July 1993, the 92 Group of Conservative MPs, which claimed a back-bench membership of 100, published its own agenda, which included a 5 per cent cut in the public sector workforce, £500 million off the £2.3 billion budget for overseas aid, £2 billion off the £62 billion paid in grants to local government, a £1 billion saving on social security benefits (with cuts in invalidity and sickness benefits and benefits for single parents), a further £1 billion saving by pulling troops out of Germany, and £500 million by cutting expenditure per head on people in Scotland, Wales and Northern Ireland to the same level as England.

The other course was to raise taxes. Two arguments were marshalled against that. One said that raising taxes would impede the recovery. The other saw it as heresy, a straight contradiction of the entrepreneurial self-help philosophy of the Thatcher years which Major was pledged to continue.

The Conservatives had won the election on the claim that, unlike their rivals, who would push taxes up, they would go on bringing them down.

"We believe," the Conservative manifesto had said, "that government should not gobble up all the proceeds of growth, and that those who create prosperity should enjoy it, through lower taxes and more opportunity to build up personal wealth . . . Keeping control of public spending will enable us to cut taxes while bringing the Government's budget back towards balance in the years ahead." And it promised: "We will make further progress towards a basic income tax rate of 20p."

If that put cuts in direct taxation out of the question — though despite the rumblings of the Conservative right, it was by no means clear that it did — there were two other possibilities. National insurance contributions, which had increased in the Thatcher years while direct taxation came down, could be increased again. Though the theory was otherwise, NICs were used in practice as a form of augmented taxation, though the cut-off point — nobody, whatever their income, was required to pay more than £420 a week — made them more regressive than tax.

Though increases had been ruled out by Major ("I have no plans to raise the top level of tax or the level of national insurance contributions" — Commons, January 28) Norman Lamont announced in his 1993 Budget an increase by 1 point to 10 per cent in 1994, netting an estimated £2,100 million. The other was Vat. It was Conservative policy to switch the emphasis in taxation from taxes on income to taxes on spending, from direct to indirect. In the 1993 Budget, Lamont proposed a progressive increase in Vat on

THE TAX HAUL showing % increase on previous year

	Taxes on income	Taxes on spending	Social security	Customs & excise	Poll tax
1983	43,344	49,500	20,780	31,651	
1984	46,655	52,576	22,322	34,997	
	7.6	6.2	7.4	10.6	
1985	51,643	56,592	24,210	38,486	
	10.7	7.6	9.0	10.0	
1986	52,239	62,947	26,165	42,509	
	1.2	11.2	8.0	10.4	
1987	55,702	69,074	28,642	46,340	
	6.6	9.8	9.5	9.1	
1988	61,861	76,133	32,106	51,445	
	11.1	10.2	12.1	11.0	
1989	70,400	79,963	32,902	54,109	586
	13.8	5.0	2.5	5.9	
1990	77,021	76,967	34,651	57,064	8,629
	9.4	-3.8	5.3	5.5	472.5
1991	75,105	83,023	36,643	63,807	8,162
	-2.5	7.8	5.7	11.8	-5.4

NATIONAL INSURANCE AND INCOME TAX
Total revenue raised at current prices and in real terms, £bn

	NI contributions[1] Current prices	NI contributions[1] 1978-9 prices	Income Tax Current prices	Income Tax 1978-79 prices
1979-80	11.8	10.1	20.6	17.7
1980-81	14.0	10.1	24.3	17.6
1981-82	16.0	10.6	28.7	19.0
1982-83	18.9	11.7	30.4	18.7
1983-84	20.8	12.3	31.1	18.3
1984-85	22.3	12.5	32.5	18.2
1985-86	24.5	13.0	35.4	18.8
1986-87	26.5	13.7	38.5	19.8
1987-88	29.1	14.2	41.4	20.2
1988-89	32.4	14.8	43.4	19.8
1989-90	32.9	14.1	48.8	20.8
1990-91	35.0	13.8	55.3	21.9
1991-92	36.3	13.5	57.5	21.3
1992-93[2]	37.4	13.4	56.5	20.3
1993-94[2]	39.1	13.6	57.5	20.1

1 excluding national insurance surcharge
2 1993-94 Financial Statement and Budget Report estimates or forecasts.

Source: written answer to A Milburn, MP March 31 1993

fuel, from the old zero rate to 8 per cent in 1994 and on to 17.5 per cent in the following year. Though it troubled some Tory back-benchers and spurned a modest back-bench revolt the Commons approved it.

The chancellor also considered other extensions of Vat to areas which, like fuel, had until then been zero-rated. Food was one, perhaps the most difficult; children's clothes, books and newspapers were among the others. Though spared in the spring 1993 Budget, they were clearly options for the first unified budget, planned for November.

The Liberal Democrats advocated increasing taxation as the only way of safeguarding essential services. In the general election they had proposed a 1p increase in tax to go to education. According to opinion polls, this was the single most popular promise made by any party in the campaign; though the fact that the Conservatives won the election must cast doubt on the long-standing finding that the British electorate would rather have better services paid for by higher taxes than tax cuts and a lesser level of services.

In the summer of 1993, the party called for a war on unpaid taxes. A written answer to the Liberal Democrat MP Matthew Taylor showed that uncollected taxes included £703 million under Schedule D, £381 million in income tax, £58 million in capital gains tax, and £33 million in national

insurance payments. The total of £1.7 billion, Taylor noted, amounted to almost twice the revenue to be collected in the first year of Vat on domestic fuel.

Labour in the campaign had advocated tax increases for the better off only, though Conservatives claimed that Labour plans would hit huge numbers of taxpayers, and not just the most prosperous. After their election defeat, Labour abandoned the commitment to higher taxation. They argued that reductions in the PSBR should come not through tax increases or public spending cuts but from growth, engineered by expansionary policies.

The unified budget

In past years, announcements on what the Government planned to spend and how it intended to pay for them had come in two separate packets. Spending plans were disclosed in an Autumn Statement, usually around November. The measures needed to pay for them were disclosed in the spring Budget. In his 1992 Budget, Lamont said he meant to end this practice and to make both statements, as logic seemed to ordain, together. He delivered his last spring Budget — and his own last Budget of any kind, as it transpired — on March 16. The first unified Budget was planned for November 30 1993, with the Finance Bill following in January 1994. ●

PROPORTION OF EARNINGS* PAID IN TAXATION (T) AND NATIONAL INSURANCE (NI) CONTRIBUTIONS

	81-82	86-87	91-92	92-93 projected
SINGLE PERSON				
half average earnings T	17.5	14.4	12.8	11.5
NI	7.7	7.0	6.2	6.2
average earnings T	23.7	21.7	18.9	18.2
NI	7.7	9.0	7.6	7.6
2 x average earnings T	27.3	25.4	22.0	22.3
NI	6.1	7.2	6.0	6.0
MARRIED MAN				
half average earnings T	10.5	6.2	6.5	5.5
NI	7.7	7.0	6.2	6.2
average earnings T	20.2	17.6	15.7	15.2
NI	7.7	9.0	7.6	7.6
2 x average earnings T	25.1	23.3	20.4	20.1
NI	6.1	7.2	6.0	6.0

(*Defined as average earnings for full-time adult male manual employees working full week on adult rates)

Source: Social Trends

GENERAL GOVERNMENT EXPENDITURE AS PROPORTION OF GDP

	%GDP		
1963-4	36	1985-6	45
1968-9	41.5	1986-7	44
1973-4	43.5	1987-8	41.75
1978-9	44	1988-9	39.25
1979-80	44	1989-90	39.75
1980-1	46.5	1990-91	40.25
1981-2	47.25	1991-92	42
1982-3	47.5	1992-93	44.75
1983-4	46. 5	1993-94 (projected)	45.5
1984-5	47		

Source: Public Expenditure Analysis

PUBLIC SECTOR BORROWING REQUIREMENT

	£bn	as % GDP
79-80	9.9	4.8
80-81	13.2	5.6
81-2	8.8	3.4
82-3	9.2	3.2
83-4	9.8	3.2
84-5	10.2	3.2
85-6	5.8	1.8
86-7	2.5	0.6
87-8	- 3.0	-0.7
88-9	-14.0	-3.0
89-90	-7.6	-1.7
90-1	-0.5	
91-2	13.7	
92-3	36.5	

THE SMILE ON THE FACE OF THE HIGHER RATE TAXPAYER

Taxpayers under the 1987-88 indexed regime	Tax liability under		Tax and national insurance liability under	
	1993-94 regime	1987-88 regime indexed to 1993-94	1993-94 regime	1987-88 regime indexed to1993-94
Top 1 per cent	9,300	12,500	9,600	12,800
Top 5 per cent	19,300	23,300	20,900	25,000
Top 10 per cent	26,000	30,600	29,300	34,100
Top 20 per cent	35,700	41,400	42,100	48,400
Top 50 per cent	52,500	60,500	65,400	75,000
Bottom 50 per cent	8,100	10,100	12,100	14,900
Bottom 20 per cent	1,000	1,400	1,700	2,300
Bottom 10 per cent	230	330	480	630
Bottom 5 per cent	60	80	160	210

Information for the bottom 1 % of taxpayers is not available. The 1987-88 income tax regime has been indexed to 1993-94 levels by reference to the statutory formula and allowing for independent taxation. For the purpose of the calculations the indexed regime of 1987-88 has been applied directly to the income base of 1993-94. In practice, retention of the 1987-88 regime, indexed as appropriate, for the intervening years would have led to changes in the income base.

Source: written answer to Donald Dewar, MP March 30 1993 HcD col 142

**AVERAGE REDUCTION IN INCOME TAX PER INDIVIDUAL* IN 1993-94 COMPARED WITH THE
1978-79 INDEXED REGIME**

Range of individual's income in 1993-94 (£)	Number of individuals 1993-94* (million)	Total reduction (£m)	Average reduction (£ per annum)
Under 5,000	3.20	450	140
5,000 to 10,000	8.00	3,000	380
10,000 to 15,000	6.10	4,500	740
15,000 to 20,000	3.70	4,000	1,100
20,000 to 30,000	3.30	5,400	1,620
30,000 to 50,000	1.20	3,000	2,520
50,000 to 80,000	0.28	2,100	7,730
Over 80,000	0.14	6,400	45,500
TOTAL	**26.00**	**28,900**	**1,100**

* Individuals liable to income tax under the 1978-79 indexed regime.

Source: written answer to Frank Field, MP April 19 1993 HcD col 7

BUDGET '92

Income Tax

Income tax reduced to 20% for the first £2,000 of taxable income.
Basic rate limit frozen at £23,700. Married couple's allowance frozen at £1,720;
wives entitled to claim half. Income support for single pensioners up by £2 a week,
for married couples £3 a week.

Alchohol

One penny on a pint of beer, 5p on a bottle of wine, 28p on a bottle of spirits

Tobacco

13p on a packet of 20 cigarettes.

Motoring

Unleaded petrol up 1.3p, leaded by 2.3p. Vehicle excise duty up from £100 to £110; tax on new
cars halved to 5%.

Inheritance/Capital Gains Tax

Inheritance tax threshold raised from £140,000 to £150,000. Capital Gains Tax exemption raised
to £5,800.

PSBR

PSBR forecast at £28 billion in 1992-93, double the 1991-92 figure.

Business

Uniform business rate reduced by 3.25%. New occupiers to inherit transitional relief.

BUDGET '93

Income Tax

No change in 25% or 40% band.
20% band extended for 1993-94 by £500 to cover first £2,500. Personal allowances for married
couples and related allowances frozen for this tax year.

Alcohol

Excise duties up by an average of 5% — 1.5p on beer and 5.5p on wine. No change in the duty
on spirits.

Tobacco

Overall increase of 6.5% but the tax structure changed. Average of 20p on 20 cigarettes but a
higher proportion on cheap small cigarettes. Packet of five small cigars rises by about 4.5p

Mortgages

No change in the £30,000 ceiling for tax relief but stamp duty threshold doubled to £60,000
immediately.

Motoring

Fuel duty increased by 10% - 12p on a gallon of unleaded and 15p on a gallon of four-star. Road Fund licence up by £15 to £125 per year.

Company Cars

The scale charge on all free fuel increased by 20% and the high-mileage discount is abolished. Other scale charges go up by 8%.

Unemployed

New Community Action programme allowing 60,000 long-term jobless to work part-time in their communities. Extra 10,000 places on Business Start-Up Scheme. 30,000 long-term unemployed to be funded for full-time vocational courses. Employers who take on those unemployed for at least two years to receive a one year subsidy.

Vat

No changes.

Business Rates

To be held for a further year to a maximum increase of 3.6%

Charities

Annual limit for tax relief under the payroll giving scheme up from £600 to £900 from April 6. Minimum gift attracting tax relief for single donations under the Gift Aid Scheme reduced from £400 to £250 from March 16.

EARLY WARNINGS

The chancellor also signalled changes he plans beyond this year.

Income Tax

From April 1994, 20% band will be extended to first £3,000. Married couple's allowance will only apply to 20% tax rate. Over 65s will get a special £200 compensatory allowance. Mortgage relief rate reduced to 20%. Tax credit on dividends down to 20%.

Energy Taxes

Domestic fuel and power will attract Vat, at 8% in 1994-95, then 17.5% from 1995-96. Road fuel tax will be increased by 3% a year in real terms.

National Insurance

Employees' and self-employed contributions to rise by 1% in 1994-95.

Company cars

Taxable value will be based on 35% on list price instead of engine capacity. Some discounts for high-mileage users. Use of company vans will be valued at £500.

FINANCE (Government Bill)
INTRODUCED: MAY 14 1992

PURPOSE:

To implement the 1992 Budget

COMMONS:

2nd reading: June 2 1992 by 308 (Con, OUP, UPUP) to 256 (Lab, Lib Dem, SNP, PC)

Report and 3rd reading: July 7-8 1992

LORDS:

All stages July 14 1992

ROYAL ASSENT:

July 16 1992

FINANCE NO. 2 (Government Bill)
INTRODUCED: March 22 1993

PURPOSE:

To implement the 1993 Budget

COMMONS:

2nd reading: April 26 1993 by 310 (Con, UPUP) to 266 (Lab, Lib Dem, SNP, PC 1 OUP)

Report and 3rd reading: July 12-13 1993

LORDS:

All stages: July 27 1993

ROYAL ASSENT:
Rebellions:

On May 10, during Committee Stage 2 Conservative MPs voted against the ending of Vat zero rating on fuel. They were N Winterton (Macclesfield) and W. Powell (Corby). At report stage Winterton, Powell and G. Dickens (Littleborough) voted for the striking out of this measure from the Bill (July 12)

THREE
INDUSTRY

From the 1992 election onwards, the Major government signalled a new approach to industrial policy and a clear break with the prevailing philosophies of the Thatcher years. Michael Heseltine, an unashamed interventionist, was installed at the Department of Trade and Industry, replacing the Thatcherite Peter Lilley.

On October 20, the prime minister appeared on the evening news bulletins to promise a new economic strategy of going for growth, though he added that this would not be the old-style intervention bent on rescuing lame ducks. Norman Lamont's Autumn Statement (November 12) was pitched to produce industrial resurgence, with extra tax on cars abolished, a mild stimulus for the housing market and temporary tax relief provisions for capital investment.

These declarations came after years of relative industrial decline, with two recessions shutting down swathes of British manufacturing industry. The first, in 1980-81, was estimated to have eliminated 18 to 20 per cent of our manufacturing base. A rise of some 45 per cent in the exchange rate over these years was alone enough to force export-based companies out of business. OECD figures for 1989 showed that manufacturing in Britain accounted for 19 per cent of GDP (Gross Domestic Product) against 22 per cent in France, 23 per cent in Italy and 31 per cent in Germany.

The 1990-92 recession brought further casualties as Britain suffered initially more than its neighbours, though this seemed likely to be alleviated as Britain also promised to be out of recession first. The 1993 World Competitiveness Report (published by the World Economic Forum) put Britain bottom out of the top 22 industrialised countries in terms of industrial production. Some industries prospered mightily. Car production in May 1993 was almost 24 per cent up on the previous year, with exports up 10 per cent. The first five months of the year showed a 9 per cent rise, with an 8.5 per cent jump in exports. It was the industry's best May for 16 years. But the one clear advantage across the board was in productivity as companies contrived to get the same amount of production out of a smaller workforce.

The figures for productivity in the summer of 1993 were looking so impressive that ministers had to bite on their tongues not to talk about a British productivity miracle. With workforces cut to the bone — in some cases, perhaps, beyond it — during the recession, and average earnings growing at a rate of under 4 per cent, productivity for the three months to May 1993 was up 8.7 per cent, the best performance for seven years, while unit wage costs were down by 5.3 per cent. This was a further help for exporters, already enjoying the fruits of the Black Wednesday devaluation. And the scent of recovery was beginning to restore to industry the long-abandoned confidence which alone could boost investment.

In practice, the new interventionism signalled by Heseltine proved to be limited. It was Heseltine who on October 19 told the Commons of British Coal's plans to close 31 pits with the loss of 30,000 jobs. There was, he suggested, nothing else to be done. There was no conceivable market for the coal these pits produced and you couldn't go on producing coal that could not be sold. And even before this — on June 16 — Lamont, unmoved by Heseltine's doubts, announced the winding-up of the National Economic Development Council, set up in 1962 by his equally ill-fated predecessor, Selwyn Lloyd, and the last surviving bastion of the tripartite approach (government, employers, unions) which Thatcherism had largely obliterated.

The privatisation programme, however, continued much as before, taking Major's government into areas which even Margaret Thatcher had stayed out of, and about whose suitability for the privatisation treatment the public, according to polls, was far from enthusiastic. The policy, as before, was driven not only by conviction but also by calculation, since the proceeds of privatisation swelled government revenues. The future of two staple industries was joined together in the British Coal and British Rail (Transfer Proposals) Bill introduced in May 1992, requiring the two organisations to prepare themselves for privatisation. Heseltine made a start on the privatisation of the Post Office service by pledging to dispose of Parcelforce, its parcel delivery business, and launching a review of the rest of the Post Office — though neither project made progress. The Government also planned to privatise bus services still in public ownership in London and 34 other towns. But in Scotland, the plans to privatise water supplies as had been done in England were stalled in the face of strong public opposition.

Some of the biggest public sector changes occurred in the civil service as, under the Next Steps programme, operations previously part of the Whitehall machine and supervised by ministers were transferred to arms length agencies. Ministers, according to this philosophy, were responsible for policy, but the day-to-day running of services was better left in the hands of others.

In a written answer on May 10, it was estimated that 19 per cent of the written questions submitted by MPs for answer by social security ministers were being answered not by ministers but by those who ran the agencies. Under a system called market testing, large parts of the civil service were opened up to competition, with people bidding against against rivals for their jobs. Bringing the market place to the heart of government, the public service minister, William Waldegrave, called it.

Among the responsibilities assigned to agencies was training, now largely in the hands of the TECs

GOVERNMENT SPENDING ON TRADE, INDUSTRY, ENERGY AND EMPLOYMENT

1 Total spending at current prices £billion
2. Total spending in real terms at 1991-2 prices £billion
3. % of government expenditure
4. % of GDP

	1978-1979	1983-1984	1984-1985	1985-1986	1986-1987	1987-1988	1988-1989	1989-1990	1990-1991	1991-1992	1992-3 (estimate)
1	4.2	7.2	8.1	8.3	8.3	6.8	8.2	7.7	7.8	7.1	7.3
2	11.2	11.4	12.3	11.9	11.5	9.0	10.1	8.9	8.3	7.1	7.0
3	5.6	5.1	5.3	5.1	4.9	3.8	4.4	3.8	3.5		
4	2.4	2.4	2.5	2.3	2.1	1.6	1.7	1.5	1.4		

PERFORMANCE OF UK MANUFACTURING

1. UK manufacturing production 1979=100   2. UK manufacturing investment 1979=100
3. Output per person in manufacturing 1979=100   4. Employees in employment, manufacturing industry (thousands)

	1	2	3	4
1980	92	88	96	6,801
1981	87	69	99	6,099
1982	87	68	106	5,751
1983	90	67	115	5,418
1984	93	79	121	5,302
1985	96	91	125	5,362
1986	97	86	129	5,227
1987	102	91	137	5,152
1988	110	102	145	5,089
1989	114	111	151	5,080
1990	114	100	152	4,994
1991	108	89	153	4,599
1992	107	91	152	4,396

Source: Annual Abstract of Statistics

(Training and Enterprise Centres). There were 82 across Britain, charged with invigorating a sector where by common consent we had failed to keep pace with our European competitors. Labour argued that "reskilling Britain" ought to be at the very heart of a strategy for sustained recovery and complained that the Government's efforts were inadequate.

Deregulation was also pushed ahead. Major promised on April 26 1993 to cut excessive regulatory burdens on industry. "Whether it comes from Brussels, from Whitehall or from town hall," he said, "there is no doubt in my mind that regulation has gone too far." But some feared deregulation would remove necessary protection from consumers and employees.

One area where deregulationary zeal was tempered was the Sunday opening of shops. Though Kenneth Clarke as home secretary favoured relaxing the law, there was strong opposition on the Tory back benches, while Labour was only willing to back legislation on the basis of safeguards for workers, which Clarke was unwilling to give.

But a Bill to resolve the matter one way or another — with the choice of whether or not to soften the law left to MPs — was promised for the autumn.●

WORLD COMPETITIVENESS LEAGUE 1993

DE - Strength of the domestic economy at a macro level
IT - Participation in international trade and investment flows
GP - Conduciveness of Government policies to competitiveness
CM - Performance of capital markets, quality of financial services
RS - Adequacy of resources and systems to serve business
ME - Management of enterprises in terms of innovation, profitability and responsibility
ST - Scientific and technological capacity, success of basic and applied research
HR - Availability and qualification of human resources

	DE	IT	GP	CM	RS	ME	ST	HR
Australia	16	16	4	10	14	17	15	12
Austria	5	4	7	12	12	10	11	6
Belg/Lux	4	1	18	9	15	6	14	15
Canada	12	20	11	3	5	14	16	11
Denmark	9	2	8	7	4	2	7	1
Finland	15	22	15	19	10	15	5	7
France	10	11	16	13	7	11	8	16
Germany	11	7	5	6	8	9	4	3
Greece	22	21	21	22	22	21	20	21
Ireland	3	8	12	14	18	12	10	14
Italy	14	18	22	20	19	18	17	7
Japan	1	9	6	2	16	1	1	2
Neth'lds	8	3	10	4	11	7	12	8
NZ	7	14	1	11	6	8	18	13
Norway	18	17	17	21	1	13	9	9
Portugal	13	6	13	15	20	22	21	19
Spain	17	13	20	16	17	20	19	20
Sweden	20	12	14	17	3	3	6	5
Switzerland	6	19	2	1	2	4	3	4
Turkey	21	15	19	18	21	19	22	22
UK	19	10	9	8	13	16	13	18
US	2	5	3	5	9	5	2	10

Source: World Competitiveness Report 1993: World Competitiveness Project

EMPLOYEES IN MANUFACTURING AND SERVICE INDUSTRIES
(thousands, June each year seasonally adjusted)

	(a) manufacturing	(b) services	ratio b:a
1979	7,113	13,222	1.9
1983	5,431	13,130	2.4
1984	5,316	13,456	2.5
1985	5,269	13,731	2.6
1986	5,138	13,918	2.7
1987	5,068	14,220	2.8
1988	5,109	14,841	2.9
1989	5,101	15,242	3.0
1990	5,018	15,573	3.1
1991	4,667	15,417	3.3
1992	4,419	15,326	3.5
1993	4,201		

Source: Monthly Digest of Statistics

BRITISH COAL AND RAIL (TRANSFER PROPOSALS) (Government Bill)
INTRODUCED: May 7 1992

PURPOSE:
To prepare the industries for privatisation. Details of privatisation plans were given in White Papers of July 14 1992 (rail) and March 25 1993 (coal)

COMMONS:
2nd reading: May 18 1992 by 325 (Con, Lib Dem, UPUP) to 256 (Lab, 1 SNP)
Report and 3rd reading: June 29 1992

LORDS:
2nd reading: July 13 1992
Report: December 15 1992
3rd reading: January 18 1993

ROYAL ASSENT:
January 18 1993

FOUR
THE CITY

You don't have to be a Queen to have an annus horribilis. The City of London had one in 1992, and another in 1993, most of all because of the turmoil in its flagship institution, Lloyd's. A loss of £2.08 billion in 1989, reported in 1992, was followed by a loss of £2.91 billion on 1990 reported on June 22 1993. (The projected loss for 1991 was put at about £1 billion.) Though fraud may have played some part, the main cause was a string of disasters — the 1987 hurricane in Britain, Hurricane Hugo in the USA, the Exxon Valdez oil spillage, the Piper Alpha rig explosion — together with expensive settlements in cases of industrial pollution and workers made terminally ill by contact with asbestos. Some of the names — the wealthy people who entered Lloyd's syndicates in the hope of making money — were ruined.

Sixteen judges and more than 90 QCs were named as substantial losers. So were more than 40 MPs, all Conservatives. At one stage it was feared that some MPs would go bankrupt, and since bankrupts cannot sit in the Commons there would then be a series of by-elections which the Government might well lose. But Mary Archer, wife of the Tory peer Lord Archer, who chaired Lloyd's Hardship Committee, said it was not Lloyd's practice to pursue the indebted into bankruptcy.

Two inquiries into the Lloyd's calamity, published on July 2 1992, were critical of the institution's system of self-regulation. One, by the City's best known regulator, Sir David Walker, said there was no evidence of systematic fraud, but standards in the market had fallen materially below best practice. Regulation had been lax, and underwriters had been guilty of "seriously flawed judgment". A second, from Sir Jeremy Morse, then chairman of Lloyds Bank, recommended changes in the system of regulation but emphasised that regulation and compliance were matters for the prudence of the market itself, with a new regulatory board behind it.

Wrangling over responsibility for the losses continued into 1993 with demands for extraordinary general meetings and even for the winding up of the organisation. Critics were not placated by the announcement on April 29 1993 of extensive changes in the way Lloyd's was run, with a "modest" contribution to help those worst hit by their losses.

The City's reputation took a further knock with the collapse of a prestige project designed to convert the City to paperless working. The Taurus project, masterminded by the chief executive of the Stock Exchange, Peter

Rawlins, proved to be a disaster and was scrapped in March 1993 with an estimated £75 million written off. Rawlins resigned.

Tempers in the City were not improved by the subsequent revelation that he had taken a 28 per cent pay increase in his final year in office, including a performance-related bonus paid at a time when Taurus was heading for the rocks, all of which substantially increased his pay-off.

The recession also claimed victims, especially in the property market. The most conspicuous casualty was Canary Wharf, a futuristic project in London's Docklands, conceived in boom years but open for business when business was bad.

The backwash of past scandals persisted, especially the collapse of BCCI in a sea of fraud and the crash of the Maxwell empire.

BCCI collapsed in 1991 leaving creditors with the hope of regaining at best 30 to 40p for every pound they were owed. A report by Lord Justice Bingham, published on October 22 1992, condemned the supervision of BCCI by the Bank of England and others as "a tragedy of errors, misunderstandings and failures of communication".

Lord Bingham was not persuaded that the Bank of England had lacked the evidence to sense what was happening at BCCI, or the power to put a halt to it. The report did, however, exonerate the Treasury, though Labour dissented. "The Treasury and its ministers knew full well there was a problem and chose to do nothing," said their spokesman, Gordon Brown, "and for this the prime minister must accept his share of the blame." Major

had been chancellor at a crucial point in the story.

Maxwell was an entrepreneur, not a man of the City, but the banks had lent him money on what, with hindsight, looked like a reckless scale. Despite some government help, the plight of the pensioners whose funds he had stolen, people far less prosperous than the stricken at Lloyd's, remained dire. All in all, the City's preference for trust in self-regulation rather than outside control was further undermined.

A series of reports appeared on aspects of the Maxwell affair. In May 1993, Andrew Large, chairman of the Securities and Investment Board, recognised that the system of self-regulation was flawed and recommended a series of regulatory arrangements, including the total exclusion of offenders from investment management, as a means of imposing control until new regulatory systems were put in place. Both he and the chairman of the Stock Exchange, Sir Andrew Hugh Smith, were now on the record as preferring a central powerful regulator with power to impose heavy civil penalties. Professor Roy Goode was due to report in September 1993 on the pensions aspects, which had also been investigated by the social security select committee of the House of Commons under Frank Field MP.

The lights often burned late at the Serious Fraud Office, which was criticised both for excessive zeal and for inadequate rigour. A series of exceptionally expensive proceedings — Guinness, Blue Arrow, BCCI — failed to produce all the hoped for convictions — not least because of the numbing complexity of the cases —

REINSURANCE (ACTS OF TERRORISM) (Government Bill)
INTRODUCED: May 6 1993

PURPOSE:

To establish Government role as re-insurer of last resort after insurance companies declined to provide cover for industrial and commercial property against loss caused by acts of terrorism.

COMMONS:

All stages May 13 1993: unopposed

LORDS:

All stages: May 27 1993

ROYAL ASSENT:

May 27 1993

or else brought convictions which were later overturned. The Office's pursuit of Asil Nadir after his Polly Peck empire collapsed led to serious charges against the SFO in the Commons from the Conservative MP Michael Mates, whose involvement in the affair cost him his ministerial job. In a personal statement to the Commons on June 29 1993, five days after his resignation, Mates complained that the SFO had orchestrated trial by media, combining with the police, the Inland Revenue and unspecified City institutions to leak information which undermined the Polly Peck share price; that its powers had been consistently exceeded; and even that it had been involved in an attempt to get the trial judge to stand down because of a supposed conspiracy to bribe him. Nadir had fled to Cyprus complaining he had no chance of a fair trial.

A further City reform designed to improve behaviour in Britain's boardrooms, the Cadbury Code, began to have an effect in 1993. Many larger companies, such as Barclays Bank, which had resisted a split between chairman and chief executive, capitulated before challenges from big institutional investors. In June 1993 Lord Hanson backed down on plans to limit shareholder democracy in the face of opposition from the large pension funds. Even so, despite the appearance of corporate governance reports in many company accounts, Cadbury appeared less than successful in stamping out larger payoffs to sacked executives and over-generous three-year pay deals among directors.

The turmoil in the City was compounded by a shift of emphasis in the IRA's mainland campaign to commercial targets and the disruption of business life. On the day after the Conservatives' election victory, a bomb in the City killed three people and people caused extensive damage to property, wrecking the Baltic Exchange. On April 24, a huge explosion in Bishopsgate caused devastation in the Square Mile, with the cost of repair initially put at close to £1 billion, though later estimates suggested it would be about half that.

The Government promised to meet most of the bill, but the consequences for City insurance costs remained menacing.●

FIVE
THE REGIONS

Those who feared that Britain had become two nations, the prosperous south and the rest, could take perverse comfort from the 1990-92 recession as that pattern began to be reversed. Past recessions had tended to hit the worst-off regions hardest. This one, destroying jobs among white-collar as well as blue-collar workers, bit most fiercely in the south, bringing unemployment and the fear of unemployment to areas which had never thought it would happen to them.

Unemployment in Greater London grew by 6.2 percentage points over the 12 years between 1981 and 1993. In the rest of the south east it increased by 4 per cent, and in the south west by 3.2 per cent. But in the north west it rose by only 0.7 per cent, in the north by 0.4 per cent. In Scotland it was static and in Wales it actually fell. Even in Northern Ireland, traditionally among the worst victims of recession, the increase was no more than 2 per cent. The result was that by 1991, the level of unemployment in Greater London was only a little short of that in the northern region, and greater than that in Wales, the north west or Yorkshire and Humberside.

Scotland, not the south, registered the biggest advance in the rate of increase of personal disposable income per head. The south was still top, but Scotland moved up from fifth place in 1987 to second. Wales fell behind Northern Ireland to take last place. House prices fell between 1991 and 1992 in Greater London, the rest of the south east, and East Anglia: in Wales, the north west, the north and Northern Ireland, they rose. The rate of repossessions grew much faster in the south than in the north.

On many other tests the pattern remained much as before. The south east and south west had the fastest-growing populations, the north and north west the slowest. The south had more people in professional jobs; Wales, the north and Yorkshire and Humberside had the fewest. The south east outside London had the highest proportion of owner-occupiers (though East Anglia had more detached houses); Scotland had fewest. The south east and south west, though also Scotland, had the highest proportion of stayers-on at school. The south east had the highest proportion of high-income taxpayers — 7 per cent with assessable incomes of over £30,000, against 2 per cent in Wales.

But even here the picture was patchy. The prosperous south east, for instance, had the highest proportion of homeless households. The overall impression was that a gap which had widened during the good years had narrowed in the bad. And that was echoed in the region by region results at the election, with swings to Labour higher across the south than in Wales, the north west, the north and Yorkshire and Humberside, and with Scotland swinging 2.5 per cent to the right.

These changes altered Government thinking about the deployment of subsidies. An analysis by the Labour MP for Darlington, Alan Milburn, based on regional public spending figures supplied by the Treasury and Ministry of Defence between 1987 and 1991, indicated a break with previous patterns of spending priority. Government spending per head fell by 3.8 per cent in Tyneside, Wearside and Northumberland and by just over 1 per cent in Scotland, Devon, Cornwall, Dorset and Somerset. The biggest rises were 11.7 per cent in East Anglia, and 4.6 per cent in London and the south east. Government spending on housing fell 39.7 per cent in the north, 41 per cent in Northern Ireland and 26.7 per cent in Scotland. It rose 263.9 per cent in the south west, 227.9 per cent in the south east, and 214 per cent in East Anglia.

Figures for road building and assistance to business showed similar shifts. (North loses out in big public spending switch/David Hencke/Guardian February 9 1993).

A revised Assisted Area Map published on July 23 mirrored the recession by including once-thriving areas of southern England and eliminating others in the north, the Midlands, Wales and Scotland (see table). The Government's original intentions had been tempered after consultations with Brussels. Towns like Brighton, excluded from the selection, complained that this had blighted their chances of aid from EC structural funds.

Despite the signs that the regional gap was narrowing, the south east had in many ways done well over the past decade. Most of the money foregone when the top rate taxes were cut went to this region. According to Treasury figures, 58.4 per cent of the benefit from tax cuts following the abolition of top rate in 1988 had gone to the south east. Only 1.1 per cent of this money went to Northern Ireland and only 1.6 per cent to the north. ●

UNEMPLOYMENT BY REGION
% unemployed, seasonally adjusted

	1979-82	1983-6	1987	1988	1989	1990	1991	1992	1993
E. Anglia	5.3	8.1	7.3	5.2	3.6	3.9	5.8	7.6	8.6
South East	4.7	7.9	7.2	5.4	3.9	4.0	7.0	9.4	10.5
South West	6.2	9.1	8.1	6.2	4.5	4.4	7.1	9.1	10.0
E. Midlands	6.1	9.8	9.0	7.1	5.4	5.1	7.2	8.9	9.7
W.Midlands	8.1	12.8	11.4	8.9	6.6	6.0	8.6	10.7	11.5
Yorks & Humb	7.4	11.9	11.3	9.3	7.4	6.7	8.7	9.9	10.6
Wales	10.2	13.3	12.0	9.8	7.3	6.6	8.7	9.7	10.3
Scotland	10.0	12.8	13.0	11.3	9.3	8.1	8.7	9.5	9.9
North West	8.8	13.6	12.5	10.4	8.5	7.7	9.4	10.5	10.9
North	10.2	15.1	14.1	11.9	9.9	8.7	10.4	11.3	12.1
N.Ireland	11.4	16.2	17.2	15.6	14.6	13.4	13.8	14.5	14.7
UK	7.9	10.8	10.0	8.1	6.3	5.8	8.1	9.7	10.6

Source: derived and updated from Regional Trends

LOSS OF HIGHER RATE TAX REVENUE BY REGION
(£million)

	1988-89	1989-90	1990-1	total	%of all
North	50	50	50	150	1.6
Yorks and H	100	150	200	450	4.7
North west	150	250	250	650	6.8
East Midlands	100	150	150	400	4.2
West Midlands	150	150	250	550	5.8
East Anglia	100	100	150	350	3.7
South east	1,600	1,800	2,150	5,500	58.4
South west	200	300	250	750	7.9
Wales	50	100	50	200	2.1
Scotland	100	100	150	350	3.7
N Ireland	*	50	50	100	1.1
UK	2,600	3,200	3,700	9,500	100

* Under £25m

Source: written answer to Alan Milburn MP

INDEX OF REGIONAL DIFFERENCES

1. Average earnings[1]   2 .Personal disposable income per head[2]   3. Perinatal mortality[3]
4. % staying on at school

	1992	**1** **1991**	**2** **1971**	**1991**	**3** **1981-2**	**4** **1991-2**
North	314.3	91.3	23.0	9.3	51.5	71.7
Yorks	307.5	93.1	22.8	8.4	53.8	73.4
E Mids	306.1	95.8	22.0	8.2	54.6	74.7
E Anglia	321.4	98.0	20.1	6.7	50.6	71.8
S East	391.9	113.7	20.5	7.6	60.8	76.7
S West	315.2	94.6	20.3	6.7	57.3	75.6
W Mids	312.1	91.8	23.7	9.8	55.6	74.8
N West	320.1	95.3	25.6	7.8	56.7	73.7
Wales	299.2	85.7	24.4	7.9	58.1	71.2
Scotland	324.6	100.5	24.5	8.6	n/a	76.8
N I	298.2	86.4	27.2	8.4	n/a	n/a

1 All full time male employees April 1992
2 On index all UK - 100
3 Rate per 10,000 live and still births

ASSISTED AREA MAP July 22 1993

New assisted areas (added to map) Alfreton and Ashfield; Alnwick and Amble; Barnstaple and Ilfracombe; Barrow; Bideford; Bridlington and Driffield; Castleford and Pontefract; Chesterfield; Clacton; Dorchester and Weymouth (part); Dover and Deal; Folkestone; Great Yarmouth; Harwich; Hastings; Isle of Wight; Park Royal, Lea Valley, west end of East London corridor, London; Louth and Mablethorpe; Mansfield (development area); Retford; Sittingbourne and Sheerness; Skegness; St Austell; Thanet (development area); Thurso; Torbay; Wakefield and Dewsbury; Whitehaven; Wisbech; Worksop.

Areas deleted from map: Accrington and Rossendale; Badenoch; Bradford; Cardiff; Corby; Cinderford and Ross-on-Wye; Darlington; Kidderminster; Lampeter and Aberavon; Manchester; Newport (eastern part); Scunthorpe; Shotton, Flint and Rhyl (part); Stewartry; Telford and Bridgnorth; Wrexham (part).

SIX
TRADE

Nobody could be sure what the effect would be of Britain's withdrawal from the Exchange Rate Mechanism and the subsequent devaluation of the pound. It looked like good news for manufacturers, who had been complaining that the parity fixed for sterling — DM2.95 — was pricing them out of world markets. Devaluation ought to give them a sharper competitive edge. But imports were sure to be dearer. With a trade deficit running — in the depths of recession, when trade deficits traditionally had tended to fall — at £12 billion for 1992-93, and projected in the Budget statement to top £17 billion in 1993-94, the calculation was crucial.

Yet for the first six months of 1993, nobody knew quite what was happening. The establishment of the European Single Market at the start of 1993, obliterating previous checks and controls, left no reliable way of monitoring trade with the European Community until July. The figures for non-EC trade, in the meantime, were not initially encouraging, with a deficit of £1,060 million in January widening to £1,334 million in February.

Subsequent months, though, went better. By the summer there were clear signs of a solid improvement in exports as the advantages of a lower exchange rate and higher productivity

fed through. Non-EC trade figures published on July exceeded the City's best expectations with the trade gap narrowing from £770 million in May to £613 million in June — a figure which would once have been seen as horrifying, yet was now saluted as the smallest deficit for two years. The volume of exports was up 15 per cent on the year. The whole of the improvement had happened since Black Wednesday.

There was worrying evidence, even so, that the weakening of Britain's industrial base had hit its trading position in much the way that a Lords select committee had predicted in Margaret Thatcher's heyday. The committee, set up in 1985 under Lord Aldington, warned of a contraction in manufacturing to a point where the successful continuation of much of our manufacturing activity would be put at risk; of an irreplaceable loss of GDP (Gross Domestic Product); of an adverse balance of payments of such dimensions that severe deflation must follow; of far higher unemployment, with little hope of reducing it; and of a stagnant economy, with inflation driven up by a falling exchange rate.

There were echoes of that in a report on the British economy published from Basle on June 14 1993 by the Bank for International Settlements

(BIS). Imports of manufactured goods, it noted, were particularly strong "suggesting the low level of manufacturing investment has led to a structural weakness as the capacity of UK manufacturing enterprises may not be sufficiently large to support the domestic market even in conditions of low demand". The BIS found it difficult to reconcile the triple objectives of enhancing growth, cutting the PSBR and improving the balance of trade. The growth needed to hold down the PSBR might push up the trade deficit; yet growth compatible with a stable current account deficit might produce an unsustainable rise in the public sector imbalance.

The depressed levels of world trade, with markets across Europe, and especially in Germany, in decline and the US recovery apparently faltering, added fresh urgency to the search for agreement in the Uruguay round of Gatt — the General Agreement on Tariffs and Trade, which since 1947 had boosted world trade by eradicating protectionist barriers. The round had begun at the Uruguayan resort of Punta del Este in September 1986, with December 1990 the target date for agreement. The aim was to extend the process successfully applied over the years to manufacturing industry, to agriculture, service industries and intellectual property.

The negotiations were dominated by conflict over agricultural subsidies between the US and the EC (especially France). December 1990 brought not the scheduled agreement but indefinite suspension. By November 1992 the gap seemed to be narrowing, but attempts to bridge it failed as fresh disagreements developed over oilseed.

The US threatened retaliation, saying swingeing tariffs on European goods — and French goods in particular — would come into force in December if no agreement was reached. Fears of a trade war were deepened by apprehension that the incoming US president, Bill Clinton, was more sympathetic to protection than his predecessor George Bush.

The election in March 1993 of a new right-wing government in France was a further complication, threatening to unpick moves towards a settlement that had been under way since November. The new French agricultural minister said planned concessions would be unacceptable to France. Tensions were high as these issues were raised yet again at Tokyo in July, where a meeting of the G7 group of industrialised nations coincided with a meeting of Gatt. Agreement on what the US negotiator called "the biggest market access package in history" might bring a boost to world trade that was desperately needed — to the tune, on one estimate, of £83 billion a year. Failure might mean a retreat into protectionism. The stakes were also high for the developing world. A deal, they were told, would offer them easier access to world markets: in practice, some feared, it might give the developed world easier, and more destructive, access to theirs.

On July 6, a deal was done which negotiators hailed as a breakthrough — "the biggest tariff cut in history", the Americans called it. The reality was rather more modest. Seven of the 114 countries involved had settled in eight areas, but 10 — including agriculture and services - remained to be resolved at later and potentially even

WHO DOES BEST IN THE EXPORT LEAGUE

Shares[1] of the main manufacturing countries[2] exports of manufactured goods (%)

	UK	USA	France	Italy	Japan	Germany[3]
1979	9.1	16.	10.5	20.8	8.3	13.7
1980	9.6	17.2	10.0	19.9	7.8	14.8
1982	8.4	18.0	9.0	19.6	7.9	17.3
1983	7.9	17.2	8.9	19.0	8.1	18.4
1984	7.5	17.4	8.6	18.1	7.7	20.0
1985	7.8	16.8	8.5	18.6	7.8	19.7
1986	7.6	14.2	8.8	20.7	8.2	19.4
1987	8.1	14.0	9.0	21.4	8.4	18.0
1988	8.3	15.1	8.8	20.6	8.1	18.0
1989	8.2	16.1	8.8	20.4	8.4	17.5
1990	8.6	15.8	9.7	20.6	8.6	15.8
1991	8.5	17.0	9.6	19.6	8.4	16.9

[1] Share of the value of exports measured in US dollars
[2] UK, US, Germany, France, Italy, Japan, Netherlands, Belgium/Luxembourg, Switzerland, Canada
[3] Includes eastern Germany from 1990

Source: written answer to Austin Mitchell, MP November 6 1992 HcD col 440

Faded glory: the Durham Miners' Gala in July '93 was no cause for celebration as the winding gear at pit heads across the country was silenced

SEVEN
EMPLOYMENT

Unemployment continued to climb long after the 1980-81 recession was over, reaching its peak, at just over 3 million, in the second quarter of 1985. The one bit of hope in a grim employment picture as Britain eased out of the 1990-92 recession was that the pick up in employment looked to be very much swifter. Unemployment, on the seasonally adjusted count, never quite topped 3 million this time, but that was due to changes in counting. On the measure of unemployment used by the ILO, the peak figure, in January 1993 would have been some 70,000 higher than the 2,992,3000 recorded by the Department of Employment on the basis of a count of claimants. (Jobless figure 'understated by 70,000' Larry Elliott/Guardian March 19 1993.)

The figures were challenged by Labour, which pointed out a sharp rise in payments of sickness and invalidity benefit, and alleged that some people claiming unemployment benefit had been advised to claim these other, more generous, benefits. Ministers denied it, though as the prime minister said about invalidity claims (in the Commons, June 15), it beggared belief that so many people had suddenly become invalids, especially when the health of the nation had improved.

Lost jobs in some industries were balanced in part by new opportunities elsewhere, but the new jobs were often not comparable with the old. The most spectacular casualties occurred in what had long been staple, and heavily unionised, industries — such as mining, with the British Coal announcement on October 13 1992 that 31 pits were to go, eliminating 30,000 jobs — as well as others in ancillary trades which depended on it. Part-time working increased: there were more new jobs for women than for men.

Some argued that Britain's best hope of salvation in a fiercely competitive world lay in its emergence as a sort of Hong Kong off the mainland of Europe. In a leader comment on June 6, the Sunday Times said: "The prime minister should state as boldly as he can his intention to turn Britain into the Hong Kong of Western Europe by the end of the decade — a low-cost, high-productivity, low-tax, high-tech offshore island whose growth and dynamism would be in marked contrast to the recession and sclerosis of the other major European economies." That meant a "leaner and meaner" working environment, greater flexibility in working practice, diminished job security, short-term contracts rather than long, and less regulation — which in turn implied fewer safeguards for workers. Already, under the system of market testing, organisations from Whitehall to the town hall had to justify themselves against rivals who cut their costs by offering lower wages and less generous working conditions.

One possible, ominous emblem of the search for salvation through cost-cutting was the Timex company at Dundee in Scotland, which, operating in a savagely competitive industry and fearing unacceptable losses to add to the £10 million it had already accumulated, announced (on Christmas Eve) that 150 of its 340 strong workforce would be laid off for six months. Shop stewards wanted to rotate the lay-offs; Timex refused; a strike was called; Timex dismissed the whole workforce. The company's cost-cutting terms for continuing their employment included a 10 per cent cut in wages and reduced conditions and benefits.

The dispute raged for a further five months, with replacement workers bused in past screaming picket lines, until on June 15 the company said it was pulling out of Dundee because of the workers' "unrealistic demands".

The Government's determination to opt out of the social chapter of the Maastricht treaty was part of the same climate. The Opposition objected that the Government wanted British workers to have fewer rights and less favourable working conditions than the rest of the Community. The Government said that to hold its own against the competitive challenge of the Far East economies, the EC would be forced to follow Britain's lead. Tory Eurosceptics said the duties Britain evaded by opting out of the chapter would in practice be applied in other ways. The EC's attempts to restrict the working week for 48 hours were made not under the chapter but through health and safety provisions, where the opt-out did not apply.

The changing employment climate was particularly menacing for the trade union movement, with old and heavily unionised industries giving way to new employment where union membership was marginal or gave no protection at all. Against bitter opposition from Labour, which saw it as number seven in a sequence of Bills since 1979 designed to disempower and marginalise unions, the Government introduced a Trade Union Reform and Employment Bill, abolishing the wages councils which since 1909 had set minimum wages in specified industries, requiring unions to give seven days' notice of a strike, and giving the public redress against unlawful union action.

When this Bill had cleared the Commons and almost completed its progress through the Lords, the Government introduced an amendment the effect of which was to reverse Appeal Court rulings in two cases brought against employers for practices which appeared to discriminate against union members. In one, the Daily Mail had decided no longer to recognise the National Union of Journalists as a collective bargainer on wages and conditions, but to negotiate personal contracts with employees individually. Only those employees who agreed to personal contracts would qualify for pay rises.

The amendment rewrote the law as the Mail (and others) had assumed

GOVERNMENT SPENDING ON EMPLOYMENT AND TRAINING

1 Total spending at current prices £billion
2. Total spending in real terms at 1991-2 prices £billion
3. % of government expenditure
4. % of GDP

	1978-1979	1983-1984	1984-1985	1985-1986	1986-1987	1987-1988	1988-1989	1989-1990	1990-1991-	1991-1992	1992-3 (estimate)
1	1.1	2.8	3.0	3.0	3.4	3.4	3.4	3.2	3.1	3.2	3.4
2	2.9	4.4	4.5	4.3	4.8	4.5	4.2	3.6	3.3	3.2	3.3
3	1.5	2.0	2.0	1.9	2.0	1.9	1.8	1.6	1.4	1.3	1.3
4	0.6	0.9	0.9	0.8	0.9	0.8	0.7	0.6	0.6	0.6	0.6

AVERAGE PAY AND CONDITIONS ACROSS EUROPE

Country	Average hrs	Maximum hrs	Hourly Pay	Minimum holidays (days)
UK	44	n/a	£6.50	n/a
France	40	39	£6.17	30
Germany	40	48	£9.78	18
Italy	39	48	£6.61	n/a
Holland	39	48	£8.08	28
Spain	41	40	£5.08	30
Portugal	42	48	£1.80	21
Belgium	38	42	£8.14	21
Greece	40	48	£3.10	28
Ireland	40	n/a	£5.65	21
Denmark	39	n/a	£10.00	30
Luxembourg	40	40	£7.97	25

Definition for hours: full-time average weekly hours worked, all employees, rounded to nearest digit in 1990
Definition for pay rates: hourly pay rates in manufacturing, including holiday pay and bonuses, but excluding social insurance and other non-wage labour costs: all figures for 1991, except Greece 1990; exchange rates may tend to distort particular figures.
Source for pay: CBI and US Bureau of Labour statistics, 1992

HOW EARNINGS ROSE
average earnings whole economy seasonally adjusted — rate of underlying increase over 12 months to nearest 0.25%

	Jan	Feb	Mar	Apr	May	Jun	Jul	Aug	Sep	Oct	Nov	Dec
1990	9.5	9.5	9.5	9.75	9.75	10	10.25	10	10	9.75	9.75	9.75
1991	9.5	9.25	9	8.75	8.75	8	7.75	7.75	7.75	7.5	7.5	7.25
1992	7.25	7.5	7.5	7	6.25	6.25	6	5.75	5.5	5.25	5	4.75
1993	4.75	4.5	4	3.75								

Source: Department of Employment Gazette

it to be. Labour and the Liberal Democrats, backed by a former Conservative employment minister, Peter Bottomley, saw this as licensed bribery, as penalising people for belonging to unions.

But employment secretary, David Hunt, described it as a necessary clarification of the law. He denied discrimination: companies would still be banned from making pay rises conditional on a worker leaving or joining a union. The Commons approved the amendment.

Events like this, and the failure of the protest against pit closures, showed yet again how comprehensively the trade unions, a great, powerful and feared estate of the realm in the 1960s and 1970s, had been humbled by the Conservatives. At the TUC, Norman Willis announced his long predicted retirement with his deputy, John Monks, named on July 19 1993 as his successor. Individual unions sought strength through merger. The AEU merged with the EETPU — bringing the electricians back into the TUC from which they had been expelled in September 1988 for collaboration with the forces of Rupert Murdoch at Wapping; Nalgo, Nupe and Cohse linked to form Unison; the TGWU considered possible mergers with the now greatly diminished NUM and with the GMB.●

UK UNEMPLOYMENT FIGURES MONTHLY SINCE JANUARY 1990 (thousands)

	1990		1991		1992		1993	
Jan	1,615.8	5.7	1,893.6	6.7	2,607.1	9.2	2,992.3	10.6
Feb	1,616.5	5.7	1,985.7	7.0	2,644.9	9.4	2,966.8	10.6
March	1,597.0	5.6	2.089.2	7.4	2,647.9	9.4	2,941.0	10.5
Apr	1,596.0	5.6	2,166.6	7.7	2,689.8	9.5	2,939.9	10.5
May	1,600.4	5.6	2,232.2	7.9	2,712.0	9.6	2,916.8	10.4
June	1,611.0	5.7	2,292.9	8.1	2,722.5	9.6	2,909.2	10.4
July	1,623.9	5.7	2,362.5	8.4	2,758.3	9.8		
Aug	1,651.8	5.8	2,422.5	8.6	2,815.7	9.9		
Sept	1,681.7	5.9	2,458.1	8.7	2,841.0	10.1		
Oct	1,723.6	6.1	2,477.1	8.8	2,868.1	10.1		
Nov	1,777.2	6.2	2,517.7	8.9	2,912.8	10.4		
Dec	1,853.1	6.5	2,551.2	9.0	2,972.4	10.6		

Source: Dept of Employment Gazette

TRADE UNION REFORM AND EMPLOYMENT RIGHTS (Government Bill)
INTRODUCED: November 5 1992

PURPOSE:
To abolish wage councils; require unions to hold strike ballots under independent scrutiny; give employers 7 days' notice of industrial action; to obtain members' assent every three years on deductions at source; to publish more information on salaries and benefits of executive members. Also to widen maternity leave to all employees and give protection against dismissal on health and safety grounds.

COMMONS:
2nd reading: November 17 1992 by 312 (Con, UPUP) to 277 (Lab, Lib Dem, SNP, PC, OUP)
Report and 3rd reading: February 16-17 1993

LORDS:
2nd reading: March 1 1993
Report: April 6, May 6 1993
3rd reading: May 24 1993

ROYAL ASSENT: July 1 1993
On December 10 1992 the employment secretary Gillian Shepherd announced that Government would no longer fund strike ballots as laid down in the 1980 Act.

DAYS LOST THROUGH STRIKES

1. Stoppages beginning in year. 2. no of workers involved (thousands) 3. working days lost

	1	2	3
1979	2,080	4,583	29,474
1980	1,330	830	11,964
1981	1,338	1,499	4,266
1982	1,528	2,101	5,313
1983	1,352	573	3,754
1984	1,206	1,436	27,135
1985	887	643	6,402
1986	1,053	538	1,920
1987	1,004	884	3,546
1988	770	759	3,702
1989	693	727	4,128
1990	620	285	1,903
1991	357	175	761
1992	240	142	528

DECLINE OF TRADE UNION MEMBERSHIP

	unions	number of members (millions)	% change in membership on year
1979	453	13.3	+ 1.3
1980	438	12.9	-2.6
1981	414	12.1	-6.5
1982	408	11.6	-4.2
1983	394	11.2	-3.1
1984	375	11.0	-2.2
1985	370	10.8	-1.6
1986	335	10.5	-2.6
1987	330	10.5	-0.6
1988	315	10.4	-0.9
1989	309	10.2	-2.1
1990	287	9.9	-2.1
1991	275	9.6	-3.6

Source: Employment Gazette

EIGHT
ENERGY

The Conservatives' election victory in April 1992 signalled the end of the Department of Energy, set up by Edward Heath in 1974 — ostensibly to speed up the search for North Sea oil, but in practice also to organise defences in the face of the miners' challenge to the Government. The department was now subsumed into the Department of Trade and Industry, whose new secretary of state, by a curious irony, was soon enmeshed in another bitter conflict with the National Union of Mineworkers (NUM). But where 20 years before the miners had been seen by some as predators, now they were almost universally seen, even in Tory heartlands, as ill-used victims.

The origin of the trouble was the fall in demand for coal, exacerbated by the privatisation of electricity. The new privatised contractors were free to place their orders where they wished; and their choice was gas. The regional electricity companies joined what came to be known as the "dash for gas", and National Power and PowerGen were expected to follow. The first signs of impending crisis came in a letter from the DTI minister Tim Sainsbury to the Treasury minister Michael Portillo, leaked to the Guardian and published on September 18 1992, which foresaw the loss of

30 pits and 25,500 jobs. The truth was worse. On October 13, six days before the Commons was due to reconvene after the summer recess, British Coal (BC) announced it was shutting 31 pits with the loss of 30,000 jobs.

The result was a quite extraordinary outcry in which people marched in defence of the miners even in places like Cheltenham, while backbench Tory MPs wondered aloud if their government had taken leave of its senses. To make things worse, it soon became clear that Heseltine had let this announcement go ahead without consulting some relevant colleagues. Even the employment secretary, Gillian Shephard, the ranks of whose unemployed clients these closures would shortly swell, was not fully aware of what was happening. When Heseltine came to the Commons on October 19 he was already on the retreat. Now there were to be only 10 immediate closures; decisions on the rest would be postponed until the New Year. Heseltine also announced an employment and training package worth £75 million over two years.

The Conservative rebels were unrequited and next day the Leader of the Lords, Lord Wakeham, announced a full and independent review of the industry's future — something Heseltine had repeatedly ruled out in the Commons the previous day. That was enough to hold the line for the Government when the Commons debated the issue on October 21. The Government had majorities of 13 on the Opposition's motion condemning its handling of the affair and of 15 on its own, approving it.

A series of inquiries followed by consultants hired by the Government and by other expert assessors. The result was a kind of broad national inquest on Government energy policy. The future of coal, it was widely argued, could not be judged except in the context of the future of other fuels, especially all-conquering gas — which might yet turn out to be less economic than coal — and the over-cosseted nuclear industry. The Government, said its Opposition critics, had made no attempt to establish a level playing field and one reason for that was its unabated desire to humble the NUM.

Two Commons select committees published condemnatory reports. On January 21, the employment committee called for a halt to the closure programme, forecast that final costs of closure to the taxpayer might reach £2,500 million and accused BC of "monstrous mistakes". On January 29, the Trade and industry committee put forward a package of proposals to revive the industry, including new subsidies, requirements for generators to place additional orders, a cut in open-cast mining and a reduction in imports from France. The benefits of expanding the coal market, it declared, far outweighed the costs. It blamed the Treasury as well as the DTI for misjudgments.

The committee's findings were tempered by the need to produce a unanimous report. Some Labour MPs thought it should have gone further, and the NUM president, Arthur Scargill, said the committee had failed to recognise that the market was rigged: it ought to have called for a halt in the dash for gas and the phasing out of nuclear power.

The Government and BC were also rebuked in the courts: on December 21 in the High Court Lord Justice Glidewell ruled that the Government and BC had acted "unlawfully and irrationally" in failing to consult the unions on closures as the law required.

The results of Heseltine's review were published in a White Paper on March 25. They fell far short of what was demanded by the unions and by Labour. Of the 31 listed pits, 12 would now close, six would be mothballed and one put into "development". Twelve were reprieved (saving 12 pits had been seen as the very least that Heseltine had to do to buy off the Tory rebels), yet their future was far from secure: there were no guarantees of survival, only a chance to prove themselves. Another 5,800 miners would join the 8,000 who had already left the industry since October. There would be £500 million in new subsidies, it was suggested, and a £200 million package of aid for regenerating the worst-afflicted communities. But the link with France would stay open and nuclear power and the dash for gas would continue. So would the £1.2 billion nuclear levy on fossil fuels. The playing field, in the view of the unions and the Opposition, stayed tilted.

GOVERNMENT REVENUE FROM OIL INDUSTRY
PETROLEUM REVENUE TAX
£ million receipts

Year	Corporation tax*	Petroleum revenue tax
1983-84	877	6,017
1984-85	2,432	7,177
1985-86	2,916	6,375
1986-87	2,676	1,188
1987-88	1,318	2,296
1988-89	1,230	1,371
1989-90	743	1,050
1990-91	971	860
1991-92	647	-216
1992-93	670	54

* Before ACT set-off

Source: written answer to A Darling, MP May 11 1993

HESELTINE'S COAL WHITE PAPER

Pits: 12 to close, 12 saved, 6 mothballed. 1 in limbo.

Another 5,800 miners to join the 8,000 who have left since October.

£13 billion, five-year contracts with the generators.

French electricity link to stay open, nuclear power and dash for gas to continue.

Government subsidy for extra coal sales.

Privatisation "at the earliest practical opportunity".

Former British Coal pits to go private.

Working practices must change. More hours underground.

£200 million package of aid for regenerating communities.

Source: the Guardian: March 26 1993

On March 29 1993, four Conservative MPs voted against a Government motion approving the Coal White Paper. The rebels were: R. Alexander, W. Cash, Mrs E Peacock, N. Winterton.
On July 5, six Conservative MPs voted against the Government in protest at the closure of two of the 12 "reprieved" pits. The Government had a majority of 22. The rebels were: R.Alexander, W.Cash, W.Churchill, Mrs E.Peacock, Mrs A. Winterton, N.Winterton.

The Tory rebellion folded. On March 29, the Commons approved the White Paper by 319 votes to 297, with four Conservative MPs voting against the Government. But even the deal Heseltine had now outlined was illusory. In practice, with miners drifting out of the industry, the outcome looked likely to be nearer the original Coal Board plans than the pattern of the White Paper. On June 8 the chairman of BC, Neil Clarke, warned of further job cuts and doubted if even the 12 reprieved pits could continue in the light of the generators' reluctance to sign up for additional cheap supplies. Ten days later miners at Rufford in Nottinghamshire, one of the reprieved pits, voted for closure. They were influenced by the knowledge that if they stayed until after Christmas, their redundancy money would be much less. In July, at the close of a year that had seen the end of 21,000 jobs in the pits, BC announced a loss of £588 million on the year — a figure inflated by the high costs of the closure programme — with the prospect of more to come.

The industry's huge improvements in productivity since the miners' strike, with a 25 per cent jump in the past year alone, had helped cost miners their jobs. With big stockpiles and new orders still not coming forward, further closures, said Clarke, were inevitable.

Other sectors were troubled, too. British Gas was in constant conflict with its regulator, Ofgas, which on March 1 1993 advocated splitting it up into 14 separate companies, on the grounds that real choice could only come from effective competition. The issue was referred to the Monopolies Commission. North Sea oil and gas were in decline — and would continue to be so, the UK oil industry argued, since changes in the 1993 budget would cut relief on exploration and appraisal costs and so limit expansion.

The nuclear industry, whose diminished attractions had caused it to be removed from the privatisation programme, with a four-year moratorium placed on all its projects except the vast new pressurised water reactor Sizewell B, faced further grim news on decommissioning costs as the time approached for the thorough review of the industry promised for 1994. On June 4 1993 the National Audit Office said the bill for closing Britain's nuclear power and waste treatment plants had shot up to £18 billion, and the final costs of closures and reprocessing spent fuel could be £40 billion. And all sectors faced the possibility of diminished demand as the ending of fuel's exemption from Vat in the 1993 Budget pushed up prices year by year.

On June 28 1993 the environment secretary, John Gummer, announced a further delay in deciding the future of THORP, the £2.8 billion nuclear processing plant at Sellafield, begun in 1978. British Nuclear Fuels were now projecting profits of no more than £500 million over 10 years, and Gummer said further thought was needed about the economic and environmental justification for going ahead. The company was outraged and responded by announcing 3,200 redundancies — though not all, it admitted, were linked with Gummer's announcement. The consultation was due to last for 10 weeks.●

COAL: PRODUCTION, EMPLOYMENT, PRODUCTIVITY AND PIT NUMBERS

1. Coal production (million tonnes) (BCC mines)
2. Total number of employees (thousands)
3. Output per man-shift (tonnes)
4. Number of operating collieries at year end

	1980/81	1985/86	1987/88	1988/89	1989/90	1990/91	1991/92	1992/93
Production	110.3	88.4	82.4	85.0	75.6	72.3	71.0	61.8
Employees	293.9	179.6	117.3	105.0	85.1	74.3	58.1	44.2
Output M/S	2.32	2.72	3.62	4.14	4.32	4.70	5.31	6.34
Collieries	211	133	94	86	73	65	50	50

What's in a name: successive disasters, such as the sinking of the Braer off the Shetlands, made Lloyd's membership a liability. Fish and wildlife weren't too pleased, either

NINE
AGRICULTURE/RURAL LIFE/FISHING

For once the discontents of the fishermen were louder and more persistent even than those of the farmers. Their problems had much in common: contracting industries, dispensations from Brussels which seemed to them to threaten their livelihoods — and a British government that had little power to help them, when so many of the decisions they railed at effectively belonged to Brussels, not London.

The troubles of the fishermen largely arose from the European Community's Common Fisheries Policy (CFP), which came into force in 1983. Their earnings in the decade since then were calculated to have fallen by nearly one-third. Now they had to contend with conservation measures they believed were stacked against them. A particular cause of wrath was the Sea Fish Conservation Act 1992, which implemented EC agreements. This sought to reduce the size of the fishing fleet by extending licensing arrangements to smaller vessels and paying compensation — critics claimed on a quite inadequate scale — where vessels were decommissioned. It also imposed stricter controls on time spent at sea. It was a kind of marine equivalent of setaside on land.

British fishermen complained that controls were tighter on them than on others: the quotas set for them implied a reduction of 19 per cent in the fishing fleet, compared to 9.5 per cent in France and 4 per cent in Spain — while Ireland was allowed a modest expansion. The quotas had been fixed to help the EC's more disadvantaged nations, but that was no consolation — especially when Spanish "quota-hoppers" were registering vessels in Britain and fishing in our waters.

The availability of cheap Russian imports of fish such as cod and haddock, at times when they could not catch them because quotas were exhausted, stirred them to fury. There were demonstrations in various ports: fishermen blockaded Teesport on September 23 in protest both against quotas and against Russian imports. But the main trouble was with the French. There were incidents at Peterhead and Grimsby on March 8 and 9 1993 and at Milford Haven on March 10, and Plymouth was blockaded with trawlers on March 26. On March 28, three members of a Royal Navy boarding party were abducted by French fishermen off Cherbourg. Forty French trawlers sailed into St Peter Port, Guernsey, on March 29: an agreement between them and local fishermen was repudiated by the British government.

When the first parliamentary order made under the provisions of the Sea Fish Conservation Bill, imposing restrictions on the number of days spent at sea, came before the Commons on May 11 1993 five Conservatives joined the opposition parties in voting against it. The order required fishermen not to spend more days at sea than they had in 1991. Since fishermen would have had no idea in 1991 that such a restriction would be imposed, the Labour spokesman Dr Gavin Strang argued, this must be an indefensibly arbitrary figure. The fisheries minister, David Curry, said the crisis in fish stocks was now so serious that nothing less would do. Even if there had been no CFP and Britain had a 200-mile limit, it would have been necessary to impose the restrictions to protect Britain's fish stock. On July 7, implementation of this order was postponed until January 1 1994 to give time for more consultations.

Farmers were hardly more cheerful. Even the 1992 Conservative election manifesto did not make their prospects sound very alluring. "World-wide pressure to reduce protectionist measures, and the need to contain the cost of the Common Agricultural Policy, mean that farmers will face reduced support and increased competition," it said. "We believe that farming in the UK can meet these challenges. But many farmers will need help to adapt to the new conditions."

Often, though, this help was judged inadequate. The inescapable prospect was further decline. A 10-year decline in farm incomes ended, even if temporarily, in 1993 — thanks to Black Wednesday, as EC farm subsidies, denominated in Ecus, shot up by 20 per cent. A modest wave of investment and re-equipment began. Not everyone benefited. Organic farmers, promised a boost to their incomes under "green" EC measures of January 1990, were disappointed.

To falling incomes, particularly among hill farmers as Government grants were cut and dropping land values, down on average by 30 per cent in a year, according to a report from the Royal Institution of Chartered Surveyors in September 1992, there was added a fresh outrage in the form of a bureaucratic exercise called the Integrated Administration and Control System (IACS), the result of changes in the Cap in May 1992. Applications for setaside payments had to be completed accurately in every detail, with penalties for delay and error. Yet the book of instructions on how to fill in the forms ran to 79 pages.

Though famous complainers, farmers had evidence to show that their worries ran deep. The suicide rate among them had climbed to twice the national average. They were not, it seemed, alone in such rural twilight. A series of studies drew attention to the plight of rural Britain, which was suffering the effects of recession just as much as the towns. A report on Communities at Risk in Wiltshire, published by the Wiltshire Community Foundation, contrasted the reality with the idyllic ideas of the countryside which seemed to exist in towns: a rising elderly population, few jobs, low pay, family breakdown, homelessness, isolation, a lack of shops, post offices and child care — and with signs of social unrest beginning to develop.

CONTRACTION OF AGRICULTURAL EMPLOYMENT

	Regular workers[1]	seasonal/casual	all
1986	208.3	95.4	303.6
1987	203.6	95.8	299.3
1988	198.5	88.3	286.7
1989	188.5	82.9	271.4
1990	181.5	78.7	260.3
1991	178.3	81.7	260.0
1992 Jun	171.3	86.2	257.5
1992 Dec[2]	160.4	63.1	223.5

figures exclude farmers, partners, directors and their spouses, salaried managers, schoolchildren, most trainees
[1]whole or part-time.
[2]figures exclude Scotland.

SEA FISH (CONSERVATION) (Government Bill)
INTRODUCED: May 22 1992

PURPOSE:

To reduce size of fishing fleet by extending licensing arrangements to smaller vessels; impose stricter controls on time spent at sea; pay compensation on decommissioned vessels

COMMONS:
2nd reading: June 8 1992 by 216 (Con, UPUP) to 187
(Lab, Lib Dem, SNP, PC, 1 SDLP)
Report and 3rd reading: July 14 1992

LORDS:
2nd reading: October 26 1992
Report: November 24 1992
3rd reading: December 3 1992

ROYAL ASSENT:
December 17 1992

REBELLIONS:

On May 11 1993, 5 Conservatives voted against the Government on an order consequent on this Bill which restricted time fishing boats could spend at sea. They were: S. Coe, D. Harris, R. Hicks, D. Porter, Sir T. Taylor

In a book called Another Country: Real Life Beyond Rose Cottage (National Council for Voluntary Organisations, London N1 9RL), James Derounian contrasted Government measures for urban and rural communities: around £775 million on urban development in 1989-90, compared with £26 million for the countryside: yet one-fifth of the population lived in the countryside.

A pilot programme for dealing with rural unemployment as part of the Action for the Countryside programme had assigned just £3.6 million to meeting the consequences of a job loss of 30,000.

But there were some issues where the House of Commons was relentless in its protection of country dwellers.

There were outraged protests from all sides of the Commons in May 1993 at a reported threat to village post offices from a system called ACT (Automated Credit Transfer) allowing pensions to be paid directly into bank accounts. In a Commons debate on May 19, the social security secretary Peter Lilley denied any threat to post offices. Even if people chose to switch, he said, post offices would not be hurt, since their incomes were based on fixed sums, not volume of business. "Our commitment to a network of sub post offices is unequivocal - we have given a triple assurance that we will maintain a viable network; no sub post office will close as a result of this" he said to loud Conservative cheers, not all of them bucolic.●

TEN
TRANSPORT

Robert Adley, the maverick back-bench Tory MP and railway buff who died on May 13 1993, predicted it might turn out to be a "poll tax on wheels". None of the Government's previous privatisation plans ran into quite as much trouble as railway privatisation. From the start there were deep divisions about how to proceed. The prime minister, it was reported, hankered for a return to the days before nationalisation, when we had regional railways, each in its distinctive livery. Malcolm Rifkind, his then transport secretary, opposed that as unworkable. The White Paper due before the 1992 election was postponed — though the manifesto remained adamant that the best way to produce "profound and lasting" improvements on the railway was to break the BR monopoly.

The White Paper which finally appeared on July 14 1992 proposed a two-way split. Lines would be franchised in batches to private sector companies until the whole network was in private operation. Franchisees would qualify for grants where they were running services which, though lossmakers, were deemed socially necessary. But they would not own the track. That would be run by an organisation called Railtrack, which would also become the residual authority responsible for running lines not yet franchised. Pure privatisation was reserved for freight and the parcels service. Two powerful new quangos would be created, one to negotiate and award franchises, the other the Railtrack regulator.

From the start this project was assailed by doubt. Even that distinguished friend of privatisation, the late Lord Ridley, did not like the look of it. The Commons select committee on transport, chaired and influenced by Adley, was especially apprehensive when it reported on April 28 on the Railways Bill. The untried form of privatisation adopted in this instance, it said, enhanced the risk that something might go badly wrong. It was possible that the taxpayer would end up paying more rather than less. Budgetary pressures might lead to service reductions and closures.

The committee was not impressed by the split between train and track: better to let private operators take control of both, it said. And BR should not, as the Bill ordained, be banned from bidding for franchises. The key to the railways' future was better public and private investment: without it, "it will scarcely matter what structure of ownership or management is put in its place". (Three Conservative members later repudiated the report.)

A report from independent consultants Steer Davies Gleave was equally downbeat: the total rail bill, it forecast on May 23, would rise between 15 and 28 per cent after privatisation, with higher fares and line closures.

The transport secretary, John MacGregor, appeared undaunted. The Bill was pushed through without any backbench rebellion until its very last stages, when a group of back-bench MPs, led by Keith Speed (Ashford), but modelling their attack on what Robert Adley had planned, demanded guarantees, which ministers had so far withheld, that the Bill would be amended to ensure that concessionary railcards for the young, elderly and disabled would continue after franchising, and that travel cards for use on rail and buses would continue in some form. A second demand, that BR be allowed to bid for franchises, was refused, with just two Conservative members, Stephen Day (Cheadle) and Hugh Dykes (Harrow E) voting with Labour. The transport secretary advertised his confidence in the enterprise by unexpectedly naming 18 more candidates for franchising to add to the seven previously announced. Later the defeat on BR participation was reversed in the Lords. MacGregor said the current culture of the railways would never change if the existing BR regime retained the upper hand. He declined to say if the Commons would be asked to strike out the change made in the Lords.

Two expensive new projects were given the go-ahead. On March 22 1993 the transport secretary at last announced the line for the Channel Tunnel rail link, which he intended should run through Kent, cross the river near Northfleet and head for St Pancras, though as yet there were no firm arrangements with the private sector to pay for it. At the CBI annual dinner on May 18 1993 the prime minister announced approval for a £1.8 billion scheme, linking Paddington and the west with Liverpool Street and the east, called Crossrail. (The Opposition objected that the Government had twice already won friendly headlines by announcing this project.) But the scheme to extend the Jubilee Line to London Docklands remained stalled. The Government had insisted it could not go ahead without private capital, and the hope of finding private capital faded with the financial collapse of Canary Wharf. Negotiations through the summer failed to break the deadlock.

MacGregor was also engaged on the privatisation of roads. A green paper (discussion document) published on May 26 raised the prospect of charging motorists for using the 2,000-mile motorway network with charges of as much as 1.5p a mile, or a £75 season ticket.

Motorways now accounted for £12 billion of the £23 billion road programme. Schemes like this, it was argued, were needed not just to raise revenue but to curb congestion: motorway traffic was expected to double by 2025. No final decisions on how the scheme would work had been taken, but toll booths were out: too slow and inconvenient. ●

GOVERNMENT SPENDING ON TRANSPORT

1 Total spending at current prices (£ billion)
2. Total spending in real terms at 1991-2 prices (£ billion)
3. % of government expenditure
4. % of GDP

	1978-1979	1983-1984	1984-1985	1985-1986	1986-1987	1987-1988	1988-1989	1989-1990	1990-1991-	1991-1992	1992-3 est.
1	3.0	5.5	5.7	5.5	5.7	5.7	5.9	6.8	8.3	9.2	10.4
2	8.1	8.7	8.6	7.9	8.0	7.5	7.2	7.9	8.9	9.2	10.8
3	4.0	3.9	3.7	3.4	3.4	3.2	3.2	3.3	3.7	3.8	4.4
4	1.8	1.8	1.7	1.5	1.5	1.3	1.2	1.3	1.5	1.6	1.8

INVESTMENT IN ROAD AND RAIL (£m)

	85-6	86-7	87-8	88-9	89-90	90-1	91-2
Road infrastructure							
public	2,037	2,112	2,310	2,613	3,140	3,606	3,876
private	-	-	9	63	56	49	na
total	2,037	2,112	2,319	2,676	3,196	3,650	na
Road rolling stock							
cars	11,200	12,800	15,600	19,100	20,400	18,600	16,200
other	2,900	3,300	3,800	4,800	5,100	3,900	3,100
total	14,100	16,100	19,400	23,900	25,500	22,500	19,300
Rail infrastructure							
BR	309	318	419	337	487	593	674
other	155	166	246	239	342	550	486
total	464	498	770	901	1,264	1,743	na
Rail rolling stock							
BR	90	81	107	208	209	265	331
other	63	71	72	77	131	157	178
TOTAL	**153**	**152**	**179**	**285**	**340**	**422**	**509**

Source: Transport Statistics, Dept of Transport.

BR CURRENT INVESTMENT £M

	current prices	1991-2 prices
1979	248	592
1980	304	608
1981	277	497
1982	243	405
1983	252	399
1984-5	280	419
1985-6	399	565
1986-7	399	547
1987-8	526	684
1988-9	545	661
1989-90	696	793
1990-1	858	919
1991-2	1,005	1,005

Source: Transport Statistics GB

GRANTS TO BRITISH RAIL

	1979	1989-90	1990-1	1991-2	1992-3	1993-4[1]
(£million at 1993/4 prices)						
Grants to BR[2]	1,363	762	844	1,129	1,346	1,000
of which:						
Public Service						
Obligation:	1,191	615	696	974	1,191	850
(£million at 1979 prices)						
Grants to BR[2]	527	295	327	437	521	387
of which:						
Public Service						
Obligation:	461	238	269	377	461	329

[1] Estimates only
[2] Includes level crossing and PTE grants

Source: Dept of Transport

THE DISPOSAL OF BRITISH RAIL

Sectors to be franchised, listed February 2 1993

East Coast Main Line:	Between King's Cross and Edinburgh
Great Western:	Paddington to Bristol and Swansea or Plymouth/Penzance
Gatwick Express	
South Western Division:	Waterloo to Exeter, Weymouth, Portsmouth
Isle of Wight	
London, Tilbury and Southend	
Scotrail	

Sectors to be franchised, listed May 23 1993

InterCity West Coast main line:	Euston to Inverness. Stations include Birmingham, Manchester, Liverpool, Preston and Glasgow.
InterCity Midland main line:	St Pancras through Luton, Leicester, Nottingham and Derby to Sheffield.
InterCity Anglia:	Liverpool Street to Norwich through Colchester, Harwich, Ipswich.
InterCity cross-country:	Long-distance service from Aberdeen in north and Penzance in south west. Stations include Plymouth, Birmingham, Leeds, Manchester, Newcastle, Glasgow and Edinburgh.
Thames line:	Paddington to Gatwick in south, Stratford-upon-Avon in Midlands and Bedwyn in Wiltshire. Other stations include Windsor and Eton, Reading and Oxford.
Chiltern line:	Marylebone and Paddington to Aylesbury and Birmingham Snow Hill. Other stations include Harrow, High Wycombe and Amersham.

Northampton and North London lines:	Links north and south London with Northampton and Bedford.
Anglia & Great Northern:	Part of Network SouthEast, linking London with East Anglia. Runs from London termini King's Cross, Moorgate, Liverpool Street and Stratford to Huntingdon, Peterborough, Cambridge.
Great Eastern:	Another Network SouthEast, London-East Anglia service out of Liverpool Street to Ipswich, Harwich and Clacton.
Thameslink:	Joining south of London destinations with Bedford and services north of the capital.
Kent services:	Serves Kent from London's Victoria, Charing Cross, Waterloo, Blackfriars, Cannon Street and London Bridge stations.
South London & Sussex coast:	Victoria/London Bridge to such places as Eastbourne, Brighton, Portsmouth and Southampton.
Northeast region:	Runs from Berwick on the Scottish border to Sheffield and Manchester. Major stations include Liverpool, Leeds, Newcastle upon Tyne, Sunderland and Middlesbrough.
Northwest region:	From Carlisle to Stoke-on-Trent,Llandudno and Wrexham. Other stations include Manchester, Sheffield and Blackpool.
Merseyrail electric services Central region:	A huge rambling part of Regional Railways covering nearly 300 stations from the coast of Wales to Lowestoft, and from Manchester to Stansted Airport.
South Wales & West region:	Another giant area covering 251 stations from Penzance to Brighton and Shrewsbury.
Cardiff Valley lines	

NEW VEHICLE REGISTRATIONS
(thousands)

	private/ light goods	public transport	cars on the road
1979	1,891.5	9.1	14,162
1983	1,989.1	7.3	15,543
1988	2,437.0	9.2	18,432
1989	2,535.2	8.0	19,248
1990	2,179.9	7.4	19,742
1991	1,708.5	5.2	19,737
1992	1,748.0	5.1	n/a

	Cars on the road 1951-1991
1951	2,095
1961	5,296
1971	10,443
1981	14,867
1991	19,737

PAYING FOR MOTORWAYS: ISSUES FOR DISCUSSION, Government Green Paper, published May 26 1993

Measures to be considered:

New combinations of existing road user taxes and tolls

Charges for motorway users;

A 1.5p per mile charge for cars and light goods vehicles and about 4.5p for lorries would generate around £700 million annually

A permit costing £50 per year or £3 per week would raise around £500 million annually

Charging extended to trunk roads of motorway standard, but not extended to isolated rural or busy urban stretches of motorway

An annual fixed-charge permit system similar to Swiss scheme would be straightforward to administer, with short-term permits available to visitors

New legislation would be necessary before introducing direct charges on the existing motorway network

Private sector could be invited to operate motorways on a "franchised" basis

RAILWAYS (Government Bill)
INTRODUCED: January 21 1993

PURPOSE:

To provide for franchising of rail services and creation of Railtrack authority.

COMMONS:

2nd reading: February 2 1993 by 302 (Con, UPUP) to 269 (Lab, Lib Dem, SNP, PC, 2 OUP)

Report and 3rd reading: May 24-25 1993

LORDS:

2nd reading: June 15 1993

Report: Scheduled for October 14 1993

3rd reading:

ROYAL ASSENT:
Rebellions:

On July 5 1993 the Lords voted by 150 to 112 to allow BR to compete for rail franchises. The amendment was moved by a former Conservative transport minister Lord Peyton.

ELEVEN
EDUCATION

The revolution in educational practice which had begun with Kenneth Baker's "Gerbil" (the Great Education Reform Bill enacted in 1988) was five years old in 1993, and was not yet over. A further Education Bill setting up powerful new quangos to take charge of funding and the curriculum was introduced by the new education secretary, John Patten, on October 30 1992.

Some Tory reforms seemed to be bedding down better than others. The number of schools given the go-ahead to opt out of local authority control reached 681 by the time the schools broke up for the 1993 summer holidays, and was forecast to hit 1,500 in 1994. There were also 14 City Technology Colleges operating outside the local authority system, with a 15th due to open in September.

A report from the Audit Commission on June 17 1993 said most schools had coped well with the change, but accountability in two-fifths of the schools had become seriously flawed, with "the green shoots of impropriety" beginning to show in some places.

Elsewhere, however, there was turbulence and discontent, over the national curriculum, over testing and over the Government's insistence on publishing "league tables" for schools.

There had been trouble over the testing of seven year olds, introduced in 1991 and radically altered and shortened in the light of experience. From the spring of 1993 there was even more serious trouble over tests for 14 year olds, particularly in the English texts which Patten stipulated must include Shakespeare. Patten's chief curriculum adviser, David Pascall, warned against tests overloading and distorting the curriculum. (His contract was not renewed: on April 19 1993 he was replaced by the former head of the Post Office, Sir Ron Dearing.)

Two of the Government's advisers, Professor Lord Skidelsky and Dr John Marenbon, resigned on the issue. Skidelsky, a Conservative peer, left the School Examinations and Assessment Council (SEAC) saying the tests were over-complicated, bureaucratic and time-consuming: he accused the department of "ineptitude".

On February 2 the National Association of Schoolmasters and Union of Women teachers (NASUWT) called for a boycott of tests, which won almost 90 per cent support in a ballot of members on a turnout of 57 per cent. The Association of Teachers and Lecturers, in April, and the National Union of Teachers, in May, also backed a boycott. Faced with similar pressures in Scotland a year before, ministers had retreated and scrapped the tests. Patten half-retreated. On April 7 he promised a streamlining of tests and a full review of tests for 11 and 14 year olds to be carried out by Dearing. But the tests for 14 year olds planned for early June must, he said, go ahead.

This failed to placate the unions, who according to a Gallup poll in the Daily Telegraph on May 10 were winning the battle for public opinion: 62 per cent of respondents sympathised with the teachers, among whom more than eight in 10 thought the boycott was justified. Only 28 per cent echoed Patten's complaint that teachers were playing politics. (Industrial action by teachers wins public's support/Anthony King/Daily Telegraph May 10 1993). The DoE published a poll showing public support for testing, but on closer inspection this backed the principle, not the practices now in dispute. Another escape route for Patten was blocked by the courts. The London borough of Wandsworth asked the High Court to rule that the boycott was illegal, but the court found against them on April 2 the Appeal Court, as did April 23.

On May 26, in a rare show of unanimity, all six teaching unions urged him to call off the tests. On June 2, Patten was given what the Guardian called "the roughest ride an education secretary has received in living memory" when head teachers and deputies at the conference of the National Association of Head Teachers greeted his speech with cries of shame, shouts of derision and muted hissing. When the tests for 14 year olds began on June 6 the boycott was near-complete: a 99.9 per cent success, said the NASUWT. The

unions were further enraged by Patten's insistence that teacher training should be made more practical and less theoretical, and by his announcement on June 9 that teachers of children aged seven and under should no longer have to be graduates.

Opposition to league tables was especially bitter. The publication of the first league tables for GCSE and A level was attacked as plainly unjust, since the figures took no account of the different abilities of intakes in different schools.

The scrapping of league tables was one of the chief recommendations in Dearing's report, published on August 2. Other concessions included extensive cuts in the testing programme. The recommendations were immediately accepted by ministers, prompting the widespread reflection that a great deal of anguish on both sides of this argument might have been spared had the case against Patten's policy been heeded earlier.

There was also trouble in higher education. Here there had been spectacular success in increasing student numbers, from 327,000 in 1979 to 578,000 in 1991, with a Government target of one in three school leavers going on to higher education. The number of university students was even further increased as former polytechnics and even a further college of higher education were accorded university status.

But the institutions complained that this huge expansion was woefully underfunded, that standards were being cut, with less individual teaching, and that more and more of their time was now being taken up with fundraising. By 1989, polytechnics

GOVERNMENT SPENDING ON EDUCATION

1 Total spending at current prices £billion
2. Total spending in real terms at 1991-2 prices £billion
3. % of government expenditure
4. % of GDP

	1978-1979	1983-1984	1984-1985	1985-1986	1986-1987	1987-1988	1988-1989	1989-1990	1990-1991	1991-1992	1992-3 (estimate)
1	9.1	15.8	16.4	17.0	18.7	20.4	22.0	24.6	26.5	29.6	32.3
2	24.7	25.2	24.9	24.4	26.0	26.9	27.1	28.4	28.4	29.6	31.0
3	12.1	11.2	10.7	10.5	11.1	11.4	11.8	12.0	11.9	12.1	12.0
4	5.4	5.2	5.0	4.7	4.8	4.8	4.6	4.8	4.8		

PATTEN'S TEST COMPROMISE, APRIL 7 1993

Mandatory tests next year at ages seven and 14 to concentrate on core subjects of English, maths and science (and Welsh in Wales). Decisions on technology at 14 after this year's tests

Testing to be streamlined, with substantial changes to "coverage and style"

Teachers testing seven year olds to concentrate on basics

National pilot to take place in 1994 for tests for 11 year olds in English, maths and science, which would be mandatory in 1995

Review by Sir Ron Dearing to consider merits of external marking in tests at 11 and 14

Tests in history and geography at 14, due in 1994, postponed pending the Dearing review

THE DEARING RECOMMENDATIONS AUGUST 2 1993

In his interim report Sir Ron Dearing recommended the following changes, to which ministers agreed:

Streamlining of classroom tests

Scrapping of school league tables of test results for seven and 14 year olds

Slimming down of the 10 national curriculum subjects

Concentration on the "three Rs"

School tests for seven and 11 year olds to be restricted to English, maths and science, plus Welsh as a first language in Wales

Freezing of national tests for 14 year olds in subjects other than the three core subjects until 1996.

were receiving 26 per cent less per pupil than they had a decade earlier. The universities escaped the squeeze in that decade, but between 1989 and 1993 they too came in for punishment, receiving 15 per cent less per pupil. It was calculated in 1990 that polytechnics were getting a book allowance of £23 per pupil — £3 less than the cost of the average academic book.

On June 6 1993 it was learned that the director of the LSE, Dr John Ashworth, had proposed that undergraduates should be charged a top-up tuition fee of up to £1,000 a year from October 1994. His colleagues voted him down. In the speculation about possible measures to cut public spending which raged through the same month, one much-floated change was a move to higher contributions by students (through long-term repayable loans).

Perhaps Patten's most acclaimed moment as Education secretary came when he told the Conservative party conference on October 7 1992 what it had long thirsted to hear: that the end was at hand for the National Union of Students "closed shop" in universities. Students would no longer be required to belong to the union if they did not wish to. Patten also intended to include in a Bill in the 1993-94 session a provision designed to ensure that money given to students unions through the university funding body should only be spent on services such as welfare and housing. Political campaigning would have to be paid for from other sources.●

ASSISTED PLACES SCHEME

Year	Places available1	Places taken up[1]	Budget estimate[2] £m	Actual Outturn[2] £m
1981-82	5,446	4,185	3.3	3.0
1982-83	11,058	8,616	9.3	8.7
1983-84	15,866	13,102	16.5	15.0
1984-85	20,699	17,386	22.5	22.2
1985-86	25,210	21,412	31.1	29.6
1986-87	29,295	24,478	37.4	37.9
1987-88	33,228	26,889	47.8	46.0
1988-89	33,217	27,083	55.1	50.9
1989-90	33,280	27,008	57.0	56.5
1990-91	33,302	26,740	60.4	63.4
1991-92	33,312	27,641	64.9	75.7

The figures are for England only
[1] Academic year [2] Financial year

Source:Written answer March 29 1993 HcD col 75

THE EXPANSION OF HIGHER EDUCATION

Academic year	Student numbers (000s)
1979	327.4
1980	340.4
1981	355.4
1982	356.9
1983	365.4
1984	370.3
1985	391.2
1986	410.3
1987	415.4
1988	438.3
1989	473.2
1990	511.5
1991	587.3

The number of students in higher education has expanded even faster than the rate of growth envisaged in the 1991 higher education White Paper. Over one in four young people were entering higher education in 1992. Government spending plans provide for an increase of 104,000 or 13 % in higher education student numbers during the next three years. This will allow the current record levels of participation to be maintained and give institutions a period during which to consolidate their recent achievements. Written answer to Nigel Evans, MP.

EDUCATION (Government Bill)
INTRODUCED: October 30 1992

PURPOSE:

To set up new funding agency for schools, taking over from local education authorities as schools opt out; allow primary schools to form "clusters" to apply for grant-maintained status; impose controls on schools identified by inspectors as "failing", with enforced closures if necessary; set up School Curriculum and Assessment Authority (SCAA) replacing National Curriculum Council and Assessment Authority; give power to education secretary to order closure of surplus school places; assist parents wishing to claim aid for children with special needs

COMMONS:

2nd reading: November 9-10 1992 by 304 (Con, 1 OUP, UPUP) to 268 (Lab, Lib Dem, SNP, PC)
Guillotined: December 15 1992
Report and 3rd reading: March 2-3 1993

LORDS:

2nd reading: March 23 1993
Report: June 10, 14 and 21 1993
3rd reading: July 6 1993

ROYAL ASSENT:

July 27 1993

TWELVE
HEALTH

In health as in education, the system was still absorbing the radical changes made in the Thatcher years. A further wave of hospitals opted: by June 1993, two- thirds of the hospital sector was managed by trusts. The number of GPs becoming fund-holders continued to grow, helped by a cut in the minimum eligible list size from 9,000 to 7,000. By June 1993, 6,000 doctors in 1,235 practices had become fund-holders.

At its annual conference, the BMA appeared to have come to terms with reforms it had previously fought. On June 28 1993 it approved a resolution lifting its opposition to GP fund-holding. But it then passed another saying the system would lead to a two-tier NHS. Later, it voted out its moderate chairman, Dr Jeremy Lee-Potter, and installed in his place Dr Sandy Macara, seen as a tougher figure. In a BBC television interview on July 4, Macara claimed that the NHS was disintegrating, and the promise that reforms would increase patient choice was "a sick joke".

Asked what he thought the NHS would be like in the year 2000, he said: "I fear that it will not be a National Health Service at all recognisable in the terms that we all, including the Government, wish by the year 2000, unless they stop now, and have a fundamental reconsideration of where we are going."

Many within the service continued to complain of chronic under-funding as demographic change, advances in medical technology and more ambitious Government targets drove up costs much faster than the rate of inflation. Part of the problem, ministers contended, was that resources were inefficiently deployed. One test of that claim came in London.

On June 24 1992 the respected independent organisation, The King's Fund, published a report which argued that while London had very inadequate primary and after care services, it had an excess of hospital capacity and 15 should be closed. A government inquiry under Sir Bernard Tomlinson, chairman of the Northern Regional Health Authority, came to much the same conclusions. With hospitals outside London now equipped to deliver services that had once been available only within the capital and the new NHS internal market pushing patients their way, it no longer made sense, it was argued, to keep beds open for them in London while the regions had resources sucked away from them. Published on October 23 1992, the Tomlinson report recommended the closure or merger of several distinguished London hospitals, of which perhaps the most contentious was Bart's (St Bartholomew's Hospital, Smithfield).

The proposals were attacked with such ferocity by some Conservative newspapers and Conservative MPs that confident forecasts began to appear that the health secretary, Virginia Bottomley, could not go through with such plans. On the eve of her decision, the London Evening Standard, a fervent campaigner for Bart's, announced that it had been saved. It hadn't. It was still on the list which the minister published on February 1993. Later, somewhat confusingly, a third report was issued, containing the findings of six specialist review teams, which recommended reprieving some threatened hospitals, but closing others that were thought to have been reprieved. The Royal Marsden, Chelsea, for instance, was named for closure by Tomlinson; not named by Bottomley; but named again by the specialty team.

The soaring cost of the service added new urgency to campaigns for preventive health measures. A White Paper published on July 8,1992 — The Health of the Nation — set targets for the reduction of coronary heart disease and strokes, to be achieved by such means as discouraging smoking and the sort of diet that made for obesity. A parallel document — Scotland's Health, A Challenge to Us All — was published in Edinburgh. Wales already had a much-admired, pace-setting document. Labour condemned the White Paper for failing to take account of the malign effects, now increasingly documented, of unemployment on health, and for funking a ban on tobacco advertising.

The Government was also committed to cutting down waiting time for hospital admission. The 1991 Patient's Charter promised that by March 31 1992, virtually all patients would be dealt with in less than two years. On April 2, at the height of the election campaign, the Department of Health claimed success. Waiting two years or more, it said, had been "virtually eliminated". Opposition parties suspected a last-minute rush to deal with cases to produce inspiring figures before polling day. Figures a year after the election produced a rather more mixed picture. The numbers waiting a year or more had fallen by 29 per cent. But the numbers waiting up to a year had grown, producing a record figure for all waiting lists of nearly 1 million.

One factor pushing up NHS costs was the drugs bill, which by 1992-93 was running at almost £2.3 billion a year. Ministers sought to recoup some of this through prescription charges, which went up on April 1 from £3.75 to £4.25 per item, netting around £278 million a year for the service. The cost of pre-payment certificates (or 12-month "season tickets", as they were known) for those requiring more than 15 items a year went up from £53.50 in 1992-93 to £60.60 in 1993-94. "A tax on illness" the BMA called it. But ministers emphasised the scale of exemptions: around 80 per cent of prescriptions, they said, came free.

Dental charges went up as well, with patients having to bear 80 per cent rather than 75 per cent of costs and the maximum payment for a single course of treatment rising from £225 to £250. The Commons select committee on health advocated on

GOVERNMENT SPENDING ON HEALTH

1 Total spending at current prices £billion
2. Total spending in real terms at 1991-2 prices £billion
3. % of government expenditure
4. % of GDP

	1978-1979	1983-1984	1984-1985	1985-1986	1986-1987	1987-1988	1988-1989	1989-1990	1990-1991-	1991-1992	1992-3 est.
1	7.8	15.5	16.7	17.6	18.9	20.7	22.8	24.7	27.7	31.5	34.6
2	21.2	24.7	25.3	25.4	26.3	27.3	28.1	28.5	29.6	31.5	33.2
3	10.4	11.0	10.9	10.9	11.1	11.6	12.2	12.0	12.4	12.9	12.94
4	4.6	5.1	5.1	4.9	4.9	4.8	4.8	4.8	5.0	5.4	5.8

PRESCRIPTION CHARGES 1971-1979

		% increase
July 1979	45p	125
April 1980	70p	56
Dec 1980	£1.00	43
April 1982	£1.30	30
April 1983	£1.40	8
April 1984	£1.60	14
April 1985	£2.00	25
April 1986	£2.20	10
April 1987	£2.40	9
April 1988	£2.60	8
April 1989	£2.80	8
April 1990	£3.05	9
April 1991	£3.40	11
April 1992	£3.75	10
April 1993	£4.25	13

% increase 1979-93

June 10 1993 that basic dental treatment and check-ups ought to be free.

Already NHS dental treatment was unobtainable in sectors of London and some areas outside, and a dispute between the dentists and the health secretary now reduced that cover still further. The Government ordered what amounted to a 7 per cent cut in dentists' fees to recoup what it said was past over-payment. In July 1992, the British Dental Association and the General Dental Practitioners Association balloted members on retaliatory action, producing large majorities (an 80 per cent "yes" in the BDA ballot, 90 per cent in the GDPA's) in favour of refusing to accept new adult NHS patients.

Unlike the BDA, which rejected it, the GDPA also voted to refuse NHS treatment to existing patients, too, except those qualifying for free care. In a written answer on May 7 1993, the health minister Dr Brian Mawhinney said that between July 22 1992 and April 23 1993, 1,842 dentists had given notification of the deregistration of 437,352 adult patients. Bottomley set up an inquiry by Sir Kenneth Bloomfield, former head of the Northern Ireland civil service, who recommended on January 18 1993 that dental services should be reconstructed as the family doctor and hospital services had been. Though accepting that dentists were unhappy about the cut in fees, he said their remuneration was at an all-time high.

Bottomley repeatedly denied any intention to privatise or otherwise alter the basic NHS principle of a service based on need and free at the point of delivery. But she talked of breaking down barriers and building bridges between the NHS and the private sector, with each augmenting the services of the other. Figures published on May 20 1993 showed an increase of 110 per cent at current prices over four years in NHS income derived from private patients, from £66,893,000 in 1987-88 to £140,834 in 1991-92. (Written answer, col 261, HCD, May 20, 1993.)

Bottomley came under ever greater pressure as the year progressed to re-examine the care in the community policy under which old institutional mental hospitals were phased out and shut and their patients transferred to their homes or to hostels. A series of cases of violence by discharged schizophrenics, some ending in murder, at last hauled the issue of schizophrenia out of its long neglect, though unhappily in a a way which wrongly suggested that schizophrenics as a group were disposed to violence. Bottomley endorsed a proposal by the Royal College of Psychiatrists for tighter controls through a system of Community Supervision Orders over mentally ill people living in the community, and especially on those who refused medication. On July 7, the Commons select committee on health said these proposals were fundamentally flawed. It also criticised the minister as inattentive to the way the community care policy operated: "we conclude that her direct responsibilities for ensuring the successful implementation of the community care changes are substantially more extensive than those recognised in the Government's response." In a letter to the Daily Telegraph on the same day, Professor Robin Murray of King's College Hospi-

NHS DRUGS BILL - ENGLAND £m

Year	FHS	HCHS	Total
1982-83	1,736	421	2,157
1983-84	1,859	438	2,297
1984-85	1,865	436	2,301
1985-86	1,892	440	2,332
1986-87	1,982	458	2,440
1987-88	2,094	480	2,574
1988-89	2,216	483	2,699
1989-90	2,316	493	2,809
1990-91	2,296	508	2,804
1991-92	2,398	612	3,010

1992-93 figures are not yet available.
FHS Family doctor services
HCHS Hospital and community services

Source:written answer to Anne Campbell, MP April 21 1993

NATIONAL HEALTH SERVICE: Average daily number of available beds, 1980-92

Regions	1980	1985	1990-1	1991-2
Northern	25,823	23,773	20,195	19,456
Yorkshire	29,298	25,676	20,387	18,968
Trent	31,516	29,391	22,882	21,723
East Anglian	13,088	12,534	10,797	10,418
North West Thames	27,116	23,816	18,105	17,414
North East Thames	28,703	26,854	20,608	18,727
South East Thames	27,720	24,297	17,333	16,442
South West Thames	25,417	22,210	16,980	16,678
Wessex	18,844	17,654	13,939	13,701
Oxford	13,422	12,555	10,220	9,693
South Western	24,245	21,932	17,511	16,677
West Midlands	35,782	33,108	26,591	24,774
Mersey	21,332	18,464	13,290	12,091
North Western	30,839	29,021	24,057	22,974
Special Health Authorities and Boards of Governors	3,376	3,086	2,544	2,619
England*	355,978	325,487	255,438	242,356

* Numbers may not add up to England total due to rounding

Source: written answer to Ms D Primarolo MP April 20 1993 HcD col 77

tal said the minister had inherited a policy which had condemned the psychotic to wander the streets in numbers unseen since the 18th century. Psychiatrists were being forced to persuade patients that they had to leave their units, not because they had recovered, but because their places were needed for people who were even more disturbed.●

WAITING LISTS 1992-1993

region	under one year		over one year	
	number	**% change**	**number**	**% change**
Northern	62,244	16.8	1,741	-56.4
Yorkshire	70,779	12.0	4,316	-33.0
Trent	79,875	4.8	6,394	-31.1
E.Anglian	38,913	7.1	3,236	-31.6
NW Thames	54,004	15.9	5,764	-37.1
NE Thames	85,235	24.0	7,544	-20.0
SE Thames	71,748	8.5	6,350	-24.2
SW Thames	55,313	25.6	2,417	4.0
Wessex	60,713	16.0	4,122	1.1
Oxford	42,377	5.0	2,596	-55.6
S Western	65,740	4.5	295	-89.4
W Midlands	96,887	14.8	3,352	-40.2
Mersey	55,915	12.6	220	-48.5
N Western	84,861	10.2	6,815	0.5
All regions	924,607	12.3	55,162	-30.3
Special HAs	11,118	-3.3	1,487*	-33.8
TOTAL	**935,725**	**12.1**	**56,599**	**-28.8**

* includes 291 Special Health Authority cases waiting more than two years

All the indications were that poverty was worst among families, especially one-parent families...

THIRTEEN
WELFARE

The main cause of the vastly bloated Public Spending Borrowing Requirement which so troubled ministers in the summer of 1993 was the vastly expanded cost of social security. And the main cause of that was recession. Diminished tax revenues and higher benefit payments — even though the value of some benefits had declined in real terms — combined to swell the biggest bill in Whitehall to ever more daunting proportions. The average cost of an unemployed worker in terms of benefits paid and tax foregone was calculated at £8,000 a year.

For a party that had so often preached the evils of dependency, the condition of society was doubly galling. The social security secretary Peter Lilley told the Commons on February 10 1993: "Excessive expenditure on social security can be doubly damaging, because when the state takes too much money from one person to give to another, it reduces the first person's incentive to work and undermines the second person's incentive to support himself. It is a double whammy of disincentive and dependency." On that basis, great swathes of the population were sunk in dependency. DSS figures given in written answers showed more than 10 million people — more than one in

six of the population — living on income support: 5.7 million claimants and 4.6 million dependants.

Lilley had arrived at the DSS with a reputation as a Thatcherite cutter. In practice, he stayed his hand (though there were suggestions that colleagues' caution had blunted his cutting edge). Through the summer of 1993, however, there was agitated speculation about where the cuts would come as the chief secretary, Michael Portillo, looked for ways of hauling down public spending. And because the DSS share of the bill was so big, it looked the likeliest candidate.

But some possible targets were shielded by manifesto pledges, and as Lilley told the Commons on February 10: "We have no intention of reneging on our manifesto pledges. Our manifesto was quite explicit. We believe that the basic pension must remain the foundation for retirement and we will protect its value against price rises. We are likewise committed to child benefit, which will continue to be paid to all families — normally to the mother — and uprated in line with prices." (Child benefit had been frozen in three of the Thatcher years.)

That was bad news for those Tory MPs who believed that child benefit illustrated all that was wrong with untargeted welfare spending, sprayed indiscriminately at rich and poor alike. A less protected target was invalidity benefit, to which claimants progressed after 28 weeks on sick benefit. A sharp increase in such claims was interpreted by Labour as evidence that claimants to unemployment benefit were being advised by offices to switch to sickness and invalidity instead, thus keeping the unemployment figures down. Though ministers denied this, they too found the figures rum. A letter from Lilley to the prime minister, leaked on June 10 1993, proposed tough new medical tests to assess if claims were genuine, with the benefit made less generous, and taxable. "Frankly it beggars belief that so many people have suddenly become invalids, especially at a time when the health of the nation has improved," the prime minister told the Commons on June 15 1993.

But if really substantial savings were going to be made, there was no way of keeping state pensions out of the argument. The government had in any case to decide what to do about pressure from Brussels — a draft directive had been issued as long ago as 1987 — to equalise retirement age between men and women. The Netherlands, Spain and Luxembourg were going for 65, Ireland for 66, Denmark for 67 and France for 60. In a consultation paper published before the election, the government had seemed inclined to choose 63. On August 3 1992, its Social Security Advisory Committee came out for 65, phased in over 15 years from 2000. The savings which would accrue by postponing women's retirement — an estimated £3 billion — should, it advised, be used to improve the pensions of the poorest and help other vulnerable groups like the long-term sick and disabled. A pamphlet published on February 8 1993 by the bright young Tory backbencher and social security specialist David Willetts (The Age of Entitlement; Social Market Foundation, 20 Queen Anne's Gate, London SW1H 9AA) suggested raising the retirement and pension age to 67. This would save at least £5 billion a year, some of which could go to provide a higher state pension for the over-80s. A decision was due in the summer, but the expectation was that 65 would be chosen, but phased in over 10-15 years.

The latest demographic arithmetic pointed strongly to such a conclusion. New projections published in February 1993 (OPCS Monitor PP2 93/1, from the Office of Population Census and Surveys) showed a steep upward revision in estimates of the growth of the elderly population. The number of those over pension age was likely to rise from 9.1 million in 1991 to 9.6 million in 2001, but then to spurt to 14.4 million (a 50 per cent increase) by 2031. The number of those over 75, who are costliest to the welfare state, which in 1991 was 3.6 million, was put at 6.1 million by 2031, 18 per cent above the previous forecast. The number of younger people available to support them, however, would fall, so that by 2031, there would be 79 dependants for every 100 people of working age. (Not so young as we were/David Brindle/Guardian March 3, 1993.)

On July 7, John Major told the G7 summit meeting in Tokyo that all the nations represented were faced with

GOVERNMENT SPENDING ON SOCIAL SECURITY

1 **Total spending at current prices £billion**
2. **Total spending in real terms at 1991-2 prices £billion**
3. **% of government expenditure**
4. **% of GDP**

	1978-1979	1983-1984	1984-1985	1985-1986	1986-1987	1987-1988	1988-1989	1989-1990	1990-1991-	1991-1992	1992-3 est.
1	17.0	36.9	40.0	43.5	46.8	48.9	50.2	53.2	59.21	70.0	79.2
2	46.0	58.8	60.6	62.5	65.2	64.6	61.7	61.5	63.32	70.0	75.9
3	22.7	26.1	26.2	26.9	27.7	27.4	26.9	26.0	26.6	28.7	29.5
4	10.0	12.1	12.3	12.2	12.1	11.4	10.5	10.3	10.7	12.0	13.2

GAINS AND LOSSES ON THE 1993 BUDGET
estimated change in net income (including 1994 and 1995 effects)
Average gain.

Poorest 10% of households	-2.47
2nd 10%	-2.12
3rd 10%	-2.49
4th 10%	-2.72
5th 10%	-2.77
6th 10%	-2.69
7th 10%	-2.63
8th 10%	-2.59
9th 10%	-2.54
Richest 10% of households	-2.20
All Households	**-2.50**

Source: IFS/The Guardian

LONE PARENTS
Local authorities with highest proportion of lone-parent families

18.1%	Knowsley	11.4%	Kingston upon Hull
16.5%	Manchester	11.3%	South Tyneside
16.2%	Hackney	11.0%	Blackburn
14.0%	Middlesbrough	10.9%	Cynon Valley
13.2%	Inner London	10.8%	Cardiff
12.5%	Greenwich	10.7%	Wolverhampton
12.4%	Halton	10.3%	Swansea
11.8%	Corby	10.1%	Easington
11.8%	Nottingham	10.0%	Arfon
11.5%	Leicester	10.0%	Bradford

Income range % of net income   *Source: 1991 CensusSource: 1991 Census*

escalating costs for social security benefits, and all would need to take "unpopular but necessary steps" to keep them in check. Next day in London, Lilley published projections of a £14 billion rise in the cost of social security benefits by the end of the century, even if unemployment fell by a quarter. A third of this increase would be in sickness and disability benefit. (The Growth of Social Security/ HMSO/£9.50.)

Any government would face these problems. They formed part of the agenda for the Commission of Social Justice which the new Labour leader John Smith set up under Sir Gordon Borrie, former director-general of Fair Trading. Labour's social justice policies had to be paid for — or modified. They had always said that pensions ought to keep pace with wages as well as with prices; but by 2030, according to one calculation, it would take a 15p rise in income tax to meet that commitment. (Our welfare arithmetic doesn't add up/Peter Kellner/Sunday Times, May 2 1993.) The figures had serious implications, too, for the new system of community care that came into force on April 1 1993, with local authorities, as purchasers, assigning old people who could not cope in their own to homes in the private or voluntary sector. The Government's first year funding of the new system, at £539 million, was alleged by the Opposition to fall £200 to £300 million short of what was needed. But clearly the coming explosion of numbers in the oldest age groups would bring even more crushing financial strains.

As it was, the gap between rich and poor was still widening. The claim that by enriching the rich you also enriched the poor — the "trickle-down" theory of the Thatcher period — had been disproved by figures produced by the Institute for Fiscal Studies (IFS) for the Commons select committee on social security. A Government publication, Households Below Average Income 1979-1990/1 (June 30 1993) documented a trend which showed no sign of being reversed. The poorest families in Britain, it said, had suffered a drop of 14 per cent in real income during the Thatcher years, while average households had a rise of 36 per cent. The less well off half of the population now received only a quarter of total income; in 1979 it took one-third. A preliminary report from the Labour Commission on Social Justice said almost two-thirds of the population had an income below the average. Drawing what it called a new map of injustice, the Commission noted that the number of homeless families had grown by 46 per cent in the 1980s, and an estimated 7 million households were unable to keep their homes warm in 1991, against 5.5 million 10 years before. (And this before Vat was attached to the cost of fuel under the terms of the 1993 Budget.)

There were conflicting claims as to how far the 1993 Budget, would further disadvantage the poorest. An IFS survey for the Guardian suggested the overall effect of the Budget would be to disadvantage the poorest families by slightly under the average. But an analysis using the LSE-Cambridge University tax and benefits model concluded that the poorest tenth of the population might be hit twice as hard as the richest tenth (The Budget: poorest could be hardest hit/Holly

INCOME SUPPORT

Number of claims to social security benefits

Benefit	1988-89	1992-93
Income Support	2,716,364	4,437,816
SF Crisis Loans[4]	496,360	837,043
SF Community Care Grants[4]	312,151	1,183,945
SF Budget Loans[4]	926,308	1,497,002
SF Maternity Payment[4]	n/a	271,598
SF Funeral Payment[4]	n/a	83,386
Sickness/Invalidity Benefit	722,321	1,085,631
Maternity Benefit	122,673	97,378
Severe Disablement Allowance	35,636	59,185
Retirement Pension	592,850	657,401
Widows Payment	n/a	56,032
Widows Benefit	41,784	44,344
Industrial Injuries Disablement Benefit	82,516	101,341
Family Credit	434,138[2]	1,154,478
War Pensions	29,216	137,567
Invalid Care Allowance	52,653	91,265
Attendance Allowance	326,734	[3]
Attendance Allowance 65-plus	[1]	499,510
Mobility Allowance	226,419	[3]
Disability Living Allowance	[1]	457,865
Disability Working Allowance	[1]	28,385
Legal Aid	n/a	371,515
Child Benefit	856,361	813,077
One-Parent Benefit	166,697	193,600
Guardians Allowance	26,746	22,826
Overseas Branch Long-Term Benefits	n/a	73,031
Overseas Branch Short-Term Benefits	n/a	2,766

1 New benefit from April 1992
2 Figures available only from August 1988 to March 1989
3 Benefit ceased
4 Relates to the number of applications rather than the
number of actual applicants

Source: written answer to Frank Field, MP May 26 1993

Sutherland/Independent, March 17 1993.) The possible effects on the old worried MPs of all parties. The Government was asked for assurances that they would be recompensed. The response sounded less than watertight.

All the indications suggested, however, that poverty was worst of all among families, especially one-parent families, whose numbers had steadily grown, and households where the head was unemployed. OPCS figures in March 1993 (Population Trends 71, HMSO) showed a record 2.2 million children being brought up by lone parents. One in 10 mothers who had never been married now had three or more children. Almost one in five children were being brought up by a single parent (nine times out of 10, a mother).

Much of this went unseen by the outside world, which was more aware of the beggars on the street, many of them young, some plainly demented. The actual numbers were always rough and ready, but they fell in 1993 as initiatives for the homeless introduced by the housing minister, Sir George Young, began to have some benefit. ●

PERMANENTLY SICK
% of workforce classed permanently sick by local authority: highest rates

11.3%	Easington	6.6%	Middlesbrough
10.8%	Blaenau Gwent	6.6%	South Tyneside
10.3%	Cynon Valley	6.4%	Blackburn
9.9%	Llanelli	6.2%	Arfon
8.4%	Knowsley	6.1%	Doncaster
7.7%	Swansea	5.7%	Bolsover
7.1%	Manchester	5.6%	Bristol
7.0%	Halton	5.4%	Cardiff
6.9%	Brecknock	5.1%	Kingston upon Hull
6.8%	Rhuddlan	5.0%	Hackney

Source: 1991 Census

HOW THE COST OF WELFARE WILL GROW
Projected cost of social security budget by 1999/2000, (£ bn)

	1992-3	1999-2000
Retirement pension- basic	25.5	25.18
- earnings related	1.4	3.7
Widow's pension	1.0	1.0
Unemployment benefit	1.8	1.5
Invalidity - basic	5.1	7.3
- earnings related	1.0	1.9
War Pensions	1.0	1.0
Attendance Allowance	1.5	2.4
Disability Living Allowance	1.9	2.8
Income support- pensioners	3.6	3.6
- non-pensioners	10.9	12.7
Child benefit	5.8	6.2
Rent allowance	2.9	4.7
Rent rebate	4.4	6.4
Council tax benefit	1.5	1.7
Other	4.8	5.7
TOTAL	**74.1**	**88.4**

Source DSS

WEEKLY RATES OF BENEFITS

	unemp loyment	sick ness	retirement pension single[1] married		invalidity benefit	child benefit
1979 Nov	18.50	18.50	23.30	37.30	23.30	4.00
1983 Nov	27.05	25.95	34.05	54.50	32.60	6.50
1984 Nov	28.45	27.25	35.80	57.30	34.25	6.85
1985 Nov	30.45	29.15	38.30	61.30	38.30	7.00
1986 Jul	30.80	29.45	38.70	61.95	38.70	7.10
1987 Apr	31.45	30.05	39.50	63.25	39.50	7.25
1988 Apr	32.75	31.30	41.15	65.90	41.15	7.25
1989 Apr	34.70	33.20	43.60	69.80	43.60	7.25
1990 Apr	37.35	35.70	46.90	75.10	46.90	7.25
1991 Apr	41.40	39.60	52.00	83.25	52.00	8.25[2]
1992 Apr	43.10	41.20	54.15	88.95	54.15	9.65[2]
1993 Apr	44.65	42.70	56.10	89.80	56.10	10.00[2][1]

1. rates of widow's pension are identical 2. first born child only. There was an interim rise to £9.25 in 1991

Source: Annual Abstract of Statistics

AGE STRUCTURE OF THE POPULATION
mid-year estimates of percentage of population falling in each group.

	under 16 %	16-39 %	40-64 %	65-79 %	80-plus %	ALL millions
1981	22.2	34.9	27.8	2.2	2.8	56.4
1991	20.3	35.2	28.7	12.0	3.7	57.6
projected						
2001	21.3	32.6	30.5	11.4	4.2	9.2
2011	20.1	30.0	33.7	11.7	4.5	60.0
2021	19.5	30.5	31.9	13.6	4.5	60.7

Source: Social Trends

GROWTH OF CLAIMS FOR RESIDENTIAL AND NURSING HOME CARE
(thousands)

	residential care homes	nursing homes	total
1979 Dec	*	*	12
1983 Dec	*	*	26
1987 May	84	32	117
1990 May	125	64	189
1991 May	137	94	231
1992 May	154	117	270
1993 March	159	122	281

Figures before 1985 are not considered reliable enough to be sub-divided between nursing and residential care homes. Figures may not add up because of rounding

Source: DSS

Out in the cold: many city centres took on the appearance of refugee camps as the numbers of homeless continued to rise

FOURTEEN
HOUSING

For many of those who, for the first time in their lives, proudly took over homes of their own during the Thatcher years and hung signs saying "Mon Repos" over the door, the late 1980s were times of bleak disillusion: more Mon Repossession than Mon Repos. According to the 1991 census, 66.4 per cent of British householders were owner-occupiers, compared with 55.8 per cent in 1981; 21.4 per cent rented from councils, against 31.1 per cent 10 years earlier.

But for many of the new owner-occupiers what had once been a pride and joy became a millstone. The cost of their mortgages soared as interest rates climbed; and the poll tax cost more than the rates. Meanwhile, the value of many properties fell to a point where people owed more to their mortgage companies than their houses were worth: the so-called "negative equity" trap. Repossessions climbed: from 44,000 in 1990 to 75,500 in 1991, though 1992 showed a sharp improvement. Rescue packages, announced by the building societies under Government pressure before the 1992 election, produced disappointing results.

The green shoots of recovery in the housing market were visible in the spring of 1993. As lending rates fell, most building societies were plotting a modest increase in prices and an increase in activity, though the largest — the Halifax — advanced less money in May than in April. The replacement of the poll tax by the council tax appeared from the public reaction to have helped more people than it hurt.

But a new threat had now appeared. The cost to the Treasury of mortgage interest relief was running in the spring of 1993 at £4.3 billion a year. In his 1993 Budget the chancellor said the rate would be cut to 20 per cent from April 1994. But against the background of an escalating Public Sector Borrowing Requirement there was clearly some temptation to come back for more. In a written answer on May 27, 1993 (HCD col 667) the financial secretary to the Treasury, Stephen Dorrell, told a Tory backbencher that the cost of MIRAS in 1994-5 was expected to be £3.6 billion. Assuming no change in the current level of interest rates, to phase it out over three years would bring savings of £1.2 billion in the first year, £2.4 billion in the second and £3.6 billion in the third.

Of the other two arms of the housing movement, one looked increasingly withered. The stock of council housing had been eroded by sales to tenants and here and there by the transfer of estates, following a local ballot, to Housing Action Trusts — though the Government's aspirations for large-scale transfers had been disappointed: five HATs (Liverpool, Tower Hamlets, Castle Vale, North Hull and Waltham Forest) had been established by June 1993. The Housing and Urban Development Bill included a rent-to-mortgages scheme, giving council tenants a part share in their homes, gradually stepping up to full ownership. Council building had all but ceased.

For those who remained council tenants there were hefty rent rises. In practice, much of the cost fell on government funds, since tenants could not afford to pay: in effect, what occurred was a boost for the DoE's funds and further inroads into the DSS's.

The role of provider of low-cost social housing was progressively transferred to housing associations, but these were difficult times for them too. The 1992 Autumn Statement brought them a windfall in the form of £577 million, made available to help shift the stock of repossessed property which was blighting the market. But it also brought a further reduction in their level of government grant.

The £577 million subvention was designed to go mainly on repossessed property. But it didn't. In their search for cost-effectiveness, associations used it instead to buy new houses which developers could not sell, including in some cases whole new estates. Only four of every 100 deals so far, it was reported in January, involved repossessions.

In the meantime the movement's grant, which in 1989-90 had been 75 per cent, was again reduced: to 67 per cent in 1993/94, 60 per cent in 1994/95 and a projected (but negotiable) 55 per cent in 1995/96. (Later the 1994/95 figure was raised to 62 per cent.) The argument was that money could be raised on the open market. So it could, but at a price. The National Federation of Housing Associations forecast a 50 per cent increase in rents by 1996 (again with much of the cost in practice transferred to the DSS).

There were other unsettling consequences. First, the way the money was to be distributed ensured that some associations would have to be merged or closed. The 567 associations had to be ranked by the Housing Corporation to help investors judge where to put their money. Of 360 associations analysed, 87 were judged acceptable, 46 needed to improve their financial performance, and 227 were excluded — including all 30 housing associations specialising in ethnic minorities.

Pressure to keep down costs was damaging housing associations in another sense, too, according to a report compiled for the Joseph Rowntree Foundation, published on April 20 1993. This said that associations were building a new generation of monolithic estates which could become the problem estates of the future. The social profile of some of the estates surveyed was lower even, said the report, than Broadwater Farm at the time of the riots in 1986.

Homelessness, however, seemed to be diminishing. Records were broken in the first quarter of 1992 when 38,460 families were accepted as homeless and the number in temporary accommodation climbed to

GOVERNMENT SPENDING ON HOUSING

1 Total spending at current prices £billion
2. Total spending in real terms at 1991-2 prices £billion
3. % of government expenditure
4. % of GDP

	1978-1979	1983-1984	1984-1985	1985-1986	1986-1987	1987-1988	1988-1989	1989-1990	1990-1991-	1991-1992	1992-3 est.
1	4.6	4.5	4.6	4.2	4.1	4.2	3.3	5.2	5.0	5.8	6.2
2	12.4	7.2	6.9	6.0	5.7	5.6	4.1	6.1	5.3	5.8	5.9
3	6.1	3.2	3.1	2.6	2.4	2.4	1.8	2.5	2.2	2.4	2.3
4	2.7	1.5	1.4	1.2	1.1	1.0	0.7	1.0	0.9	1.0	1.0

INVESTMENT HOUSING STARTS

1: gross domestic fixed capital formation £ million, 1985 prices - private and public dwellings
2: housing starts (000s) by private enterprise; housing associations; and local authorities, new towns and government departments

	Investment		housing starts			
	(a) private	(b) public	(a) private	(b) associations,	(c) LAs etc	ratio a:c
1979	9,665	3,615	144.0	15.9	65.3	2.2
1983	9,683	2,924	172.2	14.3	34.6	5.0
1984	9,737	2,825	158.3	12.7	27.4	5.8
1985	9,318	2,536	165.7	12.5	22.0	7.5
1986	10,365	2,536	180.0	13.0	20.4	8.8
1987	10,734	2,741	196.8	12.9	19.9	9.9
1988	13,999	2,549	221.4	14.4	16.3	13.6
1989	14,290	3,006	170.1	15.8	15.2	11.2
1990	10,506	3,088	135.3	18.7	8.5	15.9
1991	8,942	2,078	135.0	21.6	4.1	32.9

Source: Economic Trends Annual Supplement

61,920. But DoE figures published on March 15 1993 showed the first year-on-year drop since the new provisions on homelessness came into force in 1978. The figure for the final quarter of 1992 was 33,630. The number of households in temporary accommodation was 62,740. Use of bed and breakfast accommodation was also down: a sign, said Young, that his remedial measures were working.

At the other end of the scale, the Government moved in its Housing Urban Development Bill (later renamed the Leasehold Reform, Housing and Urban Development Bill) to give up to 750,000 leaseholders of flats the right to buy their freeholds at the market rate. This was a manifesto commitment, but it ran into opposition from Tory MPs, including several ex-ministers, as a retrospective interference with contracts freely entered into, and an attack on property rights. Britain's richest property owner, the Duke of Westminster, resigned from the party in protest. An amendment exempting stately homes was carried in the Lords and further concessions were made when the Bill returned to the Commons, limiting the right to buy. Conservative critics still thought it went too far, but the Opposition complained it had been watered down to the point of ineffectiveness.

At the other end of the market, the Government promised a Bill in the next session to give householders and the police stronger powers against squatters. Under existing law, to squat in an unoccupied house was not a criminal offence. But remedies through civil action were often slow and expensive. A new Bill would remove restrictions on criminal proceedings.●

HOUSING STRESS

year	no of mortgages at end of period number	properties repossessed number	%	mortgages 6-12 months in arrears number	%
1983	6,846,000	8,420	0.12	29,440	0.43
1984	7,313,000	12,400	0.17	48,270	0.66
1985	7,717,000	19,300	0.25	57,110	0.74
1986	8,138,000	24,090	0.30	52,080	0.64
1987	8,283,000	26,390	0.32	55,490	0.67
1988	8,564,000	18,510	0.22	42,810	0.50
1989	9,125,000	15,810	0.17	66,800	0.73
1990	9,415,000	43,890	0.47	123,110	1.31
1991	9,815,000	75,540	0.77	183,610	1.87
1992	9,922,000	68,540	0.70	205,010	2.07

Source: Council of Mortgage Lenders

HOMELESSNESS
1. households accepted as homeless by LAs under the provisions of the Housing Acts   2. households in bed and breakfast end of year. 3. households in hostels/women's refuges 4. in other temporary accommodation, including short life

| | 1 | | 2 | | 3 | 4 |
	England	London	England	London	England	England
1979	55,530	16,400	1,790	1,270	3,850	5,830
1990	140,350	36,480	11,130	7,690	9,010	25,130
1991	144,530	38,820	12,150	7,020	9,990	37,790
% increase	160.3	136.7	578.7	452.7	159.5	548.2

Source: DoE

COUNCIL RENT RISES

	Average Rent (£)	increase (%)
1979	6.41	
1980	7.70	20.1
1981	11.42	48.3
1982	13.48	18.0
1983	13.97	3.6
1984	14.66	4.9
1985	15.54	6.0
1986	16.36	5.3
1987	17.70	8.2
1988	18.82	6.3
1989	20.70	10.0
1990	23.76	14.8
1991	27.28	14.8
1992	30.57	12.1
1993 (Apr)	33.52	9.6

LEASEHOLD REFORM, HOUSING AND URBAN DEVELOPMENT (Government Bill)
Title changed from Housing and Development Bill, May 20 1993

Introduced: October 22 1992

PURPOSE:

To give new rights to certain leaseholders to purchase freehold and for council tenants to purchase their homes; introduce rent-to-mortgage schemes; extend Compulsory Competitive Tender (CCT) to management of local authority housing; and set up Urban Regeneration Agency

COMMONS:

2nd reading: November 3 1992 by 327 (Con, Lib Dem, OUP, UPUP) to 259 (Lab, SNP, PC)
Report and 3rd reading: October 9-10 1992

LORDS:

2nd reading: February 23 1993
Report: May 11, 18 and 20 1993
3rd reading: May 25 1993

ROYAL ASSENT:

July 20 1993

Rebellions:

Amendment exempting owners of 60 stately homes carried against Government in the Lords by 114 to 57.

Sixty women out of 651 MPs was a score The 300 Group was determined to improve

FIFTEEN
SOCIAL CHANGE

Though the architect of a campaign called Opportunity 2000, designed to ensure that more top jobs would go to women, John Major failed to include a woman in his first Cabinet. He did better after the election, with Virginia Bottomley going to health and Gillian Shephard to employment (she switched to agriculture in the May 1993 reshuffle) — though that still gave women only two seats out of 22. This was closely in line with the stingy proportion of women returned to Westminster at the election — 60 out of 651, the highest figure ever, but still meagre compared to some European legislatures. Though the number of Conservative seats was down, the number of women MPs was up from 17 to 20. The Liberal Democrats doubled their representation (from one to two); the best progress came from Labour, with an 80 per cent increase from 21 to 37, reflecting the increasing pressure within the party for women to have more power at every level.

On June 30 1993, the Labour National Executive approved in principle a plan to double the number of women on the Labour benches by requiring that in half of all seats where a sitting MP was retiring, or where Labour was expected to gain from other parties, there should be women-only short lists for candidate selection. Constituency parties would be required to negotiate with regional parties over which seats should be chosen, with the NEC having the right to impose a woman candidate where a region fell below its quota.

Male domination of politics extended through the civil service to the quangos (quasi-autonomous non-governmental organisations or quasi-national government organisations, according to taste) which now accounted for 20 per cent of public spending. According to the annual Cabinet Office publication, Public Bodies, 26 per cent of appointments on quangos went to women. Forty five per cent of places on boards of visitors were taken by women, but only 22 per cent of posts on executive bodies and only 7 per cent in nationalised industry boards. The proportion of women allowed to chair quangos was 15 per cent. Among the departments, the Home Office had the best record for appointing women and Defence the worst.

Kamlesh Bahl, a lawyer of Ugandan Asian origin who took over as head of the Equal Opportunities Commission on June 15 1993, said on her appointment: "Equal opportunities is now on the agenda. We have the commitment of the prime minister and of all political parties. Now we have to move on to translate the commitment into practical action." Some of that meant breaking down prejudice, but it was clear from survey research that one formidable obstacle was the lack of provision for children of working mothers. In terms of *quantity*, there had been a huge expansion in opportunities for women to work. The same was not so far true in terms of the *quality* of the jobs.

Social change in the 1960s continued to be blamed for rising crime figures, social disjunction, disruption in schools and many other maladies. Clamour for the restoration of hanging continued, with huge majorities in favour according to the polls, but for once the Commons got through a post-election year without voting on it. Nor were there further battles over abortion. On June 17 1992, the Government accepted the recommendations of the select committee on the Armed Forces Bill that homosexual activity, where legal in the rest of society, should no longer be an offence under military law. There were predictions that the Government might allow MPs a free vote if an amendment to lower the age of consent for homosexuals, at present 21, were to be tabled on the Criminal Justice Bill promised for the 1993-94 session. Major was reported to be sympathetic to a change.

The Commons remained divided over the liberalisation of the laws on Sunday trading, an issue which gained new urgency from the widespread defiance of the law by large and powerful companies. The Conservative party was split between its deregulators, who wanted to remove all restric-

tions, and its moralists, who wanted to protect the traditional Sunday. Hopes that the issue might be taken out of the Government's hands, when the European Court was asked to rule that restrictions imposed in Britain were contrary to the Treaty of Rome, were disappointed: the court saw no cause to intervene. On November 16 1992 the home secretary Kenneth Clarke promised legislation based on a choice between three options: total deregulation, broad deregulation, as in Scotland, with big shops restricted to six hours' opening but small ones allowed to open as they liked, and limited deregulation, on the lines of a private member's bill twice brought to Parliament by the Labour MP Ray Powell.

Under this option, Sunday trading would remain broadly illegal, but exemptions would be allowed for recreation, emergencies, social gatherings and travel, subject to local authority approval. Powell had introduced his Bill in the 1991-92 session, but the calling of the election killed it. He reintroduced it, but with the Government remaining opposed it failed for lack of time.

The Government promised its Bill for the start of the 1993-94 session, with its own MPs allowed a free vote between the options — now extended to four in a Government statement on July 13. Ministers were adamant, though, that they would not permit safeguards demanded by Labour, including a legal right for staff to refuse to work on Sundays and premium rates of pay.

There were some traditionalist/ moralist objections, too, though fewer than expected, to the Government's

DIVORCE

	total divorces (thousands) GB	persons divorcing per thousand married people England and Wales
1971	27.0	6.0
1976	135.4	10.1
1981	155.6	11.9
1986	166.7	12.9
1990	165.7	12.9

Source: Annual Abstract/Social Trends

LEGAL ABORTIONS (thousands) England & Wales

1971	85.8
1976	91.2
1981	112.4
1986	131.2
1991	158.1

Source: Social Trends

National Lotteries Bill. But the loudest objections came from those who thought they might suffer from the competition, including the football pools and charities, voluntary organisations and other existing good causes which feared a loss of donations and a threat to lotteries of their own.

In an unexpected reversal of normal roles, Labour condemned the Bill as a case of state power grinding down private industry: "the unacceptable face of nationalisation", said the party's spokesman, Ann Clwyd. A leaked report commissioned but not published by ministers, disclosed in the Guardian on November 27 1992, said the pools industry could suffer a drop in revenue of at least 17.5 per cent, with the loss of 1,100 jobs, unless concessions were made. The select committee on the National Heritage in a report on January 20 1993 argued for equitable treatment for the pools. Changes were made in committee to reflect these objections.

Money raised by the lottery was to be split six ways: the arts, sport, charities, the heritage, and the fund set up to celebrate the millennium would get equal shares. The final claimant was HM Treasury. The lottery's champions warned that if the Treasury was too greedy, the enterprise might founder. Twelve per cent or above was a popular definition of greed. In his 1993 Budget the chancellor Norman Lamont set the figure for the Treasury's take at 12 per cent, saying he believed this would get the lottery off to a good start.

Two other deregulation moves seemed broadly popular. On January 19 1993 Clarke announced that the law on betting shops would be relaxed to allow them to open in the evenings. On March 19, he proposed a change in the licensing laws to allow children to accompany parents into pubs certificated as suitable. And in Wales, the Welsh office announced the end of the seven yearly referendums on Sunday pub opening. With only one "dry" area left, Dwyfor in north Wales, the 1996 poll would be the last.●

WOMEN IN WESTMINSTER SINCE 1918
Women as % of MPs

	ALL	Con	Lab	Lib*	Other	all MPs	Con MPs	Lab MPs	Lib* MPs
1918	1	0	0	0	1	0.1	-	-	-
1922	2	1	0	1	0	0.3	0.6	-	1.6
1923	8	3	3	2	0	1.3	1.2	1.6	1.3
1924	4	3	1	0	0	0.7	0.7	0.7	-
1929	14	3	9	1	1	2.3	1.2	3.1	1.7
1931	15	13	0	1	1	2.4	2.8	-	3.1
1935	9	6	1	1	1	1.5	1.6	0.6	4.8
1945	24	1	21	1	1	3.8	0.5	5.3	8.3
1950	21	6	14	1	0	3.4	2.0	4.4	11.1
1951	17	6	11	0	0	2.7	1.9	3.7	-
1955	24	9	14	0	1	3.8	2.6	5.1	-
1959	25	12	13	0	0	4.0	3.3	5.0	-
1964	29	11	18	0	0	4.4	3.7	5.6	-
1966	26	7	19	0	0	4.1	2.8	5.2	-
1970	26	15	10	0	1	4.1	4.5	3.5	-
1974Feb	23	9	13	0	1	3.6	3.0	4.3	-
1974Oct	27	7	18	0	2	4.3	2.5	5.6	-
1979	19	8	11	0	0	3.0	2.4	4.1	-
1983	23	13	10	0	0	3.5	3.3	4.8	-
1987	41	17	21	2	1	6.3	4.5	9.2	9.1
1992	60	20	37**	2	1	9.2	6.0	13.7	10.0

*Liberal, Alliance, SDP, Liberal Democrat
**including Betty Boothroyd, who became Speaker.

Source: adapted from FWS Craig, British Electoral Facts 1832-1987

WOMEN ON PUBLIC BODIES
public bodies 1992: women on boards, tribunals etc

	Men	Women
All public bodies	74	26
Chairmanships	85	15
Executive bodies	78	22
Advisory	74	26
Tribunals	75	25
Boards of Visitors[1]	55	45
Nationalised Industry	93	7
Public Corporations	81	19
NHS bodies	72	28

Appointments in principal government departments[2]:

Home Office	60	40
Scottish Office	64	36
Social Security	69	31
Health	70	30
Employment	73	27
Northern.Ireland	74	26
Education	77	23
Foreign Office	77	23
National Heritage	80	20
Welsh Office	82	18
DTI	83	17
Treasury	85	15
Trade	86	14
MAFF	89	11
Cabinet Office	90	10
Defence	93	7

[1]to penal establishments in England & Wales and boards of visitors and visiting committees in N Ireland. [2] not all appointments are made by ministers. Details are given in Public Bodies.

Source: Public Bodies 1992 with additional calculations

OPTIONS FOR SUNDAY OPENING (PUBLISHED BY THE GOVERNMENT, JULY 13 1993

1. Total deregulation: all shops can open on Sundays, as in Scotland

2. Partial deregulation: smaller shops can open all day; shops over 3,000 square feet in area may open for six hours only.

3. Limited opening: convenience shops (eg corner shops, newsagents, chemists) of under 3,000 square feet may open; also estate agents, banks, travel agents. Most other shops must remain shut except on the four Sundays before Christmas.

4. Restricted opening: only small food and convenience shops permitted to open, plus DIY, garden centres, motor supply shops: all other to remain closed.

Conservative MPs will be allowed a free vote between these options, but will be whipped to oppose employee protection provisions favoured by Labour.

NATIONAL LOTTERY ETC (Government Bill)
INTRODUCED: December 16 1992

PURPOSE:

To establish a state regulated lottery with licensing and regulatory system and mechanisms for distributing the proceeds

COMMONS:

2nd reading: January 25 1993 by 339 (Con) to 203 (Lab, Lib Dem, 1 PC, OUP, DUP,UPUP)
Report and 3rd reading: April 28 1993

LORDS:

2nd reading: May 27 1993
Report: July 16 1993
3rd reading: July 23 1993

SHOPS (AMENDMENT) (Private member's bill: Ray Powell, Lab Ogmore)
INTRODUCED: June 10 1992

PURPOSE:

Revival of Bill which failed in previous session. To require shops to remain closed on Sundays except in cases where specific exemptions applied - eg those catering for recreation, emergencies, social gatherings and travel

COMMONS:

2nd reading: January 22 1993 by 214 (Con 37, Lab 154, Lib Dem 7, PC 3, OUP 9, DUP 3, UPUP 1) to 41 (Con 32, Lab 5, Lib Dem 4)
Report: July 14 1993 (adjourned)
No further progress

WELSH LANGUAGE (Government Bill)
INTRODUCED: LORDS December 17 1992

PURPOSE:

To promote the Welsh language, put the Welsh Language Board on statutory basis and open the way for equality between English and Welsh in public business and administration in Wales.

LORDS:

2nd reading: January 19 1993
Report: February 18 1993
3rd reading: February 25 1993

COMMONS:

2nd reading: May 26 1993: unopposed
Report and 3rd reading: July 15 1993

SIXTEEN

MIGRATION & RACE

The turbulence in Europe which followed the dismantling of the Berlin Wall and the progressive collapse of the Soviet system led to a wave of migration across the Continent, with an estimated 17.6 million people, twice the figure of a decade before, fleeing across borders. Even this figure underestimated what was happening, since it excluded those classed as "internally displaced", as in Bosnia.

These events triggered racial disturbances and greatly alarmed governments. The worst trouble was in Germany, where the arrival of 118,000 refugees in the first quarter of 1993, the resurgence of far-right political groups and attacks on migrant workers brought the end of the liberal "open asylum" system by a parliamentary vote on May 26. The newly elected French government was also working on tighter restrictions.

Compared with Germany's problems, Britain's were modest, with an estimated 25,000 asylum seekers in 1992, against Germany's 440,000 (or Sweden's 83,000. Although the Government agreed to take 4,000 refugees from the former Yugoslavia, it came under sharp attack after turning away 36 refugees, mostly women and children, under the terms of the Dublin Convention, an EC agreement which requires that refugees should seek asylum in the first safe country they arrive in. "A brisk exchange of words" was reported between the Foreign Office minister Baroness Chalker, worried about diplomatic repercussions, and the immigration minister, Charles Wardle. On August 12 1992 the United Nations High Commissioner for Refugees called for deportations to stop. In the spirit of international burden-sharing, it said, the UK should refrain from third country removals. Wardle promised to be more flexible.

At EC level, too, under the auspices of a committee calling itself the Expulsion Sub-group of the Ad Hoc Group on Immigration, new measures to identify and expel illegal entrants led to complaints of a "fortress Europe" mentality. The Edinburgh summit of December 1992 expressed concern that uncontrolled immigration might be destabilising and could undermine the situation of third country nationals legally resident in member states.

An Asylum Bill had been introduced in Parliament in the 1991-92 session. This was advertised as a twin-track measure, designed to clamp down on bogus asylum-seekers but to speed up progress on genuine claims. It came under sustained attack and never completed its course, falling when the general election was called — the only important measure in the Government programme to do so.

After the election this Bill was reintroduced in an altered form as the Asylum and Immigration Appeals Bill. The Government accepted the main thrust of its critics' attack by agreeing that refugees refused asylum should have a right of appeal with an oral hearing before an adjudicator — though the time scale was kept tight: 15 days at most to prepare the appeal, and in some cases only 48 hours. A second change, however, removed the right of appeal for visitors and students who were refused entry: a necessary change, said the home secretary, Kenneth Clarke, to relieve the backlog of work now imposing a two-year wait for decisions.

There were two views of the state of race relations in Britain. The prime minister told the Commons that they were by and large improving. The Commission for Racial Equality said discrimination and hostility were still unacceptably high and called for a beefing up of the Race Relations Act. Recommendations for change that it had submitted to the Government in 1985 still awaited a reply.

The Commission's claim that racial attacks were increasing was backed by Home Office figures. The worst came from south-east London, where the British National Party had established its headquarters at Welling in the London borough of Bexley. The number of racial attacks in Metropolitan police area 3, which included Bexley, had risen from 394 in 1990, shortly after the BNP moved in, to 596 in 1991 and 811 in 1992. In one widely reported incident which led to street protests, 17-year-old Stephen Lawrence, a black schoolboy, was stabbed to death in Eltham in the neighbouring borough of Greenwich in April 1992. The Conservative MP for Eltham, Peter Bottomley, complained of "complacency" over racist attacks in south London and Labour MPs said racial violence should be made a specific offence. The overall Home Office figure of 7,780 racial assaults in 1992 was attacked as a wild under-estimate. The Home Office minister Peter Lloyd told the home affairs select committee on July 14 1993 that racial attacks could be running at 130,000-140,000 a year. The British Crime survey projected a total of more than 330,000 attacks a year, though only a minority of these would be classed as serious. The Home Office figures also showed a rise in the number of prosecutions for publishing material likely to incite racial violence.

A report from the Policy Studies Institute on March 29 1993, compiled by Trevor Jones on the basis of the Government's Labour Force Survey, suggested that the "ethnic gap" in professional employment was beginning to close, with well-qualified Indian, African, Asian and Chinese men now at least as likely to hold professional jobs as white men. These groups were more likely than their white counterparts to stay on in full-time education after 16 and to be better qualified. But it found little improvement within the West Indian community, while Pakistanis and Bangladeshis remained a highly disadvantaged underclass. Where whites had an unemployment rate of 7 per cent, the rate among Afro-Caribbeans was twice that, and among Pakistanis and Bangladeshis,

DISTRICTS WITH LARGEST ETHNIC MINORITY COMMUNITIES

	%	thousands
Brent	44.9	109.1
Newham	42.4	89.1
Tower Hamlets	35.4	57.1
Hackney	33.7	61.0
Ealing	32.4	89.1
Lambeth	30.1	73.8
Haringey	29.0	58.7
Leicester	28.5	77.1
Slough	27.7	28.0
Harrow	26.3	52.6
Waltham Forest	25.6	54.3
Southwark	24.4	53.4
Hounslow	24.3	49.7
Lewisham	22.0	50.8
Birmingham	21.5	206.6
Redbridge	21.4	48.4
Westminster	21.4	37.4
Wandsworth	20.2	50.9
Luton	19.7	33.9
Islington	18.9	31.1
Wolverhampton	18.5	44.7
Barnet	18.3	53.7
Camden	17.8	30.3

Source: The Centre for Ethnic Relations Studies, University of Warwick, based on 1991 Census returns

three times that. Nearly 25 per cent of Bangladeshis in the labour market were unemployed. (Britain's Ethnic Minorities, Trevor Jones, PSI, PO Box 1496, Poole, Dorset, BH12 3LL, £15.)

Little, so far, had changed at the top. Though six MPs from ethnic communities were elected in 1992, that still accounted for only 1 per cent of the House, compared with 5.5 per cent across the community. The proportion of seats on quangos, as monitored by the Cabinet Office publication Public Bodies 1992, was just 2 per cent.

Outrageous discrimination was still in practice in corners of British industry, as was demonstrated by the successful prosecution of John Haggas plc, of Keighley, West Yorkshire, who on May 28 were ordered by an industrial tribunal to pay £229,000 compensation for discrimination against Asian night workers. All employees had been ordered to take on extra duties, but blacks, unlike whites, were told that refusal would mean dismissal. Black workers at Haggas's were not paid overtime, had four days less holiday and had no chance of promotion.

That old resentments still raged below the surface was demonstrated when on May 28 1993 Winston Churchill, Conservative MP for Davy-hulme, said in a speech at Bolton that an end must be put to the "relentless" inflow of immigrants. "With the Government continuing to bring in immigrants each year at a scale, in Mrs Thatcher's immortal phrase of 15 years ago, 'equivalent to a town the size of Grantham', a halt must be called — and urgently — if the British way of life is to be preserved," he said. The population of some of our northern cities, he claimed, was now 50 per cent immigrant.

A hail of condemnation, not least from ministers, brought a partial retraction: Churchill had meant to say "inner cities". But even that calculation was wrong, as census figures showed. The speech caused as much excitement as any on this issue since Enoch Powell's "rivers of blood" speech in April 1968. Churchill's famous name ensured him attention in spite of his backbench obscurity. The MP claimed a huge postbag in favour of his position and the letters columns of some newspapers reflected more agreement than there was among fellow MPs. The BBC's Any Answers programme was accused of censorship for failing to cover the issue.●

APPLICATIONS[1] RECEIVED FOR ASYLUM IN THE UK, EXCLUDING DEPENDANTS, AND DECISIONS2, 1989-92

Number of principal applicants

	1989	1990	1991	1992
Total applications received	11,640	22,000	44,840	24,610
Decisions[2]				
Total decisions	6,955	4,015	5,965	34,900
Recognised as refugee and granted asylum3	2,210	900	505	1,115
Not recognised as refugee, but granted exceptional leave4	3,860	2,400	2,230	15,325
Refusals				
Total refused	890	710	3,240	18,465
Refused asylum and exceptional leave after full consideration	890	710	2,185	2,680
Refused on "safe third country" grounds5			270	595
Refused under para 101 of Immigration Rules6			785	15,195

1. Includes applications made at ports on arrival and those made in country.
2. Decisions do not necessarily relate to decisions made in the same period.
3. Excluding South East Asian refugees.
4. Where it would have been unreasonable or impractical to seek to enforce return to country of origin.
5. Figures from January 1, 1991 only. Prior to this, these refusals are included in the column: Refused asylum and exceptional leave after full consideration.
6. For failure to provide evidence to support the asylum claim within a reasonable period, including failure to respond to two invitations to interview to establish identity.

Source:Written answer to Terry Dicks, MP May 18 1993 HcD col 95.

RESIDENT POPULATION BY ETHNIC GROUP
(% by origin; total groupings in thousands)

	White	Black Caribbean	Black African	Black Other	Indian	Indian Pakistani	Bangladeshi	Chinese	Other	Total groupings
North	98.7	-	-	0.1	0.3	0.3	0.1	0.2	0.3	3,027
Yorks & Humberside	95.6	0.4	0.1	0.2	0.8	2.0	0.2	0.2	0.6	4,837
East Midlands	95.2	0.6	0.1	0.3	2.5	0.4	0.1	0.2	0.6	3,953
East Anglia	97.9	0.2	0.1	0.4	0.3	0.3	0.1	0.2	0.6	2,027
South East	90.1	1.9	1.0	0.6	2.6	0.8	0.6	0.5	1.8	17,208
Gt London	79.8	4.4	2.4	1.2	5.2	1.3	1.3	0.8	3.5	6,680
Rest of South East	96.7	0.4	0.1	0.2	0.9	0.5	0.2	0.3	0.7	10,529
South West	98.6	0.3	0.1	0.1	0.2	0.1	0.1	0.1	0.4	4,609
West Midlands	91.8	1.5	0.1	0.4	3.1	1.9	0.4	0.2	0.7	5,150
North West	96.1	0.3	0.1	0.3	0.9	1.2	0.2	0.3	0.5	6,244
England	93.8	1.1	0.4	0.4	1.8	1.0	0.3	0.3	1.0	47,055
Wales	98.5	0.1	0.1	0.1	0.2	0.2	0.1	0.2	0.4	2,835
Scotland	98.7	-	0.1	0.1	0.2	0.4	-	0.2	0.3	4,999
GB	94.5	0.9	0.4	0.3	1.5	0.9	0.3	0.3	0.9	54,889

ASYLUM AND IMMIGRATION APPEALS (Government Bill)
INTRODUCED: October 22 1992

PURPOSE:

To replace Asylum Bill which failed to complete passage through previous Parliament. To curb bogus applicants while speeding up procedures to help genuine ones. New provision added to previous Bill allowing those refused asylum oral hearing before independent adjudicator; but rights of appeal for visitors and students, preserved in earlier Bill, are restricted.

COMMONS:

2nd reading: November 2 1992 by 321 (Con, UPUP) to 276 (Lab, Lib Dem, SNP, PC, OUP)
Report and 3rd reading: January 11 1993

LORDS:

2nd reading: January 26 1993
Report: March 2 and 4 1993
3rd reading: March 11 1993

ROYAL ASSENT:

July 1 1993

Rebellions :

Lords voted 274 to 226 to create statutory advisory panel to help child asylum-seekers – reversed in Commons. A Lords amendment saying children should not be fingerprinted except in presence of someone independent of immigration authorities and police was accepted by the Government.

The ass that roared: acquittals for the Guildford 4, Birmingham 6 and Judith Ward, among others, shook public faith in the justice system

SEVENTEEN
LAW AND LIBERTY

The number of criminal offences committed in England and Wales in 1992 was 5.6 million, six per cent higher than in 1991. Those figures, announced on April 28 1993, were a modest relief to ministers after the 16 per cent increase a year before. Others were more impressed by the total rise in crime over the Conservative years. A parliamentary written answer on May 7 1993 (HCD col 263) compared 1992 with 1979: an increase of 127 per cent in offences recorded, representing 10,614 offences per 1,000 population against 4,833 per 1,000 in 1979. Over the same period, the clear-up rate fell from 41 to 26 per cent. Some forces showed a surprisingly sharp fall in clear-up rates since 1990.

All crime statistics were suspect. "There are a lot of bad statistics in this world, but there are few that are more unreliable than crime statistics or anything related to it" — Kenneth Clarke, home secretary, BBC radio, February 24 1993. But the Home Office figures plainly understated the full extent of crime, since so much went unreported: the British Crime Survey, based on sample evidence, put the global figure of crime three times higher.

The reported fall in the rate of arrests and prosecutions for reported crime appeared to reflect several fac-tors. One was new cautioning proce-dures; another, falling confidence in making cases stick, influenced per-haps by the growing numbers of con-victions overturned on appeal and also by the soaring figures for com-plaints against the police, which rose from 18,149 in England and Wales in 1987 to 21,733 in 1992. Though the overall rate of juvenile crime had fall-en, police complaints that they were powerless to act against very young offenders, some of whose boastful swaggerings at the scene of their crimes had been shown on television, provoked the home secretary, Ken-neth Clarke, to announce the estab-lishment of five secure units for juve-nile offenders.

Such sturdy responses, in the view of the police, were too rare. Few home secretaries are heroes to their policemen, but Clarke seemed espe-cially unpopular, not least for his fail-ure to consult on changes he planned to make in their pay, conditions and organisation. They were subject to three inquiries. One was the Royal Commission on Criminal Justice under Lord Runciman, set up in the light of evidence from the cases of the Guild-ford Four, the Maguire Seven and the Birmingham Six, all freed on appeal, about how the police investigated and prosecuted cases. A second, chaired by Sir Patrick Sheehy, chairman of BAT, promised a shake up on pay and conditions. A third, conducted within the Home Office, dealt with amalgamations of forces, changes in the composition of police authorities and greater freedom for chief constables to manage their resources. The outcomes of all three became known in late June and early July.

The Sheehy proposals ran into fierce opposition from the police, with over 20,000 turning up at a Police Federation rally at Wembley to condemn them. The home secretary, Michael Howard, ordered urgent talks with chief constables, some of whom seemed almost as hostile as their rank and file, especially to the proposals for fixed term contracts, lower starting salaries, the later retirement age and the link between pay and performance. That Sheehy would lighten the burden on the Treasury was, they said, plain enough. What they couldn't see was how these changes would serve the imperative interest of better policing.

A similar shake-up was underway in the prison service, which on April 1 1993 became an executive agency under the Next Steps programme, with a new director-general, Derek Lewis, a former television executive with no experience of the service. Two existing prisons were privatised: the Wolds, Hull, was followed on May 25 1993 by Blakenhurst near Redditch, with a newly built prison near Doncaster destined to join them.

The privatisation of prison escort services in the East Midlands, Yorkshire and Humberside from April 5 1993 produced a spate of escapes, which made Group 4, who ran the service, the cause of much hilarity, though on June 14, when the service was 10 weeks old, the company said its loss rate for the period (0.7 per cent) compared favourably with that of the police and prison officers (2.1). On May 8, a prisoner in the care of Group 4 died of brain damage after inhaling vomit on his way back from Rotherham magistrates court to the Wolds. After complaints about the Wolds from the Prison Reform Trust, Judge Stephen Tumim, the Inspector of Prisons, went to look at it. He had earlier reported unfavourably on Cardiff ("one of the worst in Britain"), Leicester and Stafford.

The 1991 Criminal Justice Act, which came into force in October 1992, was designed to reduce prison sentences. But on May 13 1993 Clarke announced an urgent revision, to amend its rules on sentencing and repeal provisions restricting the right of the court to refer to previous convictions in sentencing property offenders. The Act contained a formula for relating fines imposed by the court to the means of the accused. Apparently bizarre anomalies — a company director until recently earning £60,000 a year fined £160 for speeding, an unemployed man aged 20 fined £1,200 for dropping litter — had led to a public outcry, with 30 magistrates (out of a total of 26,000) leaving the bench in protest.

The reversal of past prison sentences, some great and some small, continued, the most spectacular being the freeing on June 4 1993 of Judith Ward after 18 years in jail for the bombing of an army coach on the M62 in 1974. Yet again the appeal court verdict contained a damning

GOVERNMENT SPENDING ON LAW, ORDER AND PROTECTIVE SERVICES

1 Total spending at current prices £billion
2. Total spending in real terms at 1991-2 prices £billion
3. % of government expenditure
4. % of GDP

	1978-1979	1983-1984	1984-1985	1985-1986	1986-1987	1987-1988	1988-1989	1989-1990	1990-1991	1991-1992	1992-3 est.
1	2.6	5.8	6.4	6.6	7.2	8.1	9.0	10.2	11.5	13.0	14.3
2	7.0	9.2	9.8	9.5	10.0	10.7	11.0	11.8	12.3	13.0	13.7
3	3.5	4.1	4.2	4.1	4.3	4.5	4.8	5.0	5.2	5.3	5.3
4	1.5	1.9	2.0	1.9	1.9	1.9	1.9	2.0	2.1	2.2	2.4

CRIME STATISTICS 1979
**Number of crimes reported to the police, England and Wales;
proportion of crimes cleared up**

| Police force areas | 1979 | | 1992 | |
	Offences[1] per 100,000 population	Percentage cleared up	Offences[1] per 100,000 population	Percentage cleared up
Avon & Somerset	3,616	43	12,214	17
Bedfordshire	5,293	48	11,019	20
Cambridgeshire	4,050	47	9,843	27
Cheshire	3,053	58	7,944	29
Cleveland	5,769	51	14,510	32
Cumbria	3,858	56	8,739	37
Derbyshire	3,914	50	8,943	22
Devon & Cornwall	3,006	46	7,571	18
Dorset	3,769	46	7,864	32
Durham	4,150	52	10,362	30
Essex	3,708	42	7,703	29
Gloucestershire	3,095	51	11,310	24
Greater Manchester	6,052	45	14,149	35
Hampshire	3,941	46	8,934	26
Hertfordshire	4,430	54	6,916	26
Humberside	5,238	45	14,678	23

Police force areas	1979		1992	
	Offences per 100,000 population	Percentage cleared up	Offences per 100,000 population	Percentage cleared up
Kent	3,500	50	10,172	27
Lancashire	3,777	56	8,295	37
Leicestershire	3,466	54	10,741	30
Lincolnshire	3,040	60	8,110	39
City of London	2	2	171,056[3]	20
Merseyside	6,814	42	9,980	42
Metropolitan Police District	7,123	21	12,270	16
Norfolk	3,083	47	8,877	34
Northamptonshire	4,122	48	10,148	30
Northumbria	6,490	53	14,236	17
North Yorkshire	3,055	51	7,278	33
Nottinghamshire	7,174	51	15,720	26
South Yorkshire	4,055	51	10,237	26
Staffordshire	3,572	51	9,319	30
Suffolk	3,147	57	6,811	39
Surrey	3,505	47	7,076	22
Sussex	3,540	53	8,311	23
Thames Valley	4,079	45	9,885	19
Warwickshire	2,806	46	9,247	23
West Mercia	3,152	49	7,166	34
West Midlands	5,455	37	12,293	27
West Yorkshire	5,737	37	14,528	25
Wiltshire	3,654	42	7,315	37
Dyfed-Powys	2,432	62	5,632	53
Gwent	4,316	60	8,937	44
North Wales	3,663	59	7,323	33
South Wales	5,077	46	12,467	30
Total	**4,833**	**41**	**10,614**	**26**

1 Excluding criminal damage £20 and under
2 Included in the Metropolitan Police District
3 The City of London rate per 100,000 is affected by the low resident population

Source: written answer to D French MP May 7 1993 col 264

DEFENDANTS* PROCEEDED AGAINST AT MAGISTRATES' COURTS BY TYPE OF OFFENCE — EXTRACT FROM CRIMINAL STATISTICS ENGLAND AND WALES 1991
* Including "other defendants", i.e companies, public bodies, etc.
1 Total number proceeded against — thousands; **2** Number of defendants — indictable offences
3 Number of defendants — summary offences (except motoring) **4** Number of defendants — motoring **5** Percentage proceeded against — indictable offences **6** Percentage proceeded against — summary offences **(7)** Percentage proceeded against — motoring

PERSONS AGED 10 AND UNDER 17

	No. of defendants			% of defendants			
	(1)	**(2)**	**(3)**	**(4)**	**(5)**	**(6)**	**(7)**
1983	112	82	20	11	73	17	10
1984	105	78	17	9	75	16	9
1985	94	71	15	8	76	16	8
1986	75	57	11	6	76	15	8
1987	68	53	10	5	78	15	7
1988	62	48	10	4	77	16	7
1989	55	37	14	4	66	26	8
1990	54	36	13	4	67	25	8
1991	50	35	12	4	69	24	7

PERSONS AGED 18 AND UNDER 21

	No. of defendants			% of defendants			
	(1)	**(2)**	**(3)**	**(4)**	**(5)**	**(6)**	**(7)**
1983	394	149	86	159	38	22	40
1984	372	148	79	145	40	21	39
1985	364	149	75	140	41	21	38
1986	339	133	70	136	39	21	40
1987	325	140	74	110	43	23	34
1988	322	137	79	106	43	25	33
1989	324	122	90	112	38	28	35
1990	329	129	85	114	39	26	35
1991	314	132	73	110	42	23	35

ALL DEFENDANTS*

	No. of defendants			% of defendants			
	(1)	**(2)**	**(3)**	**(4)**	**(5)**	**(6)**	**(7)**
1983	2,303	530	521	1,252	23	23	54
1984	2,184	521	482	1,181	24	22	54
1985	2,147	520	469	1,158	24	22	54
1986	2,171	463	508	1,199	21	23	55
1987	1,843	488	505	850	26	27	46
1988	1,863	494	543	826	27	29	44
1989	1,864	449	568	847	24	30	45
1990	1,892	469	577	846	25	31	45
1991	1,956	489	573	894	25	29	46

Source: written answer to Joan Lestor, MP May 5 1993 HcD col 135

indictment of forensic science evidence. Convictions were also quashed on the Darvell brothers (July 14 1992), convicted of the murder of a woman in Swansea; the Cardiff Three (December 10), convicted of the murder of a prostitute; and of Michelle and Lisa Taylor (June 11 1993), convicted of the murder of a woman in London. On May 19, three retired detectives accused of falsifying evidence in the Guildford four case were acquitted.

The DPP, Barbara Mills, had ruled out proceedings against members of the now-disbanded West Midlands Serious Crime Squad arising out of allegedly fabricated confessions.

The Lord Chancellor, Lord Mackay, was also taken to court after ruling that the burgeoning costs of legal aid must be sharply cut. The qualifying level of income was cut from £145 to £61 a week from April 12 1993, removing an estimated 13 million people from eligibility.

The Commons select committee on home affairs called in vain for this decision to be reversed — as it already had been in the Lord Chancellor's native Scotland. The Law Society successfully sought a judicial review, but on June 21 the High Court ruled in the Government's favour.

The alleged bugging of royal telephones brought suspicion on the security services. Clarke dismissed this as nonsense. But on May 6 1993 the prime minister announced that MI6 would be put on a statutory basis as had MI5 in the Security Service Act of 1989. The details — including a possible remit for a parliamentary committee of privy councillors to superintend the security service — were left until later.

In a move towards open government Major named the head of MI6 as Sir Colin McColl. When Stella Rimington was appointed head of MI5 she too was named. In an extraordinary break with tradition on July 16 1993, the drapes were taken off the organisation with the publication of a £4.95 booklet called The Security Service. The numbers employed (2,000, half of them women), an address to write to, even the outfit's coat of arms, were all proudly paraded. The public was asked to send potentially useful information to PO Box 3255, London SW1P 1AE, and complaints to PO Box 18, London SE1 OTZ.●

**NOTIFIABLE OFFENCES RECORDED BY THE POLICE BY OFFENCE GROUP
ENGLAND AND WALES 1992**

NUMBER OF OFFENCES

Offence Group	Ist Qtr	2nd Qtr	3rd Qtr	4th Qtr	Total No offences
Violence against the person	45,520	53,408	53,093	49,758	201,779
Sexual offences	7,190	7,396	7,795	7,147	29,528
Robbery	12,007	12,448	13,598	14,841	52,894
Burglary	345,866	312,277	314,756	382,375	1,355,274
Theft & handling stolen goods	701,678	713,588	704,551	724,731	2,844,548
Fraud & forgery	42,425	42,889	42,662	40,654	168,000
Criminal damage	223,759	220,469	212,087	246,195	902,510
Other offences	9,856	9,670	10,264	9,593	39,383
Total	**1,388,301**	**1,372,115**	**1,358,806**	**1,475,294**	**5,594,516**

PERCENTAGE CHANGE FROM CORRESPONDING PERIOD OF PREVIOUS YEAR:

Offence Group	Ist Qtr	2nd Qtr	3rd Qtr	4th Qtr	Total No offences
Violence against the person	9	11	2	3	6
Sexual offences	8	-3	-4	1	-
Robbery	25	16	15	13	17
Burglary	16	7	9	13	11
Theft & handling stolen goods	8	2	-	3	3
Fraud & forgery	3	-3	-5	-8	-4
Criminal damage	14	3	8	14	10
Other offences	21	13	15	7	14
Total	**11**	**3**	**3**	**7**	**6**

Source: written answer to A. Michael MP May 11 1993

OFFENCES IN ENGLAND AND WALES RECORDED AS HOMICIDE
(Showing total per million population)

	recorded	per ml
1969	332	6.8
1979	546	11.1
1989	576	11.4

	initially recorded	now recorded	
1990	663	572	11.2
1991	726	675	13.0
1992	689	n/a	n/a

n/a - figures not yet available

Source: Home Office

PEOPLE IN PRISON (England and Wales)

	1990	**1991**	**1992**
Total in prison	45,400	45,600	45,500
Men	43,800	43800	43,900
Women	1,590	1,560	1,570
All on remand:			
in prison	9,439	9,474	n/a
in police cells	465	683	n/a
Total in custody -			
on remand	9,904	10,189	10,100[1]
All untried (average)	7,324	7,253[2]	n/a

1 approximate   2. provisional

Derived from H M Prison Service/Home Office

PROJECTED CHANGES IN POLICING AND CRIMINAL JUSTICE

HOME OFFICE WHITE PAPER, June 28:

Amalgamations: questionable whether 43 forces are needed in England and Wales – no plans yet to cut this number, but procedure for mergers to be simplified.

Police authorities: will have 16 members; representation of local councillors will be reduced and Home Office nominees (likely to be mainly business people) added to give 8 councillors, 3 magistrates, 5 appointees. Main task will be to devise strategy plans; will have standard spending assessments and be liable to capping.

Chief constables' powers: will be extended to give them greater control over manpower, working patterns and resources.

Special constables: 10,000 more will be appointed taking number to 30,000.

London: at present directly controlled by the home secretary; will have a new authority. But plans to give London the same kind of authority as everywhere else were rescinded after Conservative back-bench objections.

National league tables to be published, based on performance indicators.

SHEEHY REPORT, June 30: recommendations

All new officers to be appointed for fixed terms of 10 years, followed by five-yearly renewals.

Ranks of chief inspector, chief superintendent, deputy chief constable to be scrapped.

Annual index-linked pay awards to cease. Unsatisfactory officers will get no increase at all. New pay scales will reflect experience, performance, responsibility. £2,000 cut in starting rate for PCs.

No overtime except in abnormal circumstances – but cash bonuses can be paid. Housing allowances to be bought out, many other allowances to be terminated.

Retirement at 60 (up from 55). Full pensions after 40 years (up from 30).

ROYAL COMMISSION ON CRIMINAL JUSTICE, July 6: recommendations

An independent authority to investigate alleged miscarriages of justice.

Abolition of defendant's right to demand trial by jury.

Defence must disclose case pre-trial, or risk adverse comment: opposed by one member of the commission, Prof Michael Zander.

Judges may be given power to order in exceptional circumstances that three people from ethnic minorities must be included on a jury.

Abolition of committal for trial proceedings in magistrates' courts.

Tighter rules on admissibility of uncorroborated confessions: but they are not ruled out.

LAW AND LIBERTY
Main points in the home secretary's Commons statement, May 13 1993, on changes to the 1991 Criminal Justice Bill.

The mathematical formula for determining fines had proved too complex and would be abandoned. Magistrates would still be required to take an offender's means into account, but how they did it would be left to their discretion. Offenders would be asked to disclose their weekly disposable income, but in more detail than before.

Sections of the Act restricting reference to previous convictions when sentencing an offender would be repealed. This would allow courts to take account of all the offences for which the offender was before the bench and previous convictions in deciding the sentence.

A new offence of committing a crime while on bail would be introduced.

The maximum sentence for causing death by dangerous or drunken driving would be increased from five to 10 years.

CRIMINAL JUSTICE (Government Bill)
INTRODUCED: LORDS October 22 1992

PURPOSE:
To combat international fraud, drugs trade, laundering, insider dealing, etc

LORDS:
2nd reading: November 3 1992

Report: December 3 1992

3rd reading: December 10 1992

COMMONS:
2nd reading: April 14, 1993: unopposed.

Report and 3rd reading: June 29 1993

ROYAL ASSENT:
July 27 1993

EIGHTEEN
ARTS AND MEDIA

The creation after the 1992 election of the Department of National Heritage was a moment of hope for the arts, which along with sport, the heritage, broadcasting and the press were to shelter under its umbrella. All the more so because the proprietor was David Mellor, a good friend to the arts when as chief secretary to the Treasury he served as the Government's public spending monitor.

A bubbling enthusiast both for the arts and sport, equally happy discoursing on Rodney Marsh or on Medtner, his presence seemed a guarantee of championship for both at the Cabinet table. Mellor's fall from grace on September 24 1992, in the aftermath of an affair with an actress and an ill-advised free family holiday, was therefore mourned, even by some who did not like him. His successor was Peter Brooke, a connoisseur of both art and cricket, but a politician of lower profile, at a time when control of public spending was set to be tightened.

The chancellor's Autumn Statement in November 1992 had bleak implications. The news that the subsidy to the Arts Council, the central disburser of government funding of the arts, was to be cut by 5 per cent for 1994-95 sent shudders through the art world and drove Lord Rix (Brian Rix, the former master of Whitehall farce) to resign from the council. All rather different, as Mellor observed, from his own two Arts Council settlements. True, there might be rescue at hand in the shape of the national lottery, which numbered the arts, with sport, the heritage, charities and the millennium fund as beneficiaries. But apprehension persisted that other subventions might be reduced when this money arrived.

As the minister in charge of broadcasting, Brooke published on November 24 1992 a green paper on the future of the BBC. The BBC had awaited this publication uneasily, given the record of combat with the Conservative party in recent years, but what transpired was largely to its taste. No disturbing changes were threatened. The licence fee was an oddity, but suggested alternatives looked no better. Subscription could reduce choice for poorer people. Advertising could disadvantage minorities. Revenue drawn out of tax could increase the scope for political pressure. The Corporation must prune its cost and improve its efficiency, but otherwise it could stay much the same. The BBC welcomed this unThatcherite document and signalled its commitment to greater efficiency with a new round of job cuts,

1,250 over 18 months to follow the 3,000 ordered in 1991.

Brooke also had charge of the press. Here Sir David Calcutt, the author of a report in 1990 which called for tougher controls over press excess, had been called back to action by Mellor after a series of stories about the Royal family which the press's own watchdog, the Press Complaints Commission, had on June 8 1992 called intrusive, odious and prurient. On January 14 1993 Calcutt called for a statutory press complaints commission, saying self-regulation had failed.

Two other proposals were made for statutory action. The Labour backbencher Clive Soley had introduced his Freedom and Responsibility of the Press Bill, which was given a second reading on January 29 1993. This called for an Independent Press Authority with a statutory code of practice. On March 24, the select committee on the National Heritage advocated a lay-dominated commission with powers to fine newspapers, order corrections and award compensation, backed by an ombudsman. Legal aid should be allowed in cases of defamation. As a counterbalance, the press would be given greater access to information.

The Government responded cautiously. The prime minister's office let it be known when Calcutt appeared that his statutory tribunal was out. It opposed the Soley Bill, which was "talked out" by government backbenchers on April 23 1993 after the junior heritage minister, Robert Key, said it would create statutory control of the press for the first time since the 17th century.

On July 29, the Lord Chancellor, Lord Mackay, published a consultation document on privacy. It favoured a right of redress in the civil courts for invasions of privacy affecting an individual's health, communications, family and relationships, with damages of up to £10,000 for people suffering "substantial distress". Press reaction was hostile. A White Paper foreshadowing legislation on the press was expected in August.●

GOVERNMENT SPENDING ON NATIONAL HERITAGE

1 Total spending at current prices £billion
2. Total spending in real terms at 1991-2 prices £billion
3. % of government expenditure
4. % of GDP

	1978-1979	1983-1984	1984-1985	1985-1986	1986-1987	1987-1988	1988-1989	1989-1990	1990-1991	1991-1992	1992-3 (est)
1	0.7	1.3	1.4	1.5	1.6	1.8	2.0	2.3	2.5	2.5	2.7
2	2.0	2.1	2.1	2.1	2.2	2.4	2.5	2.7	2.6	2.5	2.6
3	0.9	0.9	0.9	0.9	0.9	1.0	1.1	1.1	1.1	1.0	1.0
4	0.4	0.4	0.4	0.4	0.4	0.4	0.4	0.4	0.4	0.4	0.4

ARTS SUBSIDIES 17th May 1993

Year	£ ,000
1987-88	139,300
1988-89	152,411
1989-90	155,500
1990-91	175,792
1991-92	*194,200
1992-93	221,100
1993-94	225,630

* This excludes a special payment of £10.8 million to enable the English National Opera to buy the freehold of the Coliseum.
The Government also funds the business sponsorship incentive scheme, the theatres restoration fund and various research projects. For 1993-94, total central Government expenditure additional to the Arts Council's grant-in-aid will be approximately £5.6 million.
Local authorities also fund activities, but no definitive figures on their overall expenditure are available

Source:written answer to Terry Dicks, MP May 17 1993 HcD Col 18

MOVES TO CURB PRESS EXCESS

Calcutt 2nd report, January 14 1993

A tribunal should be set up to replace the present, inadequate Press Complaints Commission, with power to impose substantial fines. This should not imperil press freedom where that freedom was used responsibly.

The tribunal should produce a code of practice and halt publication of anything breaching this code. It could also launch investigations even where no complaint had been filed; order the printing of corrections, apologies, replies and adjudications; impose fines and award compensation.

Freedom and Responsibility of the Press Bill, introduced on June 10, 1992 by Clive Soley MP (Lab, Hammersmith)

Would set up an Independent Press Authority. This would:

* produce codes of professional and ethical standards
* try to ensure that news was presented accurately
* monitor ethical standards, distribution of newspapers, ownership and control of the media, access to information and restrictions on reporting
* have statutory powers to determine factual inaccuracy and force
* newspapers to correct their errors swiftly and with equal prominence
* appoint an adviser to help complainants

Report of the Heritage select committee, March 24 1993

The Government should bring in a protection of privacy Bill to prohibit the obtaining and publishing of harmful, unauthorised or inaccurate information, or persistent invasion of privacy. Unauthorised eavesdropping and trespass in pursuit of information should be a criminal offence and intrusive surveillance devices licensed or registered.

A Press Commission should replace the Press Complaints Commission with powers to impose fines for breaches of the code and ordering compensation.

A press ombudsman should be appointed with powers to fine, award compensation and order corrections and apologies.

Consultation paper on privacy: Lord Chancellor's department, July 30 1993

Proposes establishing right of redress in civil courts against invasions of privacy affecting an individual's health, communications, family and relationships; also right to be free from harassment or molestation. Could also cover infringement of privacy by noisy neighbours, etc. Damages of up to £10,000 for people suffering "substantial distress". Legal aid would not be available.

A public interest defence would be available to newspapers.

RESPONSIBILITY OF THE PRESS
(Private member's bill: Clive Soley, Lab Hammersmith)
Introduced: June 10 1992

PURPOSE:

To set up Independent Press Authority, producing codes of conduct, seeking to ensure accurate presentation of news, monitoring ethical standards, forcing newspapers to publish corrections, with Press Complaints Adviser to aid complainants.

COMMONS:

2nd reading: January 29 1993 by 119 (11 Con, 104 Lab, 2LD, 1SNP, 1UU) to 15 (16 Listed in Hansard – 13 Con, 2 Lab, 1 UDUD)

Report:

April 23 1993 (adjourned) NO FURTHER PROGRESS

RIGHT TO KNOW (Private member's bill: Mark Fisher, Lab Stoke Central)
INTRODUCED: June 10 1992

PURPOSE:

To give the public legal right of access to information held by Whitehall, local councils, nationalised industries, NHS bodies and other agencies. To create a public interest defence against changes under the Official Secrets Act; to force companies to publish records of their compliance with environmental, safety and anti-discrimination laws. Information likely to endanger national security or personal privacy to remain protected.

COMMONS:

2nd reading: February 19 1993 by 168 (13 Con, 145 Lab, 8 LD, 1 SNP, 1 PC) to 2 (2 Con)

Report: July 2 1993 (adjourned)

NO FURTHER PROGRESS

Annus expensivus: after the Windsor Castle fire the 'peasants' revolted and the Queen ended up footing the bill

NINETEEN

THE CONSTITUTION AND GOVERNMENT

Hardly anyone doubted that the crown would see out the century. Yet in 1992-93 the monarchy became a political issue. That reflected a decline in respect not for the Queen, but for the institution, brought on above all by disputes and scandals involving the Royal family.

That the marriage of the Prince and Princess of Wales was in trouble had been evident for some time, but fresh details were uncovered in a spate of books, of which the most influential, because it most fully represented the predicament of Princess Diana, was Andrew Morton's *Diana, her True Story*, published in June and serialised in the *Sunday Times*. A bugged telephone conversation between Charles and Diana — and later, another, perhaps even more explosive, between Charles and Camilla Parker Bowles — took the public right into the royal bedroom.

On December 9 1992, the prime minister told the Commons that the couple were to separate. His statement that this did not preclude Diana from one day becoming Queen was greeted with some incredulity. In August 1992, the tabloids got hold of pictures of the Duchess of York, who had separated from the Duke in March, frolicking on a beach with a man described as her financial adviser

in circumstances which hardly appeared conducive to the discussion of gilts.

On November 20 1992 fire destroyed part of Windsor Castle. Three days later, the heritage secretary, Peter Brooke, told the Commons that the state (ie the taxpayer) would, of course, pick up the bill for refurbishment. Once that sentiment would have seemed uncontentious, but not any more. On the Opposition benches and outside the House, people asked why the taxpayer should have to subsidise someone as rich as Her Majesty, especially when, as the newspapers kept reminding them, she didn't have to pay tax. On November 25 the Public Accounts Committee of the House of Commons pointedly asked the Comptroller and Auditor General to carry out a value-for-money audit of the public funding of royal residences.

But already the previous day the Queen had appeared to recognise how public opinion had shifted. At a City lunch, she talked of the "annus horribilis" which she and her family had suffered. She had all but lost her voice, which made what she said seem even more piteous. Two days later (November 26) Major told the Commons that the Queen was now willing to pay taxes on her personal income and to take responsibility for certain Civil List payments. (The Civil List was simultaneously cut to three: the Queen, the Duke of Edinburgh and the Queen Mother. Prince Charles drew revenues from his Duchy of Cornwall.) The nation seemed gratified, but it did not go down on its knees.

The Times and Channel Four staged public debates on the future of the monarchy, which raised the issue of whether it had got one. Public opinion was still far from republican, but nonetheless it was shifting. The Royal house no longer looked unassailable. The decline in unquestioning deference was also reflected in changes to the honours system announced by Major on March 4 1993. Awards should be based on merit, he said, not on rank, connection or length of service. He planned to make it easier for ordinary people to put in nominations. The Queen's birthday honours list in June showed little sign of reform, except for the dropping of the British Empire Medal; but this, it was said, was the last of the old honours lists, not the first of the new.

Honours for political service, frequently used to reward backbenchers for loyalty (or, some said, to bribe them into it) continued, however. The row over Asil Nadir, the bankrupt businessman who fled to Cyprus on May 4 1993 to avoid facing trial, raised the question of honours in a new and more pungent form. Nadir was said to have expected that his lavish donations to Conservative party finances would bring him a knighthood. Even Conservative newspapers printed tables to show the high correlation between such donations and subsequent honours.

In 1993 Labour joined the Liberal Democrats in presenting itself as the champion of constitutional change. It now endorsed much of the agenda promulgated by the pressure group Charter 88. In a speech to this organisation on March 1, the Labour leader John Smith called for a fundamental shift from the state to "a citizen's democracy, where people have rights and powers, and where they are served by accountable and responsive government". As part of this process he proposed a Human Rights Act, incorporating the European Convention on Human Rights and backed by an independent Human Rights Commission.

Smith was much less certain about the case for electoral change, another staple of the Charter 88 campaign. A committee under Raymond (later Lord) Plant, set up by Neil Kinnock to look at electoral systems, reported on March 31 1993. It remained to the end irreconcilably split, but a majority of members favoured scrapping first-past-the-post, with the Supplementary Vote, a system devised by the Labour MP Dale Campbell-Savours, the best supported replacement. Smith at this stage expressed no preference between rival systems, but advocated that the issue should be put to a referendum.

The Conservatives remained unmoved by campaigns for constitutional change and firmly ruled out the ditching of first-past-the-post (a system which served them well). In an article in the Spectator (January 28 1993), later amplified in a pamphlet for the European Policy Forum, the education secretary, John Patten, said enormous constitutional change had been taking place under the noses of comatose constitutional commentators for the last 14 years. The transfer of power to the citizen was already under way, in reforms like grant maintained schools and GP budget-holding, which transferred decision-making from the hub to the rim of the wheel of power — and especially through the Citizen's Charter, in itself a form of rolling constitutional change. (Modernising British Government; essays by John Patten MP and Frank Vibert; European Policy Forum.)

There were now 32 Citizen's Charters, setting out people's rights, telling them how to demand them and establishing their rights to compensation when services didn't deliver. Among changes introduced under the charters, hospitals now had to offer patients fixed times for appointments, no patient should normally have to wait more than two years for an NHS operation and — a special prime ministerial interest— no motorway should be coned off for more than two and a half miles.

A written answer on May 10 (HCD col 308) recorded payments by the Benefits Agency under the charter of more than £2 million and by British Rail of around £1 million. A pilot hotline telephone scheme — Charterline — was set up in the East Midlands and was soon logging some 250 calls a day, mostly about social security benefits and the health service, and a touring "roadshow" was planned to tell people about the rights which research suggested they still didn't know they had.

In a sense this was swapping one kind of accountability for another. The Benefits Agency was the largest on a long list of government services — the prison and training services

were others — now reconstituted as separate organisations, at arm's length from government, under the Next Steps programme. The aim was to divorce policymaking (a matter for governments) from service delivery (better done by others). But that meant responsibility passed from people who could be got at (ministers at the despatch box) to people who, on the whole, could not. The new defence was the charter.

These agencies had great power. The Benefits Agency, as Vernon Bogdanor pointed out in the Times (Market must not sell democracy short/Vernon Bogdanor/The Times June 7 1993) dealt with 20 million people, many of whom were totally dependent on its decision for their income. But ministers could no longer be challenged on such decisions by MPs. From April 1992, MPs were deluged with constituents' complaints about the backlog of applications for the Disability Living Allowance. The chairman of the Commons select committee on social security described the opening year of the new allowance as the biggest chaos the social security system has ever seen. Applications far exceeded all forecasts and the agency could not cope. But questions on this score, of which there were many, were now answered not by ministers in the Commons but by agency chiefs in letters. A written answer on May 10 said 19 per cent of letters to social security ministers were now diverted to agencies.

At the same time, market testing was destined to take great swathes of activity out of the civil service into private sector hands. On November 25 1992 the public service minister,

William Waldegrave, published a White Paper proposing to put out to tender some £1.5 billion-worth of government business affecting 45,000 of the 550,000 civil service staff.

Alongside that were the quangos — bodies set up by departments and usually staffed by their nominees and disposing by 1993 of around 20 per cent of total government spending. These non-elected authorities, which usually met in secret, were set to control much of the NHS, including almost all the hospital and care in the community services and much of education and housing. Quite often they flourished at the expense of elected local government.

Under proposals by Kenneth Clarke, police authorities were to have fewer elected councillors and more nominated businessmen. Legislation like the Education Bill, the Railways Bill and the National Lotteries Bill were built around quangos. In a paper for the European Policy Forum, Prof John Stewart of Birmingham University complained of government by unelected elites. A "new magistracy", like that which existed before the establishment of local government, was being created, he said.

The Conservatives made some moves towards open government, including the naming of security service chiefs and the members of Cabinet committees, and the ending of the tradition of "purdah", which prevented Treasury ministers talking about their impending budgets. On July 15 1993, Waldegrave published a White Paper on Open Government based on a voluntary code of practice policed by the Parliamentary Ombudsman and his Northern Ireland equivalent. But no Freedom of Information Act was on the horizon.

They also proposed a transfer of power to Scotland, though this fell far short of devolutionist aspirations. A White Paper, Scotland in the Union — a Partnership for Good (March 9 1993), proposed upgrading the Scottish Grand Committee, a body made up of the 72 Scottish MPs. It would meet more often in Scotland, handle the second reading of Scottish Bills and stage Question Times involving ministers from the Lords as well as the Commons. Some Scottish Office jobs would be transferred from London to Edinburgh and the office would take on new functions, such as responsibility for the arts in Scotland (from National Heritage) and for Highlands and Islands airports (from the Civil Aviation Authority).

The Government was fortified in its firm opposition to devolution by the record of the election, when against much advice the Conservatives had fought on an anti-devolution platform and had seen their vote go up. They had, even so, taken only 25.7 per cent of the Scottish vote — an improvement of just 1.7 per cent on their year of electoral nadir, 1987.●

CITIZEN'S CHARTER INITIATIVE

Taxpayer's Charter (Operational from 13/8/92)

HM Customs and Excise

Taxpayer's entitlements to fairness and courtesy in their dealings with the Customs and Excise and Inland Revenue.

Taxpayer's Charter (13/8/91)

Inland Revenue

Performance targets including providing a substantive reply to at least 90 per cent of all correspondence within 28 days; revised and simplified forms; 'tax back' campaign to encourage rebate claims in early 1992.

Passenger's Charter (3/5/92)

British Rail

Performance targets. Paid out £1.9 million compensation and discounts April 92-March 93. Compensation due after failure in reliability (frequency of trains) and punctuality — on average over the year for season ticket holders. Name badges for staff.

London Underground Customers Charter (1/8/92 — revised 1/6/93)

London Underground Ltd

Performance targets. LU paid out £91,000 in compensation from August 92-July 93. Customers are entitled to a refund voucher if their journey is delayed by more than 20 minutes.

Benefits Agency Customer Charter (27/1/92)

Social Security Benefits Agency

£2.5 million compensation paid between April 92 and March 93. Targets on time taken to clear benefit claims; compensation paid if customer suffers financial loss due to Agency mistake. Covers England, Scotland, Wales

Tenant's Charter (24/1/92)

Department of Environment — for people living in local authority housing. Charters tell tenants how to exercise rights on security of tenure and freedom to take lodgers; encouragement to join tenants associations, management co-ops, etc.

Redundancy Payments Service Charter (1/10/92)

Employment Department — to help those who have been made redundant and explain what they are entitled to from previous employer.

Jobseekers Charter (17/12/91)

Employment Service — £89,000 compensation paid April 92 to March 93. Targets set for speed of response for ES services. Charter covers England, Scotland, Wales.

Contributor's Charter (1/8/91)

Social Security Contributions Agency — £54,500 compensation paid April 92- March 93. National insurance contributions from employees.

Employer's Charter (1/8/91)

Social Security Contributions Agency

NI contributions for employers.

Traveller's Charter (29/1/92, revised 30/3/93)

HM Customs and Excise

£9,000 compensation paid up to March 93 — standards in service and behaviour that C&E provides to those passing through customs, including offering "to help repack travellers' bags".

Patient's Charter (1/4/92)

Department of Health

Hospitals required to treat people within 1.5-2 years of joining waiting list. Quality standards in family health services.

Courts Charter (unveiled by Lord Mackay 25/11/92)

Lord Chancellor's Department, Home Office, CPS

England and Wales — guidelines on timetable for bringing cases to trial; deadlines for court staff response; time limits for court functions — ie. 10 working days for issuing summons, 15 for sending out bailiffs (no rights to compensation).

Child Support Agency Charter (5/4/92)

Child Support Agency

Parents' Charter (1/9/92)

Department of Education

For children in state schools — all parents now receive at least one written school report a year. Schools must publish exam results; local authority must make available comparative information (league tables) on schools in the area.

NORTHERN IRELAND

Railways Passenger's Charter (16/11/92)

NI Railways

£400 compensation 11/92-4/93

Northern Ireland Charter (5/2/92)

Department of Finance and Personnel

Parent's Charter (28/9/92)

Dept of Education for NI

Charter for Patients and Clients (13/3/92)

DHSS, NI

Northern Ireland Tenant's Charter (23/9/92)

NI Housing Executive

Charter for Social Security Agency Clients (24/7/92)

NI Social Security Agency

Training and Employment Agency Customer's Charter (14/9/92)

Training and Employment Agency, NI

RUC Charter (14/1/93)

Royal Ulster Constabulary

Bus Passenger's Charter (15/2/93)

Ulsterbus

Child Support Agency Charter (22/4/93)

NI Child Support Agency

SCOTLAND

Justice Charter for Scotland (1/4/92)

Scottish Office

Parent's Charter for Scotland (1/9/92)

Scottish Office

Patient's Charter for Scotland (1/4/92)

Scottish Office

Tenant's Charter for Scotland (9/12/91)

Scottish Office

WALES

Parent's Charter for Wales (1/9/92)

Welsh Office

Patient's Charter for Wales (1/4/92)

Welsh Office

Tenant's Charter for Wales (28/9/92)

Welsh Office

1. VOTES AND SEATS AT ALL ELECTIONS SINCE 1945
Share of vote and share of seats at general elections since 1945
a) share of seats in the new Parliament
b) what the share of seats would have been if the parties had taken the same share of seats as their share of the vote.

| | **ACTUAL** | | | **PROPORTIONAL** | | |
	Con	**Lab**	**Lib/All**	**Con**	**Lab**	**Lib/All**
1945*	210	393	12	253	307	58
1950**	298	315	9	271	288	57
1951**	321	295	6	300	305	16
1955**	345	277	6	313	292	17
1959**	365	258	6	311	276	37
1964**	304	317	9	273	278	71
1966**	253	364	12	264	302	54
1970	330	288	6	292	272	47
1974 (1)	297	301	14	241	236	123
1974 (2)	277	319	13	227	249	116
1979	339	269	11	279	234	88
1983	397	209	23	276	179	165
1987	376	229	22	275	200	146
1992	336	271	20	273	224	116

Source: derived from FWS Craig, British Electoral Facts & Britain Votes 4

LABOUR'S PLANT COMMISSION ON ELECTORAL SYSTEMS

The Plant Commission on electoral systems, set up by Neil Kinnock, voted by nine to seven to recommend a change to a Supplementary Vote system, proposed to the Commission by Dale Campbell-Savours MP.

The final choice was between SV, a variation of the Alternative Vote; a Mixed Member System (MMS), a variant of the German system; and First Past the Post (FPTP)

A series of votes was taken to determine the outcome. In the first, six members voted for FPTP, six for SV or AV, and four (including Lord Plant) for MMS.

On a vote between SV and AV, the result was 8-3 in favour of SV.

In the final run-off, the vote was 9-7 for SV against FPTP.

Voting for SV were Hilary Armstrong MP (PPS to John Smith), Bryan Gould MP, Ben Pimlott, historian and biographer, Graham Allen MP, party spokesman on the constitution, John Evans MP, Alistair Darling MP, Lord Plant, Richard Rosser, rail union leader, and Ken Hopkins, representing the Labour party in Wales.

Voting for FPTP were Tom Burlison of the union GMB, Lady Hollis, Margaret Beckett, deputy leader of the party, Geoff Hoon MP and MEP, and Gary Titley, MEP for Manchester, Jeff Rooker MP and Judith Church of the union MSF.

Under SV, voters would be allowed to state a second preference on the ballot paper. Any candidate taking more than 50% of the vote would be elected outright. Where the leading candidate had less than 50%, second preferences among supporters of the third, fourth and other candidates would be redistributed between the two front runners.

HONOURS UNDER THE CONSERVATIVES
Honours awarded to leading figures in companies which gave to Conservative Party funds

P=peerage, K=knighthood

company	donation £	recipient	date
AE	10,000	John Collyear (K)	1986
AGB Research	160,000	George Audley (K)	1985
Allied London Props	32,850	Geoffrey Leigh (K)	1990
Allied Lyons	991,200	Keith Showering (K)	1981
Argyll Group	192,000	Alistair Grant (K)	1992
ASDA-MFI	40,000	Arthur Stockdale (K)	1986
Barings	536,850	John Baring (K)	1983
Barratt Devs	20,000	Lawrence Barratt (K)	1981
BAT Industries	46,500	Peter Macadam (K)	1981
		Patrick Sheehy (K)	1991
BBW Partnership	51,500	Michael Bishop (K)	1991
Beecham	394,000	Graham Wilkins (K)	1980
		Ronald Halstead (K)	1985
BET	217,500	Hugh Dundas (K)	1987
Booker	5,000	Michael Caine (K)	1988
British Airways	170,000	Colin Marshall (K)	1987
Brit & Commonwealth	803,531	Sir Wm Cayzer (P)	1982
Cameron Hall	58,302	John Hall (K)	1991
Christian Salvesen	156,200	Maxwell Harper-Gow (K)	1985
		Gerald Elliott (K)	1986
Coats Paton	48,000	William Coats (K)	1985
Coats Viyella	65,000	David Alliance (K)	1989
Dawson Int	28,000	Alan Smith (K)	1982
Distillers	50,000	John Cater (K)	1984
Forte	693,700	Sir Charles Forte (P)	1982
GEC	100,000	Sir Arnold Weinstock (P)	1980
		Robert Clayton (K)	1980
		Alan Veale (K)	1984
		Robert Davidson (K)	1989
		Robert Easton (K)	1990
George Wimpey	384,675	Reginald Smith (K)	1981
		Clifford Chetwood (K)	1987
GKN	313,355	Trevor Holdsworth (K)	1982
		David Lees (K)	1991
Glaxo	691,500	Austin Bide (K)	1980
		Paul Girolami (K)	1988
Hambros	447,250	John Keswick (K)	1993

company	donation £	recipient	date
Higgs & Hill	28,500	Brian Hill (K)	1989
Inchcape	365,000	George Turnbull (K)	1990
J and J Denholm	5,000	John Denholm (K)	1989
John Brown	53,500	John Mayhew-Sanders (K)	1982
John Mowlem	186,657	Edgar Beck (K)	1988
John Swire	129,000	Adrian Swire (K)	1982
		John Swire (K)	1990
Kingfisher	210,000	Geoff Mulcahy (K)	1993
Kleinwort Benson	392,515	Martin Jacomb (K)	1985
Lancer Boss	94,212	Geo Bowman-Shaw (K)	1984
Lazard Bros	286,100	Ian Fraser (K)	1986
Lilley	13,000	Lewis Robertson (K)	1991
Littlewoods	153,000	Desmond Pitcher (K)	1992
Lucas Industries	304,500	Ronald Messervy (K)	1986
		Anthony Gill (K)	1991
MacFarlane Group	20,000	Norman MacFarlane (K)	1983
		Sir Norman MacFarlane(P)	1991
Marks & Spencer	365,000	Sir Marcus Sieff (P)	1980
		Sir Derek Rayner (P)	1983
		Richard Greenbury (K)	1992
Marley	55,000	Owen Aisher (K)	1981
Meyer Int	58,250	Harold de Ville (K)	1990
Newarthill	559,500	Sir Edwin McAlpine (P)	1980
Nickerson Group	42,350	Joseph Nickerson (K)	1983
Northern Eng Ind	427,500	Duncan MacDonald (K)	1983
Pearson	320,200	Richard Bailey (K)	1984
		Robert Lickley (K)	1984
P & O	727,500	Jeffrey Sterling (K)	1985
		Frank Lampl (K)	1990
		Bruce MacPhail (K)	1992
Racal Electronics	450,000	Ernest Harrison (K)	1981
Rank Hovis McDougall	310,000	Peter Reynolds (K)	1985
Reckitt & Colman	391,500	James Cleminson (K)	1982
Rolls-Royce	170,000	Ralph Robins (K)	1988
Scottish & Newcastle	298,500	Alick Rankin (K)	1992
Sinclair Research	39,000	Clive Sinclair (K)	1983
Slough Estates	274,000	Nigel Mobbs (K)	1986
Smiths Industries	113,900	Eric Sisson (K)	1980
Tarmac	388,500	Eric Pountain (K)	1985
Tate & Lyle	290,589	Robert Haslam (K)	1985

company	donation £	recipient	date
Taylor Woodrow	1,122,362	Sir Frank Taylor (P)	1982
		Frank Gibb (K)	1987
Thames Water	50,000	Roy Watts (K)	1992
TI Group	130,000	Christopher Lewinton (K)	1993
Timothy Taylor	15,000	Sir John Taylor (P)	1982
Trafalgar House	590,000	Victor Matthews (P)	1980
		Eric Parker (K)	1991
Transport Dev	68,450	James Duncan (K)	1981
UEI	1,600	Peter Michael (K)	1989
United Biscuits	1,004,500	Robert Clarke (K)	1993
United Newspapers	130,700	Gordon Linacre (K)	1986
Vaux	132,000	Paul Nicholson (K)	1993
Vickers	85,000	David Plastow (K)	1986
Westland	14,450	Basil Blackwell (K)	1983
YJ Lovell	3,000	Norman Wakefield (K)	1988

Source: from records compiled by Labour Research, a research organisation independent of the Labour Party.

EXECUTIVE AGENCIES
Agencies already established

	Staff		Staff
Accounts Services Agency	85	Defence Postal and Courier Services	485
ADAS Agency	2,280	Defence Research Agency [3]	11,260
Army Base Repair Org [2]	3,800	Directorate General of	
Building Research Est.	700	Defence Accounts	2,460
Cadw (Welsh Historic Monuments)	245	Driver and Vehicle Licensing Agency	4,450
Central Office of Information [3]	620	Driver and Vehicle Testing Agency	260
Central Science Laboratory	375	Driving Standards Agency	1,900
Central Statistical Office	1,235	Duke of York's Royal Military School	95
Central Veterinary Laboratory	615	DVOIT	480
Chemical and Biological		Employment Service	44,610
Defence Laboratory	600	Fire Service College [3]	285
Chessington Computer Centre [2] [3]	450	Forensic Science Service	615
Child Support Agency	3,500	Government Property Lawyers [2]	130
Civil Service College	230	Her Majesty's Prison Service [2]	37,420
Companies House [3]	1,035	Historic Royal Palaces	350
Compensation Agency [4]	150	Historic Scotland	630
Defence Analytical Services Agency	130	HMSO [3]	3,175
Defence Operational Analysis Centre	175	Hydrographic Office	815

	Staff		Staff
Insolvency Service	1,530	Scottish Agricultural Science Agency	145
Intervention Board	970	Scottish Fisheries Protection Agency	215
Laboratory of the Government Chemist	330	Scottish Office Pensions Agency[2]	185
Land Registry[3]	9,510	Scottish Prison Service[2]	4,600
Medicines Control Agency[3]	325	Scottish Record Office[2]	125
Meteorological Office	2,460	Service Children's Schools	
Military Survey	1,155	(North West Europe)[5]	1,110
National Physical Laboratory	790	Social Security Agency[4]	5,100
National Weights & Measures Laboratory	50	Social Security Benefits Agency	64,215
Natural Resources Institute	440	Social Security Contributions Agency	8,745
Naval Aircraft Repair Organisation	1,630	Social Security Information	
NEL	375	Technology Services Agency	4,090
NHS Estates	140	Social Security Resettlement Agency	455
NHS Pensions Agency	630	Teachers' Pensions Agency	290
N. Ireland Child Support Agency[2 4]	700	The Buying Agency[3]	90
Occupational Health Service	125	Training and Employment Agency[4]	1,670
Ordnance Survey	2,280	Transport Research Laboratory	685
Ordnance Survey of Northern Ireland[4]	210	United Kingdom Passport Agency	1,290
Patent Office[3]	1,015	Valuation and Lands' Agency	360
Paymaster General's Office[2]	855	Valuation Office	5,030
Pesticides Safety Directorate[2]	170	Vehicle Certification Agency	75
Planning Inspectorate	605	Vehicle Inspectorate[3]	1,780
Public Record Office	445	Veterinary Medicines Directorate	75
Queen Elizabeth II Conference Centre	60	Warren Spring Laboratory	285
Queen Victoria School	65	Wilton Park Conference Centre	25
Radiocommunications Agency	535	**89 in number** **TOTAL**	**269,570**
RAF Maintenance	12,855	Less armed forces personnel	7,730
Rate Collection Agency[4]	280	**TOTAL CIVIL SERVANTS**	**261,840**
Recruitment and Assessment		Customs & Excise [6]	
Services Agency	190	(30 Executive Units)	25,610
Registers of Scotland	1,295	Inland Revenue[6]	
Royal Mint[3]	1,005	(34 Executive Offices)	63,105
Royal Parks[2]	260	**GRAND TOTAL**	**350,555**

[1] October 1992 figures excluding casuals, except new agencies which show staffing figure at launch date. Part-time staff are counted as half units.
[2] Launched in the first week of April 1993.
[3] Trading Fund.
[4] Northern Ireland Civil Service.
[5] Excludes locally engaged staff.
[6] Departments operating fully on Next Steps lines. Staff figure for Inland Revenue.

LIST OF CANDIDATES FOR AGENCY STATUS ANNOUNCED BY MINISTERS

Army Logistics	8,440[2]	Office of Population Censuses and	
Defence Animal Centre	220	Surveys	1,995
Defence Central Services	1,385	Property Holdings Portfolio	
Directorate Information Technology		Management	1,645
Bureau Services	120	RAF Training	9,200
Driving and Vehicle Licencing (NI)[3]	150	Surveyors' General organisation	350
Equipment Test and Evaluation	2,220	Transport and Security Services	
Fisheries Research Services	270	Division	1,235
Fuel Suppliers Branch	20	War Pensions Directorate	1,250
Human Factors Research	390	Youth Treatment Service	200
Meat Hygiene Service[4]	1,800	**19 in number** **TOTAL**	**41,165**
MoD Police	5,075	Less armed forces personnel:	15765
Naval Training and Recruitment	5,200	**TOTAL CIVIL SERVANTS:**	**25,400**

[1] October 1992 figures excluding casuals. Part-time staff are counted as half units.
[2] Estimated to require 8,440 staff, drawn from a variety of sources
[3] Northern Ireland Civil Service.
[4] Estimated to require 1,800 staff, drawn from a variety of sources.

Source: written answer to H Booth, MP April 1 1993 HcD col 334

TWENTY
LOCAL GOVERNMENT

For years, as old powers were shot away, old discretions curbed and spending plans capped, as they were saddled with a system of taxation (the poll tax) which maximised the difficulties of collection, local councils must often have felt that the Government was engaging them in something uncomfortably close to war. And then who should appear, carrying what looked like a flag of truce, but John Major. On February 27 1993 the prime minister told a conference of Conservative councillors it was time the skirmishing between central and local government came to an end. "Let us stop battering one another round the head, and get on with good government," he said.

The reaction was one of relief, tinged with scepticism. Local government could not be sure that the worst was truly over. Some were groaning under Whitehall decisions on Revenue Support Grant (the amounts that government pays towards local council costs) and Standard Spending assessment (the amounts which in Whitehall's judgment each council ought to be spending), which they felt took insufficient account of their needs. Government money accounted for a huge slice of their income: the proportion of revenue raised by councils themselves had fallen to 15 per cent.

Nor had supervisory severity been relaxed with the end of the poll tax. Capping remained in place; councils were required to limit their spending increases for 1993-94 to 2.5 per cent; some faced capping if their increase exceeded 0.5 per cent. And was not the home secretary, Kenneth Clarke, contemplating at this very moment another erosion of local government, with its representation on police authorities cut and room made for appointed businessmen?

And now a new shadow had fallen over them. The newly-appointed Local Government Commission, chaired by the former head of the CBI, Sir John Banham, was drawing up a new map of local government. Their instructions were generously drafted. The Government's preference was for unitary authorities so that people looked to one town hall for all services, instead of, as under the present county and district system, to two. There would not, this time, be one big report, one broad pattern to all solutions and one big Bill to implement changes. Recommendations could vary from place to place according to local needs and preferences. Reports would be issued county by county and legislation would be piecemeal, using parliamentary orders.

But clearly there would be disruption. And as the Commission's reports began to appear, apprehension grew. The first, from the Isle of Wight, was easy, since almost everyone wanted a single authority across the island instead of the present two. But in subsequent reports a pattern appeared which was ominous for district councils. They had hoped to stay much as they were, but with powers gained from the counties. Instead, most faced amalgamation into larger units. That meant fewer council seats. Many district councillors would find themselves dispossessed. It looked on the basis of work so far as if the nostalgic cry for the resurrection of Rutland as an independent local authority — not to mention the parallel ambition for Major's Huntingdon, next door — was doomed to disappointment.

But by midsummer, it was no longer clear that the Banham Commission would complete its planned progress round England. As the protests mounted, both the Government and the Commission declared themselves prepared to reconsider its operations. Perhaps it should only go to places discontented with the status quo (as Avon, Cleveland and Humberside were assumed to have been) and leave the rest alone. Perhaps its recommendations might in some places be restricted to a simple shift of responsibilities between council and district.

In Wales the process was swifter. There was no commission, simply a statement from Welsh secretary David Hunt on March 3 1993 that the present eight counties and 37 districts would be replaced by 21 unitary authorities: four based on towns, many others reviving the former Welsh counties.

In Scotland, changes were annouced on July 8 1993 by the secretary of state Ian Lang. His statement enraged the Opposition parties, which suspected a stitch-up. Some of the new authorities planned by Lang seemed to have been designed, they objected, to produce Conservative majorities. (The implications were all the more serious should parliamentary constituency boundaries later follow those of the planned new councils.) The SNP, some of the Liberals and finally Scottish Labour MPs staged a Commons walk out. They were going to Downing Street to deliver their protests in person, said the shadow Scottish secretary, Tom Clarke. Curious, said Lang, watching them go from his side of the despatch box: they must be the only people in Britain who don't know that John Major's in Tokyo.

The change from the hated poll tax to Michael Heseltine's council tax, however, appeared to go well. A cushion for those most likely to be hit by the change helped accomplish that. At a cost of £340 million, it ensured that no household would have to pay more than £182 above its poll tax liability. This scheme would run for two years and benefit about 3.75 million households. The Department of Environment estimated that just over half of the 19 million households in England and Wales would gain from the change to council tax. About 8.75 million better-off households would lose. But for the cushion, that might have imposed heavy burdens, especially in the south.

The success of this transition, confounding predictions of yet another

MAIN SOURCES OF LOCAL AUTHORITY RECEIPTS (£M)

	central funding	rates	poll tax	TOTAL	cent funding as % of total
1979	11,272	6,567		22,043	51
1983	18,703	12,219		36,115	52
1984	19,908	12,767		37,954	53
1985	20,438	13,638		39,786	52
1986	21,813	15,251		42,862	51
1987	23,277	16,777		45,962	51
1988	23,452	18,726		48,469	48
1989	24,200	19,913	586	51,858	47
1990	38,333	5,129	8,629	59,523	64
1991	47,730	118	8,162	63,387	75

Source: Blue Book

LOCAL AUTHORITY EXPENDITURE May 17th 1993
Proportion of LA revenue expenditure met by government grants, non-domestic rates, domestic rates, community charges and council taxes

	Govt grants[1] as % of LA	Non-domestic rates[2] as % of LA expenditure	Domestic rates/ community charges[3]
1981-82	56	25	20
1982-83	53	26	21
1983-84	54	26	19
1984-85	54	26	20
1985-86	54	28	21
1986-87	50	28	22
1987-88	49	28	23
1988-89	46	28	25
1989-90	44	29	26
1990-91	42	29	28
1991-92	52	31	16
1992-93	54	29	17
1993-94	56	27	16

1 For the years 1981-82 to 1989-90 Government grants comprise Aggregate Exchequer Grant and Rate Rebate Grants. For 1990-91 to 1992-93 Government Grants are made up of Revenue Support Grant. Special Grants, Specific Grants in Aggregate External Finance, Community Charge Grant (1991-92), Teachers Pay Grant (1992-93), Community Charge Benefits and Transitional Relief/Community Charge Reduction Scheme Grants. For 1993-94 Government Grants are made up of Revenue Support Grant, Specific and Special Grants in Aggregate External Finance, Council Tax Transitional Reduction Scheme Grant.
2 For the years 1981-82 to 1989-90, this represents non-domestic rate yields net of rate relief. For the years 1990-91 to 1993-94, this represents the distributable amount from the non-domestic rates pool.
3 Net of rate rebates for the years 1981-82 to 1989-90. Net of Community Charge Benefits and Transitional Relief/Community Charge Reduction Scheme in 1990-91 to 1992-93. Net of Countil Tax Benefit and Council Tax Transitional Relief Scheme in 1993-94.

Source:written answer to Nigel Evans, MP May 26 1993

local finance revolt, was still not enough to save several hundred Conservative councillors from annihilation at the county elections on May 6 1993. Heavy losses had been expected, but the scale of the defeat made it one of the worst local government nights the party had ever experienced. They held on to only one county — Buckinghamshire — and lost Essex, Kent, Surrey, East and West Sussex, Hampshire, Dorset, Devon, Somerset, Hertfordshire, Cambridgeshire, Lincolnshire, Norfolk and Suffolk and Warwickshire. The Liberal Democrats added Cornwall and Somerset to the Isle of Wight, which they already controlled; Labour gained Northamptonshire. The Conservatives lost almost 500 seats, Labour gained more than 160 and the Liberal Democrats more than 400. Some ousted Tory councillors were openly bitter: they had paid the price, they said, not for their own shortcomings but for those of the Government and especially the chancellor.●

LOCAL GOVERNMENT COMMISSION TIMETABLE October 93 onwards

County	Review Period	Consultation Expected	Final Report
Isle of Wight	completed	completed	published
Cleveland/Durham	completed	completed	November 21 1993
Avon/Glos/Somerset	completed	completed	January 23 1994
Humber/Lincs/N Yorks	completed	completed	January 23 1994
Leicestershire	completed	8/11/93 - 9/1/94	May 8 1994
Nottinghamshire	completed	20/12/93 - 20/2/94	June 5 1994
Cumbria/Lancs	20/9/93 - 5/12/93	9/5/94 - 10/7/94	December 4 1994
Hampshire	27/9/93 - 12/12/93	16/5/94 - 17/7/94	October 30 1994
Staffordshire	22/11/93 - 6/2/94	23/5/94 - 24/7/94	November 6 1994
Devon	24/1/94 - 10/4/94	25/7/94 - 2/10/94	January 8 1995
Cambridgeshire	24/1/94 - 10/4/94	4/7/94 - 11/9/94	December 18 1994

Programme of Areas

1st Tranche	2nd Tranche	3rd Tranche	4th Tranche	5th Tranche
Isle of Wight	Leicestershire	Bedfordshire	Dorset	Cornwall
Derbyshire	Nottinghamshire	Berkshire	Essex	Hertfordshire
		Oxfordshire		
Cleveland	Cumbria	Buckinghamshire	Hereford &	Northumberland
Durham	Lancashire		Worcester	
Avon	Hampshire	Cheshire	Norfolk	Shropshire
Gloucestershire	Staffordshire	E. Sussex	Suffolk	Surrey
Somerset		W. Sussex		
Humberside	Devon	Kent	Wiltshire	Warwickshire
Lincs,	Cambridgeshire	Northamptonshire		
N. Yorks				

LOCAL GOVERNMENT COMMISSION PROPOSALS

Publication Date	County	
April 25 1993	ISLE OF WIGHT	Unitary authority to cover the whole island (final report)
May 10	CLEVELAND	Four unitary authorities based on existing districts of Hartlepool, Langbaurgh, Middlesbrough and Stockton
May 10	DURHAM	Darlington to become separate unitary authority; Co Durham unitary authority for remainder of present county, with seven districts disappearing
June 14	AVON	Avon abolished. Bristol to be unitary authority.
June 14	GLOUCESTERSHIRE	Four new unitary authorities: South Gloucs based on Kingswood and Northavon; Mid Gloucs based on Gloucester City and Stroud; East Gloucs based on Cheltenham, Cotswold and Tewkesbury; Forest of Dean
June 14	SOMERSET	Three new unitary authorities: North East Somerset based on Bath, Wansdyke and parts of N. Mendip including Frome; South & West Somerset, based on Somerset CC less parts of N.Mendip
May 17	DERBY	Derby City becomes unitary authority; rest of present county becomes another (known as the "doughnut" solution).
June 21	HUMBERSIDE	Abolished; replaced by unitary Hull & E. Riding authority based on Beverley, E. Yorks, Holderness, Selby, parts of Boothferry. For areas S. of Humber, see LINCOLNSHIRE
June 21	N. YORKSHIRE	In the North Yorkshire county area, two "ridings" — North Riding (Hambleton, Richmondshire, Ryedale, Scarborough) and West Riding (Craven, Harrogate) Selby goes to Hull & E. Riding
June 21	LINCOLNSHIRE	Two new unitary authorities on South Humberside: Cleethorpes; Grimsby and Scunthorpe with Glanford and part of Boothferry

PROPOSED NEW COUNCILS FOR SCOTLAND
(with populations):

ORKNEY	20,000
as existing islands council	
SHETLAND	22,000
as existing islands council	
WESTERN ISLES	29,000
as existing islands council	
HIGHLAND	204,000
as existing regional council	
MORAY	84,000
as existing district council	
ABERDEENSHIRE	190,000
Existing Banff & Buchan DC; Gordon DC less Westhill; Kincardine & Deeside DC less Mearns and Stonehaven-Auchenblae	
CITY OF ABERDEEN	223,000
as exisiting district plus Westhill	
ANGUS AND MEARNS	129,000
as existing Angus DC, Monfieth, Sidlaw, Mearns, Stonehaven-Auchenblae	
CITY OF DUNDEE	155,000
as existing district less Monfieth and Sidlaw	
PERTHSHIRE AND KINROSS	125,000
as existing district council	
STIRLING	81,000
as existing district council	
ARGYLL AND BUTE	91,000
as existing district plus Helensburgh	
DUMBARTON AND CLYDEBANK	99,000
as existing Clydebank DC plus Vale of Leven and Dumbarton	
E. DUNBARTONSHIRE	106,000
as existing Bearsden and Milngavie DC plus Kirkintilloch, Strathkelvin North, Bishopbriggs, South Lenzie/Waterside	
N LANARKSHIRE	334,000
as existing Cumbernauld and Kilsyth DC, Motherwell DC, Monklands DC, plus part of Chryston	

S LANARKSHIRE	317.000
as existing Clydesdale DC, Hamilton DC, E Kilbride DC, plus Toryglen/King's Park, Rutherglen/Fernhill, Cambuslang/Halfway	
CLACKMANNAN AND FALKIRK	195,000
as existing Clackmannan DC, Falkirk DC Kincardine Bridge and surrounding area	
FIFE	343,000
as existing regional council less Kincardine Bridge area	
THE LOTHIANS	255,000
as existing W Lothian and Midlothian DCs plus Musselburgh/Fisherrow and Preston/ Levenhall	
CITY OF EDINBURGH	439,000
as existing district council	
BERWICKSHIRE AND E. LOTHIAN	76,000
as existing district councils less Musselburgh/Fisherrow and Preston/Levenhall	
THE BORDERS	85,000
existing regional council less Berwickshire	
DUMFRIES AND GALLOWAY	148,000
as existing district council	
S. AYRSHIRE	113,000
as existing Kyle and Carrick DC	
N. AYRSHIRE	263,000
as existing Cumnock and Doon Valley DC, Kilmarnock and Loudoun DC, Cunninghame DC	
W. RENFEWSHIRE	265,000
as existing Inverclyde DC, Renfrew DC less Barrhead, parts of Paisley	
E. RENFREWSHIRE	88,000
as existing Eastwood DC, Barrhead, parts of Paisley	
CITY OF GLASGOW	620,000
as existing district council less Toryglen/Kings Park, Rutherglen, and Cambuslang/Halfway	

PROPOSED NEW WELSH LOCAL AUTHORITIES
(with population)

Anglesey	69,800	West Glamorgan	148,900
Aberconwy and Colwyn	108,600	Bridgend	127,600
Caernarfonshire and Merionethshire	117,500	Vale of Glamorgan	121,800
Denbighshire	110,900	Glamorgan Valleys	238,200
Flintshire	122,000	Heads of the Valleys	155,100
Wrexham	123,600	Caerphilly	153,100
Cardiganshire	66,700	Torfaen	91,200
Powys	109,800	Monmouthshire	76,600
Carmarthenshire	170,400	Newport	135,400
Pembrokeshire	113,700	Cardiff	295,400
Swansea	230,100		

COUNCIL TAX: valuation bands

band	valuation	% of tax payable
A	up to £40,000	100
B	£40,001-52,000	117
C	£52,001-68,000	133
D	£68,001-88,000	150
E	£88,001-120,000	183
F	£120,001-160,000	217
G	£160,001-320,000	250
H	above £320,000	300

TWENTY ONE
INNER CITIES

Eleven years separated Lord Scarman from Benjamin Stanley: Scarman, the former law lord, identifying as ignitable ingredients in his report on Brixton after the riots unemployment, poor housing and an education system that did not meet young people's needs; Benjamin, a Manchester schoolboy, shot dead in Moss Side, Manchester, the casualty of an inner city culture of guns and drugs of which he was no part. In 1993, the Government embarked on yet another initiative to redeem inner cities: an Urban Regeneration Agency headed by the former Welsh secretary Peter, now Lord, Walker, dispensing some £300 million a year and designed to establish a partnership between Government, business and local councils as the Welsh Development Agency had done.

The original design was Michael Heseltine's. He had envisaged a kind of English Development Agency, taking over the whole machinery of local development corporations and urban programmes from existing agencies. The new agency established in the Leasehold Reform, Housing and Urban Development Bill was less ambitious, though it did incorporate the Derelict Land Grant and City Grant schemes, as well as English Estates, the Government property agency. But

now it would work alongside existing local agencies like that in London Docklands, mopping up areas of need which they did not cover.

The agency was created in a time of debate as to whether all the multifarious government efforts since Labour's 1968 initiative had done very much good. A Policy Studies Institute inquiry published on July 13 1992 concluded that "surprisingly little" had changed for the better in the deprived inner city. A series of indicators — the proportion of families living in property, rates of premature death, employment training schemes, pupil-teacher ratios — showed these areas falling even further below national averages. The bulk of the money spent on urban development corporations had gone to Docklands; spending on the urban programme had fallen in real terms — though rescue might yet be at hand from the promised Regeneration Agency and the City Challenge programme.

A more upbeat assessment came from Professor Brian Robson of Manchester University in his presidential address to the Institute of British Geographers (January 5 1993). Urban aid had reduced unemployment in priority areas; urban development corporations had attracted new capital — even if government had never been generous and had all too often been incoherent and mean-spirited. Robson warned of a "nightmare scenario" in which inner cities became ghettos of poor and disadvantaged people guarded by armed police. That had already become reality in his own city. The notion of areas out of control was a very real prospect in most big cities. Yet much could be done by coherent programmes of urban generation — as cities like Hamburg, Amsterdam and Dortmund had shown. The sadness was that Britain's urban programme was not being adequately sustained.

Robson had in mind two recent decisions. The first was the freezing of the urban programme, started in the 1970s, expanded after the 1980 riots, and now covering 9,900 projects in 57 inner city areas. Norman Lamont's Autumn Statement had precluded the funding of further projects: some £80 million-worth of activity, it was unofficially estimated, would be brought to a halt. The programme was being halted, the Department of Environment explained, because the chancel-lor had lifted the ban on councils spending revenues raised by the sale of land and buildings. The department also pointed to £20 million now made available for the Urban Partnership Programme.

The other was the cancellation of the planned third stage of Heseltine's City Challenge project, under which the 57 Urban Programme authorities could compete for a kitty of money that would go to those which made the best case. (Labour complained that some of the money to fund this adventure had been taken from the urban programme.) Eleven councils had qualified in phase one; 20 more lucky winners were named on July 16 1992.

But on November 27, the department confirmed reports that phase three had been scrapped. The environment secretary, Michael Howard, would assess the evidence of the first two rounds before he staged another. In any case, the Urban Programme list of 57 areas suffering from deprivation had been compiled on the basis of the 1981 census and the findings of the 1991 census might lead to changes.●

CITY CHALLENGE

City Challenge area	Population (a)	Area (hectares) (b)	Unemployment rate(%) (c)
Pacemakers			
Bradford	42,997	1,400	36.0
Dearne Valley	76,000	5,750	16.0
Lewisham	28,000	494	20.8
Liverpool	4,000	138	27.0
Manchester	10,000	110	31.0
Middlesbrough	40,300	792	20.0
Newcastle	35,200	580	25.0
Nottingham	25,000	405	24.4
Tower Hamlets	13,500	145	21.8
Wirral	29,000	683	29.0
Wolverhampton	22,000	560	n/a
Round 2:			
Barnsley	17,000	850	12.5
Birmingham	12,000	265	26.5
Blackburn	19,500	400	22.0
Bolton	19,500	506	17.0
Brent	20,000	320	30.0
Derby	26,000	240	25.0
Hackney	23,000	215	23.6
Hartlepool	11,200	280	22.7
Kensington	25,000	216	18.1
Kirklees	20,000	550	10.8*
Lambeth	30,000	250	29.0
Leicester	13,600	370	13.6
Newham	17,000	518	20.8
North Tyneside	36,000	1,128	15.4
Sandwell	27,000	606	16.0
Sefton	29,000	800	36.0
Stockton	23,600	695	22.8
Sunderland	37,000	2,950	16.1*
Walsall	15,000	470	17.2
Wigan	20,000	800	16.0

* DoE estimate

Sources: (a) and (b) Original Pacemaker and Round 2 Bid Documents and Action Plans; (c) Original Pacemaker and Round 2 Bid Documents and Action Plans .(Since their submission, the unemployment rate may have changed); written answer to Simon Hughes, MP

URBAN PROGRAMME ALLOCATION (1993-94)

	£m		£m
Newcastle	5.340	Wolverhampton	3.522
Gateshead	5.272	The Wrekin	0.634
Hartlepool	1.309	Derby	0.837
Langbaurgh	1.331	Leicester	3.143
Middlesbrough	3.325	Nottingham	3.350
North Tyneside	2.231	Barnsley	1.342
South Tyneside	3.158	Bradford	3.002
Stockton	1.280	Doncaster	1.288
Sunderland	3.317	Hull	3.265
Manchester	9.048	Kirklees	0.724
Salford	4.529	Leeds	3.473
Blackburn	2.115	Rotherham	1.486
Bolton	2.253	Sheffield	3.940
Burnley	1.396	Hackney	3.425
Oldham	2.554	Islington	5.873
Preston	1.210	Lambeth	5.863
Rochdale	2.475	Brent	1.436
Wigan	1.704	Greenwich	1.112
Liverpool	12.364	Hammersmith & Fulham	1.707
Halton	0.968	Haringey	2.012
Knowsley	2.615	Kensington & Chelsea	1.202
St Helens	1.185	Lewisham	1.530
Sefton	1.000	Newham	1.974
Wirral	2.340	Southwark	1.826
Birmingham	14.847	Tower Hamlets	3.083
Coventry	3.065	Wandsworth	2.110
Dudley	1.030	Bristol	1.109
Sandwell	3.148	Plymouth	0.925
Walsall	1.051	**TOTAL**	**162.834**

Source: written answer to David Evans, MP/March 30 1993

TWENTY TWO
THE ENVIRONMENT

Another European election, another Green party triumph? Perhaps not. At the 1989 European elections, the Green party came from nowhere to take 15 per cent of the votes, knocking the Liberal Democrats into fourth place and setting off a minor stampede among other parties to paint themselves green in the hope of catching this new national mood. There seems little chance of the Greens repeating that feat at the 1994 elections. The party has faded badly, its membership down from around 19,000 at peak to 6,000-8,000. At a strife-ridden annual conference at Wolverhampton in September 1992 it lost two of its most famous figures: Jonathon Porritt, who said that from now on he would cease to play an active role in the party, and Sara Parkin, who said that it had become "a liability to Green politics". One of her more abrasive critics said that all the members he knew had "danced with joy" at the news of Ms Parkin's departure.

But interest in green issues had generally declined, as had happened before, with the onset of recession, which made growth once more look desirable. Pressure groups like Friends of the Earth and Greenpeace continued to run high memberships — though new direct action groups

such as Earth First complained that organisations like Friends of the Earth had grown too complacent, too close in with government. There was no shortage of protesters to take up causes, especially when they involved the destruction of the countryside to make way for roads, as at Twyford Down near Winchester, Hampshire, or Oxleas Wood in south east London — the best-reported cases, perhaps because they were closest to newspaper offices. Plans to enlarge the M25 alarmed not only environmentalists but Tory MPs, whose constituents feared the loss of homes as well as of green spaces. Friends of the Earth accused the transport ministry of surreptitiously building an orbital motorway outside the M25 ring, by creating dual carriageways which would one day be linked to form the new road. The department denied it.

Sometimes these pressures succeeded. A threatened beauty spot near Hindhead in Surrey was reprieved. So in the end was Oxleas Wood: the scheme failed to meet the high environmental standards his department now applied to road schemes, said the transport secretary, John MacGregor. But plans to enhance the M25 by adding extra lanes — or in places, link roads running alongside the motorway for the benefit of local traffic — were confirmed. And 160 Sites of Special Scientific Interest still faced invasion by the motor car.

Yet polls suggested that the environment was falling back on most voters' agendas, unable to hold its own with the economy, health and education. Donations to environmental charities fell.

Interest flickered back into life with the Earth Summit — more properly, the UN Conference on Environment and Development (UNCED) — in Rio (June 3-14 1992). Its main decisions included:

• A binding treaty — the Biological Diversity Convention — requiring states to safeguard ecologically valuable areas and species; to come into force when ratified by 30 states. The US declined to sign the Convention.

• A second binding treaty, the Framework Convention on Climate Change, requiring states to limit the emission of greenhouse gases, especially carbon dioxide, a principal culprit for global warming. Rio endorsed the target already agreed by the European Community: stabilisation of emissions at the level of 1990 by 2000.

• A statement of Forest Principles, to defend threatened forests

• A new Sustainable Development Commission under UN auspices to monitor progress towards Rio objectives. Funding for Third World countries saddled with massive debt to help them achieve these targets would be organised through a new Global Environmental Facility.

A document called Agenda 21 set out measures which ought to be taken to ensure sustainable development.

In the Commons on June 15 the prime minister said Britain had taken a leading part in making these agreements possible. The UK had been responsible for launching the Biodiversity initiative, for setting in hand a global technology partnership with a UK conference in 1994, and for proposing a global forum, also in Britain in 1994, to help non-governmental organisations such as Oxfam plan campaigns. Labour said Britain's principal influence had been in watering commitments down.

Twelve months on, Britain had yet to ratify the two binding treaties. There was also controversy over the strength of Britain's commitment to limiting CO_2 emissions. Major had told the Commons that Britain was willing to go beyond the Rio agreement if others would do the same by making a firm commitment to reduce emissions of CO_2 and other greenhouse gases to 1990 levels by 2000. Because of US objections, that "firm commitment" had been lacking in Rio. The Government, however, continued to resist calls for a carbon tax, which some other governments saw as essential to meet that target. On April 23 1993, Britain, alone of the EC member states, refused to accept the need for a Community energy tax.

Britain had already made its contribution, its representatives argued, by ending the zero-rating of fuel in the Budget. This step was frequently quoted as evidence of green credentials. It made no sense for the Government to commit Britain to lower CO_2 emissions, but at the same time to be the only EC government with no Vat on domestic fuel, Major told the Global Technology Partnership Conference on March 24.

The return of London smog, long thought to have been banished, revived fears of pollution, and on April 8 1993 Her Majesty's Inspectorate of Pollution announced stringent limits on 29 coal and oil power stations. Brussels, which so often set the pace on environmental issues, was pressing the British to set more ambitious targets than the projected 60 per cent cut in sulphur emissions (at 1980 levels) by 2003 and 30 per cent in nitrous oxide emissions by 1998.

It had often been argued that tighter controls would be damaging to industry, but industry by now was demonstrating a far greater environmental consciousness, and a sharper eye for commercial advantage from environmental advance. At a conference in London in May, representatives of industry joined forces with environmentalists in demanding more resolute action from government on global warming. There were calls for a cut in company car perks, greater investment in public transport and a carbon tax.

John Gummer, appointed environment secretary in the post-Lamont reshuffle, was beginning to talk that language too. A consultative paper — UK Strategy for Sustainable Development, required of the Government by the terms of the Rio agreement — was published on July 21 1993. In language unlikely to endear itself to Gummer's colleagues in the Department of Transport, this argued that if public health and the countryside were to be safeguarded and pollution quelled, the motor car would have to be tamed. It called for a "major nation-al debate" on curbing traffic growth.

Plans for a new environmental agency, contained in the Conservative manifesto, failed to appear in the parliamentary programme. The agency was to combine the Inspectorate of Pollution and the National Rivers Authority and to take over from local government its waste regulation functions. The legislation was not now expected to surface until 1995.

In the meantime, though, people could at least look forward to the prospect of Gummer splashing about in one of the seas now under his command.

He had promised to swim in the sea off Blackpool during the party conference of October 1993 to dispel any fears aroused by a European Court censure on the British government for failing to ensure that the sea at Blackpool and Southport met EC standards of cleanliness.

The courts said the water was polluted by sewage. The DoE said the ruling was "technical"; the water was being brought up to scratch and would certainly pass muster by 1995.

There seemed little hope, however, of the nation's drinking water being brought up to Brussels' requirements, since the Government's water regulator, Ian Byatt, estimated in July 1993 that to do so would mean an average increase on customers' bills of £54 a year until 1998 — on top of increases of 5 per cent a year above inflation already required to meet British water quality legislation. He thought ministers should not have accepted the EC requirement and should now renegotiate it.●

Night shift: revolt and counter revolt continued to threaten Government attempts to pass the Maastricht Bill

TWENTY THREE
EUROPE

Though it was never very high on voters' lists of priorities, Europe dominated the 1992-93 parliamentary session, dividing both the main parties and at times even raising the possibility — against which the foreign secretary, Douglas Hurd, specifically warned at the party conference — that the Conservative party might even split on the issue, as it had over the corn laws and tariff reform. In each case, Hurd reminded them, the party had been out of power for 10 years thereafter,

In 1986 a European Communities (Amendment) Bill, implementing the Single European Act, had sailed through the Commons with little excitement or disturbance. But the European Communities (Amendment) Bill of 1992, through which the Commons assented to the agreement reached at Maastricht on December 9-10 1991, gave the Government months of trouble and even at some stages appeared likely to threaten its life. It ate up much of the parliamentary session — 204 hours of debate, 163 of them in a 23-day committee stage — and became for some MPs the most ardent political cause of their lives.

Labour and the Liberal Democrats supported the Maastricht agreement, though both opposed the opt-out John Major had obtained for Britain from the social chapter. The Liberal Democrats had the longest and deepest commitment to European integration, though even they had one Maastricht rebel, the new MP for North Devon, Nick Harvey. Labour under Neil Kinnock had come round to the European cause, but a sturdy opposition remained to the integrationist logic of Maastricht: some still wanted to see Britain leave the European Community.

At the start of the party conference at Blackpool in October, Bryan Gould, a long-standing Eurosceptic and the defeated candidate in the leadership election, resigned from the shadow Cabinet in order to declare his opposition to the leadership's policies on the economy and on Europe (September 27). Earlier that day, Gould had been on the losing side when the Labour party's National Executive voted 22-3 against a referendum on Maastricht.

But because they were the Government and it was they who had to get the Bill through, the Conservatives had the most intractable difficulties. Their divisions affected the party at every level, from the Cabinet, where Michael Howard, Peter Lilley and Michael Portillo — and perhaps even the chancellor, Norman Lamont —

were regarded by back-bench Eurosceptics as sympathetic to their cause, through the junior ranks of the ministry, across the back benches and out to the party in the country, particularly those troubled by the loss of national sovereignty. Long-held doubts about closer integration in Europe had been exacerbated by the experience of the ERM, which was seen as having deepened and prolonged recession, impeded recovery, and discredited the party with the electorate. Black Wednesday, in this sense, was seen as a liberation.

So the passage of the European Communities Amendment Bill 1992 — a measure which did not, as was sometimes suggested, ratify the Maastricht treaty, but accommodated it in British law — was always going to be a perilous undertaking. The Government sought to quell dissent by a combination of cajolement and menace. Doubters were assured that, far from making integration more likely, Maastricht had begun the process of rolling it back. That which they feared could never now happen. "You are shutting your eyes to what is in the treaty because you wish to haunt yourself with what is not in the treaty," Hurd told one of the most dedicated of the anti-Maastricht MPs, Richard Shepherd.

A crucial change, it was said, was the growing acceptance of the doctrine of subsidiarity, under which decisions were best taken at the lowest practicable level. On that score power ought, wherever possible, to be exercised in national parliaments rather than Brussels. This, ministers argued, was part of the spirit of Maastricht, to be taken further at coming summits under Britain's presidency.

The pressures were applied both at Westminster, where there were cases of MPs reduced to tears in encounters with whips, and in the constituencies. Rebel MPs complained of dirty tricks — even including threats to publicise less than saintly private lives. Constituency chairmen were asked to be firm with disobedient members. Some were; others retorted with warm endorsements of their member's rebellion.

The second reading debate was held on May 20 and 21 1992. Labour had tabled a reasoned amendment deploring both Britain's opt-out from the protocol which embodied the social chapter and the opt-out on Economic and Monetary Union which, its amendment said, would preclude any chance of the European Monetary Institute or the European Central Bank coming to London. The amendment was defeated. Then, in a vote where Labour MPs were instructed by the whips to abstain, the Bill got its second reading by 336 to 92. Those against were 22 Conservatives, 59 Labour MPs and 11 MPs from the two Northern Ireland Unionist parties.

But its progress was then suspended after Danish voters rejected the treaty terms in a referendum (June 2 1992) and put the whole future of the treaty in doubt. It remained stalled through the summer. In September, the prime minister promised to bring it back to the House when two conditions had been met: progress on subsidiarity and a decision from Denmark on how to proceed after the referendum defeat. In response to Labour pressure, Major promised to resume the Bill's progress with what came to be known as a "paving motion" — in essence, a vote by the House saying it wanted to proceed.

There was no requirement, and no precedent, for such a debate, and as the time approached the promise began to look fatal. The mood of the party conference in Brighton, though not exactly hostile to the European project, had been far from enthusiastic. The party appeared delighted at having escaped the ERM, and determined not to be reimprisoned. Warnings of what might happen if Britain were left behind in the European process clearly worried representatives, but the merest reference to supranationalism, even the word Delors, seemed to stir the place to a frenzy.

On October 6, Norman (nowadays Lord) Tebbit got a roaring, stamping ovation from about one-third of the hall. Do you want other countries interfering, he asked them, in our immigration controls, our industrial negotiations, in every bit of our lives? Major, he said, should raise the flag of patriots all over Europe: "let's launch the drive for Maastricht Two, a treaty with no mention of Brussels, no mention of economic and monetary and political union". Lady Thatcher, an opponent of Maastricht with an even greater pull on the hearts of a Tory audience, did not speak at the conference, but she still got her message though, with an article in the European.

Any hopes that the whips would be able to invoke the mood of the party to get rebel MPs on board for the paving vote faded in Brighton. As the day approached, reports from Egypt, where Major had gone for a ceremony to mark the anniversary of El Alamein, suggested he might resign if defeated. The paving debate was staged on November 4 and 5. Labour, despite its pro-Maastricht sentiments, voted against the Government, on the grounds that the tests Major had set for reviving the Bill had not been met. The Liberal Democrats, though opponents warned them that they might save the life of an unpopular government, declared that the cause of Europe ought to come first, and voted with the Conservatives.

The Government defeated the Labour amendment by six votes, and won its own motion by three. Twenty six Tory MPs voted against the Government and at least 16 abstained. But for the Liberal Democrats, the Bill would have stayed in limbo and the Government, on some assessments, might even have finished. The majorities would have been even narrower had Major not promised the Conservative member for Great Yarmouth, Michael Carttiss, that the third reading debate would not take place until the outcome was known of Denmark's repeat referendum thus, to the rage of some other member states, still further delaying the earliest possible date for a British ratification.

The Committee stage began on December 1 as it meant to go on — with 90 minutes of points of order. (Like all major constitutional bills, this one was taken on the floor of the House, allowing all MPs to take part in debates.) Government hopes of reducing the ranks of potential rebels rose when Major got most of what he wanted from the EC summit in Edinburgh (December 11-12). An interim summit called by Major at Birmingham on October 16 had initially been

trailed as the opportunity for a reso-
nant new commitment to subsidiarity:
but little had emerged from it. Edinburgh, though, made progress on several fronts. In particular, it agreed concessions designed to allay the fears of
Danish voters in time for a fresh referendum. and — crucially for the internal Conservative party debate — settled new procedures to apply the
principle of subsidiarity.

But the core of 40 or so Conservative rebels were unmoved. The most
dedicated declared they were ready to
see the Government fall rather than
agree any further transfer of power to
Brussels. The most potent issue of all
was the social protocol, on which
Labour had tabled Amendment 27,
requiring the opt-out on the chapter
to be dropped. But dropping the opt-
out would mean departing from the
terms enshrined in the treaty. On January 20 the Foreign Office minister
Tristan Garel-Jones warned the
House: "Under the terms of the
amendment, United Kingdom law
would not conform to the treaty's provisions, so it would be impossible for
the United Kingdom to ratify the
treaty."

That was no doubt meant to shock
Labour, which wanted Maastricht to
go through, into dropping its amendment. The Tory rebels, however, were
overjoyed. Although as opposed as
the Government to the social chapter
provisions, they were happy to back
any course of action that would rule
out ratification. With Labour and the
Liberal Democrats standing firm, the
Government looked destined for
defeat.

Four weeks later, however, Garel-
Jones's advice was suddenly super-
seded by advice from the Government's Law Officers which said precisely the opposite. On February 15
Hurd disclosed that the attorney-general, Sir Nicholas Lyell, had advised
that the treaty could still be ratified
even if the Government lost the vote
on the social chapter. At one moment
the vote on the social chapter men-
aced the Government's future and
possibly threatened the whole European enterprise: at the next it became
a mere distracting irrelevance.

A second rebel tactic was to press
for a referendum. As ministers and
pro-Europe MPs champed at the
snail's pace progress of the Bill in the
committee, the rebels said they'd be
only too ready to help if only the Government agreed to give the final say to
the British people. Though the Euro-
fervent Liberal Democrat leader Paddy
Ashdown favoured a referendum and
opinion polls showed three-quarters
or more of the British electorate want-
ing one too, the Conservative and
Labour back benches remained resolutely against it. On April 21 1993 the
Commons rejected a referendum by
363 to 124.

On other issues, though, the Government had to bend. On March 8, it
lost a vote on the composition of EC
committees representing the regions.
Labour, backed by the Liberal
Democrats and Ulster Unionist MPs,
wanted the UK contingent drawn
from elected councillors. The Government wanted room to be left for nominees. Though nationalists were persuaded by concessions on other
issues to vote with the Government,
the defection of 42 Tories ensured
defeat. On other amendments placing
new duties on ministers and on the

Bank of England to report to MPs on progress towards economic union, the Government simply conceded rather than risk defeat (April 20).

And in the end it bent on the social chapter, too. At one point the Commons, bizarrely, seemed to have lost the right to vote on the issue. On April 15 the Deputy Speaker, Michael Morris, ruled that although the relevant amendment had been debated, no vote could be taken on it. Instead, the House could vote on a fresh arrival (clause 75) tabled by two Labour backbenchers, forbidding the Government from transferring further powers to Brussels until there had been a separate debate on the social chapter. (The vote would come after Royal Assent, but before ratification.) It was then revealed that the Government had accepted Clause 75, so that would not be voted on either.

This decision, which by tradition the Deputy Speaker was not required to explain, produced back-bench outrage and the left-wing Labour MP Tony Benn tabled a motion which condemned it as "profoundly mistaken". After a heated debate on April 21, the House rejected Benn's motion by 450 to 81. That ruled out all hope of a vote on amendment 27 in committee.

The Government looked to be safe. But on May 4 the Speaker, Betty Boothroyd, announced that a vote could be taken when the Bill came back on Report Stage. Thus was averted the ludicrous and demeaning prospect of the House of Commons being denied a vote on one of the political issues of the day. Inescapably faced with defeat and firm in their conviction — based on Lyell's advice — that it didn't matter anyway, minis-

ters accepted the hated Labour amendment, which thus became part of their Bill.

The purpose of its proponents, the foreign secretary told the Commons on May 5 1993, was "quite simply to inflict defeat on the Government, regardless of the unnecessary confusion this would introduce into British law. The Government will not give them that satisfaction. When it comes down to it, the amendment is pointless. It is tiresome and undesirable, but in practice irrelevant . . . The Government is prepared to acquiesce in the amendment on the basis that I have explained, rather than give its push-me-pull-you opponents the entirely synthetic victory that they crave".

The Bill which got its third reading on the night of May 20 was thus rather different, swollen as it was by the changes forced on the Government, from the one introduced a year before. The Commons' consent was less than full-hearted. The vote was 229 in favour (well under half the House) and 112 against. Again, Labour was whipped to abstain, but 66 Labour MPs voted against the Government while five voted with it.. There were 41 Tory rebels — nearly twice as many as on the second reading — a mark of the Government's failure to reassure or to bulldoze its dissidents into compliance.

More excitements were predicted in the Lords, but though senior Eurosceptics like Thatcher and Tebbit made muscular speeches, the Bill made much swifter progress than it had in the Commons. When on July 14 the rebels reached the amendment to impose a referendum, peers who rarely frequented the House flooded in from all quarters, home and abroad, to prevent it. The amendment was lost by 445 to 176.

The Maastricht Bill had riven the Conservative party, setting brother (of sorts) against brother in what had sometimes become snarling confrontation. "These people," the former Tory prime minister and senior Europhile Edward Heath said of the rebels, "are going to be hated for all time." One of the offences for which a junior minister, Edward Leigh, was sacked in the May reshuffle was allegedly giving aid and comfort to Euro-rebels. No continuing rebel was included in Major's new team, though two former Euro-troublemakers, who had voted against the Government on the Single European Act but had toed the line over Maastricht, were posted to the whips' office.

The Bill completed its final stages on July 20 and was given Royal Assent. But that wasn't the end of the story. Both Houses now had to handle Labour's "ticking time bomb": the requirement accepted during the Commons committee stage that before the new law became effective, Parliament must resolve the issue of Britain's opt-out on the social policy protocol, more familiarly known as the social chapter.

Both Houses debated the issue on July 22 amid frenetic manoeuvring. The Government taunted Labour and the Liberal Democrats as traitors to their European professions by putting ratification in doubt. But no defections were likely there. To win on the night, Major had either to reduce the ranks of the Tory rebels, or recruit fresh support — and the only hope of that lay

in wooing the nine Ulster Unionists.

On the first count, progress was made, but not enough. Nine of the 30 most persistent Maastricht rebels voted with the Government against the Labour amendment, including such hardliners as Nicholas Winterton (tempted over by an assurance that the Government was in no rush to rejoin the ERM), and the rebels' unofficial whip throughout the fight against Maastricht, James Cran. But too many others remained irreconcilable. By the time the vote was called, however, the Ulster Unionist vote, for reasons which no one would give, was safely in Major's pocket.

Two votes were required. The first on a Labour amendment saying the Government should not ratify Maastricht until Brussels had been informed that we did, after all, assent to the social chapter. The result was a tie: 317-317. The Speaker, required by precedent to stick to the status quo, gave her vote to the Government. They were home by one. (In fact, it later transpired that it wasn't a tie after all. In the excitement, one Labour member too many had been counted: the Speaker's vote should not have been necessary.)

The second vote was on the Government's own anodyne motion, noting the Government's policy on the social chapter. And here the Tory rebellion swelled from 18, which was just containable, to a fatal 23. The House had failed to reach a resolution; the issue was now in limbo.

Immediately Major announced a debate on a motion of confidence, linking the social chapter opt-out to the Government's survival. If they voted him down this time, the rebels knew, there was likely to be an election which the Tories, now lying third on some polls, looked certain to lose. On Friday 23, the Government won its two votes — the first on Labour's amendment, the second expressing confidence in Government policy on the social policy protocol — by sturdy majorities. No Conservative voted against them. Only one abstained.

Even then, one hurdle stood in the way of ratification. Lord Rees-Mogg, cross-bench peer, newspaper columnist and former editor of the Times, had been given leave to challenge the Government in the courts. The basis on which the Government intended to ratify Maastricht, he said, was legally and constitutionally flawed.

The Government, it was argued, had erred in three ways: by not obtaining Parliamentary approval for protocols, two of which enhanced the powers of the European Parliament; by taking the attorney-general's advice that the social protocol could be ratified by use of the royal prerogative, which advice was wrong; and by requiring the Crown to transfer foreign policy and treaty-making powers to Brussels, which the Crown could not legally do. On July 30, the High Court ruled against Rees-Mogg, but he still had the option of taking his case to appeal. In the end he decided against it. On August 2, after a merciless battering from speculators, the ERM collapsed. That, said Rees-Mogg, removed a key pillar of Maastricht. Britain ratified the treaty later the same day. ●

EUROPEAN COMMUNITIES (AMENDMENT) (Government Bill)
Introduced: May 7 1992

PURPOSE:

To incorporate the Maastricht treaty in UK law.

COMMONS:

2nd reading: May 20-21 1992 by 336 (Con, Lib Dem, SNP, SDLP, PC, UPUP) to 92 (22 Con, 59 Labour, OUP, DUP)

Motion relating to progress ("Paving" motion) November 4 1992. Carried by 319 (Con, 18 LD, UPUP) to 316 (Lab, 26 Con, 1 LD, SNP, PC, UU, DUP, SDLP)

Referendum Vote: on the night of April 21-22, the Commons rejected a referendum on Maastricht by 363 (Con 265, Lab 91, LD 6, UPUP 1) to 124 (Con 38, Lab 63, LD 14, SNP 3, OUP 5, DUP 1)

Report: May 4-5 1993

3rd reading: May 20 1993 by 292 to 112, with 41 Conservatives voting against the Government. Labour abstained but 66 MPs voted against the Government and 5 with the Government. Liberal Democrats supported the Government but N Harvey voted against. J Molyneaux, W Ross and D Trimble (OUP) and I. Paisley (DUP) voted against.

LORDS

2nd reading: June 7-8 1993

Referendum Vote: on July 14 1993 the Lords rejected a referendum on Maastricht by 445 votes to 176. This was thought to be the highest number of peers voting in a division this century.

Report: July 12-14 1993

3rd reading: July 20 1993

ROYAL ASSENT: July 20 1993

On July 22, the Government was defeated on its own motion on the Maastricht social charter by 324 to 316, having earlier won the vote on a Labour amendment by the casting vote of the Speaker after a tied vote of 317 to 317. On July 23 the Government had a majority of 40 on a motion expressing confidence in Government policy on the social chapter.

Rebellions.

On March 8 1993 the Government was defeated by 314 to 292 in a vote on the composition of the EC Committee of the Regions; 26 Conservatives voted against the Government and 22 others abstained or did not vote.

The Government also accepted Labour amendments in the Commons opposing the opt-out on the social chapter, requiring a vote on that issue before Royal Assent and requiring reports to be made by ministers and the Bank of England on progress towards EMU.

VOTES ON MAASTRICHT

Voting in divisions on the European Communities (Amendment) Bill 1992-3

1. 2nd reading: Labour amendment. May 21 1992, division no 18
2. 2nd reading. May 21, 1992 division 19
3. Paving motion: Labour amendment. November 4 1992, division no 82
4. Paving motion. November 4 1992, division no 83
5. Government defeat in vote on committee of the regions. March 8 1993, division no 174
6. New clause 49: referendum must be held before Act takes effect. April 21 1993, division no 248.
7. 3rd reading, May 20 1993, division no 277.

KEY:
A denotes vote with the Government.
X denotes vote against the Government.
O denotes that the MP did not vote. Deliberate abstentions are not recorded: failure to vote may be due to illness, absence, on parliamentary work abroad, etc.
S denotes Speaker or Deputy Speaker, who do not vote.
d denotes the death of an MP before the vote was taken.
(A) denotes a teller for the Government.(X) denotes a teller for the Opposition.

For voting on the Social Chapter opt-out after the passage of the Bill had been completed, see separate table below.

CONSERVATIVE

ADLEY, R	Christchurch	A	A	A	A	A	A	d
AINSWORTH, P	Surrey E	A	A	A	A	A	A	A
AITKEN, J	Thanet S	A	A	A	A	A	A	A
ALEXANDER, R	Newark	A	A	A	A	A	A	A
ALISON, M.	Selby	A	A	A	A	A	A	A
ALLASON, R	Torbay	A	X	A	A	O	X	X
AMESS, D	Basildon	A	A	A	A	A	A	A
ANCRAM, M	Devizes	A	A	A	A	A	A	A
ARBUTHNOT, J	Wanstead	A	A	A	A	A	A	A
ARNOLD, J	Gravesham	A	A	A	A	A	A	A
ARNOLD, Sir T	Hazel Grove	A	A	A	A	A	A	A
ASHBY, D	Leics NW	A	A	A	A	A	A	A
ASPINWALL, J	Wansdyke	A	A	A	A	A	A	A
ATKINS, R	S Ribble	A	A	A	A	A	O	A
ATKINSON, D	Bournemouth E	A	A	A	A	A	A	A
ATKINSON, P	Hexham	A	A	A	A	A	A	A
BAKER, K	Mole Valley	A	A	A	A	O	O	O
BAKER, N	Dorset N	A	A	A	A	A	A	A
BALDRY, T	Banbury	A	A	A	A	A	A	A
BANKS, M	Southport	A	A	A	A	A	A	A
BANKS, R	Harrogate	A	A	A	A	A	A	A
BATES, M	Langbaurgh	A	A	A	A	A	A	A
BATISTE, S	Elmet	A	A	A	A	A	A	A
BELLINGHAM, H	Norfolk NW	A	A	A	A	A	A	A

BENDALL, V	Ilford N	A	A	O	A	O	X	X
BERESFORD, Sir P	Croydon C	A	A	A	A	A	A	A
BIFFEN, J	Shropshire N	A	X	X	X	X	O	X
BLACKBURN, J	Dudley W	A	A	A	A	A	A	A
BODY, Sir R	Holland	A	X	X	X	X	O	X
BONSOR, Sir N	Upminster	A	A	A	A	O	X	X
BOOTH, H	Finchley	A	A	A	A	A	A	A
BOSWELL, T	Daventry	A	A	A	A	A	A	A
BOTTOMLEY, V	Surrey SW	A	A	A	A	A	A	A
BOTTOMLEY, P	Eltham	A	A	A	A	A	A	A
BOWDEN, A	Brighton Kemptown	A	A	A	A	A	A	A
BOWIS, J	Battersea	A	A	A	A	A	A	A
BOYSON, Sir R	Brent N	A	A	A	A	A	X	X
BRANDRETH, G	Chester	A	A	A	A	A	A	A
BRAZIER, J	Canterbury	A	A	A	A	A	A	A
BRIGHT, G	Luton S	A	A	A	A	A	O	A
BROOKE, P	City of London	A	A	A	A	A	A	A
BROWN, M	Brigg	A	A	A	A	A	A	A
BROWNING, A	Tiverton	A	A	A	A	A	A	A
BRUCE, I	Dorset S	A	A	A	A	A	A	A
BUDGEN, N	W'hampton SW	A	X	X	X	X	X	X
BURNS, S	Chelmsford	A	A	A	A	A	A	A
BURT, A	Bury N	A	A	A	A	A	A	A
BUTCHER, J	Coventry SW	A	X	X	X	O	O	X
BUTLER, P	Milton Keynes NE	A	A	A	A	A	A	A
BUTTERFILL, J	Bournemouth W	A	A	A	A	A	A	A
CARLISLE, J	Luton N	A	X	O	X	X	X	X
CARLISLE, K	Lincoln	A	A	A	A	A	A	A
CARRINGTON, M	Fulham	A	A	A	A	A	A	A
CARTTISS, M	Gt Yarmouth	A	X	A	A	O	X	X
CASH, W	Stafford	A	X	X	X	X	X	X
CHANNON, P	Southend W	A	A	A	A	A	A	A
CHAPLIN, J	Newbury	A	A	A	A	d	d	d
CHAPMAN, S	Chipping Barnet	(A)	(A)	(A)	(A)	(A)	(A)	(A)
CHURCHILL, W	Davyhulme	A	A	A	A	A	A	O
CLAPPISON, J	Hertsmere	A	A	A	A	A	A	A
CLARK, Dr M	Rochford	A	A	X	X	A	O	O
CLARKE, K	Rushcliffe	A	A	A	A	A	A	A
CLIFTON-BROWN, G	Cirencester	A	A	A	A	A	A	A
COE, S	Falmouth	A	A	A	A	A	A	A
COLVIN, M	Romsey	A	A	A	A	A	A	A

CONGDON, D	Croydon NW	A	A	A	A	A	A	A
CONWAY, D	Shrewsbury	A	A	A	A	A	A	A
COOMBS, A	Wyre Forest	A	A	A	A	A	A	O
COOMBS, S	Swindon	A	A	A	A	A	A	A
COPE, Sir J	Northavon	A	A	A	A	A	A	A
CORMACK, P	Staffs S	A	A	A	A	A	A	A
COUCHMAN, J	Gillingham	A	A	A	A	A	A	A
CRAN, J	Beverley	A	X	X	X	X	X	X
CRITCHLEY, J	Aldershot	A	A	A	A	A	O	O
CURRIE, E	Derbyshire S	A	A	A	A	A	A	A
CURRY, D	Skipton	A	A	A	A	A	A	A
DAVIES, Q	Stamford	A	A	A	A	A	A	A
DAVIS, D	Boothferry	A	A	A	A	A	A	A
DAY, S	Cheadle	A	A	A	A	A	A	A
DEVA, N	Brentford	A	A	A	A	A	X	A
DEVLIN, T	Stockton S	A	A	A	A	A	A	A
DICKENS, G	Littleborough	A	A	A	A	A	A	A
DICKS, T	Hayes	A	A	A	A	A	O	A
DORRELL, S	Loughborough	A	A	A	A	A	A	A
DOUGLAS-HAMILTON Ld J	Edinburgh W	A	A	A	A	A	A	A
DOVER, D	Chorley	A	A	A	A	A	A	A
DUNCAN, A	Rutland	A	A	A	A	A	A	A
DUNCAN-SMITH, I	Chingford	A	O	X	X	O	X	X
DUNN, R	Dartford	A	A	A	A	A	X	A
DURANT, Sir A	Reading W	A	A	A	A	A	A	A
DYKES, H	Harrow E	A	A	A	A	A	A	A
EGGAR, T	Enfield N	A	A	A	A	A	A	A
ELLETSON, H	Blackpool N	A	A	A	A	A	A	A
EMERY, Sir P	Honiton	A	A	A	A	A	A	A
EVANS, D	Welwyn	A	A	A	A	A	A	A
EVANS, J	Brecon	A	A	A	A	A	A	A
EVANS, N	Ribble Valley	A	A	A	A	A	A	A
EVANS, R	Monmouth	A	A	A	A	A	A	A
EVENNETT, D	Erith	A	A	A	A	A	A	A
FABER, D	Westbury	A	A	A	A	A	A	A
FABRICANT, M	Mid Staffs	A	A	A	A	A	A	A
FAIRBAIRN, Sir N	Perth	A	A	A	A	A	A	O
FENNER, Dame P	Medway	A	A	A	A	A	A	A
FIELD, B	Isle of Wight	A	A	A	A	A	A	A
FISHBURN, D	Kensington	A	A	A	A	A	A	A
FOOKES, Dame J	Plymouth Drake	S	S	S	S	S	S	S

FORMAN, N	Carshalton	A	A	A	A	A	A	A
FORSYTH, M	Stirling	A	A	A	A	A	A	A
FORTH, E	Worcs Mid	A	A	A	A	A	A	O
FOWLER, Sir N	Sutton C'field	A	A	A	A	A	A	A
FOX, Dr L	Woodspring	A	A	A	A	A	A	A
FOX, Sir M	Shipley	A	A	A	A	A	A	A
FREEMAN, R	Kettering	A	A	A	A	A	A	A
FRENCH, D	Gloucester	A	A	A	A	A	A	A
FRY, P	Wellingborough	A	A	A	A	O	X	X
GALE, R	Thanet N	A	A	A	A	A	A	A
GALLIE, P	Ayr	A	A	A	A	A	A	A
GARDINER, Sir G	Reigate	A	A	A	A	X	X	X
GAREL-JONES, T	Watford	A	A	A	A	A	A	A
GARNIER, E	Harborough	A	A	A	A	A	A	A
GILL, C	Ludlow	A	X	X	X	X	X	X
GILLAN, C	Chesham	A	A	A	A	A	A	A
GOODLAD, A	Eddisbury	A	A	A	A	A	A	A
GOODSON-WICKES, C	Wimbledon	A	A	A	A	A	A	A
GORMAN, T	Billericay	A	X	X	X	X	X	X
GORST, J	Hendon N	A	A	A	A	A	A	A
GRANT, Sir A	Cambs SW	A	A	A	A	A	A	A
GREENWAY, H	Ealing N	A	X	A	A	A	X	X
GREENWAY, J	Ryedale	A	A	A	A	A	A	O
GRIFFITHS, P	Portsmouth N	A	A	A	A	A	O	A
GRYLLS, Sir M	Surrey NW	A	A	A	A	O	A	A
GUMMER, J	Suffolk Coastal	A	A	A	A	A	A	A
HAGUE, W	Richmond, Yorks	A	A	A	A	A	A	A
HAMILTON, A	Epsom	A	A	A	A	A	A	A
HAMILTON, N	Tatton	A	A	A	A	A	A	A
HAMPSON, Dr K	Leeds NW	A	A	A	A	A	A	A
HANLEY, J	Richmond	A	A	A	A	A	O	A
HANNAM, J	Exeter	A	A	A	A	A	A	A
HARGREAVES, A	B'ham Hall Green	A	A	A	A	A	A	A
HARRIS, D	St Ives	A	A	A	A	A	A	A
HASELHURST, A	Saffron Walden	A	A	A	A	A	A	A
HAWKINS, N	Blackpool S	A	A	A	A	A	A	A
HAWKSLEY, W	Halesowen	O	O	O	O	X	O	X
HAYES, J	Harlow	A	A	A	A	A	A	A
HEALD, O	Herts N	A	A	A	A	A	A	A
HEATH, Sir E	Old Bexley	A	A	A	A	A	O	A
HEATHCOAT-AMORY, D	Wells	A	A	A	A	A	A	A

HENDRY, C	High Peak	A	A	A	A	A	A	A
HESELTINE, M	Henley	A	A	A	A	A	O	A
HICKS, R	Cornwall SE	A	A	A	A	A	A	A
HIGGINS, T	Worthing	A	A	A	A	A	A	A
HILL, J	So'ton Test	A	A	A	A	A	A	A
HOGG, D	Grantham	A	A	A	A	A	A	A
HORAM, J	Orpington	A	A	A	A	A	A	A
HORDERN, Sir P	Horsham	A	A	A	A	A	A	A
HOWARD, M	Folkestone	A	A	A	A	A	A	A
HOWARTH, A	Stratford	A	A	A	A	A	A	A
HOWELL, D	Guildford	A	A	A	A	O	A	A
HOWELL, R	Norfolk N	A	A	A	A	O	O	A
HUGHES, R	Harrow W	A	A	A	A	A	A	A
HUNT, D	Wirral W	A	A	A	A	A	A	A
HUNT, Sir J	Ravensbourne	A	A	A	A	A	A	A
HUNTER, A	Basingstoke	A	X	A	A	X	O	O
HURD, D	Witney	A	A	A	A	A	A	A
JACK, M	Fylde	A	A	A	A	A	A	A
JACKSON, R	Wantage	A	A	A	A	A	A	A
JENKIN, B	Colchester N	A	A	O	O	O	X	X
JESSEL, T	Twickenham	A	X	X	X	X	X	X
JOHNSON-SMITH, G	Wealden	A	A	A	A	A	A	O
JONES, G	Cardiff N	A	A	A	A	A	A	A
JONES, R	Herts W	A	A	O	A	A	A	O
JOPLING, M	Westmorland	A	A	A	A	A	A	O
KELLETT-BOWMAN, Dame E	Lancaster	A	A	A	A	A	A	A
KEY, R	Salisbury	A	A	A	A	A	A	A
KING, T	Bridgwater	A	A	A	A	A	A	A
KIRKHOPE, T	Leeds NE	A	A	A	A	A	(A)	A
KNAPMAN, R	Stroud	A	O	X	X	X	X	X
KNIGHT, Dame J	B'ham Edgbaston	A	A	A	A	A	A	O
KNIGHT, A	Erewash	A	A	A	A	A	A	A
KNIGHT, G	Derby N	A	A	A	A	A	A	A
KNOX, D	Staffs Moorlands	A	A	A	A	A	A	A
KYNOCH, G	Kincardine	A	A	A	A	A	A	A
LAIT, J	Hastings	A	A	A	A	A	A	A
LAMONT, N	Kingston	A	A	A	A	A	O	A
LANG, I	Galloway	A	A	A	A	A	A	A
LAWRENCE, Sir I	Burton	A	A	O	O	X	X	O
LEGG, B	Milton Keynes SW	A	A	X	X	O	X	X
LEIGH, E	Gainsborough	A	A	A	A	A	A	A

LENNOX-BOYD, M	Morecambe	A	A	A	A	A	A	A
LESTER, J	Broxtowe	A	A	A	A	A	A	A
LIDINGTON, D	Aylesbury	A	A	A	A	A	A	A
LIGHTBOWN, D	Staffs SE	(A)	A	A	O	(A)	A	(A)
LILLEY, P	St Albans	A	A	A	A	A	A	A
LLOYD, P	Fareham	A	A	A	A	A	A	A
LORD, M	Suffolk Central	A	A	O	X	X	X	X
LUFF, P	Worcester	A	A	A	A	A	A	A
LYELL, Sir N	Beds Mid	A	A	A	A	A	A	A
MacGREGOR, J	Norfolk S	A	A	A	A	A	A	A
MACKAY, A	Berks E	A	A	A	A	A	A	A
MACLEAN, D	Penrith	A	A	A	A	A	A	A
MADEL, D	Beds SW	A	A	A	A	A	A	A
MAITLAND, Lady O	Sutton	A	A	A	A	A	A	A
MAJOR, J	Huntingdon	A	A	A	A	A	A	A
MALONE, G	Winchester	A	A	A	A	A	A	A
MANS, K	Wyre	A	A	A	A	A	A	A
MARLAND, P	Gloucs W	A	A	A	A	A	A	A
MARLOW, A	Northampton N	A	X	X	X	X	X	X
MARSHALL, J	Hendon S	A	A	A	A	A	A	A
MARSHALL, Sir M	Arundel	A	A	A	A	A	A	O
MARTIN, D	Portsmouth S	A	A	A	A	A	A	A
MATES, M	Hants E	A	A	A	A	O	A	O
MAWHINNEY, Dr B	Peterborough	A	A	A	A	A	A	A
MAYHEW, Sir P	Tunbridge Wells	A	A	A	A	A	O	A
McLOUGHLIN, P	Derbyshire W	A	A	A	A	A	A	A
McNAIR-WILSON,Sir P	New Forest	A	A	A	A	O	O	O
MELLOR, D	Putney	A	A	A	A	A	A	O
MERCHANT, P	Beckenham	A	A	A	A	A	A	A
MILLIGAN, S	Eastleigh	A	A	A	A	A	A	A
MILLS, I	Meriden	A	A	A	A	A	A	A
MITCHELL, A	Gedling	A	A	A	A	A	A	A
MITCHELL, Sir D	Hants NW	A	A	A	A	A	A	A
MOATE, Sir R	Faversham	A	O	A	A	O	X	X
MONRO, Sir H	Dumfries	A	A	A	A	A	A	A
MONTGOMERY, Sir F	Altrincham	A	A	A	A	A	A	A
MORRIS, M	Northampton S	S	S	S	S	S	S	S
MOSS, M	Cambs NE	A	A	A	A	A	A	A
NEEDHAM, R	Wilts N	A	A	A	A	O	O	A
NELSON, A	Chichester	A	A	A	A	A	A	A
NEUBERT, Sir M	Romford	A	A	A	A	A	A	A

NEWTON, T	Braintree	A	A	A	A	A	A	A
NICHOLLS, P	Teignbridge	A	A	A	A	A	A	A
NICHOLSON, D	Taunton	A	A	A	A	A	A	A
NICHOLSON, E	Devon W	A	A	A	A	A	A	A
NORRIS, S	Epping Forest	A	A	A	A	A	O	A
ONSLOW, C	Woking	A	A	A	A	A	A	A
OPPENHEIM, P	Amber Valley	A	A	A	A	A	A	A
OTTAWAY, R	Croydon S	A	A	A	A	A	A	A
PAGE, R	Herts SW	A	A	A	A	A	A	A
PAICE, J	Cambs SE	A	A	A	A	A	A	A
PATNICK, I	Sheffield Hallam	A	(A)	(A)	(A)	A	A	A
PATTEN, J	Oxford W	A	A	A	A	A	A	A
PATTIE, Sir G	Chertsey	A	A	A	A	A	A	A
PAWSEY, J	Rugby	A	A	A	A	A	X	X
PEACOCK, E	Batley	A	A	A	A	A	A	A
PICKLES, E	Brentwood	A	A	A	A	A	A	A
PORTER, B	Wirral S	A	A	A	A	A	A	A
PORTER, D	Waveney	A	X	A	X	O	O	X
PORTILLO, M	Enfield Southgate	A	A	A	A	A	A	A
POWELL, W	Corby	A	A	A	A	A	A	A
RATHBONE, T	Lewes	A	A	A	A	A	A	A
REDWOOD, J	Wokingham	A	A	A	A	A	A	A
RENTON, T	Sussex Mid	A	A	A	A	A	A	A
RICHARDS, R	Clwyd NW	A	A	A	A	A	A	A
RIDDICK, G	Colne Valley	A	A	A	A	A	A	A
RIFKIND, M	Edinburgh P'lands	A	A	A	A	A	O	O
ROBATHAN, A	Blaby	A	A	A	A	A	A	X
ROBERTS, Sir W	Conwy	A	A	A	A	A	A	A
ROBERTSON, R	Aberdeen S	A	A	A	A	A	A	A
ROBINSON, M	Somerton	A	A	A	A	A	A	A
ROE, M	Broxbourne	A	A	A	A	A	O	A
ROWE, A	Kent Mid	A	A	A	A	A	A	A
RUMBOLD, Dame A	Mitcham	A	A	A	A	A	A	A
RYDER, R	Norfolk Mid	A	A	A	A	A	A	A
SACKVILLE, T	Bolton W	A	A	A	A	A	A	A
SAINSBURY, T	Hove	A	A	A	A	A	A	A
SCOTT, N	Chelsea	O	A	A	A	A	A	A
SHAW, D	Dover	A	A	A	A	A	A	A
SHAW, Sir G	Pudsey	A	A	A	A	A	A	A
SHEPHARD, G	Norfolk SW	A	A	A	A	A	A	A
SHEPHERD, C	Hereford	A	A	A	A	A	A	A

SHEPHERD, R	Aldridge	A	X	X	X	X	X	X
SHERSBY, M	Uxbridge	A	A	A	A	A	A	A
SIMS, R	Chislehurst	A	A	A	A	A	A	A
SKEET, Sir T	Beds N	A	X	X	X	X	X	X
SMITH, Sir D	Warwick	A	A	A	A	A	A	A
SMITH, T	Beaconsfield	A	A	A	A	A	A	A
SOAMES, N	Crawley	A	A	A	A	A	A	A
SPEED, Sir K	Ashford	A	A	A	A	A	A	A
SPENCER, Sir D	Brighton Pavilion	A	A	A	A	A	A	A
SPICER, Sir J	Dorset W	A	A	A	A	A	A	A
SPICER, M	Worcs S	A	X	X	X	X	X	X
SPINK, Dr R	Castle Point	A	A	A	A	A	A	A
SPRING, R	Bury St E	A	A	A	A	A	A	A
SPROAT, I	Harwich	A	A	A	A	A	A	A
SQUIRE, R	Hornchurch	A	A	A	A	A	A	A
STANLEY, Sir J	Tonbridge	A	A	A	A	O	A	A
STEEN, A	S Hams	A	A	A	A	A	A	A
STEPHEN, M	Shoreham	A	A	A	A	A	A	A
STERN, M	Bristol NW	A	A	A	A	A	A	A
STEWART, A	Eastwood	A	A	A	A	A	A	A
STREETER, G	Plymouth Sutton	A	A	A	A	A	A	A
SUMBERG, D	Bury S	A	A	A	A	A	A	A
SWEENEY, W	Vale of Glam	A	A	O	O	X	X	X
SYKES, J	Scarborough	A	A	A	A	A	A	A
TAPSELL, Sir P	Lindsey E	A	A	X	X	A	X	X
TAYLOR, I	Esher	A	A	A	A	A	A	A
TAYLOR, J	Solihull	A	A	A	A	A	A	A
TAYLOR, Sir T	Southend E	A	X	X	X	X	X	X
TEMPLE-MORRIS, P	Leominster	A	A	A	A	A	A	A
THOMASON, R	Bromsgrove	A	A	A	A	A	A	A
THOMPSON, Sir D	Calder Valley	A	A	A	A	A	A	A
THOMPSON, P	Norwich N	A	A	A	A	A	A	A
THORNTON, Sir M	Crosby	A	A	A	A	A	A	A
THURNHAM, P	Bolton NE	A	A	A	A	A	A	A
TOWNEND, J	Bridlington	A	A	A	A	O	X	X
TOWNSEND, C	Bexleyheath	A	A	A	A	A	A	A
TRACEY, R	Surbiton	A	A	A	A	A	A	A
TREDINNICK, D	Bosworth	A	A	A	A	A	A	A
TREND, M	Maidenhead	A	A	A	A	A	A	A
TROTTER, N	Tynemouth	A	A	A	A	A	A	A
TWINN, Dr I	Edmonton	A	A	A	A	A	A	A

VAUGHAN, Sir G	Reading E	A	A	O	O	A	O	O
VIGGERS, P	Gosport	A	A	A	A	A	A	O
WALDEGRAVE, W	Bristol W	A	A	A	A	A	A	A
WALDEN, G	Buckingham	A	A	A	A	O	A	A
WALKER, B	Tayside N	A	O	X	X	X	X	X
WALLER, G	Keighley	A	A	A	A	A	A	A
WARD, J	Poole	A	A	A	A	A	A	A
WARDLE, C	Bexhill	A	A	A	A	A	A	A
WATERSON, N	Eastbourne	A	A	A	A	A	A	A
WATTS, J	Slough	A	A	A	A	A	A	A
WELLS, B	Hertford	A	A	A	A	A	A	A
WHEELER, Sir J	Westminster N	A	A	A	A	A	A	A
WHITNEY, R	Wycombe	A	A	A	A	A	A	A
WHITTINGDALE, J	Colchester S	A	A	O	O	O	X	X
WIDDECOMBE, A	Maidstone	A	A	A	A	A	A	A
WIGGIN, Sir J	Weston-s-Mare	A	A	A	A	A	A	A
WILKINSON, J	Ruislip	A	A	X	X	X	X	X
WILLETTS, D	Havant	A	A	A	A	A	A	A
WILSHIRE, D	Spelthorne	A	A	A	A	A	O	O
WINTERTON, A	Congleton	A	X	X	X	X	X	X
WINTERTON, N	Macclesfield	A	X	X	X	X	X	X
WOLFSON, M	Sevenoaks	A	A	A	A	A	A	A
WOOD, T	Stevenage	A	A	A	A	A	A	A
YEO, T	Suffolk S	A	A	A	A	A	A	A
YOUNG, Sir G	Acton	A	A	A	A	A	A	A
LABOUR								
ABBOTT, D	Hackney N	X	X	X	X	X	X	X
ADAMS, I	Paisley N	O	O	X	X	X	X	X
AINGER, N	Pembroke	X	O	X	X	X	O	O
AINSWORTH, R	Coventry NE	X	O	X	X	X	O	O
ALLEN, G	Nottingham N	X	O	X	X	X	A	O
ANDERSON, D	Swansea E	X	O	X	X	X	A	O
ANDERSON, J	Rossendale	X	O	X	X	X	O	O
ARMSTRONG, H	Durham NW	X	O	X	X	X	A	O
ASHTON, J	Bassetlaw	X	O	X	X	X	O	O
AUSTIN-WALKER, J	Woolwich	X	X	X	X	X	O	X
BANKS, T	Newham NW	X	A	X	X	X	O	O
BARNES, H	Derbyshire NE	X	X	X	X	X	X	X
BARRON, K	Rother Valley	O	O	X	X	X	A	O
BATTLE, J	Leeds W	X	O	X	X	X	A	O

BAYLEY, H	York	X	O	X	X	X	A	O
BECKETT, M	Derby S	X	O	X	X	X	A	O
BELL, S	Middlesbrough	X	O	X	X	X	A	O
BENN, T	Chesterfield	O	X	X	X	X	X	X
BENNETT, A	Denton	X	X	X	X	X	X	X
BENTON, J	Bootle	X	O	X	X	X	O	O
BERMINGHAM, G	St Helens S	X	O	X	X	X	X	O
BERRY, Dr R	Kingswood	X	X	X	X	X	O	X
BETTS, C	Sheffield A'cliffe	X	O	X	X	X	O	O
BLAIR, A	Sedgefield	X	O	X	X	X	A	O
BLUNKETT, D	Sheffield B'side	X	O	X	X	X	O	O
BOATENG, P	Brent S	X	O	X	X	X	A	O
BOYCE, J	Rotherham	X	O	X	X	X	O	X
BOYES. R	Houghton	X	O	X	X	X	O	O
BRADLEY, K	M'chester Withingt	X	O	X	X	X	A	O
BRAY, Dr J	Motherwell S	X	O	X	X	X	O	O
BROWN, G	Dunfermline E	X	O	X	X	X	A	O
BROWN, N	Newcastle E	X	O	X	X	X	A	O
BURDEN, R	B'ham Northfield	X	O	X	X	X	O	O
BYERS, S	Wallsend	X	O	X	X	X	O	O
CABORN, R	Sheffield C	X	O	X	X	X	O	O
CALLAGHAN, J	Heywood	X	X	X	X	X	X	X
CAMPBELL, A	Cambridge	X	O	X	X	X	X	O
CAMPBELL, R	Blyth Valley	O	X	X	X	X	O	X
C-SAVOURS, D	Workington	X	O	X	X	X	A	O
CANAVAN, D	Falkirk W	O	X	X	X	X	X	X
CANN, J	Ipswich	O	X	X	X	X	X	X
CHISHOLM, M	Edinburgh Leith	X	X	X	X	X	X	X
CLAPHAM, M	Barnsley W	X	O	X	X	X	O	X
CLARK, Dr D	S Shields	X	O	X	X	X	A	O
CLARKE, E	Midlothian	X	X	X	X	X	X	O
CLARKE, T	Monklands W	X	O	X	X	X	A	O
CLELLAND, D	Tyne Bridge	X	O	X	X	X	O	O
CLWYD, A	Cynon Valley	X	O	X	X	X	A	O
COFFEY, A	Stockport	X	O	X	X	X	O	O
COHEN, H	Leyton	X	X	X	X	X	X	O
CONNARTY, M	Falkirk E	X	X	X	X	X	X	X
COOK, F	Stockton N	X	O	X	X	X	O	O
COOK, R	Livingston	X	O	X	X	X	O	O
CORBETT, R	B'ham Edgbaston	X	O	X	X	X	O	O
CORBYN, J	Islington N	O	X	X	X	X	X	X

CORSTON, Ms J	Bristol E	X	X	X	X	X	X	X
COUSINS, J	Newcastle C	X	O	X	X	X	A	O
COX, T	Tooting	X	O	X	X	X	O	O
CRYER, R	Bradford S	X	(X)	X	X	X	(X)	X
CUMMINGS, J	Easington	X	X	X	X	X	O	O
CUNLIFFE, L	Leigh	X	O	X	X	X	O	O
CUNNINGHAM, Jim	Coventry SE	X	O	X	X	X	O	O
CUNNINGHAM, John	Copeland	X	O	X	X	X	A	O
DALYELL, T	Linlithgow	X	A	X	X	X	O	O
DARLING, A	Edinburgh C	X	O	X	X	X	A	O
DAVIDSON, I	Glasgow Govan	X	O	X	X	X	X	X
DAVIES, B	Oldham C	X	O	X	X	X	O	O
DAVIES, D	Llanelli	X	X	X	X	X	X	X
DAVIES, R	Caerphilly	X	O	X	X	X	A	O
DAVIS, T	B'ham Hodge Hill	X	X	X	X	X	X	X
DENHAM, J	Southampton Itchen	X	O	X	X	X	O	O
DEWAR, D	Glasgow Garscadden	X	O	X	X	X	A	O
DIXON, D	Jarrow	X	O	X	X	X	A	O
DOBSON, F	Holborn	X	O	X	X	X	O	O
DONOHOE, B	Cunninghame S	X	O	X	X	X	X	X
DOWD, J	Lewisham W	X	O	X	X	X	O	O
DUNNACHIE, J	Glasgow Pollok	X	O	X	X	X	O	O
DUNWOODY, G	Crewe	X	X	X	X	X	X	X
EAGLE, A	Wallasey	X	O	X	X	X	O	O
EASTHAM, K	M'chester Blackley	X	O	X	X	X	O	O
ENRIGHT, D	Hemsworth	X	O	X	X	X	A	O
ETHERINGTON, W	Sunderland N	X	X	X	X	X	A	X
EVANS, J	St Helens N	X	O	X	X	X	O	O
FATCHETT, D	Leeds C	X	O	X	X	X	A	O
FAULDS, A	Warley E	X	A	X	X	X	O	A
FIELD, F	Birkenhead	X	O	X	X	X	X	X
FISHER, M	Stoke C	X	O	X	X	X	O	O
FLYNN, P	Newport W	O	O	X	X	X	O	O
FOSTER, D	Bishop Auckland	X	O	X	X	X	A	O
FOULKES, G	Carrick	X	O	X	X	X	A	O
FRASER, J	Norwood	X	O	X	X	X	A	O
FYFE, Mrs M	Glasgow Maryhill	X	O	X	X	X	A	O
GALBRAITH, S	Strathkelvin	X	O	X	X	X	A	O
GALLOWAY, G	Glasgow Hillhead	X	X	X	X	X	X	O
GAPES, M	Ilford S	X	O	X	X	X	O	O
GARRETT, J	Norwich S	X	O	X	X	X	A	O

GEORGE, B	Walsall S	O	O	X	X	X	O	O
GERRARD, N	Walthamstow	X	X	X	X	X	O	X
GILBERT, Dr J	Dudley E	O	O	X	X	X	O	O
GODMAN, Dr N	Greenock	X	O	X	X	X	O	X
GODSIFF, R	B'ham Small Heath	X	O	X	X	X	O	O
GOLDING, L	Newcastle-u-Lyme	X	O	X	X	X	A	O
GORDON, M	Bow	X	X	X	X	X	O	X
GOULD, B	Dagenham	X	O	X	X	X	X	X
GRAHAM, T	Renfrew W	X	O	X	X	X	X	O
GRANT, B	Tottenham	X	X	X	X	X	X	O
GRIFFITHS, N	Edinburgh S	X	O	X	X	X	A	O
GRIFFITHS, W	Bridgend	X	O	X	X	X	A	O
GROCOTT, B	Wrekin	X	O	X	X	X	O	O
GUNNELL, J	Leeds S	X	O	X	X	X	A	O
HAIN, P	Neath	X	X	X	X	X	O	X
HALL, M	Warrington S	X	X	X	X	X	X	X
HANSON, D	Delyn	X	O	X	X	X	A	O
HARDY, P	Wentworth	X	O	X	X	X	A	O
HARMAN, H	Peckham	X	O	X	X	X	A	O
HATTERSLEY, R	B'ham Sparkbrook	X	O	X	X	X	O	O
HENDERSON, D	Newcastle N	X	O	X	X	X	A	O
HEPPELL, J	Nottingham E	X	O	X	X	X	A	O
HILL, K	Streatham	X	O	X	X	X	A	O
HINCHCLIFFE, D	Wakefield	X	X	X	X	X	O	O
HOEY, K	Vauxhall	X	O	X	X	X	O	X
HOGG, N	Cumbernauld	X	O	X	X	X	O	O
HOME ROBERTSON, J	Lothian	X	O	X	X	X	A	A
HOOD, J	Clydesdale	X	X	X	X	X	X	O
HOON, G	Ashfield	X	O	X	X	X	A	O
HOWARTH, G	Knowsley N	X	X	X	X	X	X	X
HOWELLS, K	Pontypridd	X	O	X	X	X	O	O
HOYLE, D	Warrington N	X	X	X	X	X	O	O
HUGHES, K	Doncaster N	X	O	X	X	X	O	X
HUGHES, Rbt	Aberdeen N	X	O	X	X	X	A	O
HUGHES, Roy	Newport E	X	X	X	X	X	O	X
HUTTON, J	Barrow	X	O	X	X	X	O	O
ILLSLEY, E	Barnsley C	X	O	X	X	X	A	O
INGRAM, E	E Kilbride	X	O	X	X	X	A	O
JACKSON, G	Hampstead	X	O	X	X	X	O	O
JACKSON, H	Sheffield Hillsborough	X	O	X	X	X	O	O
JAMIESON, D	Plymouth D'port	X	O	X	X	X	O	O

JANNER, G	Leicester W	X	O	X	X	X	O	O
JONES, J O	Cardiff C	O	O	X	X	X	O	O
JONES, Dr L	B'ham Selly Oak	X	X	X	X	X	X	X
JONES, M	Clwyd SW	(X)	O	(X)	(X)	X	O	O
JONES, B	Alyn	X	O	X	X	X	A	O
JOWELL, T	Dulwich	X	O	X	X	X	O	O
KAUFMAN, G	M'chester Gorton	X	O	X	X	X	A	O
KEEN, A	Feltham	X	O	X	X	X	O	O
KENNEDY, Mrs J	L'pool Broad Green	X	O	X	X	X	X	O
KHABRA, P	Southall	X	O	X	X	X	O	O
KILFOYLE, P	L'pool Walton	X	O	X	X	X	O	O
KINNOCK, N	Islwyn	X	O	X	X	X	O	O
LEIGHTON, R	Newham NE	X	(X)	X	X	X	X	(X)
LESTOR, J	Eccles	X	O	X	X	X	O	O
LEWIS, T	Worsley	X	X	X	X	X	X	X
LITHERLAND, R	M'chester C	X	X	X	X	X	O	X
LIVINGSTONE, K	Brent E	O	X	X	X	X	X	X
LLOYD, A	Stretford	X	O	X	X	X	A	O
LOFTHOUSE, G	Pontefract	S	S	S	S	S	S	S
LOYDEN, E	L'pool Garston	X	X	X	X	X	X	O
McALLION, J	Dundee E	X	X	X	X	X	X	X
McAVOY, T	Glasgow Rutherglen	X	O	X	X	X	A	O
McCARTNEY, I	Makerfield	O	O	X	X	X	O	O
MACDONALD, C	Western Isles	X	O	X	X	X	A	A
McFALL, J	Dumbarton	X	O	X	X	X	A	O
McKELVEY, W	Kilmarnock	X	O	X	X	X	X	X
MACKINLAY, A	Thurrock	X	O	X	X	(X)	O	O
McLEISH, H	Fife C	X	O	X	X	X	A	O
McMASTER, G	Paisley S	X	O	X	X	X	O	O
McNAMARA, K	Hull N	X	O	X	X	X	A	O
McWILLIAM, J	Blaydon	X	O	X	X	O	X	X
MADDEN, M	Bradford W	X	X	X	X	X	X	X
MAHON, A	Halifax	X	X	X	X	X	X	O
MANDELSON, P	Hartlepool	X	O	X	X	X	O	O
MAREK, Dr J	Gloucestershire W	X	O	X	X	X	X	O
MARSHALL, D	G'gow Shettleston	X	O	X	X	X	O	X
MARSHALL, J	Leicester S	X	O	X	X	X	A	X
MARTIN, M	Glasgow Springburn	X	O	X	X	X	A	O
MARTLEW, E	Carlisle	X	O	X	X	X	O	O
MAXTON, J	Glasgow Cathcart	X	O	X	X	X	O	O
MEACHER, M	Oldham W	X	O	X	X	X	O	O

MEALE, A	Mansfield	X	O	(X)	(X)	X	A	O
MICHAEL, A	Cardiff S	X	O	X	X	X	A	O
MICHIE, W	Sheffield Heeley	X	X	X	X	X	X	X
MILBURN, A	Darlington	X	O	X	X	X	A	O
MILLER, A	Ellesmere Port	X	O	X	X	X	A	O
MITCHELL, A	Grimsby	X	X	X	X	X	(X)	X
MOONIE, Dr L	Kirkcaldy	X	O	X	X	X	A	O
MORGAN, R	Cardiff W	X	O	X	X	X	A	O
MORLEY, E	Glanford	X	O	X	X	X	O	O
MORRIS, A	M'chester W'shawe	X	O	X	X	X	O	O
MORRIS, E	B'ham Yardley	X	O	X	X	X	A	O
MORRIS, J	Aberavon	X	O	X	X	X	O	O
MOWLAM, Dr M	Redcar	X	O	X	X	X	A	O
MUDIE, G	Leeds E	X	O	X	X	X	O	X
MULLIN, C	Sunderland S	X	X	X	X	X	X	O
MURPHY, P	Torfaen	X	O	X	X	X	A	O
OAKES, G	Halton	X	O	X	X	X	O	O
O'BRIEN, M	Warwickshire N	X	O	X	X	X	O	O
O'BRIEN, W	Normanton	X	O	X	X	X	A	O
O'HARA, E	Knowsley S	X	O	X	X	X	O	O
OLNER, W	Nuneaton	X	O	X	X	X	O	X
O'NEILL, M	Clackmannan	X	O	X	X	X	A	O
ORME, S	Salford E	X	O	X	X	X	O	O
PARRY, R	L'pool Riverside	X	X	X	X	X	O	X
PATCHETT, T	Barnsley E	X	X	X	X	O	O	O
PENDRY, T	Stalybridge	X	O	X	X	X	A	O
PICKTHALL, C	Lancs W	X	X	X	X	X	X	X
PIKE, P	Burnley	X	O	X	X	X	A	O
POPE, G	Hyndburn	X	O	X	X	X	O	X
POWELL, R	Ogmore	X	O	X	X	X	O	O
PRENTICE, B	Lewisham E	X	O	X	X	X	O	X
PRENTICE, G	Pendle	X	O	X	X	X	X	X
PRESCOTT, J	Hull E	X	O	X	X	X	A	O
PRIMAROLO, D	Bristol S	X	X	X	X	O	O	O
PURCHASE, K	Wolverhampton NE	X	O	X	X	X	O	O
QUIN, J	Gateshead E	X	O	X	X	X	A	O
RADICE, G	Durham N	X	O	X	X	X	A	A
RANDALL, S	Hull W	X	O	X	X	X	O	O
RAYNSFORD, N	Greenwich	X	O	X	X	X	O	O
REDMOND, M	Don Valley	X	X	X	X	X	O	X
REID, Dr J	Motherwell N	X	O	X	X	X	A	O

RICHARDSON, J	Barking	X	O	X	X	O	O	X
ROBERTSON, G	Hamilton	X	O	X	X	X	A	O
ROBINSON, G	Coventry NW	X	O	X	X	X	O	O
ROCHE, B	Hornsey	X	O	X	X	X	O	O
ROGERS, A	Rhondda	X	O	X	X	X	A	O
ROOKER, J	B'ham Perry Barr	X	O	X	X	X	A	O
ROONEY, T	Bradford N	O	O	X	X	X	X	O
ROSS, E	Dundee W	X	O	X	X	X	O	O
ROWLANDS, E	Merthyr	X	X	X	X	X	X	X
RUDDOCK, J	L'sham Deptford	X	O	X	X	X	O	O
SEDGEMORE, B	Hackney S	X	O	X	X	X	O	A
SHEERMAN, B	Huddersfield	X	O	X	X	X	A	O
SHELDON, R	Ashton-u-Lyne	X	O	X	X	X	O	O
SHORE, P	Bethnal Green	X	X	X	X	X	X	X
SHORT, C	B'ham Ladywood	X	O	X	X	X	A	O
SIMPSON, A	Nottingham S	X	X	X	X	X	X	X
SKINNER, D	Bolsover	O	X	X	X	X	X	X
SMITH, A	Oxford E	X	O	X	X	X	A	O
SMITH, C	Islington S	X	O	X	X	X	A	O
SMITH, J	Monklands E	X	O	X	X	X	A	O
SMITH, L	Blaenau Gwent	X	X	X	X	X	X	X
SNAPE, P	W Bromwich E	X	O	X	X	X	O	O
SOLEY, C	Hammersmith	X	O	X	X	X	O	O
SPEARING, N	Newham S	O	X	X	X	X	X	(X)
SPELLAR, J	Warley W	X	O	X	X	X	O	O
SQUIRE, R	Dunfermline W	X	O	X	X	X	O	O
STEINBERG, G	Durham	X	O	X	X	X	X	O
STEVENSON, G	Stoke S	X	O	X	X	X	X	X
STOTT, R	Wigan	X	O	X	X	X	A	O
STRANG, Dr G	Edinburgh E	X	O	X	X	X	A	O
STRAW, J	Blackburn	X	O	X	X	X	A	O
TAYLOR, A	Dewsbury	X	O	X	X	X	A	O
THOMPSON, J	Wansbeck	(X)	O	X	X	(X)	O	O
TIPPING, P	Sherwood	X	O	X	X	X	A	O
TURNER, D	W'hampton SE	X	O	X	X	X	O	O
VAZ, K	Leicester E	X	O	X	X	X	A	O
WALKER, Sir H	Doncaster C	O	O	X	X	X	X	O
WALLEY, J	Stoke N	X	O	X	X	X	A	O
WARDELL, G	Gower	X	X	X	X	X	O	O
WAREING, R	L'pool W Derby	X	O	X	X	X	X	O
WATSON, M	Glasgow C	X	O	X	X	X	X	X

WICKS, M	Croydon NW	X	O	X	X	X	O	O
WILLIAMS, A J	Swansea W	X	X	X	X	X	X	X
WILLIAMS, Dr A W	Carmarthen	X	O	X	X	X	O	O
WILSON, B	Cunninghame N	X	O	X	X	X	O	O
WINNICK, D	Walsall N	X	X	X	X	X	X	X
WISE, A	Preston	X	X	X	X	X	X	X
WORTHINGTON, T	Clydebank	X	O	X	X	X	A	O
WRAY, J	Glasgow Provan	X	X	X	X	X	X	O
WRIGHT, Dr A	Cannock	X	O	X	X	X	X	O
YOUNG, D	Bolton SE	X	O	X	X	X	X	O

LIBERAL DEMOCRATS

ALTON, D	L'pool Mossley H	A	A	A	A	A	X	A
ASHDOWN, P	Yeovil	A	A	A	A	X	X	A
BEITH, A	Berwick	A	A	A	A	X	X	A
BRUCE, M	Gordon	A	A	A	A	X	O	O
CAMPBELL, M	Fife NE	A	A	A	A	X	X	A
CARLILE, A	Montgomery	A	A	A	A	X	A	O
FOSTER, D	Bath	A	A	A	A	X	X	A
HARVEY, N	Devon N	O	O	X	X	X	X	X
HUGHES, S	Southwark	A	A	A	A	X	X	A
JOHNSTON, Sir R	Inverness	A	A	A	A	X	A	A
JONES, N	Cheltenham	A	A	A	A	X	X	A
KENNEDY, C	Ross	O	O	A	A	X	X	A
KIRKWOOD, A	Roxburgh	A	A	A	A	X	A	A
LYNNE, L	Rochdale	A	A	A	A	X	X	O
MACLENNAN, R	Caithness	A	A	A	A	X	A	A
MICHIE, Mrs R	Argyll	A	A	A	A	X	X	A
RENDEL, D	Newbury	-	-	-	-	-	-	A
STEEL, Sir D	Tweeddale	A	A	A	A	O	A	A
TAYLOR, M	Truro	A	A	A	A	X	X	A
TYLER, P	Cornwall N	A	A	A	A	X	X	A
WALLACE, J	Orkney	A	A	A	A	X	X	A

SNP

EWING, M	Moray	X	A	X	X	A	X	O
SALMOND, A	Banff	X	A	X	X	A	X	O
WELSH, A	Angus E	X	A	X	X	A	X	O

PLAID CYMRU

DAFIS, C	Ceredigion	X	A	X	X	A	O	O
JONES, I W	Ynys Mon	X	A	X	X	A	O	A
LLWYD, E	Meirionnydd	X	A	X	X	A	O	A
WIGLEY, D	Caernarfon	X	A	X	X	A	O	A

THE SPEAKER

BOOTHROYD, B	W Bromwich W	S	S	S	S	S	S	S

NORTHERN IRELAND MEMBERS

Ulster Unionists

BEGGS, R	Antrim E	A	X	X	X	X	X	O
FORSYTHE, C	Antrim S	A	X	X	X	O	O	O
MAGINNIS, K	Fermanagh	A	X	X	X	O	O	O
MOLYNEAUX, J	Lagan Valley	A	X	X	X	O	X	X
ROSS, W	Londonderry E	A	X	X	X	X	X	X
SMYTH, Rev M	Belfast S	A	X	O	O	O	X	O
TAYLOR, J D	Strangford	A	X	X	X	X	X	O
TRIMBLE, D	Upper Bann	A	X	X	X	X	O	X
WALKER, C	Belfast N	O	O	X	X	O	O	O

Democratic Unionists

McCREA, Rev W	Ulster Mid	A	X	X	X	O	O	O
PAISLEY, Rev I	Antrim N	A	X	X	X	X	O	X
ROBINSON, P	Belfast E	A	X	X	X	X	X	O

UPUP

KILFEDDER, Sir J	Down N	A	A	A	A	A	A	O

SDLP

HENDRON, Dr J	Belfast W	X	A	X	X	O	O	O
HUME, J	Foyle	X	A	X	X	O	O	O
McGRADY, E	Down S	X	A	X	X	O	O	O
MALLON, S	Newry	X	A	X	X	O	O	O

CONSERVATIVE REBELS IN THE SOCIAL PROTOCOL VOTES, July 22 1993

Key: A- vote with Government. X- vote against Government. O - did not vote.

	On Labour amendment	On Government motion
R.Allason (Torbay)	O	O
Sir R.Body (Holland)	X	X
N.Budgen (Wolverhampton SW)	O	X
J.Butcher (Coventry SW)	X	X
W.Cash (Stafford)	X	X
J.Cran (Beverley)	A	X
I. Duncan-Smith (Chingford)	A	X
Sir G.Gardiner (Reigate)	O	X
C.Gill (Ludlow)	O	X
T.Gorman (Billericay)	X	X
W.Hawksley (Halesowen)	O	A
T.Jessel (Twickenham)	X	X
Sir I.Lawrence (Burton)	O	X
B.Legg (Milton Keynes SW)	O	X
E.Leigh (Gainsborough)	X	X
T.Marlow (Northampton)	X	X
R.Shepherd (Aldridge)	X	X
Sir T.Skeet (Beds N)	X	X
M.Spicer (Worcs S)	O	X
W.Sweeney (Vale of Glamorgan)	X	X
Sir P.Tapsell (Lindsey E)	X	X
Sir T.Taylor (Southend E)	X	X
B.Walker (Tayside N)	X	X
J.Wilkinson (Ruislip)	X	X
Mrs A.Winterton (Congleton)	X	X

One Conservative, R.Allason, abstained in both votes on Friday 23. All other Conservatives voted with the Government.

TWENTY FOUR
FOREIGN AFFAIRS

The premiership of John Major seemed likely to mark the moment at which Britain finally had to say goodbye to its cherished "special relationship" with the United States. In reality, that relationship had been fading for 40 years; compared with the Churchill-Roosevelt era it was little more then a sentimental pretence. Personal chemistry had done more than political necessity to keep it alive, but Bush-Thatcher was never the same as Reagan-Thatcher, and Bush-Major, despite the close and successful collaboration of the Gulf war, meant still less.

Clinton-Major marked a further decline. The efforts of Conservative Central Office to help the Bush campaign — backed by a trawl of Home Office records at the Republicans' suggestion in the hope of finding something discreditable about Clinton's time in England — rankled with the new president, and though spokesmen were wheeled on to say it had all been forgiven and forgotten, Major's long wait for a date with Clinton told a different story. A further cause of possible trouble was Ireland, with Clinton committed by a campaign pledge to despatch a peace envoy to the North — though once he was in the White House, that promise was whittled away.

Few, even so, were fooled by both sides' assurances after Major and Clinton at last met in Washington in February 1993 that nothing had really changed. "The relationship is special to me personally and will be special to the United States as long as I am serving here," the president said on February 24, to Major's obvious delight. Major, unlike his predecessor, saw Britain's future in Europe; but espousing Europe did not mean renouncing Atlanticism.

To the extent that Britain was often more likely than some of its European Community partners to understand, even to share, US preoccupations, Britain could still hope to be *primus inter pares*, and the Gulf war served to reinforce the old conviction that of all America's allies, Britain was the trustiest and most enduring. Yet for any US president, old ties with Britain could no longer carry much weight. It was one of a number of middle-ranking countries which mattered to the Americans, but on any president's scale, Germany now was likely to count for more.

Britain could hardly mediate as European and American views diverged over Bosnia. At the start, the fate of the former Yugoslavia was identified in the US as Europe's problem; but through American eyes,

Europe's response seemed uncertain and incoherent. Clinton favoured tougher measures to enforce the air exclusion zone. Along with the Germans (and Margaret Thatcher) he also favoured lifting the sanctions on arms sales to the Bosnian Muslims. Here Britain was his firmest adversary, successfully, but frustratingly, counselling caution, underlining military warnings of the dangers of getting bogged down inextricably in a war that could not be won.

Major's immediate, approving reaction to the air strike against Iraq in June 1993 was by contrast all that any American president could have asked. Off the record, though, London was sceptical, and Major was said to have privately urged a limited and proportionate response. The opposition parties were publicly hostile.

Yugoslavia

Britain had never wanted to recognise Croatia: but in the end, German pressure prevailed. That led to the recognition of Bosnia-Herzegovina, which the ever-cautious British foreign secretary, Douglas Hurd, saw as a potentially lethal — if unhappily now unavoidable — error. And throughout the dreadful events that followed, Britain's attitude to the problems of the former Yugoslavia remained one of dogged caution. Though largely echoed by the Labour leadership, it left many other people, watching the drama unravel nightly on their television screens, angry, disturbed and frustrated.

Britain hoped from the start, and persisted in hoping even when the prospects looked bleakest, that Serbs,

Croats and Muslims could yet be reconciled by diplomacy. On a British initiative, a conference was called in London in August 1992 which led to the establishment of continuing peace talks in Geneva. The EC peace initiative begun by Lord Carrington and now taken on by David, now Lord, Owen was merged with the initiative which the UN had entrusted to the former US secretary of state Cyrus Vance.

The Vance-Owen process produced much negotiation, occasional short-lived ceasefires, and eventually a doomed plan for the cantonisation of Bosnia. But the fighting and the slaughter grew worse.

There were two agreed courses of action. First, an international attempt to bring *humanitarian aid* to the most severely stricken areas. On February 21 1992, the Security Council approved the establishment of a UN Protection Force (UNProFor). On August 18, John Major announced that Britain had offered the UN 1,800 troops: they were despatched in October and their number eventually grew to nearly 3,000. And second, the *imposition of sanctions* on the Serbs, who were commonly identified as the worst aggressors — a course which the UN Security Council approved on May 30, 1992. Sanctions alone, it was recognised, were never likely to be enough, especially when at the start they were easily evaded — as Labour, who in other respects did not quarrel with Government policy, repeatedly complained.

Once the Russian referendum was out of the way (the Russians were more sympathetic to the Serbs than

**OFFICIAL DEVELOPMENT ASSISTANCE FROM OECD MEMBERS
AS % OF DONOR GNP**

	1980	1985	1991
Canada	0.43	0.49	0.45
Denmark	0.74	0.80	0.96
France	0.63	0.78	0.62
Germany	0.44	0.47	0.41
Italy	0.15	0.26	0.30
Japan	0.32	0.29	0.32
Sweden	0.78	0.86	0.92
United Kingdom	0.35	0.33	0.32
United States	0.27	0.24	0.20

The UK's record in detail 1979-1991

79	83	84	85	86	87	88	89	90	91
0.52	0.35	0.33	0.33	0.31	0.28	0.32	0.31	0.27	0.32

Source: World Development Report 1993

TOP 10 RECIPIENTS OF UK OVERSEAS AID FROM 1979
(Individual years may be unrepresentative because of response to particular crises).

Average 1981-85		Average 1986-90		1991 (£m)	
1. India	120.7	India	102.1	India	114.0
2. Kenya	36.4	Bangladesh	45.1	Bangladesh	66.4
3. Sudan	34.8	Kenya	53.9	Zimbabwe	53.4
4. Bangladesh	31.7	Malawi	33.4	Kenya	49.5
5. Zambia	28.0	Pakistan	29.2	Ghana	43.2
6. Tanzania	27.7	Ghana	28.6	Zambia	41.8
7. Sri Lanka	26.5	Tanzania	27.4	Tanzania	40.3
8. Zimbabwe	25.9	Sudan	25.0	Nigeria	38.6
9. Indonesia	21.4	Zambia	24.4	Pakistan	37.1
10. Pakistan	18.9	Mozambique	21.8	Malawi	37.0

Source: derived from Annual Abstract of Statistics

others on the Security Council) sanctions were duly tightened. They progressively bit on the Serb economy and in the spring of 1993 produced, as intended, Serb pressure on Bosnia's Serbs to settle with the Croats and Muslims. By the summer, sanctions, according to the foreign secretary, Douglas Hurd, were bringing "slow ruin" to Serbia.

As the plight of Bosnia worsened, a sort of impromptu "war party" appeared in Britain clamouring for stronger action. Its line-up was unexpected; the former Conservative prime minister Margaret Thatcher, the former Labour leader Michael Foot, and the Liberal Democrat leader Paddy Ashdown were among those who called for tough action — though on different lines. A group of Labour left wingers demanded military action.

Impatience with the Government's caution came to a head after the massacre at Srebrenica on April 13 1993. The following night after television film from Srebrenica, Margaret Thatcher denounced Europe's inactivity in a series of TV interviews. "I am ashamed of the European Community, that this is happening in the heart of Europe and they have not done anything about it," she said. "There is no conscience. We have been like accomplices to massacre."

Thatcher demanded that the arms embargo imposed in September 1991 should be lifted to give the embattled Bosnian Muslims a better chance to defend themselves. An ultimatum should be delivered to the Serbs, she said, to accept the plans for cantonisation drawn up by Vance and Owen, or face retaliation through air strikes or even troop deployment on the ground. The Labour leader, John Smith, called for the first time for air strikes against Serbian supply lines.

The groundswell of concern evoked by the Thatcher interviews drew from the foreign secretary, Douglas Hurd, a characteristic exposition of the Government's policy. "We are all conscious of the moral and public pressures on the international community to do more, to intervene more actively to stop the carnage," he told the Commons on April 29. "Those pressures are sincere and must be taken seriously. However we also have to remember the nature of this problem. We are witnessing a civil war in Bosnia which is encouraged and overwhelmingly fuelled by Belgrade. We should not pretend that, from outside, we can ensure a solution. Even a prolonged military commitment by the international community could not guarantee that."

The options for tougher action most often put forward fell into three groups:

● *Air strikes* — against supply lines, against artillery positions, or even within Serbia. But apart from the difficulties of picking out military targets efficiently enough to avoid the slaughter of civilians, air strikes could imperil troops on the ground and would mean abandoning the UN's humanitarian aid effort.

● *The lifting of the arms embargo* — advocated by Thatcher, but strongly opposed by Ashdown. But the British government remained resolutely opposed. The effect, Hurd had argued in a letter to the Daily Telegraph, would merely be to establish "a level

GROSS UK PUBLIC EXPENDITURE ON AID TO DEVELOPING COUNTRIES

year	amount £m
1987-88	1,410
1988-89	1,607
1989-90	1,733
1990-91	1,883
1991-92	2,021

Source: written answer, May 17 1993

REBELLIONS AGAINST THE GULF WAR

MPs voting against armed intervention against Iraq, January 21 1993 (on a motion for the adjournment):

Mrs I.Adams, T.Benn, A.F.Bennett, D.Canavan, M.Chisholm, H.Cohen, J.Corbyn, T.Dalyell, T.Davis, G.Galloway, B.Grant, J.Hood, K.Livingstone, E.Loyden, J.McAllion, M.Madden, Mrs A.Mahon, C.Pickthall, A.Simpson, D. Skinner, Mrs A. Wise. Tellers H.Barnes, R Cryer (all Labour)

killing field". Later there were sharp public differences on this issue between the Americans and Germans, who favoured ending the embargo, and the French and Germans who did not. Disagreements came to a head at an EC summit in Copenhagen on June 21. It was noted that the countries which favoured lifting the embargo did not have troops in the area: those who opposed to it did.

● Deploying many more *troops on the ground* — that more troops might need to be sent, to police a settlement if the Vance-Owen process achieved one, or to defend such safe havens as the UN might establish, was generally agreed, but in the context of a prior agreement between the warring parties. That troops should be sent in the sort of numbers which could halt the fighting by military means alone, or make possible the establishment of a UN protectorate for Bosnia, seemed to most MPs an unacceptable risk and one which public opinion would not tolerate.

The most compelling factor holding the Government back from further involvement was the strong and consistent advice of the military, who in Britain as in the United States feared being bogged down for years, perhaps with little to show for it. For them, the parallel was not Kuwait, or the Falklands, but Vietnam. But there was also sometimes detectable a kind of world-weary cynicism. The chairman of the Commons select committee on foreign affairs, David Howell, told the House on April 29: "I confess that I used to think that this was just another Balkan mess, that they have been at it for hundreds of years — we

can all remember Balkan wars — and if we could somehow put a ring fence around all that, we could stand aside and walk away." But Europe had fallen into a major diplomatic ambush and allowed premature recognition of Croatia and then the independent state of Bosnia — "probably the biggest diplomatic blunders since the second world war". We could not, he now concluded, walk away after that; and we could not walk away from genocide.

But the most characteristic Government note — sad, perhaps fatalistic — came from the Foreign Office minister, Douglas Hogg, on May 24 1993, immediately after a foreign minister's meeting in Washington which appeared tacitly to endorse the end of any hopes for the tripartite division of Bosnia envisaged by Vance and Owen, and acceptance that the Serbs and Croatians would take what they wanted and leave the Bosnian Muslims with the meagre remainder. Patrick Cormack (Staffordshire S), a back-bench Conservative who had argued the Bosnian Muslim case with great passion over many months, asked at the end of Hogg's bleak statement whether there was anything he could say which might sustain hope. "My honourable friend is right to say this is the greatest tragedy, the greatest crime, Europe has seen since the end of the second world war," Hogg replied. "He has fairly asked whether I can bring comfort. The answer is: I cannot. I wish that I could."

Hong Kong

Worsted in electoral battle by the Liberal Democrats in April 1992, the former Conservative party chairman Chris Patten found himself six months later locked in jarring conflict with the might of China.

Patten's appointment as Governor signalled a startling change both in style and content. Until now, Britain had shown little passion for the cause of democratisation in the colony: Patten put it at the very head of his agenda.

Until now negotiations with the Chinese had been largely conducted in a sort of twilight zone, away from prying eyes, by diplomats who prided themselves on knowing the Chinese mind. "Quiet but tenacious negotiation with Beijing in the interest of Hong Kong, pressing hard, but avoiding open breaches and trials of strength for which Hong Kong will have to pay," as one old hand, Sir Percy Cradock, described it. Now they were in the hands of a politician, not a diplomat, and a politician who believed in bringing issues into the open and involving public opinion.

So the Governor's use of his maiden policy speech on October 7 1992 to outline changes designed to shift Hong Kong, in its final years before China took over, sharply towards democracy, were greeted with outrage — and not only by the Chinese. Some old hands thought the Governor's tactics were doomed. A former acting governor, Sir David Akers-Jones, signed up as an adviser to the Chinese government, declaring that in his view the commitment to democracy was quite wrong.

Patten's aim was to alter the system as drastically as he could without infringing China's Basic Law drawn up for application after the hand-over. He was not permitted to open up all 60 seats on the Legislative Council to direct election. The limit was 20. But he could change the rules for the 30 seats elected by "functional constituencies" — mainly white-collar professionals — by redefining these constituencies to include most of Hong Kong's working population. And he could reconstitute the electoral committee which would fill another 10 seats. That was what he proposed.

Well within the Basic Law, Patten contended. Indefensibly outside it, said China. On the letter of the law, Patten was right; but the spirit of the law was a different matter, since China had seen the Basic Law as a defence against the growth of democracy, something its leaders did not wish to see encouraged by example on the mainland. Why was it, they asked with asperity, that when Britain had been in unchallenged command it had no commitment to democracy, but when China was due to take over, the issue became all-important? (There had been no direct elections to the Legislative Council at all until 1991.) Whatever the merits of that, however, one thing was clear: the thirst for democratic institutions now ran high in Hong Kong and the Governor's determination to go as far as he could kept his popularity ratings equally high.

Negotiations between the two sides came to a virtual standstill. Four times Patten postponed putting his Bill before the Legislative Council to give China more time. But deadlock continued, and to further Chinese protests he published it on March 12, 1993.

At one level, the enterprise appeared doomed. From July 1 1997, when it assumed full control, China would have the power to dismantle such democratic edifices as Britain's last Governor-General might have chosen to create. But Patten's supporters believed that it wouldn't, for fear of imperilling policies of economic modernisation, attracting capital, maximising foreign exchange earnings; also for fear of impeding any hope of peaceful reunion with Taiwan.

On April 14 a deal was done which allowed talks to resume. Patten conceded Chinese demands that Hong Kong should not be directly represented: government officials would be there as advisers, not members of the negotiating teams. But suspicions of British duplicity ran higher than ever. Hopes of bringing the issue back to the Legislative Council before it broke for the summer recess in late July were abandoned.

The Gulf and after

The aftermath of the Gulf war of 1991 troubled the Government both abroad and at home. On August 18 1992, in the same statement which announced the despatch of troops to Yugoslavia, the prime minister said that RAF Tornados had been committed to the Gulf to enforce a no-fly zone over southern Iraq. On June 27 1993, Major gave strong public support (despite private Whitehall reservations) for rocket attacks ordered by Clinton on Saddam Hussein's security headquarters. Clinton said the US had evidence of an Iraqi plot to assassinate former presi-

dent George Bush in Kuwait in April. Both Labour and the Liberal Democrats condemned the US action, which Labour's spokesman, George Robertson, called "dubious in legality, questionable in morality, haphazard in its military impact, and potentially devastating in diplomacy".

At home, Major's government found itself in serious trouble over arms sold to Iraq before the Gulf war. Allegations on this score had appeared from time to time in the press. When the Sunday Times accused the former Department of Trade and Industry minister, Alan Clark of turning a blind eye to arms sales which broke Government guidelines on sales to Iraq, Clark threatened to sue.

But Clark's evidence, on November 4 1992 in the course of an Old Bailey trial, appeared to confirm the allegation completely. The court was hearing the case against three executives of a company called Matrix Churchill, charged with deceiving the DTI by falsely describing the use to which exported equipment was to be put. The executives told the court that the DTI had known all along that the equipment was not for peaceful purposes. Clark confirmed their story. Asked about a minute which recorded him as saying that the cargo was "for general engineering purposes", Clark — echoing a celebrated line of Sir Robert Armstrong during the Falklands war — replied: "Well, it's our old friend, being economical, isn't it." "With the truth?" he was asked. "With the actualité," he replied.

On November 9 the prosecution said that in the light of this evidence it could not proceed. The three executives were acquitted. Next day, the attorney-general, Sir Nicholas Lyell, announced an inquiry into arms licensing policy as it concerned Iraq. Lord Justice Scott was appointed to conduct the inquiry, whose terms of reference allowed it to look at other cases besides that of Matrix Churchill. Many of the issues the inquiry would be asked to resolve were rehearsed in a Commons debate on November 23. These were among them:

● The guidelines to which the Government said it was working were those laid down in 1985 by the then foreign secretary, Sir Geoffrey Howe. As late as December 1990 a DTI minister, Tim Sainsbury, told the Commons: "The guidelines are clear. They were set out in 1985 and since then they have been scrupulously observed and carefully followed in the issuing of licences."

● Yet evidence in the Matrix Churchill case had shown that the guidelines were relaxed at the end of 1988, a decision confirmed at a ministerial meeting in April 1989. (A former trade and industry secretary, Paul Channon, was to tell the Scott inquiry on May 19 1993 that the policy was repeatedly changed without adjusting the guidelines: "I think they changed the rules as they went on," he said.) So why had the public and parliament not been told — or indeed been led to believe, as by Sainsbury, that nothing had altered?

● Why, when ministers knew all this, had the prosecution of the three Matrix Churchill executives — one of whom, to compound the embarrassment, now turned out to have been working for British Intelligence — been allowed to proceed, with nothing done to save them from possible conviction?

● And why, even more specifically, had four ministers — Michael Heseltine, Kenneth Clarke, Malcolm Rifkind and Tristan Garel-Jones — signed Public Interest Immunity Certificates asking the court that certain government information should not be disclosed? As it happened the court disagreed; and in any case, Clark's testimony aborted the trial. But that could not have been foreseen; and in other circumstances, it might have made a wrongful conviction more likely. The documents the ministers had tried to suppress proved vital to the defence at the trial.

The Opposition, whose pursuit of ministers over Matrix Churchill was as vigorous as anything it managed all year, compiled a lengthening list of alleged ministerial culprits. Clark — though in a sense, having finally told the truth, he was also a hero. The four signatories of the Public Interest Immunity certificates — plus the attorney-general, who told them it was their duty to do it, a ruling others challenged. William Waldegrave of the Foreign Office and Lord Trefgarne of the DTI, who had been at vital meetings when the guidelines shifted.

Also the two ripest targets of all: Margaret Thatcher, who as prime minister must, it was argued, have chaired crucial meetings; and Major, since as foreign secretary his department was closely involved. Thatcher, too, had told the Commons in November 1989: "Supplies of British defence equipment to Iraq and Iran continue to be

governed by the guidelines introduced in 1985." Major had told them
in November 1992: "From 1985 until
the Iraqi invasion of Kuwait (1990) the
Government operated under guidelines set out by the then foreign secretary."

And Matrix Churchill were not the
only casualties. Stuart Blackledge, a
former director of the Ordtec military
engineering firm, had been convicted
and given a suspended sentence on
another Customs prosecution for
evading export controls. Peter
Mitchell, managing director of Walter
Somers, and Chris Cowley, an engi-
neer, had been arrested during Customs inquiries into the export of
British made parts for an Iraqi supergun and charged with breaking the
arms embargo. Cowley spent 15 days
in jail on remand. The Tory MP Sir Hal
Miller said he had discussed the
supergun with the relevant government agencies which had let it go
ahead. He was ready to testify, but the
prosecutions of Mitchell and Cowley
were suddenly dropped. On May 24
1993 Miller told the Scott inquiry of a
conversation with the then attorney-
general Sir Patrick Mayhew in the
lobby of the House of Commons
about this affair and his willingness to
give evidence for the accused. "You
wouldn't do that, would you?" Mayhew had replied. In evidence to the
Scott inquiry, he repudiated this
account. He denied he had put any
pressure on Sir Hal to withhold his
evidence.

Overseas aid

Major's government stuck faithfully to
the traditions of governments before it
— pledging to meet the UN target of
an aid budget equivalent to 0.7 per
cent of gross national product, while
doing nothing to suggest that this target would be achieved in the lifetime
of most voters. It would be done "as
soon as possible" Major told the Rio
Earth Summit. Labour railed against
this delay, but though they could fairly say that Britain's performance had
slipped since 1979 (when the level
was 0.52 per cent) they had never
come close to the target themselves.
The best that could be said was that
the cuts predicted in the autumn programme did not occur. A concession
to popular concern, said a spokesman
for the main aid charities. But perhaps
the fear of something worse had been
created to reconcile people to what
was in fact announced: aid to be sustained at the present level, but to be
frozen there for three years, implying
cuts in real terms. Based on recent
expenditure figures, said the World
Development Movement, it would
take Britain 95 years to reach the UN
target.

Even that was a minor matter in
the context of third world debt.

Six MPs, two from each of the
three main parties, set out the statistics
in a letter to the Times. A quarter of all
exports, the equivalent of $10 billion a
year, was being drained out of Africa
simply to service the debt. Africa was
spending four times as much on debt
repayments as on health care. Since
1980, its debt burden had trebled to
$183 million, the equivalent of 109 per
cent of its GNP. In Zambia, every
man, woman and child owed foreign
creditors twice the national average
wage. Since the G7 first acknowl-

edged the urgency of the issue (1987) the debt had increased by $30 billion. The MPs called for immediate implementation of the Trinidad two-thirds formula. (Letter to the Times, July 6 1993 from David Howell, Con, Guildford; Simon Hughes, LibDem, Bermondsey; Jim Lester, Con, Broxtowe; Michael Meacher, Lab, Oldham W; Sir David Steel, LibDem, Tweeddale; and Mike Watson, Lab, Glasgow Central.) ●

Betrayed: Alan Clark's admission that he had been economical with the *realité* kept Paul Henderson of Matrix Churchill out of prison

TWENTY FIVE
DEFENCE

The end of the cold war, it was sometimes euphorically predicted, would give birth to a New World Order; also, as swords were beaten back into ploughshares, a Peace Dividend. But the New World Order proved to be riddled with disorder, and the Peace Dividend blossomed only fitfully. In a curious way, the cold war period began to be mourned as a time of vanished stability. Menace had made way not for tranquility but for confusion and doubt. The defence secretary, Malcolm Rifkind, caught the mood when he presented his White Paper, Defending Our Future, to the Commons on July 5 1993. "The certainty has vanished, to be replaced by a broad spectrum of risk and uncertainty" he said.

To the Opposition parties, which had demanded a full-scale defence review, ministers were able to say that a review compiled as the Evil Empire breathed its last would already have looked inappropriate a mere two years later. Instead, the Government offered a "major restructuring", proceeding by stages, and built round new concepts like mobility, flexibility and responsiveness rather than granite confrontation.

The progress began with Options for Change (1990) which cut manpower by 20 per cent to match a defence budget set to decline by 12 per cent over five years. The army suffered most, because the first obvious move was to halve the size of the British Army of the Rhine, which for 40 years had been committed to Nato's defence of Western Germany. Later, though, the cuts were modified, restoring two infantry regiments.

The 1993 White Paper was designed to cope with a further budgetary cut of £1 billion, to meet new Government expenditure targets set out in the Autumn Statement nine months before. This time, redressing the balance, the navy and air force took the worst of the punishment. The surface fleet was to be reduced from "about 40" destroyers and frigates to "about 35". Four submarines of the Upholder class, newly built at a cost of almost £900 million, would be sold or mothballed. The naval manpower target fell for the second time in a few months, from 55,000 to 52,500. The air force faced a cut of 22 Tornado F3 fighters, with one squadron — now enforcing the no-fly zone over Bosnia — destined to disappear. Its manpower would be cut from 75,000 to 70,000. The third phase of the army's multiple launch rocket system programme, on which some £100 million had been spent, would also be scrapped.

The one conspicuous omission in

this restructuring was the nuclear weapons programme. The context of defence strategy might have changed utterly, but the policy of nuclear deterrence remained sacrosanct. The White Paper described it as "the ultimate guarantee of the United Kingdom's security". But even as these words were published, a blow was struck at the programme by a distant hand. The US president, Bill Clinton, imposed a moratorium on nuclear testing in Nevada until September 1994, with the clear implication that it might continue thereafter, preparing the way for the signing of the long-awaited Comprehensive Test Ban treaty in 1996. Britain, eager to resume tests — safety factors were cited as the reason — had lobbied vigorously against this restraint. This might even, some suggested, be the beginning of the end for Britain's role as a nuclear power, which all three main parties had been committed at the 1992 election to maintain.

The 1993 White Paper was ill-received by some of the back-bench Tory MPs who specialised in defence. Already before it was published the Commons select committee on defence had argued that the services would be stretched to meet their commitments on the level of resources now available. Rifkind's restructuring, they argued, seemed to owe rather more to Treasury stringency than to the assessments of present risk set out in its pages. "Thus far, and no further" these MPs growled.

At other times, the cuts in defence spending announced between 1990 and 1993 might have won a readier welcome from Labour. But they fell in a time of heavy unemployment, to which they seemed certain to add not just through direct manpower reductions but through the knock-on effects in ancillary industries. The problem of this negative peace dividend was illustrated on June 24 1993, shortly before the White Paper appeared, when the Government ended weeks of debate and speculation about which of the naval dockyards would get the £5 billion job of refitting the navy's nuclear-powered Trident submarines. The two contenders were Devonport, Plymouth, and Rosyth in Scotland. The choice seemed likely to turn partly on judgments of expertise; partly on cost (Devonport's bid was lower on the Government's calculations by £64 billion, though a late undercutting bid from Rosyth was ruled out on technical grounds); and partly on political calculation. Which would be worse, ministers asked themselves: the boost to SNP and Labour support in Scotland if Rosyth was rejected — or the further lift in support for the Liberal Democrats in the south west if Devonport was disappointed?

The outcome was a compromise. Devonport got the nuclear refitting, but Rosyth was offered a consolation prize in the form of a promise to allocate 12 years of work on surface ships to its yard. Rifkind told the Commons on June 24 1993 that because of this concession only 450 of the 3,700 jobs at Rosyth would be lost. Next day, however, the management estimated that job losses might reach 1,000.●

GOVERNMENT SPENDING ON DEFENCE

1 Total spending at current prices £billion
2. Total spending in real terms at 1991-2 prices £billion
3. % of government expenditure
4. % of GDP

	1978-1979	1983-1984	1984-1985	1985-1986	1986-1987	1987-1988	1988-1989	1989-1990	1990-1991	1991-1992	1992-3 (estimate)
1	7.6	15.7	17.4	18.2	18.4	18.9	19.2	20.8	21.8	23.0	23.8
2	20.5	25.1	26.3	26.2	25.7	25.0	23.6	24.0	23.3	23.0	22.8
3	10.1	11.1	11.4	11.3	10.9	10.6	10.3	10.1	9.8	9.4	8.9
4	4.5	5.2	5.3	5.1	4.8	4.4	4.0	4.0	3.9	4.0	4.0

DEFENCE SPENDING AS % OF GDP

Defence expenditure 1992

	£ per head	%
United States	820	5.2
Norway	605	3.4
France	538	3.4
UK	506	4.1
Denmark	366	1.9
Germany	358	2.2
Netherlands	350	2.5
Italy	286	2.0
Canada	278	2.0
Greece	276	5.5
Belgium	274	1.9
Luxembourg	211	1.2
Spain	166	1.7
Portugal	155	2.9
Turkey	65	3.9

BRITAIN'S DEFENCE ROLES, AS DEFINED IN 1992 AND 1993 WHITE PAPERS:

ONE: Protection and security of UK and dependent territories even where there is no major external threat; surveillance and policing of territorial waters and airspace; military support to machinery of government in war; support to civil power (as in N Ireland). Nuclear forces "provide the ultimate guarantee of the United Kingdom's security".

TWO: Insure against major external threat to UK and allies - discharged through NATO.

THREE: Promoting wider security interests through maintenance of international peace and stability, including participation in UN operations, eg in former Yugoslavia.

1993 WHITE PAPER: THE DECISIONS

NAVY

Frigates down from "about 40" to "about 35"

Minesweepers and minehunters reduced by nine.

Four new Upholder submarines to be sold or leased.

No further war role for Royal Yacht Britannia.

Manpower down from 55,000 to 52,500.

RAF

Tornado F3 fighters down from 122 to 100; 23 Squadron to be axed

Extra resources for support helicopters and transport aircraft

The £32 billion Eurofighter 2000 cornerstone of future capability

Plans for advanced missile defence system on British coast to replace the Bloodhound anti-aircraft system.

Tanker and transport planes to fall from 93 to 90

Queen's Flight of three BAe 146 jets and two Wessex helicopters remain on call for casualty evacuation

Manpower down from 75,000 to 70,000

ARMY

Orders expected for a further 200 Challenger 2s

Manpower up from 116,000 to 119,000 because of earlier decision to keep two infantry regiments earmarked for removal in Options for Change

1993 WHITE PAPER: THE FORCES THAT REMAIN

Showing strengths in 1990; as reduced in Options for Change; as further reduced in the White Paper

	1990	Options for Change	White Paper
NAVY			
Nuclear powered ballistic Missile submarines	4	4	4
Nuclear powered submarines	14	12	12
Conventionally powered submarines	10	4	0
Aircraft carriers	3	3	3
Destroyers/frigates	44	40*	35*
Helicopter carrier	0	1	1
Landing platform decks	2	2	2
Landing ships logistic	5	5	5
Minesweepers	38	34	25
RM Commando brigades	3	3	3
Sea harriers	24	22	22
ARMY			
Infantry battalions	55	38	40
Armoured regiments	13	8	8
Armoured recce regiments	5	2	2
Artillery regiments	20	15	15
Engineer regiments	13	10	10
Army Air Corps regiments	4	5	5
AIR FORCE			
Tornado F3	92	122	100
Phantoms	65	0	0
Hawks	72	52	50
Awacs	0	7	6
Tornado GR 1/1a/1b	148	112	112
Harriers	74	52	52
Jaguars	40	40	40
Buccaneers	30	0	0
Nimrods	35	27	27
Support helicopters	93	90	90
Transport and tanker aircraft	94	93	90

*approx. Precise figuires withheld by MoD

Front line: IRA outrages on mainland Britain diverted public attention away from the killing fields of Northern Ireland, right

TWENTY SIX
NORTHERN IRELAND

The death toll from the troubles in Northern Ireland, which passed 3,000 in August 1992, continued to climb though 1993 on the same often arbitrary pattern. The biggest shift had been the increase in murders committed by "loyalists", which in 1992 overtook the number ascribed to Republicans but neither crimes against people nor crimes against property got the same attention if committed across the water as they did when they happened on the mainland. The bomb that went off in Warrington on March 20 1993 fired the nation's anger as little had done since Eniskillen, mainly because two children were killed — Tim Parry, who was 12, and Johnathan Ball, who was three.

People marched in Dublin and in mainland cities and once again it was claimed that something, deep down, had changed, that patience with terrorist violence had this time run its course, that the hopes of ordinary people for an end to senseless killing must now prevail. The Warrington bomb prompted less response in Northern Ireland, which had grown used to such tragedies. Little was printed in London about the death of four Catholics in the hitherto unheard of village of Castlerock, Co Londonderry, five days later and in a week when "loyalists" murdered six people

in 48 hours. That was almost routine.

Yet there had been a shift in IRA activity, with the mainland bombing campaign stepped up in the knowledge that attacks in England would get greater publicity. Targets on the mainland were chosen, as they had for a long while been in the province, for the disruption they caused to commercial life and the spectacular cost of repairing the damage. One man, a freelance photographer, was killed by the bomb in the City of London on April 24 1993 which caused even greater damage than the City bomb days after the 1992 election. The cost of the bombings in Belfast, Portadown and Magherafelt on May 20, 22 and 23, though minor compared with the cost in the City, was stunning on any other scale: some £28 million.

There were few new initiatives even to be considered. In what looked like a vote of no confidence in the previous arrangements, the home secretary Kenneth Clarke transferred the lead responsibility for intelligence work against the IRA from the Special Branch of the Metropolitan Police to MI5. And there were security successes, including the interception of a bomb meant for Canary Wharf.

But those who aspired to government had, for most of this period, little new to offer. In the 1992 election,

Northern Ireland was scarcely mentioned. Labour wanted a united Ireland — but only on the basis of consent. The Liberal Democrats seemed to say the same thing the other way round: they accepted that Northern Ireland should remain part of the UK until the free consent of a majority was expressed for change. The Conservatives, though the party of union, did not always sound very different. "Many people," said the new Northern Ireland secretary Sir Patrick Mayhew in a somewhat unguarded interview with Die Zeit, "believe that we would not want to release Northern Ireland. To be honest, we would, with pleasure!" And then, recollecting himself: "No, not with pleasure, I take that back. But we would not stand in the way if that was the will of the majority."

Later he went on to marvel at the cost of the province: "three billion pounds for one and a half million people! None of our strategic or economic interests are at stake there. But as long as the majority wishes to remain in the United Kingdom, we will pay the £3 billion without complaining."

No mainland party favoured withdrawal. Every year, the Government proposed to renew the Prevention of Terrorism Act and Labour opposed it, arguing that even some of the Government's own advisers had told them to drop it; the Government in return accused Labour of being soft on terrorism. That was now little more than ritual. Elsewhere there were few open disagreements.

All mainland parties backed the Anglo-Irish Agreement and the process of talks begun by Peter Brooke, now taken over by Mayhew. In terms

of breaking historic taboos, these made significant advances after the 1992 election. On June 14 1992 a meeting took place between representatives of Northern Ireland opinion and representatives of the Irish government. On June 30 detailed talks began in London between Northern Ireland politicians and ministers from the Republic. Most remarkable of all, on September 21, an Ulster Unionist leader, James Molyneaux, arrived for talks in Dublin — the first such visit by a Unionist leader since 1922. (Dr Ian Paisley's Democratic Unionists boycotted the occasion.)

That such dialogue even began represented an advance. But the talks got nowhere, as Mayhew had to report to the Commons on November 11. By then Paisley and his colleagues had become semi-detached from the discussions, insisting that the Republic must make the first move in eliminating articles 2 and 3 of its constitution, which laid claim to Northern Ireland. In fact, the Labour leader in the Republic, Dick Spring, who was both deputy premier and foreign minister in the new Finna Fail/Labour coalition, had made it plain that articles 2 and 3 were no longer sacrosanct. But the Government in the Republic was not prepared to contemplate their abandonment of them unilaterally; only in the context of a more comprehensive package. In any case, there would have to be a referendum first. To Unionists that sounded too much like an enhanced Anglo-Irish Agreement.

In the spring of 1993 the British Government's position shifted. Until now it had held the ring while the parties talked. But on April 23, Mayhew

HOW NORTHERN IRELAND COSTS MORE

Identifiable general government spending per head by area & function
£ per head — totals from 1992 territorial analysis

	England	Scotland	Wales	N Ireland
Agriculture, fisheries, food, forestry	20	49	51	115
Trade, industry, energy, employment	70	162	147	299
Roads and transport	118	142	145	91
Housing	78	127	112	154
Other environmental	116	152	172	182
Law, order, protective services	184	182	139	480
Education & science	455	605	454	660
National heritage	22	25	19	(3)
Health, personal social services	558	703	603	661
Social security	985	1,027	1,092	1,115
Miscellaneous		28	19	35
TOTAL	**2,604**	**3,202**	**2,953**	**3,832**
as % England	100	123	113	147

laid out in a speech at Liverpool the lines of a Government initiative: a "substantial" transfer of power from Whitehall to politicians in Northern Ireland, with a select committee to monitor powers retained in London. He specifically ruled out a joint Anglo-Irish authority. The SDLP was not pleased. Its leader, John Hume, had been holding exploratory talks, much attacked by the Unionist parties, with Gerry Adams of Sinn Fein. The two men now issued a statement rejecting an internal settlement "because it does not deal with all the relationships at the heart of the problem".

And then, quite suddenly, the political picture started to change, destroying bi-partisanship and abruptly ending an unusual period of harmony between London and Dublin symbolised by their commitment to the Brooke-Mayhew talks.

On June 29, the Guardian and the Irish Times carried reports that a document had been prepared by the Labour front bench spokesman on Northern Ireland, Kevin McNamara, advocating joint control over the province by London and Dublin. This was no new suggestion, but until now the Westminster parties had kept well clear of it.

McNamara's document was essentially a strategy for an incoming Labour government. The inter-party talks should be allowed to continue, it said, but if no progress was made within six months, a Labour government should open discussions with the Irish government about a system of shared responsibility, to run for 20 years. The Queen and the Irish president would be joint heads of state. The document admitted that this solu-

tion would need to be imposed against the wishes of the majority of Northern Irish citizens.

This was not a shadow Cabinet document, but the Government treated it as if it contained the secret thoughts of John Smith. John Major called it "a recipe for disaster", and Paisley "a recipe for civil war", Conservatives and Unionists called on Smith to sack McNamara, but although keeping his distance from the document, he did not.

Major now began to take a more militant tone in defence of the union - partly in response to McNamara, no doubt, but also because by now he needed Unionist votes to save him from defeat over Europe. Next, Spring suggested direct negotiations between London and Dublin, by-passing the province's politicians, with any solution which might be arrived at put to an all-Ireland referendum. These proposals surfaced in an interview in the Guardian on a day when Spring and Mayhew were due to meet, and they dominated the proceedings, with Mayhew declaring them unacceptable.

All this became interwoven with Major's attempts to recruit supporters for the night of the Commons vote on the Maastricht social chapter. Paisley's Democratic Unionists kept out of the bargaining, but rumours built up throughout the day that a deal had been done. When the nine Ulster Unionists voted with the Government, saving it from defeat on the first of the night's two votes, that suspicion hardened. But what were the terms of the deal? The setting up of a Commons select committee on Northern Ireland seemed imminent. But what else? A change in the ramshackle system

VICTIMS OF THE TROUBLES

Deaths in Northern Ireland 1969-93

	civilian	police	army	UDR
1969	12	1	0	0
1970	23	2	0	0
1971	115	11	43	5
1972	321	17	103	26
1973	171	13	58	8
1974	166	15	28	7
1975	216	11	14	6
1976	245	23	14	15
1977	69	14	15	14
1978	50	10	14	7
1979	51	14	38	10
1980	50	9	8	9
1981	57	21	10	13
1982	57	12	21	7
1983	44	18	5	10
1984	36	9	9	10
1985	25	23	2	4
1986	37	12	4	8
1987	66	16	3	8
1988	54	6	21	12
1989	39	9	12	2
1990	49	13	7	8
1991	75	6	5	8
1992	75	3	6*	-
1993 (to Aug 8)	30	3	6*	-

* Includes Royal Irish Regiment

Source: Northern Ireland Office

ELECTIONS IN NORTHERN IRELAND

Share of the vote 1985-90

	District** 1985	General* 1987	District** 1989	European** 1989	General* 1992	District** 1993
UUP	29.8	37.8	31.0	22.2	34.5	29.0
DUP	23.4	11.7	17.8	29.9	13.1	17.2
SDLP	17.6	21.1	20.9	25.5	23.5	21.9
Sinn Fein	11.8	11.4	11.1	9.2	10.0	12.5
Alliance	7.1	10.0	6.9	5.2	8.7	7.7

* First-past-the-post voting   ** Proportional representation

Source: Conservative Campaign Guide

which meant Northern Ireland legislation was largely processed by orders, debated late at night? More powers for district councils? Or action to diminish, if not to eliminate, the Anglo-Irish agreement? In Commons exchanges next morning, Major denied the lot. "Nothing was asked for, nothing was offered, and nothing was given," he said. Few on the Opposition benches believed him. But the suspicion developed that the Unionists would be backing the Government not just on the European issue but on others, effectively shoring up the prime minister's dwindling Commons majority. Some Tory MPs suggested that what had turned the Unionists was the spectre of McNamara as Northern Ireland secretary. ●

NORTHERN IRELAND TALKS SINCE THE 1992 ELECTION

April 27 - Inter-Governmental Conference met, London, announced suspension of its meetings to allow talks to be resumed

April 29 - First plenary session after election. Meetings in plenary and sub-committees through June.

STRAND TWO	STRAND THREE
June 19 - agenda setting meeting chaired by Sir Ninian Stephen, London	June 30 — first Strand Three meeting, London
July 6 - opening plenary session, London, chaired by Stephen	
July 15 Strand Two resumes in Belfast	
July 24 adjourned until September	July 28 - opening Strand Three plenary, Dublin,co-chairedby British and Irish
	Sept 1 - resume with meetings of business committee
	Sept 2 - plenary meetings resume, Belfast
Sept 10 - Continues with only token DUP representation	Sept 11 - resumes with plenary session, London
Sept 16 - DUP boycotts talks as protest against placing articles 2 and 3 last on agenda	
Sept 21 continues in Dublin without DUP	Sept 22 - continues in Dublin

Sept 25 - meeting between PM and Taoiseach in London announced final extension in suspension of Inter-Governmental Conference

Nov 10 - statement on progress to date: the two governments and the four NI parties agree further dialogue is necessary and desirable.

Nov 11 - Sir Patrick Mayhew says British Government is determined to persevere.

June 16 1993 - PM and Taoiseach meet, London. Call on political parties in NI to help in search for political progress; agree to continue active contacts with parties

ANALYSIS & MISCELLANY

CONTENTS

INDEX OF CONSTITUENCIES

Belfast South	SMYTH, Rev Martin	UU
Belfast West	HENDRON, Dr Joe	SDLP
Berkshire East	MACKAY, Andrew	Con
Berwick-upon-Tweed	BEITH, Alan	LD
Bethnal Green & Stepney	SHORE, Peter	Lab
Beverley	CRAN, James	Con
Bexhill & Battle	WARDLE, Charles	Con
Bexleyheath	TOWNSEND, Cyril	Con
Billericay	GORMAN, Mrs Teresa	Con
Birkenhead	FIELD, Frank	Lab
Birmingham Edgbaston	KNIGHT, Dame Jill	Con
Birmingham Erdington	CORBETT, Robin	Lab
Birmingham Hall Green	HARGREAVES, Andrew	Con
Birmingham Hodge Hill	DAVIS, Terry	Lab
Birmingham Ladywood	SHORT, Ms Clare	Lab
Birmingham Northfield	BURDEN, Richard	Lab
Birmingham Perry Barr	ROOKER, Jeff	Lab
Birmingham Selly Oak	JONES, Dr Lynne	Lab
Birmingham Small Heath	GODSIFF, Roger	Lab
Birmingham Sparkbrook	HATTERSLEY, Roy	Lab
Birmingham Yardley	MORRIS, Ms Estelle	Lab
Bishop Auckland	FOSTER, Derek	Lab
Blaby	ROBATHAN, Andrew	Con
Blackburn	STRAW, Jack	Lab
Blackpool North	ELLETSON, Harold	Con
Blackpool South	HAWKINS, Nicholas	Con
Blaenau Gwent	SMITH, Llew	Lab
Blaydon	McWILLIAM, John	Lab
Blyth Valley	CAMPBELL, Ronnie	Lab
Bolsover	SKINNER, Dennis	Lab
Bolton North East	THURNHAM, Peter	Con
Bolton South East	YOUNG, David	Lab
Bolton West	SACKVILLE, Tom	Con
Boothferry	DAVIS, David	Con
Bootle	BENTON, Joe	Lab
Bosworth	TREDINNICK, David	Con
Bournemouth East	ATKINSON, David	Con
Bournemouth West	BUTTERFILL, John	Con
Bow & Poplar	GORDON, Mrs Mildred	Lab
Bradford North	ROONEY, Terry	Lab
Bradford South	CRYER, Bob	Lab

Bradford West	MADDEN, Max	Lab
Braintree	NEWTON, Tony	Con
Brecon & Radnor	EVANS, Jonathan	Con
Brent East	LIVINGSTONE, Ken	Lab
Brent North	BOYSON, Sir Rhodes	Con
Brent South	BOATENG, Paul	Lab
Brentford & Isleworth	DEVA, Nirj	Con
Brentwood & Ongar	PICKLES, Eric	Con
Bridgend	GRIFFITHS, Win	Lab
Bridgwater	KING, Tom	Con
Bridlington	TOWNEND, John	Con
Brigg & Cleethorpes	BROWN, Michael	Con
Brighton Kemptown	BOWDEN, Andrew	Con
Brighton Pavilion	SPENCER, Sir Derek	Con
Bristol East	CORSTON, Ms Jean	Lab
Bristol North West	STERN, Michael	Con
Bristol South	PRIMAROLO, Ms Dawn	Lab
Bristol West	WALDEGRAVE, William	Con
Bromsgrove	THOMASON, Roy	Con
Broxbourne	ROE, Mrs Marion	Con
Broxtowe	LESTER, Jim	Con
Buckingham	WALDEN, George	Con
Burnley	PIKE, Peter	Lab
Burton	LAWRENCE, Sir Ivan	Con
Bury North	BURT, Alistair	Con
Bury South	SUMBERG, David	Con
Bury St Edmunds	SPRING, Richard	Con
Caernarfon	WIGLEY, Dafydd	PlC
Caerphilly	DAVIES, Ron	Lab
Caithness & Sutherland	MACLENNAN, Robert	LD
Calder Valley	THOMPSON, Sir Donald	Con
Cambridge	CAMPBELL, Mrs Anne	Lab
Cambridgeshire North East	MOSS, Malcolm	Con
Cambridgeshire South East	PAICE, James	Con
Cambridgeshire South West	GRANT, Sir Anthony	Con
Cannock & Burntwood	WRIGHT, Dr Tony	Lab
Canterbury	BRAZIER, Julian	Con
Cardiff Central	JONES, Jonathan Owen	Lab
Cardiff North	JONES, Gwilym	Con
Cardiff South	MICHAEL, Alun	Lab
Cardiff West	MORGAN, Rhodri	Lab

Carlisle	MARTLEW, Eric	Lab
Carmarthen	WILLIAMS, Dr Alan W	Lab
Carrick Cumnock & Doon Valley	FOULKES, George	Lab
Carshalton & Wallington	FORMAN, Nigel	Con
Castle Point	SPINK, Dr Robert	Con
Ceredigion & Pembroke North	DAFIS, Cynog	PIC
Cheadle	DAY, Stephen	Con
Chelmsford	BURNS, Simon	Con
Chelsea	SCOTT, Nicholas	Con
Cheltenham	JONES, Nigel	LD
Chertsey & Walton	PATTIE, Sir Geoffrey	Con
Chesham & Amersham	GILLAN, Ms Cheryl	Con
Chester, City of	BRANDRETH, Giles	Con
Chesterfield	BENN, Tony	Lab
Chichester	NELSON, Anthony	Con
Chingford	DUNCAN SMITH, Iain	Con
Chipping Barnet	CHAPMAN, Sydney	Con
Chislehurst	SIMS, Roger	Con
Chorley	DOVER, Den	Con
Christchurch	MADDOCK Diana	LD
Cirencester & Tewkesbury	CLIFTON-BROWN, Geoffrey	Con
City of London & Westminster South	BROOKE, Peter	Con
Clackmannan	O'NEILL, Martin	Lab
Clwyd North West	RICHARDS, Rod	Con
Clwyd South West	JONES, Martyn	Lab
Clydebank & Milngavie	WORTHINGTON, Tony	Lab
Clydesdale	HOOD, Jimmy	Lab
Colchester North	JENKIN, Bernard	Con
Colchester South & Maldon	WHITTINGDALE, John	Con
Colne Valley	RIDDICK, Graham	Con
Congleton	WINTERTON, Mrs Ann	Con
Conwy	ROBERTS, Sir Wyn	Con
Copeland	CUNNINGHAM, John	Lab
Corby	POWELL, William	Con
Cornwall North	TYLER, Paul	LD
Cornwall South East	HICKS, Robert	Con
Coventry North East	AINSWORTH, Robert	Lab
Coventry North West	ROBINSON, Geoffrey	Lab
Coventry South East	CUNNINGHAM, James	Lab
Coventry South West	BUTCHER, John	Con
Crawley	SOAMES, Nicholas	Con

Crewe & Nantwich	DUNWOODY, Mrs Gwyneth	Lab
Crosby	THORNTON, Sir Malcolm	Con
Croydon Central	BERESFORD, Sir Paul	Con
Croydon North East	CONGDON, David	Con
Croydon North West	WICKS, Malcolm	Lab
Croydon South	OTTAWAY, Richard	Con
Cumbernauld & Kilsyth	HOGG, Norman	Lab
Cunninghame North	WILSON, Brian	Lab
Cunninghame South	DONOHOE, Brian	Lab
Cynon Valley	CLWYD, Mrs Ann	Lab
Dagenham	GOULD, Bryan	Lab
Darlington	MILBURN, Alan	Lab
Dartford	DUNN, Robert	Con
Daventry	BOSWELL, Timothy	Con
Davyhulme	CHURCHILL, Winston	Con
Delyn	HANSON, David	Lab
Denton & Reddish	BENNETT, Andrew	Lab
Deptford see Lewisham Deptford		
Derby North	KNIGHT, Gregory	Con
Derby South	BECKETT, Mrs Margaret	Lab
Derbyshire North East	BARNES, Harry	Lab
Derbyshire South	CURRIE, Mrs Edwina	Con
Derbyshire West	McLOUGHLIN, Patrick	Con
Devizes	ANCRAM, Michael	Con
Devon North	HARVEY, Nick	LD
Devon West & Torridge	NICHOLSON, Mrs Emma	Con
Dewsbury	TAYLOR, Mrs Ann	Lab
Don Valley	REDMOND, Martin	Lab
Doncaster Central	WALKER, Sir Harold	Lab
Doncaster North	HUGHES, Kevin	Lab
Dorset North	BAKER, Nicholas	Con
Dorset South	BRUCE, Ian	Con
Dorset West	SPICER, Sir James	Con
Dover	SHAW, David	Con
Down North	KILFEDDER, Sir James	UPUP
Down South	McGRADY, Eddie	SDLP
Dudley East	GILBERT, Dr John	Lab
Dudley West	BLACKBURN, John	Con
Dulwich	JOWELL, Ms Tessa	Lab
Dumbarton	McFALL, John	Lab
Dumfries	MONRO, Sir Hector	Con

Dundee East	McALLION, John	Lab
Dundee West	ROSS, Ernest	Lab
Dunfermline East	BROWN, Gordon	Lab
Dunfermline West	SQUIRE, Ms Rachel	Lab
Durham, City of	STEINBERG, Gerry	Lab
Durham North	RADICE, Giles	Lab
Durham North West	ARMSTRONG, Ms Hilary	Lab
Ealing Acton	YOUNG, Sir George	Con
Ealing North	GREENWAY, Harry	Con
Ealing Southall	KHABRA, Piara	Lab
Easington	CUMMINGS, John	Lab
East Kilbride	INGRAM, Adam	Lab
East Lothian	HOME ROBERTSON, John	Lab
Eastbourne	WATERSON, Nigel	Con
Eastleigh	MILLIGAN, Stephen	Con
Eastwood	STEWART, Allan	Con
Eccles	LESTOR, Ms Joan	Lab
Eddisbury	GOODLAD, Alastair	Con
Edinburgh Central	DARLING, Alistair	Lab
Edinburgh East	STRANG, Dr Gavin	Lab
Edinburgh Leith	CHISHOLM, Malcolm	Lab
Edinburgh Pentlands	RIFKIND, Malcolm	Con
Edinburgh South	GRIFFITHS, Nigel	Lab
Edinburgh West	DOUGLAS-HAMILTON, Lord Jas	Con
Edmonton	TWINN, Dr Ian	Con
Ellesmere Port & Neston	MILLER, Andrew	Lab
Elmet	BATISTE, Spencer	Con
Eltham	BOTTOMLEY, Peter	Con
Enfield North	EGGAR, Tim	Con
Enfield Southgate	PORTILLO, Michael	Con
Epping Forest	NORRIS, Steve	Con
Epsom & Ewell	HAMILTON, Archie	Con
Erewash	KNIGHT, Mrs Angela	Con
Erith & Crayford	EVENNETT, David	Con
Esher	TAYLOR, Ian	Con
Exeter	HANNAM, John	Con
Falkirk East	CONNARTY, Michael	Lab
Falkirk West	CANAVAN, Dennis	Lab
Falmouth & Camborne	COE, Sebastian	Con
Fareham	LLOYD, Peter	Con
Faversham	MOATE, Sir Roger	Con

Feltham & Heston	KEEN, Alan	Lab
Fermanagh & South Tyrone	MAGINNIS, Kenneth	UU
Fife Central	McLEISH, Henry	Lab
Fife North East	CAMPBELL, Menzies	LD
Finchley	BOOTH, Hartley	Con
Folkestone & Hythe	HOWARD, Michael	Con
Foyle	HUME, John	SDLP
Fulham	CARRINGTON, Matthew	Con
Fylde	JACK, Michael	Con
Gainsborough & Horncastle	LEIGH, Edward	Con
Galloway & Upper Nithsdale	LANG, Ian	Con
Gateshead East	QUIN, Ms Joyce	Lab
Gedling	MITCHELL, Andrew	Con
Gillingham	COUCHMAN, James	Con
Glanford & Scunthorpe	MORLEY, Elliot	Lab
Glasgow Cathcart	MAXTON, John	Lab
Glasgow Central	WATSON, Mike	Lab
Glasgow Garscadden	DEWAR, Donald	Lab
Glasgow Govan	DAVIDSON, Ian	Lab
Glasgow Hillhead	GALLOWAY, George	Lab
Glasgow Maryhill	FYFE, Mrs Maria	Lab
Glasgow Pollok	DUNNACHIE, Jimmy	Lab
Glasgow Provan	WRAY, James	Lab
Glasgow Rutherglen	McAVOY, Tommy	Lab
Glasgow Shettleston	MARSHALL, David	Lab
Glasgow Springburn	MARTIN, Michael	Lab
Gloucester	FRENCH, Douglas	Con
Gloucestershire West	MARLAND, Paul	Con
Gordon	BRUCE, Malcolm	LD
Gosport	VIGGERS, Peter	Con
Gower	WARDELL, Gareth	Lab
Grantham	HOGG, Douglas	Con
Gravesham	ARNOLD, Jacques	Con
Great Grimsby	MITCHELL, Austin	Lab
Great Yarmouth	CARTTISS, Michael	Con
Greenock & Port Glasgow	GODMAN, Dr Norman	Lab
Greenwich	RAYNSFORD, Nick	Lab
Guildford	HOWELL, David	Con
Hackney North & Stoke Newington	ABBOTT, Ms Diane	Lab
Hackney South & Shoreditch	SEDGEMORE, Brian	Lab
Halesowen & Stourbridge	HAWKSLEY, Warren	Con

Halifax	MAHON, Mrs Alice	Lab
Halton	OAKES, Gordon	Lab
Hamilton	ROBERTSON, George	Lab
Hammersmith	SOLEY, Clive	Lab
Hampshire East	MATES, Michael	Con
Hampshire North West	MITCHELL, Sir David	Con
Hampstead & Highgate	JACKSON, Ms Glenda	Lab
Harborough	GARNIER, Edward	Con
Harlow	HAYES, Jerry	Con
Harrogate	BANKS, Robert	Con
Harrow East	DYKES, Hugh	Con
Harrow West	HUGHES, Robert G	Con
Hartlepool	MANDELSON, Peter	Lab
Harwich	SPROAT, Iain	Con
Hastings & Rye	LAIT, Ms Jacqui	Con
Havant	WILLETTS, David	Con
Hayes & Harlington	DICKS, Terry	Con
Hazel Grove	ARNOLD, Sir Tom	Con
Hemsworth	ENRIGHT, Derek	Lab
Hendon North	GORST, John	Con
Hendon South	MARSHALL, John	Con
Henley	HESELTINE, Michael	Con
Hereford	SHEPHERD, Colin	Con
Hertford & Stortford	WELLS, Bowen	Con
Hertfordshire North	HEALD, Oliver	Con
Hertfordshire South West	PAGE, Richard	Con
Hertfordshire West	JONES, Robert	Con
Hertsmere	CLAPPISON, James	Con
Hexham	ATKINSON, Peter	Con
Heywood & Middleton	CALLAGHAN, James	Lab
High Peak	HENDRY, Charles	Con
Holborn & St Pancras	DOBSON, Frank	Lab
Holland with Boston	BODY, Sir Richard	Con
Honiton	EMERY, Sir Peter	Con
Hornchurch	SQUIRE, Robin	Con
Hornsey & Wood Green	ROCHE, Mrs Barbara	Lab
Horsham	HORDERN, Sir Peter	Con
Houghton & Washington	BOYES, Roland	Lab
Hove	SAINSBURY, Tim	Con
Huddersfield	SHEERMAN, Barry	Lab
Hull East	PRESCOTT, John	Lab

Hull North	McNAMARA, Kevin	Lab
Hull West	RANDALL, Stuart	Lab
Huntingdon	MAJOR, John	Con
Hyndburn	POPE, Gregory	Lab
Ilford North	BENDALL, Vivian	Con
Ilford South	GAPES, Mike	Lab
Inverness, Nairn & Lochaber	JOHNSTON, Sir Russell	LD
Ipswich	CANN, Jamie	Lab
Isle of Wight	FIELD, Barry	Con
Islington North	CORBYN, Jeremy	Lab
Islington South	SMITH, Chris	Lab
Islwyn	KINNOCK, Neil	Lab
Jarrow	DIXON, Don	Lab
Keighley	WALLER, Gary	Con
Kensington	FISHBURN, Dudley	Con
Kent Mid	ROWE, Andrew	Con
Kettering	FREEMAN, Roger	Con
Kilmarnock & Loudoun	McKELVEY, William	Lab
Kincardine & Deeside	KYNOCH, George	Con
Kingston-upon-Thames	LAMONT, Norman	Con
Kingswood	BERRY, Dr Roger	Lab
Kirkcaldy	MOONIE, Dr Lewis	Lab
Knowsley North	HOWARTH, George	Lab
Knowsley South	O'HARA, Eddie	Lab
Lagan Valley	MOLYNEAUX, James	UU
Lancashire West	PICKTHALL, Colin	Lab
Lancaster	KELLETT-BOWMAN,Dame Elaine	Con
Langbaurgh	BATES, Michael	Con
Leeds Central	FATCHETT, Derek	Lab
Leeds East	MUDIE, George	Lab
Leeds North East	KIRKHOPE, Timothy	Con
Leeds North West	HAMPSON, Dr Keith	Con
Leeds South & Morley	GUNNELL, John	Lab
Leeds West	BATTLE, John	Lab
Leicester East	VAZ, Keith	Lab
Leicester South	MARSHALL, James	Lab
Leicester West	JANNER, Greville	Lab
Leicestershire North West	ASHBY, David	Con
Leigh	CUNLIFFE, Lawrence	Lab
Leominster	TEMPLE-MORRIS, Peter	Con
Lewes	RATHBONE, Tim	Con

Lewisham Deptford	RUDDOCK, Ms Joan	Lab
Lewisham East	PRENTICE, Mrs Bridget	Lab
Lewisham West	DOWD, Jim	Lab
Leyton	COHEN, Harry	Lab
Lincoln	CARLISLE, Kenneth	Con
Lindsey East	TAPSELL, Sir Peter	Con
Linlithgow	DALYELL, Tam	Lab
Littleborough & Saddleworth	DICKENS, Geoffrey	Con
Liverpool Broadgreen	KENNEDY, Mrs Jane	Lab
Liverpool Garston	LOYDEN, Eddie	Lab
Liverpool Mossley Hill	ALTON, David	LD
Liverpool Riverside	PARRY, Robert	Lab
Liverpool Walton	KILFOYLE, Peter	Lab
Liverpool West Derby	WAREING, Robert	Lab
Livingston	COOK, Robin	Lab
Llanelli	DAVIES, Denzil	Lab
Londonderry East	ROSS, William	UU
Loughborough	DORRELL, Stephen	Con
Ludlow	GILL, Christopher	Con
Luton North	CARLISLE, John	Con
Luton South	BRIGHT, Graham	Con
Macclesfield	WINTERTON, Nicholas	Con
Maidstone	WIDDECOMBE, Miss Ann	Con
Makerfield	McCARTNEY, Ian	Lab
Manchester Blackley	EASTHAM, Kenneth	Lab
Manchester Central	LITHERLAND, Robert	Lab
Manchester Gorton	KAUFMAN, Gerald	Lab
Manchester Withington	BRADLEY, Keith	Lab
Manchester Wythenshawe	MORRIS, Alf	Lab
Mansfield	MEALE, Alan	Lab
Medway	FENNER, Dame Peggy	Con
Meirionnydd Nant Conwy	LLWYD, Elfyn	PIC
Meriden	MILLS, Iain	Con
Merthyr Tydfil & Rhymney	ROWLANDS, Ted	Lab
Middlesbrough	BELL, Stuart	Lab
Midlothian	CLARKE, Eric	Lab
Milton Keynes North East	BUTLER, Peter	Con
Milton Keynes South West	LEGG, Barry	Con
Mitcham & Morden	RUMBOLD, Dame Angela	Con
Mole Valley	BAKER, Kenneth	Con
Monklands East	SMITH, John	Lab

Monklands West	CLARKE, Tom	Lab
Monmouth	EVANS, Roger	Con
Montgomery	CARLILE, Alex	LD
Moray	EWING, Mrs Maggie	SNP
Morecambe & Lunesdale	LENNOX-BOYD, Mark	Con
Motherwell North	REID, Dr John	Lab
Motherwell South	BRAY, Dr Jeremy	Lab
Neath	HAIN, Peter	Lab
New Forest	McNAIR-WILSON,Sir Patrick	Con
Newark	ALEXANDER, Richard	Con
Newbury	RENDEL, David	LD
Newcastle-under-Lyme	GOLDING, Mrs Llin	Lab
Newcastle-upon-Tyne Central	COUSINS, Jim	Lab
Newcastle-upon-Tyne East	BROWN, Nicholas	Lab
Newcastle-upon-Tyne North	HENDERSON, Douglas	Lab
Newham North East	LEIGHTON, Ron	Lab
Newham North West	BANKS, Tony	Lab
Newham South	SPEARING, Nigel	Lab
Newport East	HUGHES, Roy	Lab
Newport West	FLYNN, Paul	Lab
Newry & Armagh	MALLON, Seamus	SDLP
Norfolk Mid	RYDER, Richard	Con
Norfolk North	HOWELL, Sir Ralph	Con
Norfolk North West	BELLINGHAM, Henry	Con
Norfolk South	MacGREGOR, John	Con
Norfolk South West	SHEPHARD, Mrs Gillian	Con
Normanton	O'BRIEN, Bill	Lab
Northampton North	MARLOW, Tony	Con
Northampton South	MORRIS, Michael	Con
Northavon	COPE, Sir John	Con
Norwich North	THOMPSON, Patrick	Con
Norwich South	GARRETT, John	Lab
Norwood	FRASER, John	Lab
Nottingham East	HEPPELL, John	Lab
Nottingham North	ALLEN, Graham	Lab
Nottingham South	SIMPSON, Alan	Lab
Nuneaton	OLNER, William	Lab
Ogmore	POWELL, Ray	Lab
Old Bexley & Sidcup	HEATH, Sir Edward	Con
Oldham Central & Royton	DAVIES, Bryan	Lab
Oldham West	MEACHER, Michael	Lab

Orkney & Shetland	WALLACE, Jim	LD
Orpington	HORAM, John	Con
Oxford East	SMITH, Andrew	Lab
Oxford West & Abingdon	PATTEN, John	Con
Paisley North	ADAMS, Mrs Irene	Lab
Paisley South	McMASTER, Gordon	Lab
Peckham	HARMAN, Ms Harriet	Lab
Pembroke	AINGER, Nick	Lab
Pendle	PRENTICE, Gordon	Lab
Penrith & the Border	MACLEAN, David	Con
Perth & Kinross	FAIRBAIRN, Sir Nicholas	Con
Peterborough	MAWHINNEY, Dr Brian	Con
Plymouth Devonport	JAMIESON, David	Lab
Plymouth Drake	FOOKES, Dame Janet	Con
Plymouth Sutton	STREETER, Garry	Con
Pontefract & Castleford	LOFTHOUSE, Geoffrey	Lab
Pontypridd	HOWELLS, Kim	Lab
Poole	WARD. John	Con
Portsmouth North	GRIFFITHS, Peter	Con
Portsmouth South	MARTIN, David	Con
Preston	WISE, Mrs Audrey	Lab
Pudsey	SHAW, Sir Giles	Con
Putney	MELLOR, David	Con
Ravensbourne	HUNT, Sir John	Con
Reading East	VAUGHAN, Sir Gerry	Con
Reading West	DURANT, Sir Anthony	Con
Redcar	MOWLAM, Dr Mo	Lab
Reigate	GARDINER, Sir George	Con
Renfrew West & Inverclyde	GRAHAM, Tommy	Lab
Rhondda	ROGERS, Allan	Lab
Ribble Valley	EVANS, Nigel	Con
Richmond & Barnes	HANLEY, Jeremy	Con
Richmond (Yorks)	HAGUE, William	Con
Rochdale	LYNNE, Ms L	LD
Rochford	CLARK, Dr Michael	Con
Romford	NEUBERT, Sir Michael	Con
Romsey & Waterside	COLVIN, Michael	Con
Ross, Cromarty & Skye	KENNEDY, Charles	LD
Rossendale & Darwen	ANDERSON, Ms Janet	Lab
Rother Valley	BARRON, Kevin	Lab
Rotherham	BOYCE, James	Lab

Roxburgh & Berwickshire	KIRKWOOD, Archy	LD
Rugby & Kenilworth	PAWSEY, James	Con
Ruislip-Northwood	WILKINSON, John	Con
Rushcliffe	CLARKE, Kenneth	Con
Rutland & Melton	DUNCAN, Alan	Con
Ryedale	GREENWAY, John	Con
Saffron Walden	HASELHURST, Alan	Con
St Albans	LILLEY, Peter	Con
St Helens N	EVANS, John	Lab
St Helens S	BERMINGHAM, Gerry	Lab
St Ives	HARRIS, David	Con
Salford East	ORME, Stanley	Lab
Salisbury	KEY, Robert	Con
Scarborough	SYKES, John	Con
Sedgefield	BLAIR, Tony	Lab
Selby	ALISON, Michael	Con
Sevenoaks	WOLFSON, Mark	Con
Sheffield Attercliffe	BETTS, Clive	Lab
Sheffield Brightside	BLUNKETT, David	Lab
Sheffield Central	CABORN, Richard	Lab
Sheffield Hallam	PATNICK, Irvine	Con
Sheffield Heeley	MICHIE, Bill	Lab
Sheffield Hillsborough	JACKSON, Mrs Helen	Lab
Sherwood	TIPPING, Paddy	Lab
Shipley	FOX, Sir Marcus	Con
Shoreham	STEPHEN, Michael	Con
Shrewsbury & Atcham	CONWAY, Derek	Con
Shropshire North	BIFFEN, John	Con
Skipton & Ripon	CURRY, David	Con
Slough	WATTS, John	Con
Solihull	TAYLOR, John M	Con
Somerton & Frome	ROBINSON, Mark	Con
South Hams	STEEN, Anthony	Con
South Ribble	ATKINS, Robert	Con
South Shields	CLARK, Dr David	Lab
Southall- see Ealing Southall		
Southgate-see Enfield Southgate		
Southampton Itchen	DENHAM, John	Lab
Southampton Test	HILL, James	Con
Southend East	TAYLOR, Sir Teddy	Con
Southend West	CHANNON, Paul	Con

Southport	BANKS, Matthew	Con
Southwark & Bermondsey	HUGHES, Simon	LD
Spelthorne	WILSHIRE, David	Con
Stafford	CASH, William	Con
Staffordshire Mid	FABRICANT, Michael	Con
Staffordshire Moorlands	KNOX, Sir David	Con
Staffordshire South	CORMACK, Patrick	Con
Staffordshire South East	LIGHTBOWN, David	Con
Stalybridge & Hyde	PENDRY, Tom	Lab
Stamford & Spalding	DAVIES, Quentin	Con
Stevenage	WOOD, Timothy	Con
Stirling	FORSYTH, Michael	Con
Stockport	COFFEY, Mrs Anne	Lab
Stockton North	COOK, Frank	Lab
Stockton South	DEVLIN, Tim	Con
Stoke-on Trent South	STEVENSON, George	Lab
Stoke-on-Trent Central	FISHER, Mark	Lab
Stoke-on-Trent North	WALLEY, Ms Joan	Lab
Strangford	TAYLOR, John D	UU
Stratford-on-Avon	HOWARTH, Alan	Con
Strathkelvin & Bearsden	GALBRAITH, Sam	Lab
Streatham	HILL, Keith	Lab
Stretford	LLOYD, Tony	Lab
Stroud	KNAPMAN, Roger	Con
Suffolk Central	LORD, Michael	Con
Suffolk Coastal	GUMMER, John	Con
Suffolk South	YEO, Timothy	Con
Sunderland North	ETHERINGTON, William	Lab
Sunderland South	MULLIN, Chris	Lab
Surbiton	TRACEY, Richard	Con
Surrey East	AINSWORTH, Peter	Con
Surrey North West	GRYLLS, Sir Michael	Con
Surrey South West	BOTTOMLEY, Mrs Virginia	Con
Sussex Mid	RENTON, Tim	Con
Sutton Coldfield	FOWLER, Sir Norman	Con
Sutton & Cheam	MAITLAND, Lady Olga	Con
Swansea East	ANDERSON, Donald	Lab
Swansea West	WILLIAMS, Alan J	Lab
Swindon	COOMBS, Simon	Con
Tatton	HAMILTON, Neil	Con
Taunton	NICHOLSON, David	Con

Tayside North	WALKER, Bill	Con
Teignbridge	NICHOLLS,Patrick	Con
Thanet North	GALE, Roger	Con
Thanet South	AITKEN, Jonathan	Con
Thurrock	MACKINLAY, Andrew	Lab
Tiverton	BROWNING, Mrs Angela	Con
Tonbridge & Malling	STANLEY, Sir John	Con
Tooting	COX, Tom	Lab
Torbay	ALLASON, Rupert	Con
Torfaen	MURPHY, Paul	Lab
Tottenham	GRANT, Bernie	Lab
Truro	TAYLOR, Mathew	LD
Tunbridge Wells	MAYHEW, Sir Patrick	Con
Tweeddale, Ettrick & Lauderdale	STEEL, Sir David	LD
Twickenham	JESSEL, Toby	Con
Tyne Bridge	CLELLAND, David	Lab
Tynemouth	TROTTER, Neville	Con
Ulster Mid	McCREA, Rev William	DUP
Upminster	BONSOR, Sir Nicholas	Con
Upper Bann	TRIMBLE, David	UU
Uxbridge	SHERSBY, Michael	Con
Vale of Glamorgan	SWEENEY, Walter	Con
Vauxhall	HOEY, Ms Kate	Lab
Wakefield	HINCHCLIFFE, David	Lab
Wallasey	EAGLE, Ms Angela	Lab
Wallsend	BYERS, Stephen	Lab
Walsall North	WINNICK, David	Lab
Walsall South	GEORGE, Bruce	Lab
Walthamstow	GERRARD, Neil	Lab
Wansbeck	THOMPSON, Jack	Lab
Wansdyke	ASPINWALL, Jack	Con
Wanstead & Woodford	ARBUTHNOT, James	Con
Wantage	JACKSON, Robert	Con
Warley East	FAULDS, Andrew	Lab
Warley West	SPELLAR, John	Lab
Warrington North	HOYLE, Doug	Lab
Warrington South	HALL, Mike	Lab
Warwick & Leamington	SMITH, Sir Dudley	Con
Warwickshire North	O'BRIEN, Michael	Lab
Watford	GAREL-JONES, Tristan	Con
Waveney	PORTER, David	Con

Wealden	JOHNSON SMITH, Geoffrey	Con
Wellingborough	FRY, Peter	Con
Wells	HEATHCOAT-AMORY, David	Con
Welwyn Hatfield	EVANS, David	Con
Wentworth	HARDY, Peter	Lab
West Bromwich East	SNAPE, Peter	Lab
West Bromwich West	BOOTHROYD, Ms Betty	Spk
Westbury	FABER, David	Con
Western Isles	MacDONALD, Calum	Lab
Westminster North	WHEELER, Sir John	Con
Westmorland & Lonsdale	JOPLING, Michael	Con
Weston-Super-Mare	WIGGIN, Sir Jerry	Con
Wigan	STOTT, Roger	Lab
Wilts North	NEEDHAM, Richard	Con
Wimbledon	GOODSON-WICKES, Charles	Con
Winchester	MALONE, Gerald	Con
Windsor & Maidenhead	TREND, Michael	Con
Wirral South	PORTER, Barry	Con
Wirral West	HUNT, David	Con
Witney	HURD, Douglas	Con
Woking	ONSLOW, Cranley	Con
Wokingham	REDWOOD, John	Con
Wolverhampton North East	PURCHASE, Kenneth	Lab
Wolverhampton SE	TURNER, Dennis	Lab
Wolverhampton SW	BUDGEN, Nicholas	Con
Woodspring	FOX, Dr Liam	Con
Woolwich	AUSTIN-WALKER, John	Lab
Worcester	LUFF, Peter	Con
Worcestershire Mid	FORTH, Eric	Con
Worcestershire South	SPICER, Michael	Con
Workington	CAMPBELL-SAVOURS, Dale	Lab
Worsley	LEWIS, Terry	Lab
Worthing	HIGGINS, Sir Terence	Con
Wrekin, The	GROCOTT, Bruce	Lab
Wrexham	MAREK, Dr John	Lab
Wycombe	WHITNEY, Ray	Con
Wyre	MANS, Keith	Con
Wyre Forest	COOMBS, Anthony	Con
Yeovil	ASHDOWN, Paddy	LD
Ynys Mon	JONES, Ieuan Wyn	PlC
York	BAYLEY, Hugh	Lab

MPs AND THEIR CONSTITUENCIES

	PARTY	CONSTIT	% MAJ	BIRTH DATE	FIRST ELECTED
ABBOTT Diane	Lab	Hackney N	30.9	27.9.53	1987
ADAMS Irene	Lab	Paisley N	27.4	1948	1990*
AINGER Nick	Lab	Pembroke	1.2	24.10.49	1992
AINSWORTH Peter	Con	Surrey E	37.0	16.11.56	1992
AINSWORTH Robert	Lab	Coventry NE	24.6	19.6.52	1992
AITKEN Jonathan	Con	Thanet S	23.6	30.8.42	1974 F
ALEXANDER Richard	Con	Newark	14.6	29.6.34	1979
ALISON Michael	Con	Selby	15.4	27.6.26	1964
(MP for Barkston Ash 1964-83, Selby 1983-)					
ALLASON Rupert	Con	Torbay	10.1	8.11.51	1987
ALLEN Graham	Lab	Nottingham N	20.6	11.1.53	1987
ALTON David	LD	L'pl Mossley Hill	6.3	15.3.51	1979*
(MP for Liverpool Edge Hill 1979-1983)*					
AMESS David	Con	Basildon	2.8	26.3.52	1983
ANCRAM Michael	Con	Devizes	26.9	7.7.45	1979 R
(MP for Berwickshire 1974F-O, Edinburgh S 1979-87, Devizes 1992-)					
ANDERSON Donald	Lab	Swansea E	52.5	17.6.39	1966 R
(MP for Monmouth 1966-70; Swansea E 1974O-)					
ANDERSON Janet	Lab	Rossendale	0.2	6.12.49	1992
ARBUTHNOT James	Con	Wanstead	38.6	4.8.52	1987
ARMSTRONG Hilary	Lab	Durham NW	30.3	30.11.45	1987
ARNOLD Jacques	Con	Gravesham	9.3	27.8.47	1987
ARNOLD Sir Tom	Con	Hazel Grove	1.7	25.1.47	1974O
ASHBY David	Con	Leics NW	1.6	14.5.40	1983
ASHDOWN Paddy	LD	Yeovil	14.7	27.7.41	1983
ASHTON Joe	Lab	Bassetlaw	18.4	9.10.33	1968*
ASPINWALL Jack	Con	Wansdyke	20.5	5.2.33	1983
ATKINS Robert	Con	S Ribble	9.2	5.2.46	1979
ATKINSON David	Con	Bournemouth E	27.1	24.3.40	1977*
ATKINSON Peter	Con	Hexham	28.2	19.1.43	1992
AUSTIN-WALKER John	Lab	Woolwich	5.6	21.8.44	1992
BAKER Kenneth	Con	Mole Valley	29.1	3.11.34	1968*
(MP for Acton 1968-70; St Marylebone 1970-83; Mole Valley 1983-)*					
BAKER Nicholas	Con	Dorset N	16.1	23.11.38	1979
BALDRY Tony	Con	Banbury	28.6	10.7.50	1983
BANKS Matthew	Con	Southport	5.5	21.6.61	1992
BANKS Robert	Con	Harrogate	21.2	18.1.37	1974 F
BANKS Tony	Lab	Newham NW	35.2	8.4.43	1983
BARNES Harry	Lab	Derbyshire NE	10.6	22.7.36	1987
BARRON Kevin	Lab	Rother Valley	33.6	26.10.46	1983
BATES Michael	Con	Langbaurgh	2.4	26.5.61	1992
BATISTE Spencer	Con	Elmet	5.6	5.6.45	1983
BATTLE John	Lab	Leeds W	29.0	26.4.51	1987
BAYLEY Hugh	Lab	York	9.9	9.1.52	1992
BECKETT Margaret	Lab	Derby S	13.8	15.1.43	1974 OR
BEGGS Roy	UUP	Antrim E	18.9	20.2.36	1983
BEITH Alan	LD	Berwick	11.6	20.4.43	1973*
BELL Stuart	Lab	Middlesbrough	38.4	16.5.38	1983
BELLINGHAM Henry	Con	Norfolk NW	18.5	29.3.55	1983

	PARTY	CONSTIT	% MAJ	BIRTH DATE	FIRST ELECTED
BENDALL Vivian	Con	Ilford N	19.8	14.12.38	1978*
BENN Tony	Lab	Chesterfield	11.5	3.4.25	1950*R
(MP for Bristol SE 1950-60 and 1963-83; Chesterfield 1984-)*					
BENNETT Andrew	Lab	Denton	23.0	9.3.39	1974 F
(MP for Stockport N 1974 F-83; Denton 1983-)					
BENTON Joe	Lab	Bootle	58.6	28.9.33	1990*
BERESFORD Sir Paul	Con	Croydon C	24.1	6.4.46	1992
BERMINGHAM Gerald	Lab	St Helens S	36.6	20.8.40	1983
BERRY Dr Roger	Lab	Kingswood	3.9	4.7.48	1992
BETTS Clive	Lab	Sheff. A'cliffe	31.2	13.1.50	1992
BIFFEN John	Con	Shropshire N	25.2	3.11.30	1961*
BLACKBURN Dr John	Con	Dudley W	8.1	2.9.33	1979
BLAIR Tony	Lab	Sedgefield	31.6	6.5.53	1983
BLUNKETT David	Lab	Sheffield B'side	53.6	6.6.47	1987
BOATENG Paul	Lab	Brent S	27.0	14.6.51	1987
BODY Sir Richard	Con	Holland	26.1	18.5.27	1955 R
(MP for Billericay 1955-59; Holland 1966-)					
BONSOR Sir Nicholas	Con	Upminster	26.8	9.12.42	1979
(MP for Nantwich 1979-83; Upminster 83-)					
BOOTH Dr Hartley	Con	Finchley	15.5	17.7.46	1992
BOOTHROYD Betty	Spkr	W Bromwich W	19.3	8.10.29	1973*
BOSWELL Timothy	Con	Daventry	34.1	2.12.42	1987
BOTTOMLEY Peter	Con	Eltham	4.1	30.7.44	1975*
BOTTOMLEY Virginia	Con	Surrey SW	25.0	12.3.48	1984*
BOWDEN Andrew	Con	Brighton Kemptown	7.0	8.4.30	1970
BOWIS John	Con	Battersea	9.3	2.8.45	1987
BOYCE James	Lab	Rotherham	40.2	6.9.47	1992
BOYES Roland	Lab	Houghton	37.2	12.2.37	1983
BOYSON Sir Rhodes	Con	Brent N	24.4	11.5.25	1974 F
BRADLEY Keith	Lab	M'chester Withgtn	21.4	17.5.50	1987
BRANDRETH Gyles	Con	Chester	2.1	8.3.48	1992
BRAY Dr Jeremy	Lab	Motherwell S	36.8	29.6.30	1962*
(MP for Middlesbrough W 1962-70; Motherwell and Wishaw 1974 O-1983; Motherwell S 1983-)*					
BRAZIER Julian	Con	Canterbury	18.4	24.7.53	1987
BRIGHT Graham	Con	Luton S	1.4	2.4.42	1979
BROOKE Peter	Con	City of London	38.5	3.3.34	1977*
BROWN Gordon	Lab	Dunfermline E	46.0	20.2.51	1983
BROWN Michael	Con	Brigg	14.4	3.7.51	1979
BROWN Nicholas	Lab	Newcastle E	34.3	13.6.50	1983
BROWNING Angela	Con	Tiverton	18.8	4.12.46	1992
BRUCE Ian	Con	Dorset S	23.2	14.3.47	1987
BRUCE Malcolm	LD	Gordon	0.5	17.11.44	1983
BUDGEN Nicholas	Con	W'verhmpton SW	9.4	3.11.37	1974 F
BURDEN Richard	Lab	B'ham N'field	1.2	1.9.54	1992
BURNS Simon	Con	Chelmsford	25.9	6.9.52	1987
BURT Alistair	Con	Bury N	8.1	25.5.55	1983
BUTCHER John	Con	Coventry SW	2.8	13.2.46	1979
BUTLER Peter	Con	Milton Keynes NE	27.9	10.6.51	1992
BUTTERFILL John	Con	Bournemouth W	22.4	14.2.41	1983
BYERS Stephen	Lab	Wallsend	33.7	13.4.53	1992
CABORN Richard	Lab	Sheffield C	52.2	6.10.43	1983
CALLAGHAN James	Lab	Heywood	18.8	28.1.27	1974 F

	PARTY	CONSTIT	% MAJ	BIRTH DATE	FIRST ELECTED
CAMPBELL Anne	Lab	Cambridge	1.1	6.4.40	1992
CAMPBELL Menzies	LD	Fife NE	7.9	22.5.41	1987
CAMPBELL Ronnie	Lab	Blyth Valley	16.3	14.8.43	1987
CAMPBELL-SAVOURS Dale	Lab	Workington	22.3	23.8.43	1979
CANAVAN Dennis	Lab	Falkirk W	25.5	8.8.42	1974 O
(MP for W Stirlingshire 1974 O- 1983; Falkirk W Edinburgh1983-)					
CANN Jamie	Lab	Ipswich	0.5	28.6.46	1992
CARLILE Alex	LD	Montgomery	15.8	12.2.48	1983
CARLISLE John	Con	Luton N	20.8	28.8.42	1979
CARLISLE Kenneth	Con	Lincoln	3.3	25.3.41	1979
CARRINGTON Matthew	Con	Fulham	16.4	19.10.47	1987
CARTTISS Michael	Con	Gt Yarmouth	10.0	11.3.38	1983
CASH William	Con	Stafford	17.6	10.5.40	1984*
CHANNON Paul	Con	Southend W	23.8	9.10.35	1959*
CHAPMAN Sydney	Con	C.Barnet	31.1	17.10.35	1970 R
(MP for B'ham Handsworth 1970-74 F; for Barnet 1979-)					
CHISHOLM Malcolm	Lab	E'burgh Leith	12.4	7.3.49	1992
CHURCHILL Winston	Con	Davyhulme	8.8	10.10.40	1970
(MP for Stretford 1970-83; Davyhulme 1983-)					
CLAPHAM Michael	Lab	Barnsley W	30.2	15.5.43	1992
CLAPPISON James	Con	Hertsmere	33.1	14.9.56	1992
CLARK Dr David	Lab	S.Shields	32.4	19.10.39	1970 R
(MP for Colne Valley 1970-74 F; S Shields 1979-)					
CLARK Dr Michael	Con	Rochford	40.8	8.8.35	1983
CLARKE Eric	Lab	Midlothian	22.0	9.4.33	1992
CLARKE Kenneth	Con	Rushcliffe	31.2	2.7.40	1970
CLARKE Tom	Lab	Monklands W	44.7	10.1.41	1983*
CLELLAND David	Lab	Tyne Bridge	45.7	27.6.43	1985*
CLIFTON-BROWN Geoffrey	Con	Cirencester	22.2	23.3.53	1992
CLWYD Ann	Lab	Cynon Valley	56.2	21.3.37	1984*
COE Sebastian	Con	Falmouth	5.7	29.9.56	1992
COFFEY Ann	Lab	Stockport	3.0	31.8.46	1992
COHEN Harry	Lab	Leyton	29.8	10.12.49	1983
COLVIN Michael	Con	Romsey	22.3	27.9.32	1979
(MP for Bristol NW 1979-83, Romsey 1983-)					
CONGDON David	Con	Croydon NE	16.1	16.10.49	1992
CONNARTY Michael	Lab	Falkirk E	20.0	3.9.47	1992
CONWAY Derek	Con	Shrewsbury	18.8	15.2.53	1983
COOK Frank	Lab	Stockton N	19.6	3.11.35	1983
COOK Robin	Lab	Livingston	17.8	28.2.46	1974 F
(MP for Edinburgh C 1974 F-83; Livingston 83-)					
COOMBS Anthony	Con	Wyre Forest	17.1	18.11.52	1987
COOMBS Simon	Con	Swindon	3.9	21.2.47	1983
COPE Sir John	Con	Northavon	16.9	13.5.37	1974 F
(MP for S Gloucestershire 1974 F-83, Northavon 83-)					
CORBETT Robin	Lab	B'ham Erdington	12.9	22.12.33	1974OR
(MP for Hemel Hempstead 1974 O-83, Erdington 1983-)					
CORBYN Jeremy	Lab	Islington N	33.8	26.5.49	1983
CORMACK Patrick	Con	Staffs S	33.5	18.5.39	1970
(MP for Cannock 1970-74 F, SW Staffs 1974 F-83, S Staffs 1983-)					
CORSTON Jean	Lab	Bristol E	5.4	5.5.42	1992
COUCHMAN James	Con	Gillingham	28.8	11.2.42	1983

	PARTY	CONSTIT	% MAJ	BIRTH DATE	FIRST ELECTED
COUSINS Jim	Lab	Newcastle C	12.4	23.2.44	1987
COX Tom	Lab	Tooting	8.0	1928	1970
CRAN James	Con	Beverley	25.5	28.1.44	1987
CRITCHLEY Julian	Con	Aldershot	29.8	8.12.30	1959 R
(MP for Rochester 1959-64, Aldershot 1970-)					
CRYER Bob	Lab	Bradford S	9.3	3.12.34	1974 FR
(MP for Keighley 1974 F-83, Bradford S 87-)					
CUMMINGS John	Lab	Easington	56.0	6.7.43	1987
CUNLIFFE Lawrence	Lab	Leigh	35.8	23.3.29	1979
CUNNINGHAM Jim	Lab	Coventry SE	3.6	4.2.41	1992
CUNNINGHAM Dr John	Lab	Copeland	5.3	4.8.39	1970
CURRIE Edwina	Con	Derbyshire S	6.6	13.10.46	1983
CURRY David	Con	Skipton	31.4	13.6.44	1987
DAFIS Cynog	PC/GP	Ceredigion	6.2	1.4.38	1992
DALYELL Tam	Lab	Linlithgow	14.6	9.8.32	1962*
(MP for W Lothian 1962-83, for Linlithgow 1983-)*					
DARLING Alistair	Lab	Edinburgh C	5.4	28.11.53	1987
DAVIDSON Ian	Lab	Glasgow Govan	11.8	8.9.50	1992
DAVIES Bryan	Lab	Oldham C	18.9	9.11.39	1974 FR
(MP for Enfield N 1974-9, for Oldham C 1992-)					
DAVIES Denzil	Lab	Llanelli	38.1	9.10.38	1970
DAVIES Quentin	Con	Stamford	37.5	29.5.44	1987
DAVIES Ron	Lab	Caerphilly	45.5	6.8.46	1983
DAVIS David	Con	Boothferry	27.2	23.12.48	1987
DAVIS Terry	Lab	B'h'm Hodge Hill	17.3	5.1.38	1971*R
(MP for Bromsgrove 1971-74 F, Stechford 1979-83, Hodge Hill 83-)*					
DAY Stephen	Con	Cheadle	28.3	30.10.48	1987
DENHAM John	Lab	So'ton Itchen	1.0	15.7.53	1992
DEVA Nirj	Con	Brentford	3.9	11.5.48	1992
DEVLIN Tim	Con	Stockton S	5.4	13.6.59	1987
DEWAR Donald	Lab	G'gow G'scadden	45.4	21.8.37	1966 R
(MP for Aberdeen S 1966-70, Glasgow Garscadden 1978-)*					
DICKENS Geoffrey	Con	Littleborough	8.4	26.8.31	1983
DICKS Terry	Con	Hayes	0.1	17.3.37	1983
DIXON Don	Lab	Jarrow	38.4	6.3.29	1979
DOBSON Frank	Lab	Holborn	26.6	15.3.40	1979
DONOHOE Brian	Lab	Cunninghame S	28.7	10.9.48	1992
DORRELL Stephen	Con	Loughborough	18.4	25.3.52	1979
D-HAMILTON Ld James	Con	Edinburgh W	1.8	31.7.42	1974 O
DOVER Den	Con	Chorley	6.5	4.4.38	1979
DOWD Jim	Lab	Lewisham W	4.2	5.3.51	1992
DUNCAN Alan	Con	Rutland	39.0	31.3.57	1992
DUNCAN-SMITH Iain	Con	Chingford	34.4	9.4.54	1992
DUNN Robert	Con	Dartford	17.1	14.7.46	1979
DUNNACHIE James	Lab	Glasgow Pollok	24.1	17.11.30	1987
DUNWOODY Gwyneth	Lab	Crewe	4.4	12.12.30	1966 R
(MP for Exeter 1966-70, Crewe 1974 Feb-)					
DURANT Sir Anthony	Con	Reading W	25.1	9.1.28	1974 F
(MP for Reading N 1974 F-83, Reading W 1983-)					
DYKES Hugh	Con	Harrow E	19.1	17.5.39	1970
EAGLE Angela	Lab	Wallasey	7.0	17.2.61	1992
EASTHAM Kenneth	Lab	M'chester Blackley	32.4	11.8.27	1979

	PARTY	CONSTIT	% MAJ	BIRTH DATE	FIRST ELECTED
EGGAR Tim	Con	Enfield N	18.0	19.12.51	1979
ELLETSON Harold	Con	Blackpool N	6.7	8.12.60	1992
EMERY Sir Peter	Con	Honiton	25.8	27.2.26	1959 R
(MP for Reading 1959-66, Honiton 1967-)*					
ENRIGHT Derek	Lab	Hemsworth	52.2	2.8.35	1991*
ETHERINGTON William	Lab	Sunderland N	33.9	17.7.41	1992
EVANS David	Con	Welwyn	13.9	23.4.35	1987
EVANS John	Lab	St Helens N	29.5	19.10.30	1974 F
(MP for Newton 1974 F-83, St Helens N 1983-)					
EVANS Jonathan	Con	Brecon	0.3	2.6.50	1992
EVANS Nigel	Con	Ribble Valley	11.7	10.11.57	1992
EVANS Roger	Con	Monmouth	6.3	18.3.47	1992
EVENNETT David	Con	Erith	5.0	3.6.49	1983
EWING Margaret	SNP	Moray	6.2	1.9.45	1974O R
(As Margaret Bain, MP for Dunbartonshire E 1974 O- 79 and MP for Moray 1987-)					
FABER David	Con	Westbury	17.4	7.7.61	1992
FABRICANT Michael	Con	Staffs Mid	9.9	12.6.50	1992
FAIRBAIRN Sir Nicholas	Con	Perth	4.2	24.12.33	1974 F
(MP for Kinross & W Perthshire 1974F-83, Perth & Kinross 1983-)					
FATCHETT Derek	Lab	Leeds C	39.5	22.8.45	1983
FAULDS Andrew	Lab	Warley E	21.0	1.3.23	1966
(MP for Smethwick 1966-74F, Warley E 1974F-)					
FENNER Dame Peggy	Con	Medway	17.7	12.11.22	1970
(MP for Rochester and Chatham 1970-74O and 1979-83, Medway 83-)					
FIELD Barry	Con	Isle of Wight	2.3	4.7.46	1987
FIELD Frank	Lab	Birkenhead	38.5	16.7.42	1979
FISHBURN Dudley	Con	Kensington	11.5	8.6.46	1988*
FISHER Mark	Lab	Stoke C	30.1	29.10.44	1983
FLYNN Paul	Lab	Newport W	17.1	9.2.35	1987
FOOKES Dame Janet	Con	Plymouth Drake	5.2	21.2.36	1970
(MP for Merton 1970-74F, Plymouth Drake 1974F-)					
FORMAN Nigel	Con	Carshalton	18.8	25.3.43	1976*
FORSYTH Michael	Con	Stirling	1.5	16.10.54	1983
FORSYTHE Clifford	UUP	Antrim S	58.1	24.8.29	1983
FORTH Eric	Con	Worcs Mid	14.4	9.9.44	1983
FOSTER Derek	Lab	Bishop Auckland	18.2	25.6.37	1979
FOSTER Don	LD	Bath	7.2	31.3.47	1992
FOULKES George	Lab	Carrick	39.1	21.1.42	1979
(MP for Ayrshire S 1979-83, Carrick 1983-)					
FOWLER Sir Norman	Con	Sutt C'field	45.9	2.2.38	1970
(MP for Nottingham S 1970-74F, Sutton Coldfield 74F-)					
FOX Liam	Con	Woodspring	27.1	22.9.61	1992
FOX Sir Marcus	Con	Shipley	21.9	11.6.27	1970
FRASER John	Lab	Norwood	20.9	30.6.34	1966
FREEMAN Roger	Con	Kettering	19.9	27.5.42	1983
FRENCH Douglas	Con	Gloucester	9.4	20.3.44	1987
FRY Peter	Con	Wellingboro'	19.5	26.5.31	1969*
FYFE Maria	Lab	Glasgow Maryhill	42.5	25.11.38	1987
GALBRAITH Sam	Lab	Strathkelvin	6.3	18.10.45	1987
GALE Roger	Con	Thanet N	33.7	20.8.43	1983
GALLIE Phil	Con	Ayr	0.2	3.6.39	1992
GALLOWAY George	Lab	Glasgow Hillhead	12.3	16.8.54	1987

	PARTY	CONSTIT	% MAJ	BIRTH DATE	FIRST ELECTED
GAPES Mike	Lab	Ilford S	0.9	4.9.52	1992
GARDINER Sir George	Con	Reigate	31.3	3.3.35	1974 F
GAREL-JONES Tristan	Con	Watford	16.1	28.2.41	1979
GARNIER Edward	Con	Harborough	21.6	26.10.52	1992
GARRETT John	Lab	Norwich S	12.1	8.9.31	1974F R
(MP for Norwich S 1974F-83, regained seat in 1987)					
GEORGE Bruce	Lab	Walsall S	6.3	1.6.42	1974F
GERRARD Neil	Lab	Walthamstow	8.5	3.7.42	1992
GILBERT Dr John	Lab	Dudley E	16.3	5.5.27	1970
GILL Christopher	Con	Ludlow	25.4	28.10.36	1987
GILLAN Cheryl	Con	Chesham	38.8	21.4.52	1992
GODMAN Dr Norman	Lab	Greenock	39.0	19.4.37	1983
GODSIFF Roger	Lab	B'h'm Small H	40.2	28.6.46	1992
GOLDING Llin	Lab	N'castle-u-Lyme	18.4	21.3.33	1986*
GOODLAD Alastair	Con	Eddisbury	20.5	4.7.43	1974F
GOODSON-WICKES Dr Chas	Con	Wimbledon	29.7	7.11.45	1987
GORDON Mildred	Lab	Bow	22.5	24.8.23	1987
GORMAN Teresa	Con	Billericay	34.0	30.9.31	1987
GORST John	Con	Hendon N	18.4	28.6.28	1970
GOULD Bryan	Lab	Dagenham	16.0	11.2.39	1974O R
(MP for Southampton Test 1974-9, Dagenham 1983-)					
GRAHAM Tommy	Lab	Renfrew W	3.7	5.12.43	1987
GRANT Sir Anthony	Con	Cambs SW	28.8	29.5.25	1964
(MP for Harrow C 1964-83, Cambs SW 1983-)					
GRANT Bernie	Lab	Tottenham	26.7	17.2.44	1987
GREENWAY Harry	Con	Ealing N	11.9	4.10.34	1979
GREENWAY John	Con	Ryedale	25.9	15.2.46	1987
GRIFFITHS Nigel	Lab	Edinburgh S	9.4	20.5.55	1987
GRIFFITHS Peter	Con	Portsm'th N	22.6	24.5.28	1964 R
(MP for Smethwick 1964-66, Portsmouth N 1979-)					
GRIFFITHS Win	Lab	Bridgend	15.6	11.2.43	1987
GROCOTT Bruce	Lab	Wrekin	9.5	1.11.40	1974O R
(MP for Lichfield 1974O-79, Wrekin 1987-)					
GRYLLS Sir Michael	Con	Surrey NW	43.4	21.2.34	1970
(MP for Chertsey 1970-74F, NW Surrey 74F-)					
GUMMER John	Con	Suffolk Coastal	29.8	26.11.39	1970 R
(MP for Lewisham W 1970-74F, Eye 1979-83, for Suffolk Coastal 1983-)					
GUNNELL John	Lab	Leeds S	16.1	1.10.33	1992
HAGUE William	Con	Richmond Yorks	36.2	26.3.61	1989*
HAIN Peter	Lab	Neath	52.8	16.2.50	1991*
HALL Michael	Con	Warrington S	0.3	20.9.52	1992
HAMILTON Archibald	Con	Epsom	36.7	30.12.41	1978*
HAMILTON Neil	Con	Tatton	27.6	9.3.49	1983
HAMPSON Dr Keith	Con	Leeds NW	15.2	14.8.43	1974F
HANLEY Jeremy	Con	Richmond & B	8.6	17.11.45	1983
HANNAM Sir John	Con	Exeter	4.9	2.8.29	1970
HANSON David	Lab	Delyn	3.7	5.7.57	1992
HARDY Peter	Con	Wentworth	46.7	17.7.31	1970
HARGREAVES Andrew	Con	B'ham Hall Green	7.8	15.5.55	1987
HARMAN Harriet	Lab	Peckham	38.2	30.7.50	1982*
HARRIS David	Con	St Ives	2.9	1.11.37	1983
HARVEY Nicholas	LD	Devon N	1.4	3.8.61	1992

NAME	PARTY	CONSTIT	% MAJ	BIRTH DATE	FIRST ELECTED
HASELHURST Alan	Con	Saffron Walden	28.0	23.6.37	1970 R
(MP for Middleton 1970-74F, Saffron Walden 1977*-)					
HATTERSLEY Roy	Lab	B'ham Sparkbrook	39.3	28.12.32	1964
HAWKINS Nicholas	Con	Blackpool S	3.8	27.3.57	1992
HAWKSLEY Warren	Con	Halesowen	15.0	10.3.43	1979R
(MP for the Wrekin 1979-87, Halesowen 1992-)					
HAYES Jerry	Con	Harlow	5.2	20.4.53	1983
HEALD Oliver	Con	Herts N	24.4	15.12.54	1992
HEATH Sir Edward	Con	Old Bexley	38.7	9.7.16	1950
HEATHCOAT-AMORY David	Con	Wells	11.5	21.3.49	1983
HENDERSON Douglas	Lab	Newcastle N	17.6	9.6.49	1987
HENDRON Dr Joseph	SDLP	Belfast W	1.5	12.11.32	1992
HENDRY Charles	Con	High Peak	8.0	6.5.59	1992
HEPPELL John	Lab	Nottingham E	16.1	3.11.48	1992
HESELTINE Michael	Con	Henley	35.6	21.3.33	1966
(MP for Tavistock 1966-74F, Henley 1974F-)					
HICKS Robert	Con	Cornwall SE	12.8	18.1.38	1970 R
(MP for Bodmin 1970-74 F; regained seat 1974O-1983, MP for Cornwall SE 1983-)					
HIGGINS Sir Terence	Con	Worthing	27.5	18.1.28	1964
HILL James	Con	Southampton Test	1.0	21.12.26	1970 R
(MP for Southampton Test 1970-74 O, regained seat 1979)					
HILL Keith	Lab	Streatham	5.7	28.7.43	1992
HINCHCLIFFE David	Lab	Wakefield	12.4	14.10.48	1987
HOEY Kate	Lab	Vauxhall	26.9	21.6.46	1989*
HOGG Douglas	Con	Grantham	29.6	5.2.45	1979
HOGG Norman	Lab	Cumbernauld	25.1	12.3.38	1979
HOME ROBERTSON John	Lab	E Lothian	18.3	5.12.48	1978*
HOOD James	Lab	Clydesdale	21.2	16.5.48	1987
HOON Geoffrey	Lab	Ashfield	22.3	6.12.53	1992
HORAM John	Con	Orpington	27.0	7.3.39	1970 R
(Lab MP for Gateshead W 1970-81, SDP MP for Gateshead W 1981-3. Con MP for Orpington 1992-)					
HORDERN Sir Peter	Con	Horsham	36.7	18.4.29	1964
HOWARD Michael	Con	Folkestone	17.0	7.7.41	1983
HOWARTH Alan	Con	Stratford	33.7	11.6.44	1983
HOWARTH George	Lab	Knowsley N	63.1	29.6.49	1986*
HOWELL David	Con	Guildford	22.1	18.1.36	1966
HOWELL Sir Ralph	Con	Norfolk N	20.8	25.5.23	1970
HOWELLS Dr Kim	Lab	Pontypridd	40.5	27.11.46	1989*
HOYLE Doug	Lab	Warrington N	20.8	17.2.30	1974O R
(MP for Nelson 1974 O-79, Warrington 1981*-83, Warrington N 1983-)					
HUGHES Kevin	Lab	Doncaster N	35.9	15.12.52	1992
HUGHES Robert	Lab	Aberdeen N	23.1	3.1.32	1970
HUGHES Robert G	Con	Harrow W	32.7	14.7.51	1987
HUGHES Roy	Lab	Newport E	23.6	9.6.25	1966
HUGHES Simon	LD	Southwark	26.1	17.5.51	1983*
HUME John †	SDLP	Foyle	25.1	18.1.37	1983
HUNT David	Con	Wirral W	21.7	21.5.42	1976*
HUNT Sir John	Con	Ravensbourne	42.4	27.10.29	1964
HUNTER Andrew	Con	Basingstoke	30.9	8.1.43	1983
HURD Douglas	Con	Witney	35.1	8.3.30	1974F

	PARTY	CONSTIT	% MAJ	BIRTH DATE	FIRST ELECTED
HUTTON John	Lab	Barrow	6.4	6.5.55	1992
ILSLEY Eric	Lab	Barnsley C	49.6	9.4.55	1987
INGRAM Adam	Lab	E Kilbride	23.4	1.2.47	1987
JACK Michael	Con	Fylde	42.1	17.9.46	1987
JACKSON Glenda	Lab	Hampstead	3.4	9.5.36	1992
JACKSON Helen	Lab	Sheffield H'borough	11.8	19.5.39	1992
JACKSON Robert	Con	Wantage	29.2	24.9.46	1983
JAMIESON David	Lab	Plymouth Devonport	14.5	18.5.47	1992
JANNER Greville	Lab	Leicester W	8.2	11.7.28	1970
JENKIN Bernard	Con	N Colchester	24.1	9.4.59	1992
JESSEL Toby	Con	Twickenham	10.7	11.7.34	1970
JOHNSON SMITH Sir Geoff	Con	Wealden	34.7	16.4.24	1959 R
(MP for Holborn 1959-64, East Grinstead 1965-83, for Wealden 1983-)					
JOHNSTON Sir Russell	LD	Inverness	0.9	28.7.32	1964
JONES Barry	Lab	Alyn	16.2	26.6.38	1970
(MP for East Flint 1970-83, Alyn 1983-)					
JONES Gwilym	Con	Cardiff N	6.2	1947	1983
JONES Ieuan Wyn	PIC	Ynys Mon	2.6	22.5.49	1987
JONES Jon Owen	Lab	Cardiff C	8.1	19.4.54	1992
JONES Dr Lynne	Lab	B'h'm Selly O	3.7	26.4.51	1992
JONES Martyn	Lab	Clwyd SW	10.0	1.3.47	1987
JONES Nigel	LD	Cheltenham	2.6	30.3.48	1992
JONES Robert	Con	Herts W	21.5	26.9.50	1983
JOPLING Michael	Con	Westmorland	29.4	10.12.30	1964
JOWELL Tessa	Lab	Dulwich	5.5	17.9.47	1992
KAUFMAN Gerald	Lab	M'chester Gorton	42.9	21.6.30	1970
KEEN Alan	Lab	Feltham	3.3	25.11.37	1992
KELLETT-BOWMAN Dme Elaine	Con	Lancaster	6.4	8.7.24	1970
KENNEDY Charles	LD	Ross Cromarty	18.6	25.11.59	1983
KENNEDY Jane	Lab	L'pool Broad Green	16.8	4.5.58	1992
KEY Robert	Con	Salisbury	14.8	22.4.45	1983
KHABRA Piara	Lab	Ealing Southall	13.9	20.11.24	1992
KILFEDDER Sir James	UPUP	Down N	11.0	16.7.28	1964R
(UU MP for Belfast W 1964-66; UU MP for Down N 1970-79; re-elected defeating Official Unionist 1979-80; UPUP MP 1980-)					
KILFOYLE Peter	Lab	L'pool Walton	59.9	9.6.46	1991*
KING Tom	Con	Bridgwater	17.1	13.6.33	1970
KINNOCK Neil	Lab	Islwyn	59.4	28.3.42	1970
(MP for Bedwellty 1970-83, Islwyn 1983- . He was leader of the Labour Party 1983-92)					
KIRKHOPE Tim	Con	Leeds NE	8.6	29.4.45	1987
KIRKWOOD Archy	LD	Roxburgh	12.6	22.4.46	1983
KNAPMAN Roger	Con	Stroud	19.2	20.2.44	1987
KNIGHT Angela	Con	Erewash	9.0	31.10.50	1992
KNIGHT Gregory	Con	Derby N	7.5	4.4.49	1983
KNIGHT Dame Jill	Con	B'ham Edgbaston	11.4	9.7.23	1966
KNOX Sir David	Con	Staffs Moorlands	11.8	30.5.33	1970
(MP for Leek 1970-83, Staffs Moorlands 1983-)					
KYNOCH George	Con	Kincardine	8.6	7.10.46	1992
LAIT Jacqui	Con	Hastings	12.3	16.12.47	1992
LAMONT Norman	Con	Kingston	25.4	8.5.42	1972*
LANG Ian	Con	Galloway	5.5	27.6.40	1979
LAWRENCE Sir Ivan	Con	Burton	9.7	24.12.36	1974F

	PARTY	CONSTIT	% MAJ	BIRTH DATE	FIRST ELECTED
LEGG Barry	Con	Milton K SW	9.2	30.5.49	1992
LEIGH Edward	Con	Gainsborough	27.9	20.7.50	1983
LEIGHTON Ron	Lab	Newham NE	27.8	24.1.30	1979
LENNOX-BOYD Mark	Con	Morecambe	26.0	4.5.43	1979
LESTER Jim	Con	Broxtowe	16.2	23.5.32	1974F
(MP for Beeston 1974-83, Broxtowe 1983-)					
LESTOR Joan	Lab	Eccles	27.5	13.11.31	1966 R
(MP for Eton & Slough 1966-83, Eccles 1987-)					
LEWIS Terry	Lab	Worsley	17.8	29.12.35	1983
LIDINGTON David	Con	Aylesbury	29.7	30.6.56	1992
LIGHTBOWN David	Con	Staffs SE	12.5	30.11.32	1983
LILLEY Peter	Con	St Albans	26.5	23.8.43	1983
LITHERLAND Bob	Lab	Manchester C	56.2	23.6.30	1979*
LIVINGSTONE Ken	Lab	Brent E	16.3	17.6.45	1987
LLOYD Tony	Lab	Stretford	29.7	25.2.50	1983
LLOYD Peter	Con	Fareham	36.4	12.11.37	1979
LLWYD Elfyn	PlC	Meirionnydd	17.5	26.9.51	1992
LOFTHOUSE Geoffrey	Lab	Pontefract	48.9	18.12.25	1978*
LORD Michael	Con	Suffolk Central	24.1	17.10.38	1983
LOYDEN Eddie	Lab	Liverpool Garston	30.2	3.5.23	1974F
LUFF Peter	Con	Worcester	10.2	18.2.55	1992
LYELL Sir Nicholas	Con	Beds Mid	36.4	6.12.38	1979
(MP for Hemel Hempstead 1979-83, Beds Mid 1983-)					
LYNNE Elizabeth	LD	Rochdale	3.5	22.1.48	1992
McALLION John	Lab	Dundee E	10.7	13.2.48	1987
McAVOY Thomas	Lab	Glasgow R'glen	38.5	14.12.43	1987
McCARTNEY Ian	Lab	Makerfield	33.3	25.5.51	1987
McCREA Rev William	DUP	Ulster Mid	11.3	6.8.48	1983
MacDONALD Calum	Lab	Western Isles	10.6	7.5.56	1987
McFALL John	Lab	Dumbarton	13.9	4.10.44	1987
McGRADY Eddie	SDLP	Down S	10.3	3.6.35	1987
MacGREGOR John	Con	Norfolk S	25.6	14.2.37	1974F
MACKAY Andrew	Con	Berks E	39.0	27.8.49	1977* R
(MP for B'ham Stechford 1977-79, Berkshire E 1983-)*					
McKELVEY William	Lab	Kilmarnock	14.1	July 1934	1979
MACKINLAY Andrew	Lab	Thurrock	2.2	24.4.49	1992
MACLEAN David	Con	Penrith	31.4	16.5.53	1983*
McLEISH Henry	Lab	Fife C	25.3	15.6.48	1987
MACLENNAN Robert	LD	Caithness	24.1	26.6.36	1966
(Lab MP for Caithness 1966-81, SDP MP 81- 88 and leader of SDP 87-88; Lib Dem MP 1988-)					
McLOUGHLIN Patrick	Con	Derbyshire W	31.0	30.11.57	1986*
McMASTER Gordon	Lab	Paisley S	26.6	13.2.60	1990*
McNAIR-WILSON Sir Patrick	Con	New Forest	33.5	28.5.29	1964 R
(MP for Lewisham W 1964-66, New Forest 1968-)*					
McNAMARA Kevin	Lab	Hull N	32.3	5.9.34	1966*
McWILLIAM John	Lab	Blaydon	26.0	16.5.41	1979
MADDEN Max	Lab	Bradford W	19.4	29.10.41	1974F R
(MP for Sowerby 1974F-79, Bradford W 1983-)					
MADDOCK Diana	LD	Christchurch	62.2	19.5.45	29.7.1993
MADEL David	Con	Beds SW	32.4	6.8.38	1970

	PARTY	CONSTIT	% MAJ	BIRTH DATE	FIRST ELECTED
MAGINNIS Ken	UUP	Fermanagh	25.6	21.1.38	1983
MAHON Alice	Lab	Halifax	0.8	28.9.37	1987
MAITLAND Lady Olga	Con	Sutton	21.4	23.5.44	1992
MAJOR John	Con	Huntingdon	49.3	29.3.43	1979
MALLON Seamus	SDLP	Newry	13.5	17.8.36	1986*
MALONE Gerald	Con	Winchester	12.3	21.7.50	1983 R
(MP for Aberdeen S 1983-7, Winchester 1992-)					
MANDELSON Peter	Lab	Hartlepool	17.0	21.10.53	1992
MANS Keith	Con	Wyre	21.6	10.2.46	1987
MAREK Dr John	Lab	Wrexham	13.1	24.12.40	1983
MARLAND Paul	Con	Gloucs W	7.4	19.3.40	1979
MARLOW Tony	Con	N'hampton N	7.2	17.6.40	1979
MARSHALL David	Lab	Glasgow Shett	41.5	May 1941	1979
MARSHALL James	Lab	Leicester S	17.7	13.3.41	1974O R
(MP for Leicester S 1974O- 83, regained seat 1987-)					
MARSHALL John	Con	Hendon S	34.4	19.8.40	1987
MARSHALL Sir Michael	Con	Arundel	32.5	21.6.30	1974F
MARTIN David	Con	Portsmouth S	0.5	5.2.45	1987
MARTIN Michael	Lab	Glasgow S'burn	48.2	3.7.45	1979
MARTLEW Eric	Lab	Carlisle	7.1	3.1.49	1987
MATES Michael	Con	Hants E	39.4	9.6.34	1974O
(MP for Petersfield 1974O-83, Hants E 83-)					
MAWHINNEY Dr Brian	Con	Peterborough	8.2	26.7.40	1979
MAXTON John	Lab	G'gow Cathcart	23.7	5.5.36	1979
MAYHEW Sir Patrick	Con	Tonbridge Wells	28.6	11.9.29	1974F
MEACHER Michael	Lab	Oldham W	20.4	4.11.39	1970
MEALE Alan	Lab	Mansfield	21.3	31.7.49	1987
MELLOR David	Con	Putney	15.6	12.3.49	1979
MERCHANT Piers	Con	Beckenham	33.0	2.1.51	1983 R
(MP for Newcastle C 1983-7, Beckenham 1992-)					
MICHAEL Alun	Lab	Cardiff S	21.9	22.8.43	1987
MICHIE Ray	LD	Argyll	7.2	4.2.34	1987
MICHIE William	Lab	Sheffield Heeley	29.7	24.11.35	1983
MILBURN Alan	Lab	Darlington	5.1	27.1.58	1992
MILLER Andrew	Lab	Ellesmere Pt	3.3	23.3.49	1992
MILLIGAN Stephen	Con	Eastleigh	23.3	12.5.48	1992
MILLS Iain	Con	Meriden	24.2	21.4.40	1979
MITCHELL Andrew	Con	Gedling	18.7	23.3.56	1987
MITCHELL Austin	Lab	Great Grimsby	14.8	19.9.34	1977*
MITCHELL Sir David	Con	Hants NW	30.2	20.6.28	1964
(MP for Basingstoke 1964-83, Hants NW 1983-)					
MOATE Sir Roger	Con	Faversham	25.0	12.5.38	1970
MOLYNEAUX James	UUP	Lagan Valley	48.1	27.8.20	1970
(MP for Antrim S 1970-83, Lagan Valley 1983-)					
MONRO Sir Hector	Con	Dumfries	13.1	4.10.22	1964
MONTGOMERY Sir Fergus	Con	Altrincham	31.6	25.11.27	1959 R
(MP for Newcastle E 1959-64, Brierley Hill 1967-74F, Altrincham 74 O-)*					
MOONIE Dr Lewis	Lab	Kirkcaldy	23.5	25.2.47	1987
MORGAN Rhodri	Lab	Cardiff W	20.3	29.9.39	1987
MORLEY Elliot	Lab	Glanford	14.5	6.7.52	1987

	PARTY	CONSTIT	% MAJ	BIRTH DATE	FIRST ELECTED
MORRIS Alf	Lab	M'chester W'shawe	32.1	23.3.28	1964
MORRIS Estelle	Lab	B'ham Yardley	0.4	6.6.52	1992
MORRIS John	Lab	Aberavon	53.2	5.11.31	1959
MORRIS Michael	Con	N'hampton S	25.4	25.11.36	1974F
MOSS Malcolm	Con	Cambs NE	23.8	6.3.43	1987
MOWLAM Dr Marjorie	Lab	Redcar	23.8	18.9.49	1987
MUDIE George	Lab	Leeds E	29.4	6.2.45	1992
MULLIN Chris	Lab	Sunderland S	28.6	12.12.47	1987
MURPHY Paul	Lab	Torfaen	43.8	25.11.48	1987
NEEDHAM Richard	Con	Wilts N	23.4	29.1.42	1979
NELSON Anthony	Con	Chichester	32.7	11.6.48	1974 O
NEUBERT Sir Michael	Con	Romford	27.1	3.9.33	1974F
NEWTON Anthony	Con	Braintree	26.6	29.8.37	1974F
NICHOLLS Patrick	Con	Teignbridge	14.2	14.11.48	1983
NICHOLSON David	Con	Taunton	5.2	17.8.44	1987
NICHOLSON Emma	Con	Devon W	5.8	16.10.41	1987
NORRIS Steven	Con	Epping Forest	37.1	24.5.45	1983 R
(MP for Oxford E 1983-87, Epping Forest 1988*)					
OAKES Gordon	Lab	Halton	31.0	22.6.31	1964 R
(MP for Bolton W 1964-70, Widnes 1971*-83, Halton 1983-)					
O'BRIEN Michael	Lab	Warks N	2.4	19.6.54	1992
O'BRIEN William	Lab	Normanton	17.9	25.1.29	1983
O'HARA Edward	Lab	Knowsley S	47.3	1.10.37	1990*
OLNER Bill	Lab	Nuneaton	2.7	9.5.42	1992
O'NEILL Martin	Lab	Clackmannan	22.2	6.1.45	1979
ONSLOW Sir Cranley	Con	Woking	31.0	8.6.26	1964
OPPENHEIM Philip	Con	Amber Valley	1.2	20.3.56	1983
ORME Stanley	Lab	Salford E	33.2	5.5.23	1964
OTTAWAY Richard	Con	Croydon S	40.7	24.5.45	1983 R
(MP for Nottingham N 1983-87, Croydon S 1992-)					
PAGE Richard	Con	Herts SW	33.9	22.2.41	1976* R
(MP for Workington 1976*-79, Herts SW 1979*-)					
PAICE James	Con	Cambs SE	37.6	24.4.49	1987
PAISLEY Rev Ian †	DUP	Antrim N	32.8	6.4.26	1970
PARRY Bob	Lab	Liverpool Riverside	64.4	8.1.33	1970
PATCHETT Terry	Lab	Barnsley E	63.0	11.7.40	1983
PATNICK Irvine	Con	Sheff Hallam	12.4	October 1929	1987
PATTEN John	Con	Oxford W	6.4	17.7.45	1979
PATTIE Sir Geoffrey	Con	Chertsey	40.2	17.1.36	1974F
PAWSEY James	Con	Rugby	20.3	21.8.33	1979
PEACOCK Elizabeth	Con	Batley	2.3	4.9.37	1983
PENDRY Tom	Lab	Stalybridge	17.6	10.6.34	1970
PICKLES Eric	Con	Brentwood	27.2	20.4.52	1992
PICKTHALL Colin	Lab	Lancs W	3.2	13.9.44	1992
PIKE Peter	Lab	Burnley	22.4	26.6.37	1983
POPE Gregory	Lab	Hyndburn	4.0	29.8.60	1992
PORTER David	Con	Waveney	9.7	16.4.48	1987
PORTER Barry	Con	Wirral S	16.3	11.6.39	1979
PORTILLO Michael	Con	Enfield Southgate	31.7	26.5.53	1984*
POWELL Raymond	Lab	Ogmore	56.6	19.6.28	1979
POWELL William	Con	Corby	0.6	3.8.48	1983
PRENTICE Bridget	Lab	Lewisham E	2.5	28.12.52	1992

	PARTY	CONSTIT	% MAJ	BIRTH DATE	FIRST ELECTED
PRENTICE Gordon	Lab	Pendle	4.0	28.1.51	1992
PRESCOTT John	Lab	Hull E	39.1	31.5.38	1970
PRIMAROLO Dawn	Lab	Bristol S	17.8	2.5.54	1987
PURCHASE Ken	Lab	W'hampton NE	8.1	8.1.39	1992
QUIN Joyce	Lab	Gateshead E	39.1	26.11.44	1987
RADICE Giles	Lab	Durham N	35.0	4.10.36	1973*
RANDALL Stuart	Lab	Hull W	28.7	22.6.38	1983
RATHBONE Tim	Con	Lewes	20.1	17.3.33	1974F
RAYNSFORD Nick	Lab	Greenwich	3.8	28.1.45	1986* R
(MP for Fulham 1986*-87, Greenwich 1992-)					
REDMOND Martin	Lab	Don Valley	23.3	15.8.37	1983
REDWOOD John	Con	Wokingham	36.3	15.6.51	1987
REID Dr John	Lab	Motherwell N	43.0	8.5.47	1987
RENDEL David	LD	Newbury	65.1	15.4.49	6.5.1993
RENTON Tim	Con	Sussex Mid	30.7	28.5.32	1974F
RICHARDS Roderick	Con	Clwyd NW	11.4	12.3.47	1992
RICHARDSON Jo	Lab	Barking	17.7	28.8.23	1974F
RIDDICK Graham	Con	Colne Vall	12.2	26.8.55	1987
RIFKIND Malcolm	Con	E'burgh P'lds	9.6	21.6.46	1974F
ROBATHAN Andrew	Con	Blaby	37.2	17.7.51	1992
ROBERTS Sir Wyn	Con	Conwy	2.4	10.7.30	1970
ROBERTSON George	Lab	Hamilton	35.4	12.4.46	1978*
ROBERTSON Raymond	Con	Aberdeen S	3.7	11.12.59	1992
ROBINSON Geoffrey	Lab	Coventry NW	16.4	25.5.39	1976*
ROBINSON Mark	Con	Somerton	7.4	26.12.46	1983 R
(MP for Newport W 1983-87, Somerton 1992-)					
ROBINSON Peter	DUP	Belfast E	21.8	29.12.48	1979
ROCHE Barbara	Lab	Hornsey	9.3	13.4.54	1992
ROE Marion	Con	Broxbourne	41.6	15.7.36	1983
ROGERS Allan	Lab	Rhondda	62.7	24.10.32	1983
ROOKER Jeff	Lab	B'h'm Perry B	16.6	5.6.41	1974F
ROONEY Terence	Lab	Bradford N	15.7	11.11.50	1990*
ROSS Ernie	Lab	Dundee W	25.3	27.7.42	1979
ROSS William	UUP	Londonderry E	35.1	4.2.36	1974F
ROWE Andrew	Con	Kent Mid	33.1	11.9.35	1983
ROWLANDS Ted	Lab	Merthyr	60.3	23.1.40	1966 R
(MP for Cardiff N 1966-70, Merthyr 1972*-)					
RUDDOCK Joan	Lab	L'sham Deptford	33.0	28.12.43	1987
RUMBOLD Dame Angela	Con	Mitcham	3.4	11.8.32	1982*
RYDER Richard	Con	Norfolk Mid	28.9	4.2.49	1983
SACKVILLE Tom	Con	Bolton W	1.8	26.10.50	1983
SAINSBURY Tim	Con	Hove	24.5	11.6.32	1973*
SALMOND Alex	SNP	Banff	8.9	31.12.54	1987
SCOTT Nicholas	Con	Chelsea	47.7	5.8.33	1966 R
(MP for Paddington S 1966-74F, Chelsea 1974 O-)					
SEDGEMORE Brian	Lab	Hackney S	24.4	17.3.37	1974F R
(MP for Luton W 1974F- 79, for Hackney S 1983-)					
SHAW David	Con	Dover	1.4	14.11.50	1987
SHAW Sir Giles	Con	Pudsey	14.6	16.11.31	1974F
SHEERMAN Barry	Lab	Huddersfield	14.8	17.8.40	1979
SHELDON Robert	Lab	Ashton-u-Lyne	25.2	13.9.23	1964
SHEPHARD Gillian	Con	Norfolk SW	27.5	22.1.40	1987

	PARTY	CONSTIT	% MAJ	BIRTH DATE	FIRST ELECTED
SHEPHERD Colin	Con	Hereford	6.0	13.1.38	1974 O
SHEPHERD Richard	Con	Aldridge	21.1	6.12.42	1979
SHERSBY Michael	Con	Uxbridge	27.1	17.2.33	1972*
SHORE Peter	Lab	Bethnal Gn	33.6	20.5.24	1964
SHORT Clare	Lab	B'h'm Ladywood	40.7	15.2.46	1983
SIMPSON Alan	Lab	Nottingham S	5.9	20.9.48	1992
SIMS Roger	Con	Chislehurst	36.0	27.1.30	1974F
SKEET Sir Trevor	Con	Beds N	19.7	28.1.18	1959 R
(MP for Willesden W 1959-64, Bedford 1970-83, Beds N 1983-)					
SKINNER Dennis	Lab	Bolsover	39.2	11.2.32	1970
SMITH Andrew	Lab	Oxford E	16.0	1.2.51	1987
SMITH Chris	Lab	Islington S	26.4	24.7.51	1983
SMITH Sir Dudley	Con	Warwick	15.4	14.11.26	1959 R
(MP for Brentford 1959-66, Warwick 1968-)*					
SMITH John	Lab	Monklands E	43.2	13.9.38	1970
SMITH Llew †	Lab	Blaenau Gwent	69.2	16.4.44	1992
SMITH Tim	Con	Beaconsfield	44.6	5.10.47	1977* R
(MP for Ashfield 1977-79, for Beaconsfield 1982*-)*					
SMYTH Rev Martin	UUP	Belfast S	30.0	15.6.31	1982*
SNAPE Peter	Lab	W Brom E	6.6	12.2.42	1974F
SOAMES Nicholas	Con	Crawley	12.5	12.2.48	1983
SOLEY Clive	Lab	Hammersmith	14.0	7.5.39	1979
SPEARING Nigel	Lab	Newham S	8.1	8.10.30	1974*
SPEED Sir Keith	Con	Ashford	30.5	11.3.34	1968 R
(MP for Meriden 1968-70, for Ashford 1974O-)*					
SPELLAR John	Lab	Warley W	13.0	5.8.47	1982* R
(MP for Birmingham Northfield 1982-1983, 1992-)*					
SPENCER Sir Derek	Con	Brighton Pav	8.3	31.3.36	1983 R
(MP for Leicester S 1983-87, Brighton Pavilion 1992-)					
SPICER Sir James	Con	Dorset W	14.7	4.10.25	1974F
SPICER Michael	Con	Worcs S	25.1	22.1.43	1974F
SPINK Dr Robert	Con	Castle Point	31.6	1.8.48	1992
SPRING Richard	Con	Bury St Edmunds	30.0	24.9.46	1992
SPROAT Iain	Con	Harwich	27.5	8.11.38	1970 R
(MP for Aberdeen S 1970-83; transferred to Roxburgh 1983 but defeated; MP for Harwich 1992-)					
SQUIRE Rachel	Lab	Dunfermline W	19.2	13.7.54	1992
SQUIRE Robin	Con	Hornchurch	19.0	12.7.44	1979
STANLEY Sir John	Con	Tonbridge	33.7	19.1.42	1974F
STEEL Sir David	LD	Tweeddale	8.2	31.3.38	1965*
(MP for Roxburgh 1965-83, Tweeddale 1983- . Leader of the Liberal Party 1976-88)*					
STEEN Anthony	Con	S Hams	20.4	22.7.39	1974F R
(MP for L'pool Wavertree 1974F-83, South Hams 1983-)					
STEINBERG Gerald	Lab	Durham	29.6	20.4.45	1987
STEPHEN Michael	Con	Shoreham	24.7	25.9.42	1992
STERN Michael	Con	Bristol NW	0.1	3.8.42	1983
STEVENSON George †	Lab	Stoke S	13.0	30.8.38	1992
STEWART Allan	Con	Eastwood	22.7	1.6.42	1979
STOTT Roger	Lab	Wigan	39.4	7.8.43	1973*
STRANG Dr Gavin	Lab	Edinburgh E	21.4	10.7.43	1970
STRAW Jack	Lab	Blackburn	11.0	3.8.46	1979

	PARTY	CONSTIT	% MAJ	BIRTH DATE	FIRST ELECTED
STREETER Gary	Con	Plymouth Sutton	21.8	2.10.55	1992
SUMBERG David	Con	Bury S	1.5	2.6.41	1983
SWEENEY Walter	Con	Vale of Glam	0.0	23.4.49	1992
SYKES John	Con	Scarborough	19.9	24.8.56	1992
TAPSELL Sir Peter	Con	Lindsey E	19.0	1.2.30	1959 R
(MP for Nottingham W 1959-64, Horncastle 1966-83, Lindsey E 1983-)					
TAYLOR Ann	Lab	Dewsbury	1.1	2.7.47	1974O R
(Taylor was MP for Bolton W 1974 O-83, Dewsbury 1987-)					
TAYLOR Sir Teddy	Con	Southend E	31.3	18.4.37	1964 R
(Taylor was MP for Glasgow Cathcart 1964-79, for Southend E 1980-)*					
TAYLOR Ian	Con	Esher	42.8	18.4.45	1987
TAYLOR John D	UUP	Strangford	19.9	24.12.37	1983
TAYLOR John M	Con	Solihull	39.9	19.8.41	1983
TAYLOR Matthew	LD	Truro	12.2	3.1.63	1987*
TEMPLE-MORRIS Peter	Con	Leominster	28.8	12.2.38	1974F
THOMASON Roy	Con	Bromsgrove	23.4	14.12.44	1992
THOMPSON Sir Donald	Con	Calder Valley	8.0	13.11.31	1979
THOMPSON Patrick	Con	Norwich N	0.5	21.10.35	1983
THOMPSON John	Lab	Wansbeck	36.1	27.8.28	1983
THORNTON Sir Malcolm	Con	Crosby	21.8	3.4.39	1979
(Thornton was MP for Liverpool Garston 1979-83, Crosby 1983-)					
THURNHAM Peter	Con	Bolton NE	0.4	21.8.38	1983
TIPPING Paddy	Lab	Sherwood	4.6	24.10.49	1992
TOWNEND John	Con	Bridlington	24.7	12.6.34	1979
TOWNSEND Cyril	Con	Bexleyheath	29.7	21.12.37	1974F
TRACEY Richard	Con	Surbiton	27.6	8.2.43	1983
TREDINNICK David	Con	Bosworth	28.3	19.1.50	1987
TREND Michael	Con	Windsor	20.5	19.4.52	1992
TRIMBLE David	UUP	Upper Bann	35.5	15.10.44	1990*
TROTTER Neville	Con	Tynemouth	1.0	27.1.32	1974F
TURNER Dennis	Lab	W'hampton SE	25.0	26.8.42	1987
TWINN Dr Ian	Con	Edmonton	1.2	26.4.50	1983
TYLER Paul	LD	Cornwall N	3.1	29.10.41	1974F R
(MP for Bodmin 1974F-74O, Cornwall N 1992-)					
VAUGHAN Sir Gerard	Con	Reading E	26.9	11.6.23	1970
VAZ Keith	Lab	Leicester E	22.8	26.11.56	1987
VIGGERS Peter	Con	Gosport	30.5	13.3.38	1974F
WALDEGRAVE William	Con	Bristol W	11.6	15.8.46	1979
WALDEN George	Con	Buckingham	41.9	15.9.39	1983
WALKER Cecil	UUP	Belfast N	26.8	17.12.24	1983
WALKER Bill	Con	Tayside N	9.2	20.2.29	1979
WALKER Harold	Lab	Doncaster C	20.9	12.7.27	1964
WALLACE James	LD	Orkney	24.4	25.8.54	1983
WALLER Gary	Con	Keighley	6.6	24.6.45	1979
(MP for Brighouse 1979-83, Keighley 1983-)					
WALLEY Joan	Lab	Stoke N	27.5	23.1.49	1987
WARD John	Con	Poole	20.4	8.3.25	1979
WARDELL Gareth	Lab	Gower	15.0	29.11.44	1982*
WARDLE Charles	Con	Bexhill	31.3	23.8.39	1983
WAREING Bob	Lab	L'pool W Derby	51.6	20.8.30	1983

	PARTY	CONSTIT	% MAJ	BIRTH DATE	FIRST ELECTED
WATERSON Nigel	Con	Eastbourne	8.9	12.10.50	1992
WATSON Mike	Lab	G'gow C	36.3	1.5.49	1989*
WATTS John	Con	Slough	0.9	19.4.47	1983
WELLS Bowen	Con	Hertford	32.5	4.8.35	1979
WELSH Andrew	SNP	Angus E	2.0	19.4.44	1974O R
(MP for Angus S 1974 O-1979, Angus E 1987-)					
WHEELER Sir John	Con	Westminster N	8.4	1.5.40	1979
WHITNEY Ray	Con	Wycombe	30.2	28.11.30	1978*
WHITTINGDALE John	Con	Colchester S	31.9	16.10.59	1992
WICKS Malcolm	Lab	Croydon NW	3.8	1.7.47	1992
WIDDECOMBE Ann	Con	Maidstone	27.9	4.10.47	1987
WIGGIN Sir Jerry	Con	Weston-s-Mare	8.5	24.2.37	1969*
WIGLEY Dafydd	PIC	Caernarfon	39.9	1.4.43	1974F
WILKINSON John	Con	Ruislip	44.6	23.9.40	1970 R
(MP for Bradford W 1970-74F, Rusilip 1979-)					
WILLETTS David	Con	Havant	30.0	9.3.56	1992
WILLIAMS Alan	Lab	Swansea W	21.6	14.10.30	1964
WILLIAMS Dr Alan W	Lab	Carmarthen	5.1	21.12.45	1987
WILSHIRE David	Con	Spelthorne	35.6	16.9.43	1987
WILSON Brian	Lab	Cunninghame N	6.9	13.12.48	1987
WINNICK David	Lab	Walsall N	7.3	26.6.33	1966 R
(MP for Croydon S 1966-70, Walsall N 1976-)*					
WINTERTON Ann	Con	Congleton	18.7	6.3.41	1983
WINTERTON Nicholas	Con	Macclesfield	36.1	31.3.38	1971*
WISE Audrey	Lab	Preston	26.5	4.1.35	1974F
WOLFSON Mark	Con	Sevenoaks	33.1	7.4.34	1979
WOOD Tim	Con	Stevenage	8.4	13.8.40	1983
WORTHINGTON Tony	Lab	Clydebank	33.8	11.10.41	1987
WRAY James	Lab	G'gow Provan	44.8	28.4.38	1987
WRIGHT Dr Anthony	Lab	Cannock	2.5	11.3.48	1992
YEO Tim	Con	Suffolk S	24.9	20.3.45	1983
YOUNG David	Lab	Bolton SE	25.6	12.10.28	1974F
YOUNG Sir George	Con	Ealing Acton	15.7	16.7.41	1974F

1974F indicates February 1974 election; 1974 indicates October election; * indicates by-election; R indicates a "retread" — the parliamentary term for an MP who re-enters the Commons after a period out of it; † denotes also a member of European Parliament. For full names of constituencies and of those MPs abbreviated here, see table: Index of Constituencies

GENERAL ELECTION 1992 IN BRIEF

House of Commons

UK:

			cand	seat	lost* deposits
Conservatives	14093007	41.9	645	336	4
Labour	11560094	34.4	634	271	1
Liberal Democrat	5999606	17.8	632	20	11
Scottish National	629564	1.9	72	3	0
Plaid Cymru **	156796	0.5	38	4	23
Green**	170047	0.5	253	0	253
Liberal	64744	0.2	73	0	72
Natural Law	62888	0.2	309	0	309
Ulster Unionist	271049	0.8	13	0	9
Democratic Unionist	103039	0.3	7	0	3
Popular Unionist	19305	0.1	1	1	0
SDLP	184445	0.5	13	4	0
Sinn Fein	78291	0.2	14	0	5
Alliance	68665	0.2	16	0	5
Others	152534	0.5	229	0	218
TOTAL	**33614074**		**2949**	**651**	**901**

* includes 11 in NI   ** joint Pl C-Green counted as Pl C votes
Turnout 77.7%

REGIONAL

	Con	**Lab**	**LDem**	**Nat**	**Other**	**Total**
ENG	12796772	9551910	5398293		401531	28148506
SCOT	751950	1142911	383856	629564	23417	2931698
WALES**	499677	865663	217457	156747	9233	1748777
NI	44608				740485	785093

**joint PlC-Green counted as Pl C votes
GB shares of vote (%)   42.8   35.2   18.3   2.4   1.3

PARTY PERCENTAGES BY REGION

	Con	Lab	LDem	Nat	Other
ENG	45.5	33.9	19.2	-	1.4
Nth	33.4	50.6	15.6	-	0.5
YH	37.9	44.3	16.8	-	0.9
EM	46.6	37.4	15.3	-	0.7
EA	51.0	28.0	19.5	-	1.5
GL	45.3	37.1	15.1	-	2.5
SE	54.5	20.8	23.3	-	1.4
SW	47.6	19.2	31.4	-	1.8
WM	44.8	38.8	15.0	-	1.5
NW	37.8	44.9	15.8	-	1.5
Wales	28.6	49.5	12.4	9.0	0.5
Scot	25.6	39.0	13.1	21.5	0.8
NIre	5.7				94.3

changes since 1987

	Con	Lab	LDem	Nat	Others
ENG	-0.8	+4.4	-4.7		+1.0
Nh	+1.1	+4.2	-5.5		+0.2
YH	+0.5	+3.7	-4.8		+0.6
EM	-2.0	+7.4	-5.7		+0.3
EA	-1.1	+6.3	-6.2		+1.0
GL	-1.2	+5.6	-6.2		+1.7
SE	-1.1	+4.0	-3.8		+0.9
SW	-3.0	+3.3	-1.6		+1.3
WM	-0.8	+5.5	-5.8		+1.1
NW	-0.2	+3.7	-4.8		+1.3
Wales	-0.9	+4.4	-5.5	+1.7	+0.3
Scot	+1.6	-3.4	-6.1	+7.4	+0.5
GB	-0.5	+3.7	-4.8	+0.7	+0.9

CON LOST:

To Labour- Barrow, Birmingham Northfield, Birmingham Selly Oak, Birmingham Yardley, Bristol E, Cambridge, Cannock, Cardiff C, Croydon NW, Darlington, Delyn, Dulwich, Ellesmere Pt, Feltham, Hampstead, Hornsey, Hyndburn, Ilford S, Ipswich, Kingswood, Lancashire W, Lewisham E, Lewisham W, Nottingham E, Nottingham S, Nuneaton, Pembroke, Pendle, Rossendale, Sherwood, Southampton Itchen, Stockport, Streatham, Thurrock, Wallasey, Walthamstow, Warrington S, Warwickshire N, Wolverhampton NE, York (40)

To LibDem — Bath, Cheltenham, Cornwall N, Devon N (4)

LABOUR LOST:

To Conservative — Aberdeen S (1)

LIB DEMS LOST:

To Conservative — Brecon, Southport (2)

To Plaid Cymru — Ceredigion (1)

SDP LOST:

To Labour — Greenwich, Plymouth Devonport, Woolwich (3)

SINN FEIN LOST:

To SDLP — Belfast W (1)

What next?: John Smith's attempts at party reform, particularly one member one vote, met with considerable resistance from the trades unions, who adopted the battle cry 'no say, no pay'

THE 1992 ELECTION RESULT IN DETAIL

These tables show how the parties fared in the constituencies on April 9 1992. The left-hand side of the table shows the parties' numerical votes; the right-hand side shows the proportion they took of the total vote in the constituency. The size of the qualified electorate, and the turnout (the proportion of those qualified to vote who actually did so) are shown in the final two columns. (For the names of successful candidates see: Index of Constituencies.)

The results given here largely follow Britain Votes 5, compiled and edited by Colin Rallings and Michael Thrasher (Parliamentary Research Services) and incorporate many changes since the results published immediately after the election, discovered by checking with the Home Office and with returning officers. Most of the changes are in figures for total electorates, but in some cases the votes initially attributed to the parties have been corrected. In Pudsey, for instance, the Conservative majority over Labour is now stated to have been 8,372 (14.6%), not 8,972 (15.8%), as published at the time.

Columns headed "Others" shows the aggregate vote for all candidates of parties other than those specifically listed. Where the vote of a candidate from one of the "other" parties topped 5%, this is noted underneath the constituency result. The best performances by "other" candidates were: *J.Kilfedder (UPUP, Down N) 42.9% — elected; *J.Cartwright (SDP, Woolwich) 38.6%; *R.Barnes (SDP, Greenwich) 37.2%; *D.Nellist (Ind Lab, Coventry SE) 28.9%; T.Sheridan (Scottish Militant, Glasgow Pollok) 19.3 per cent. (* denotes the former MP for the constituency.) In Winchester, J.Browne, who fought as an independent Conservative after being de-selected by his local party, polled only 4.7%.

Northern Ireland seats are listed at the end of the tables on pages 324-325

Constituency	Con	Lab	LDem	Nat	Other	Votes	maj
Aberavon	5567	26877	4999	1919	707	40069	21310
Aberdeen N	6836	18845	4772	9608		40061	9237
Aberdeen S	15808	14291	4767	6223		41089	1517
Acton	22579	15572	5487		986	44624	7007
Aldershot	36974	8552	17786		1038	64350	19188
Aldridge	28431	17407	6503			52341	11024
Altrincham	29066	12275	11601		212	53154	16791
Alyn & Deeside	17355	25206	4687	551	633	48432	7851
Amber Valley	27418	26706	5294			59418	712
Angus East	18052	5994	3897	19006	449	47398	954
Argyll	10117	4946	12739	8689		36491	2622
Arundel	35405	8321	15542		1796	61064	19863
Ashfield	19031	32018	7291			58340	12987
Ashford	31031	11365	13672		773	56841	17359
Ashton-u-Lyne	13615	24550	4005		1196	43366	10935
Aylesbury	36500	8517	17640		941	63598	18860
Ayr	22172	22087	4067	5949	132	54407	85
Banbury	32215	15495	10602		250	58562	16720
Banff	17846	3803	2588	21954		46191	4108
Barking	11956	18224	5133			35313	6268
Barnsley C	7687	27048	4321			39056	19361
Barnsley E	5569	30346	3399			39314	24777
Barnsley W & P	13461	27965	5610		970	48006	14504
Barrow	22990	26568	6089			55647	3578
Basildon	24159	22679	6963			53801	1480
Basingstoke	37521	16323	14119		714	68677	21198
Bassetlaw	19064	29061	6340			54465	9997
Bath	21950	4102	25718		801	52571	3768
Batley & Spen	27629	26221	6380		628	60858	1408
Battersea	26390	21550	3659		682	52281	4840
Beaconsfield	33817	7163	10220		1679	52879	23597
Beckenham	26323	11038	8038		886	46285	15285
Beds Mid	40230	15092	11957		1861	69140	25138
Beds North	29970	18302	10014		821	59057	11668
Beds SW	37498	16225	10988		928	65639	21273
Berks E	43898	14458	15218			73574	28680
Berwick	14240	9933	19283			43456	5043

Con	Lab	LDem	Nat	Other	% maj	Electors	Turnout
13.9%	67.1%	12.5%	4.8%	1.8%	53.2%	51655	77.6%
17.1%	47.0%	11.9%	24.0%	0.0%	23.1%	59911	66.9%
38.5%	34.8%	11.6%	15.1%	0.0%	3.7%	58881	69.8%
50.6%	34.9%	12.3%	0.0%	2.2%	15.7%	58688	76.0%
57.5%	13.3%	27.6%	0.0%	1.6%	29.8%	81755	78.7%
54.3%	33.3%	12.4%	0.0%	0.0%	21.1%	63404	82.6%
54.7%	23.1%	21.8%	0.0%	0.4%	31.6%	66248	80.2%
35.8%	52.0%	9.7%	1.1%	1.3%	16.2%	60478	80.1%
46.1%	44.9%	8.9%	0.0%	0.0%	1.2%	70156	84.7%
38.1%	12.6%	8.2%	40.1%	0.9%	2.0%	63170	75.0%
27.7%	13.6%	34.9%	23.8%	0.0%	7.2%	47921	76.1%
58.0%	13.6%	25.5%	0.0%	2.9%	32.5%	79299	77.0%
32.6%	54.9%	12.5%	0.0%	0.0%	22.3%	72528	80.4%
54.6%	20.0%	24.1%	0.0%	1.4%	30.5%	71768	79.2%
31.4%	56.6%	9.2%	0.0%	2.8%	25.2%	58702	73.9%
57.4%	13.4%	27.7%	0.0%	1.5%	29.7%	79090	80.3%
40.8%	40.6%	7.5%	10.9%	0.2%	0.2%	65534	83.0%
55.0%	26.5%	18.1%	0.0%	0.4%	28.6%	71847	81.5%
38.6%	8.2%	5.6%	47.5%	0.0%	8.9%	64472	71.6%
33.9%	51.6%	14.5%	0.0%	0.0%	17.7%	50480	70.0%
19.7%	69.3%	11.1%	0.0%	0.0%	49.6%	55374	70.5%
14.2%	77.2%	8.6%	0.0%	0.0%	63.0%	53956	72.9%
28.0%	58.3%	11.7%	0.0%	2.0%	30.2%	63391	75.7%
41.3%	47.7%	10.9%	0.0%	0.0%	6.4%	67835	82.0%
44.9%	42.2%	12.9%	0.0%	0.0%	2.8%	67442	79.8%
54.6%	23.8%	20.6%	0.0%	1.0%	30.9%	82962	82.8%
35.0%	53.4%	11.6%	0.0%	0.0%	18.4%	68583	79.4%
41.8%	7.8%	48.9%	0.0%	1.5%	7.2%	63838	82.4%
45.4%	43.1%	10.5%	0.0%	1.0%	2.3%	76387	79.7%
50.5%	41.2%	7.0%	0.0%	1.3%	9.3%	68207	76.7%
64.0%	13.5%	19.3%	0.0%	3.2%	44.6%	66899	79.0%
56.9%	23.8%	17.4%	0.0%	1.9%	33.0%	59469	77.8%
58.2%	21.8%	17.3%	0.0%	2.7%	36.4%	81950	84.4%
50.7%	31.0%	17.0%	0.0%	1.4%	19.7%	73789	80.1%
57.1%	24.7%	16.7%	0.0%	1.4%	32.4%	80120	81.9%
59.7%	19.7%	20.7%	0.0%	0.0%	39.0%	90414	81.4%
32.8%	22.9%	44.4%	0.0%	0.0%	11.6%	54937	79.1%

Constituency	Con	Lab	LDem	Nat	Other	Votes	maj
Bethnal Gn	6507	20350	8120		1466	36443	12230
Beverley	34503	12026	17986		199	64714	16517
Bexhill	31330	4883	15023		784	52020	16307
Bexleyheath	25606	11520	10107		170	47403	14086
Billericay	37406	13880	14912			66198	22494
Birkenhead	11485	29098	4417		733	45733	17613
B'hm Edgbaston	18529	14222	4419		643	37813	4307
B'hm Erdington	13814	18549	4398			36761	4735
B'hm Hall Gn	21649	17984	7342			46975	3665
B'hm Hodge Hill	14827	21895	3740		370	40832	7068
B'hm Ladywood	9604	24887	3068			37559	15283
B'hm Northfield	23803	24433	5431			53667	630
B'hm Perry Barr	18917	27507	5261			51685	8590
B'hm Selly Oak	23370	25430	5679		797	55276	2060
B'hm Small H	8686	22675	2515		824	34700	13989
B'hm Sparkbrook	8544	22116	3028		833	34521	13572
B'hm Yardley	14722	14884	12899		192	42697	162
Bp Auckland	17676	27763	10099			55538	10087
Blaby	39498	14151	13780		781	68210	25347
Blackburn	20606	26633	6332		1407	54978	6027
Blackpool N	21501	18461	4786		303	45051	3040
Blackpool S	19880	18213	5675		173	43941	1667
Blaenau Gwent	4266	34333	2774	2099		43472	30067
Blaydon	13685	27028	10602			51315	13343
Blyth Valley	7691	24542	16498		470	49201	8044
Bolsover	13323	33978	5368			52669	20655
Bolton NE	21644	21459	4971		181	48255	185
Bolton SE	14215	26906	5244		3184	49548	12691
Ind Lab candidate took 2894 votes (5.8%)							
Bolton W	26452	25373	7529		240	59594	1079
Boothferry	35266	17731	11388			64385	17535
Bootle	8022	37464	3301		1438	50225	29442
Bosworth	36618	17524	12643		716	67501	19094
Bournemouth E	30820	7541	15998		329	54688	14822
Bournemouth W	29820	9423	17117		232	56592	12703
Bow & Poplar	6876	18487	10083		1877	37323	8404
Bradford N	15756	23420	9133		654	48963	7664

Con	Lab	LDem	Nat	Other	% maj	Electors	Turnout
17.9%	55.8%	22.3%	0.0%	4.0%	33.6%	55675	65.5%
53.3%	18.6%	27.8%	0.0%	0.3%	25.5%	81033	79.9%
60.2%	9.4%	28.9%	0.0%	1.5%	31.3%	65829	79.1%
54.0%	24.3%	21.3%	0.0%	0.4%	29.7%	57684	82.2%
56.5%	21.0%	22.5%	0.0%	0.0%	34.0%	80287	82.5%
25.1%	63.6%	9.7%	0.0%	1.6%	38.5%	62673	73.0%
49.0%	37.6%	11.7%	0.0%	1.7%	11.4%	53058	71.3%
37.6%	50.5%	12.0%	0.0%	0.0%	12.9%	52414	70.1%
46.1%	38.3%	15.6%	0.0%	0.0%	7.8%	60103	78.2%
36.3%	53.6%	9.2%	0.0%	0.9%	17.3%	57581	70.9%
25.6%	66.3%	8.2%	0.0%	0.0%	40.7%	56995	65.9%
44.4%	45.5%	10.1%	0.0%	0.0%	1.2%	70563	76.1%
36.6%	53.2%	10.2%	0.0%	0.0%	16.6%	72186	71.6%
42.3%	46.0%	10.3%	0.0%	1.4%	3.7%	72195	76.6%
25.0%	65.3%	7.2%	0.0%	2.4%	40.2%	55233	62.8%
24.8%	64.1%	8.8%	0.0%	2.4%	39.3%	51682	66.8%
34.5%	34.9%	30.2%	0.0%	0.4%	0.4%	54755	78.0%
31.8%	50.0%	18.2%	0.0%	0.0%	18.2%	72573	76.5%
57.9%	20.7%	20.2%	0.0%	1.1%	37.2%	81791	83.4%
37.5%	48.4%	11.5%	0.0%	2.6%	11.0%	73337	75.0%
47.7%	41.0%	10.6%	0.0%	0.7%	6.7%	58142	77.5%
45.2%	41.4%	12.9%	0.0%	0.4%	3.8%	56829	77.3%
9.8%	79.0%	6.4%	4.8%	0.0%	69.2%	55643	78.1%
26.7%	52.7%	20.7%	0.0%	0.0%	26.0%	66044	77.7%
15.6%	49.9%	33.5%	0.0%	1.0%	16.3%	60975	80.7%2
25.3%	64.5%	10.2%	0.0%	0.0%	39.2%	66551	79.1%
44.9%	44.5%	10.3%	0.0%	0.4%	0.4%	58660	82.3%
28.7%	54.3%	10.6%	0.0%	6.4%	25.6%	65600	75.5%
44.4%	42.6%	12.6%	0.0%	0.4%	1.8%	71345	83.5%
54.8%	27.5%	17.7%	0.0%	0.0%	27.2%	80561	79.9%
16.0%	74.6%	6.6%	0.0%	2.9%	58.6%	69308	72.5%
54.2%	26.0%	18.7%	0.0%	1.1%	28.3%	80260	84.1%
56.4%	13.8%	29.3%	0.0%	0.6%	27.1%	75131	72.8%
52.7%	16.7%	30.2%	0.0%	0.4%	22.4%	74729	75.7%
18.4%	49.5%	27.0%	0.0%	5.0%	22.5%	56685	65.8%
32.2%	47.8%	18.7%	0.0%	1.3%	15.7%	66711	73.4%

Constituency	Con	Lab	LDem	Nat	Other	Votes	maj
Bradford S	20283	25185	7243		156	52867	4902
Bradford W	16544	26046	5150		1206	48946	9502
Braintree	34415	16921	13603		855	65794	17494
Brecon & Radnor	15977	11634	15847	418	393	44269	130
Brent E	13416	19387	3249		644	36696	5971
Brent N	23445	13314	4149		674	41582	10131
Brent S	10957	20662	3658		645	35922	9705
Brentford	24752	22666	5683		927	54028	2086
Brentwood	32145	6080	17000		555	55780	15145
Bridgend	16817	24143	4827	1301		47088	7326
Bridgwater	26610	12365	16894		1041	56910	9716
Bridlington	33604	15263	17246			66113	16358
Brigg	31673	22494	9374		790	64331	9179
Brighton K'town	21129	18073	4461		230	43893	3056
Brighton Pavilion	20630	16955	5606		1066	44257	3675
Bristol E	19726	22418	7903		270	50317	2692
Bristol NW	25354	25309	8498		729	59890	45
Bristol S	16245	25164	7822		892	50123	8919
Bristol W	22169	12992	16098		1231	52490	6071
Bromsgrove	31709	18007	8090		856	58662	13702
Broxbourne	36094	12124	9244		198	57660	23970
Broxtowe	31096	21205	8395		293	60989	9891
Buckingham	29496	7662	9705		353	47216	19791
Burnley	15693	27184	8414			51291	11491
Burton	30845	24849	6375			62069	5996
Bury N	29266	24502	5010		163	58941	4764
Bury S	24873	24085	4832		228	54018	788
Bury St Edmunds	33554	14767	13814		550	62685	18787
Caernarfon	6963	5641	2101	21439	173	36317	14476
Caerphilly	9041	31713	4247	4821		49822	22672
Caithness	4667	3483	10032	4049		22231	5365
Calder Valley	27753	22875	9842		622	61092	4878
Cambridge	19459	20039	10037		978	50513	580
Cambs NE	34288	8746	19195		1225	63454	15093
Cambs SE	36693	12688	12883		1067	63331	23810
Cambs SW	38902	9378	19263		924	68467	19639
Cannock	26633	28139	5899		469	61140	1506

Con	Lab	LDem	Nat	Other	% maj	Electors	Turnout
38.4%	47.6%	13.7%	0.0%	0.3%	9.3%	69930	75.6%
33.8%	53.2%	10.5%	0.0%	2.5%	19.4%	70017	69.9%
52.3%	25.7%	20.7%	0.0%	1.3%	26.6%	78880	83.4%
36.1%	26.3%	35.8%	0.9%	0.9%	0.3%	51564	85.9%
36.6%	52.8%	8.9%	0.0%	1.8%	16.3%	53436	68.7%
56.4%	32.0%	10.0%	0.0%	1.6%	24.4%	58923	70.6%
30.5%	57.5%	10.2%	0.0%	1.8%	27.0%	56054	64.1%
45.8%	42.0%	10.5%	0.0%	1.7%	3.9%	72193	74.8%
57.6%	10.9%	30.5%	0.0%	1.0%	27.2%	65884	84.7%
35.7%	51.3%	10.3%	2.8%	0.0%	15.6%	58518	80.5%
46.8%	21.7%	29.7%	0.0%	1.8%	17.1%	71575	79.5%
50.8%	23.1%	26.1%	0.0%	0.0%	24.7%	84950	77.8%
49.2%	35.0%	14.6%	0.0%	1.2%	14.3%	83510	77.0%
48.1%	41.2%	10.2%	0.0%	0.5%	7.0%	57649	76.1%
46.6%	38.3%	12.7%	0.0%	2.4%	8.3%	57618	76.8%
39.2%	44.6%	15.7%	0.0%	0.5%	5.4%	62659	80.3%
42.3%	42.3%	14.2%	0.0%	1.2%	0.1%	72760	82.3%
32.4%	50.2%	15.6%	0.0%	1.8%	17.8%	64403	77.8%
42.2%	24.8%	30.7%	0.0%	2.3%	11.6%	70945	74.0%
54.1%	30.7%	13.8%	0.0%	1.5%	23.4%	71085	82.5%
62.6%	21.0%	16.0%	0.0%	0.3%	41.6%	72127	79.9%
51.0%	34.8%	13.8%	0.0%	0.5%	16.2%	73124	83.4%
62.5%	16.2%	20.6%	0.0%	0.7%	41.9%	56064	84.2%
30.6%	53.0%	16.4%	0.0%	0.0%	22.4%	69128	74.2%
49.7%	40.0%	10.3%	0.0%	0.0%	9.7%	75293	82.4%
49.7%	41.6%	8.5%	0.0%	0.3%	8.1%	69531	84.8%
46.0%	44.6%	8.9%	0.0%	0.4%	1.5%	65793	82.1%
53.5%	23.6%	22.0%	0.0%	0.9%	30.0%	79462	78.9%
19.2%	15.5%	5.8%	59.0%	0.5%	39.9%	45348	80.1%
18.1%	63.7%	8.5%	9.7%	0.0%	45.5%	64555	77.2%
21.0%	15.7%	45.1%	18.2%	0.0%	24.1%	30677	72.5%
45.4%	37.4%	16.1%	0.0%	1.0%	8.0%	74418	82.1%
38.5%	39.7%	19.9%	0.0%	1.9%	1.1%	69011	73.2%
54.0%	13.8%	30.3%	0.0%	1.9%	23.8%	79991	79.3%
57.9%	20.0%	20.3%	0.0%	1.7%	37.6%	78601	80.6%
56.8%	13.7%	28.1%	0.0%	1.3%	28.7%	84419	81.1%
43.6%	46.0%	9.6%	0.0%	0.8%	2.5%	72522	84.3%

Constituency	Con	Lab	LDem	Nat	Other	Votes	maj
Canterbury	29827	8936	19022		950	58735	10805
Cardiff C	14549	18014	9170	748	435	42916	3465
Cardiff N	21547	18578	6487	916	207	47735	2969
Cardiff S	15958	26383	3707	776	676	47500	10425
Cardiff W	15015	24306	5002	1177	184	45684	9291
Carlisle	17371	20479	5740		190	43780	3108
Carmarthen	12782	20879	5353	17957		56971	2922
Carrick Cumnock	8516	25182	2005	6910		42613	16666
Carshalton	26243	9333	16300		880	52756	9943
Castle Point	29629	12799	10208		683	53319	16830
Ceredigion	12718	9637	12827		16020	51202	3193
Cheadle	32504	6442	16726		168	55840	15778
Chelmsford	39043	10010	20783		769	70605	18260
Chelsea	17471	4682	4101		573	26827	12789
Cheltenham	28683	4077	30351		996	64107	1668
Chertsey	34164	10793	11344		444	56745	22820
Chesham	36273	5931	14053		1008	57265	22220
Chester	23411	22310	6867		546	53134	1101
Chesterfield	9473	26461	20047			55981	6414
Chichester	37906	7192	17019		1757	63874	20887
Chingford	25730	10792	5705		1218	43445	14938
Chipping Barnet	25589	11638	7247		435	44909	13951
Chislehurst	24761	9485	6683		1501	42430	15276
Chorley	30715	26469	7452		402	65038	4246
Christchurch	36627	6997	13612		418	57654	23015
Cirencester	40258	7262	24200		736	72456	16058
City of London	20938	7569	5392		813	34712	13369
Clackmannan	6638	18829	2567	10326		38360	8503
Clwyd NW	24488	18438	7999	1888	158	52971	6050
Clwyd SW	16549	21490	6027	4835	506	49407	4941
Clydebank	6650	19642	3216	7207	112	36827	12435
Clydesdale	11231	21418	3957	11084	342	48032	10187
Colchester N	35213	13870	18721		610	68414	16492
Colchester S	37548	14158	15727		1028	68461	21821
Colne Valley	24804	17579	15953		720	59056	7225
Congleton	29163	11927	18043		399	59532	11120

Con	Lab	LDem	Nat	Other	% maj	Electors	Turnout
50.8%	15.2%	32.4%	0.0%	1.6%	18.4%	75180	78.1%
33.9%	42.0%	21.4%	1.7%	1.0%	8.1%	57780	74.3%
45.1%	38.9%	13.6%	1.9%	0.4%	6.2%	56757	84.1%
33.6%	55.5%	7.8%	1.6%	1.4%	21.9%	61490	77.2%
32.9%	53.2%	10.9%	2.6%	0.4%	20.3%	58936	77.5%
39.7%	46.8%	13.1%	0.0%	0.4%	7.1%	55140	79.4%
22.4%	36.6%	9.4%	31.5%	0.0%	5.1%	68920	82.7%
20.0%	59.1%	4.7%	16.2%	0.0%	39.1%	55332	77.0%
49.7%	17.7%	30.9%	0.0%	1.7%	18.8%	65209	80.9%
55.6%	24.0%	19.1%	0.0%	1.3%	31.6%	66229	80.4%
24.8%	18.8%	25.1%	31.3%	0.0%	6.2%	66166	77.4%
58.2%	11.5%	30.0%	0.0%	0.3%	28.3%	66131	84.4%
55.3%	14.2%	29.4%	0.0%	1.1%	25.9%	83440	84.6%
65.1%	17.5%	15.3%	0.0%	2.1%	47.7%	42372	63.3%
44.7%	6.4%	47.3%	0.0%	1.6%	2.6%	79806	80.3%
60.2%	19.0%	20.0%	0.0%	0.8%	40.2%	70675	80.3%
63.3%	10.4%	24.5%	0.0%	1.8%	38.8%	69898	81.9%
44.1%	42.0%	12.9%	0.0%	1.0%	2.1%	63319	83.9%
16.9%	47.3%	35.8%	0.0%	0.0%	11.5%	71685	78.1%
59.3%	11.3%	26.6%	0.0%	2.8%	32.7%	82126	77.8%
59.2%	24.8%	13.1%	0.0%	2.8%	34.4%	55466	78.3%
57.0%	25.9%	16.1%	0.0%	1.0%	31.1%	57150	78.6%
58.4%	22.4%	15.8%	0.0%	3.5%	36.0%	53783	78.9%
47.2%	40.7%	11.5%	0.0%	0.6%	6.5%	78514	82.8%
63.5%	12.1%	23.6%	0.0%	0.7%	39.9%	71469	80.7%
55.6%	10.0%	33.4%	0.0%	1.0%	22.2%	88413	82.0%
60.3%	21.8%	15.5%	0.0%	2.3%	38.5%	54830	63.3%
17.3%	49.1%	6.7%	26.9%	0.0%	22.2%	48362	79.3%
46.2%	34.8%	15.1%	3.6%	0.3%	11.4%	67352	78.6%
33.5%	43.5%	12.2%	9.8%	1.0%	10.0%	60607	81.5%
18.1%	53.3%	8.7%	19.6%	0.3%	33.8%	47337	77.8%
23.4%	44.6%	8.2%	23.1%	0.7%	21.2%	61914	77.6%
51.5%	20.3%	27.4%	0.0%	0.9%	24.1%	86479	79.1%
54.8%	20.7%	23.0%	0.0%	1.5%	31.9%	86406	79.2%
42.0%	29.8%	27.0%	0.0%	1.2%	12.2%	72029	82.0%
49.0%	20.0%	30.3%	0.0%	0.7%	18.7%	70475	84.5%

Constituency	Con	Lab	LDem	Nat	Other	Votes	maj
Conwy	14250	10883	13255	3108	751	42247	995
Copeland	19889	22328	3508		148	45873	2439
Corby	25203	24861	5792		784	56640	342
Cornwall N	27775	4103	29696		1066	62640	1921
Cornwall SE	30565	5536	22861		1026	59988	7704
Coventry NE	13220	24896	5306		4008	47430	11676

J. Hughes, former Labour MP, stood as Ind Lab, took 4,008 votes (8.5%)

Coventry NW	13917	20349	5070			39336	6432
Coventry SE	10591	11902	3318		10724	36535	1311

D Nellist, former Labour MP, stood as Ind Lab, took 10,551 (28.9%)

Coventry SW	23225	21789	4666		1193	50873	1436
Crawley	30204	22439	8558		766	61967	7765
Crewe	25370	28065	7315		651	61401	2695
Crosby	32267	17461	16562		1763	68053	14806
Croydon C	22168	12518	5342			40028	9650
Croydon NE	23835	16362	6186			46383	7473
Croydon NW	17626	19153	3728			40507	1527
Croydon S	31993	6444	11568		239	50244	20425
Cumbernauld	4143	19855	2118	10640		36756	9215
Cunninghame N	14625	17564	2864	7813		42866	2939
Cunninghame S	6070	19687	2299	9007	128	37191	10680
Cynon Valley	4890	26254	2667	4186		37997	21364
Dagenham	15295	22029	4824			42148	6734
Darlington	23758	26556	4586		355	55255	2798
Dartford	31194	20880	7584		503	60161	10314
Daventry	34734	14460	9820		422	59436	20274
Davyhulme	24216	19790	5797		665	50468	4426
Delyn	22940	24979	6208	1414		55541	2039
Reddish	16937	29021	4953		1650	52561	12084
Deptford	10336	22574	4181			37091	12238
Derby N	28574	24121	5638		686	59019	4453
Derby S	18981	25917	5198			50096	6936
Derbyshire NE	22590	28860	7675			59125	6270
Derbyshire S	34266	29608	6236		291	70401	4658
Derbyshire W	32879	13528	14110			60517	18769
Devizes	39090	13060	19378		1770	73298	19712
Devon N	26620	3410	27414		765	58209	794

Con	Lab	LDem	Nat	Other	% maj	Electors	Turnout
33.7%	25.8%	31.4%	7.4%	1.8%	2.4%	53668	78.7%
43.4%	48.7%	7.6%	0.0%	0.3%	5.3%	54911	83.5%
44.5%	43.9%	10.2%	0.0%	1.4%	0.6%	68334	82.9%
44.3%	6.6%	47.4%	0.0%	1.7%	3.1%	76333	82.1%
51.0%	9.2%	38.1%	0.0%	1.7%	12.8%	73028	82.1%
27.9%	52.5%	11.2%	0.0%	8.5%	24.6%	64788	73.2%
35.4%	51.7%	12.9%	0.0%	0.0%	16.4%	50671	77.6%
29.0%	32.6%	9.1%	0.0%	29.4%	3.6%	48797	74.9%
45.7%	42.8%	9.2%	0.0%	2.3%	2.8%	63475	80.1%
48.7%	36.2%	13.8%	0.0%	1.2%	12.5%	78268	79.2%
41.3%	45.7%	11.9%	0.0%	1.1%	4.4%	75001	81.9%
47.4%	25.7%	24.3%	0.0%	2.6%	21.8%	82538	82.5%
55.4%	31.3%	13.3%	0.0%	0.0%	24.1%	55947	71.5%
51.4%	35.3%	13.3%	0.0%	0.0%	16.1%	64874	71.5%
43.5%	47.3%	9.2%	0.0%	0.0%	3.8%	57821	70.1%
63.7%	12.8%	23.0%	0.0%	0.5%	40.7%	64895	77.4%
11.3%	54.0%	5.8%	28.9%	0.0%	25.1%	46515	79.0%
34.1%	41.0%	6.7%	18.2%	0.0%	6.9%	54856	78.1%
16.3%	52.9%	6.2%	24.2%	0.3%	28.7%	49025	75.9%
12.9%	69.1%	7.0%	11.0%	0.0%	56.2%	49696	76.5%
36.3%	52.3%	11.4%	0.0%	0.0%	16.0%	59656	70.7%
43.0%	48.1%	8.3%	0.0%	0.6%	5.1%	66094	83.6%
51.8%	34.7%	12.6%	0.0%	0.8%	17.1%	72373	83.1%
58.4%	24.3%	16.5%	0.0%	0.7%	34.1%	71830	82.7%
48.0%	39.2%	11.5%	0.0%	1.3%	8.8%	62667	80.5%
41.3%	45.0%	11.2%	2.5%	0.0%	3.7%	66593	83.4%
32.2%	55.2%	9.4%	0.0%	3.1%	23.0%	68463	76.8%
27.9%	60.9%	11.3%	0.0%	0.0%	33.0%	57062	65.0%
48.4%	40.9%	9.6%	0.0%	1.2%	7.5%	73177	80.7%
37.9%	51.7%	10.4%	0.0%	0.0%	13.8%	66329	75.5%
38.2%	48.8%	13.0%	0.0%	0.0%	10.6%	73320	80.6%
48.7%	42.1%	8.9%	0.0%	0.4%	6.6%	83104	84.7%
54.3%	22.4%	23.3%	0.0%	0.0%	31.0%	71201	85.0%
53.3%	17.8%	26.4%	0.0%	2.4%	26.9%	89746	81.7%
45.7%	5.9%	47.1%	0.0%	1.3%	1.4%	68991	84.4%

Constituency	Con	Lab	LDem	Nat	Other	Votes	maj
Devon W	29627	5997	26013		1039	62676	3614
Dewsbury	24962	25596	6570		1277	58405	634
Don Valley	18474	32008	6920		803	58205	13534
Doncaster C	17113	27795	6057		184	51149	10682
Doncaster N	14322	34135	6787			55244	19813
Dorset N	34234	4360	24154			62748	10080
Dorset S	29319	12298	15811		864	58292	13508
Dorset W	27766	7082	19756			54604	8010
Dover	25395	24562	6212		1421	57590	833
Dudley E	20606	29806	5400		675	56487	9200
Dudley W	34729	28940	7446			71115	5789
Dulwich	15658	17714	4078			37450	2056
Dumbarton	13126	19255	3425	8127	192	44125	6129
Dumfries	21089	14674	5749	6971	419	48902	6415
Dundee E	7549	18761	1725	14197	372	42604	4564
Dundee W	7746	20498	3132	9894	591	41861	10604
Dunfermline E	6248	23692	2262	5746		37948	17444
Dunfermline W	8890	16374	6122	7563		38949	7484
Durham	12037	27095	10915		812	50859	15058
Durham N	13930	33567	8572			56069	19637
Durham NW	12747	26734	6728			46209	13987
Ealing N	24898	18932	5247		1011	50088	5966
Easington	7879	34269	5001			47149	26390
E Kilbride	9781	24055	5377	12063		51276	11992
E Lothian	15501	25537	6126	7776		54940	10036
Eastbourne	31792	2834	26311		687	61624	5481
Eastleigh	38998	15768	21296			76062	17702
Eastwood	24124	12436	8493	6372	146	51571	11688
Eccles	14131	27357	5835		791	48114	13226
Eddisbury	31625	18928	10543		890	61986	12697
Edinbgh C	13063	15189	4500	5539	865	39156	2126
Edinbgh E	8235	15446	3432	6225	424	33762	7211
Edinbgh Leith	8496	13790	4975	8805	4238	40304	4985
Edinbgh Pentlands	18128	13838	5597	6882	111	44556	4290
Edinbgh S	14309	18485	5961	5727	108	44590	4176
Edinbgh W	18071	8759	17192	4117	639	48778	879
Edmonton	22076	21483	3940		207	47706	593

Con	Lab	LDem	Nat	Other	% maj	Electors	Turnout
47.3%	9.6%	41.5%	0.0%	1.7%	5.8%	76936	81.5%
42.7%	43.8%	11.2%	0.0%	2.2%	1.1%	72833	80.2%
31.7%	55.0%	11.9%	0.0%	1.4%	23.3%	76328	76.3%
33.5%	54.3%	11.8%	0.0%	0.4%	20.9%	68890	74.2%
25.9%	61.8%	12.3%	0.0%	0.0%	35.9%	74733	73.9%
54.6%	6.9%	38.5%	0.0%	0.0%	16.1%	76719	81.8%
50.3%	21.1%	27.1%	0.0%	1.5%	23.2%	75802	76.9%
50.8%	13.0%	36.2%	0.0%	0.0%	14.7%	67260	81.2%
44.1%	42.6%	10.8%	0.0%	2.5%	1.4%	68954	83.5%
36.5%	52.8%	9.6%	0.0%	1.2%	16.3%	75355	75.0%
48.8%	40.7%	10.5%	0.0%	0.0%	8.1%	86633	82.1%
41.8%	47.3%	10.9%	0.0%	0.0%	5.5%	55275	67.8%
29.7%	43.6%	7.8%	18.4%	0.4%	13.9%	57252	77.1%
43.1%	30.0%	11.8%	14.3%	0.9%	13.1%	61189	79.9%
17.8%	44.1%	4.1%	33.4%	0.7%	10.7%	58959	72.3%
18.5%	49.0%	7.5%	23.6%	1.4%	25.3%	59953	69.8%
16.5%	62.4%	6.0%	15.1%	0.0%	46.0%	50180	75.6%
22.8%	42.0%	15.7%	19.4%	0.0%	19.2%	50949	76.4%
23.7%	53.3%	21.5%	0.0%	1.6%	29.6%	68166	74.6%
24.8%	59.9%	15.3%	0.0%	0.0%	35.0%	73702	76.1%
27.6%	57.9%	14.6%	0.0%	0.0%	30.3%	61168	75.5%
49.7%	37.8%	10.5%	0.0%	2.0%	11.9%	63528	78.8%
16.7%	72.7%	10.6%	0.0%	0.0%	56.0%	65062	72.5%
19.1%	46.9%	10.5%	23.5%	0.0%	23.4%	64100	80.0%
28.2%	46.5%	11.2%	14.2%	0.0%	18.3%	66700	82.4%
51.6%	4.6%	42.7%	0.0%	1.1%	8.9%	76146	80.9%
51.3%	20.7%	28.0%	0.0%	0.0%	23.3%	91760	82.9%
46.8%	24.1%	16.5%	12.4%	0.3%	22.7%	63658	81.0%
29.4%	56.9%	12.1%	0.0%	1.6%	27.5%	64911	74.1%
51.0%	30.5%	17.0%	0.0%	1.4%	20.5%	75081	82.6%
33.4%	38.8%	11.5%	14.1%	2.2%	5.4%	56689	69.1%
24.4%	45.7%	10.2%	18.4%	1.3%	21.4%	45785	73.7%
21.1%	34.2%	12.3%	21.8%	10.5%	12.4%	56654	71.1%
40.7%	31.1%	12.6%	15.4%	0.2%	9.6%	55646	80.1%
32.1%	41.5%	13.4%	12.8%	0.2%	9.4%	61547	72.4%
37.0%	18.0%	35.2%	8.4%	1.3%	1.8%	59078	82.6%
46.3%	45.0%	8.3%	0.0%	0.4%	1.2%	63052	75.7%

Constituency	Con	Lab	LDem	Nat	Other	Votes	maj
Ellesmere Port	25793	27782	5944		694	68213	1989
Elmet	27677	24416	6144			58237	3261
Eltham	18813	17147	4804		165	40929	1666
Enfield N	27789	18359	5817		565	52530	9430
Epping Forest	32407	12219	9265		552	54443	20188
Epsom & Ewell	32861	8577	12840		334	54612	20021
Erewash	29907	24204	8606		645	63362	5703
Erith & Crayford	21926	19587	5657			47170	2339
Esher	31115	5685	10744			47544	20371
Exeter	25543	22498	12059		1981	62081	3045
Falkirk E	8279	18423	2775	10454		39931	7969
Falkirk W	7558	19162	2414	9350		38484	9812
Falmouth	21150	16732	17883		1579	57344	3267
Fareham	40482	8766	16341		818	66407	24141
Faversham	32755	16404	15896		294	65349	16351
Feltham & Heston	25665	27660	6700			60025	1995
Fife C	7353	21036	2892	10458		41739	10578
Fife NE	16122	2319	19430	3589	379	41839	3308
Finchley	21039	14651	4568		823	41081	6388
Folkestone	27437	6347	18527		123	52434	8910
Fulham	21438	14859	3339		534	40170	6579
Fylde	30639	9382	9648		239	49908	20991
Gainsborough	31444	11619	15199			58262	16245
Galloway	18681	5766	3826	16213		44486	2468
Gateshead E	11570	30100	5720			47390	18530
Gedling	30191	19554	6863		168	56776	10637
Gillingham	30201	13563	13509		438	57711	16638
Glanford	22226	30637	4186		996	58045	8411
Ggow Cathcart	8264	16265	2614	6107	441	33691	8001
Ggow Central	4208	17341	1921	6322	541	30333	11019
Ggow G'scad	3385	18920	1425	5580	61	29371	13340
Ggow Govan	3458	17051	1227	12926	181	34843	4125
Ggow Hillhead	6728	15148	10322	6484	691	39373	4826
Ggow Maryhill	3248	19452	2215	6033	608	31556	13419
Ggow Pollok	5147	14170	1932	5107	6287	32643	7883

T. Sheridan, Scottish Militant Labour, took 6,287 votes (19.3%)

Constituency	Con	Lab	LDem	Nat	Other	Votes	maj
Ggow Provan	1865	15885	948	5182		23880	10703

Con	Lab	LDem	Nat	Other	% maj	Electors	Turnout
42.8%	46.1%	9.9%	0.0%	1.2%	3.3%	71572	84.1%
47.5%	41.9%	10.5%	0.0%	0.0%	5.6%	70711	82.4%
46.0%	41.9%	11.7%	0.0%	0.4%	4.1%	51989	78.7%
52.9%	34.9%	11.1%	0.0%	1.1%	18.0%	67422	77.9%
59.5%	22.4%	17.0%	0.0%	1.0%	37.1%	67600	80.5%
60.2%	15.7%	23.5%	0.0%	0.6%	36.7%	68138	80.1%
47.2%	38.2%	13.6%	0.0%	1.0%	9.0%	75729	83.7%
46.5%	41.5%	12.0%	0.0%	0.0%	5.0%	59214	79.7%
65.4%	12.0%	22.6%	0.0%	0.0%	42.8%	58862	80.8%
41.1%	36.2%	19.4%	0.0%	3.2%	4.9%	77134	80.5%
20.7%	46.1%	6.9%	26.2%	0.0%	20.0%	51224	78.0%
19.6%	49.8%	6.3%	24.3%	0.0%	25.5%	49434	77.8%
36.9%	29.2%	31.2%	0.0%	2.8%	5.7%	70712	81.1%
61.0%	13.2%	24.6%	0.0%	1.2%	36.4%	81125	81.9%
50.1%	25.1%	24.3%	0.0%	0.4%	25.0%	82037	79.7%
42.8%	46.1%	11.2%	0.0%	0.0%	3.3%	82133	73.1%
17.6%	50.4%	6.9%	25.1%	0.0%	25.3%	56092	74.4%
38.5%	5.5%	46.4%	8.6%	0.9%	7.9%	53836	77.7%
51.2%	35.7%	11.1%	0.0%	2.0%	15.5%	52908	77.6%
52.3%	12.1%	35.3%	0.0%	0.2%	17.0%	65856	79.6%
53.4%	37.0%	8.3%	0.0%	1.3%	16.4%	52945	75.9%
61.4%	18.8%	19.3%	0.0%	0.5%	42.1%	63599	78.5%
54.0%	19.9%	26.1%	0.0%	0.0%	27.9%	72038	80.9%
42.0%	13.0%	8.6%	36.4%	0.0%	5.5%	54500	81.6%
24.4%	63.5%	12.1%	0.0%	0.0%	39.1%	64355	73.6%
53.2%	34.4%	12.1%	0.0%	0.3%	18.7%	68954	82.3%
52.3%	23.5%	23.4%	0.0%	0.8%	28.8%	71851	80.3%
38.3%	52.8%	7.2%	0.0%	1.7%	14.5%	73404	79.1%
24.5%	48.3%	7.8%	18.1%	1.3%	23.7%	44779	75.2%
13.9%	57.2%	6.3%	20.8%	1.8%	36.3%	48159	63.0%
11.5%	64.4%	4.9%	19.0%	0.2%	45.4%	41214	71.3%
9.9%	48.9%	3.5%	37.1%	0.5%	11.8%	45879	75.9%
17.1%	38.5%	26.2%	16.5%	1.8%	12.3%	57331	68.7%
10.3%	61.6%	7.0%	19.1%	1.9%	42.5%	48479	65.1%
15.8%	43.4%	5.9%	15.6%	19.3%	24.1%	46190	70.7%
7.8%	66.5%	4.0%	21.7%	0.0%	44.8%	36579	65.3%

Constituency	Con	Lab	LDem	Nat	Other	Votes	maj
Ggow Rutherglen	6692	21962	4470	6470	62	39656	15270
Ggow Shettleston	5396	21665	1881	6831		35773	14834
Ggow Springburn	2625	20369	1242	5863		30099	14506
Gloucester	29870	23801	10978			64649	6069
Gloucs W	29232	24274	13366		247	67119	4958
Gordon	21884	6682	22158	8445		59169	274
Gosport	31094	7275	14776		332	53477	16318
Gower	16437	23485	4655	1639	636	46852	7048
Grantham	37194	17606	9882		1500	66182	19588
Gravesham	29322	23829	5269		634	59054	5493
Gt Grimsby	18391	25897	6475			50761	7506
Gt Yarmouth	25505	20196	7225		284	53210	5309
Greenock	4479	22258	4359	7279		38375	14979
Greenwich	6960	14630			14076	35666	1357

R. Barnes, former SDP MP, took 13,273 votes (37.2%)

Constituency	Con	Lab	LDem	Nat	Other	Votes	maj
Guildford	33516	6781	20112		234	60643	13404
Hackney N & SN	9356	20083	3996		1289	34724	10727
Hackney S	10714	19730	5533		998	36975	9016
Halesowen	32312	22730	7941		908	63891	9582
Halifax	24637	25115	7364		649	57765	478
Halton	16821	35005	6104		736	58666	18184
Hamilton	8250	25849	3515	9246		46860	16603
Hammersmith	12575	17329	3380		676	33960	4754
Hants E	47541	6840	18376		1278	74035	29165
Hants NW	34310	7433	16462		825	59030	17848
H'stead & H'gate	17753	19193	4765		801	42512	1440
Harborough	34280	7483	20737		328	62828	13543
Harlow	26608	23668	6375			56651	2940
Harrogate	32023	7230	19434		780	59467	12589
Harrow E	30752	19654	6360		1403	58169	11098
Harrow W	30240	12343	11050		1151	54784	17897
Hartlepool	18034	26816	6860			51710	8782
Harwich	32369	14511	15210		279	62369	17159
Hastings & Rye	25573	8458	18939		808	53778	6634
Havant	32233	10968	14649		793	58643	17584
Hayes & H'ton	19489	19436	4472			43397	53
Hazel Grove	24479	6390	23550		204	54623	929

Con	Lab	LDem	Nat	Other	% maj	Electors	Turnout
16.9%	55.4%	11.3%	16.3%	0.2%	38.5%	52719	75.2%
15.1%	60.6%	5.3%	19.1%	0.0%	41.5%	51913	68.9%
8.7%	67.7%	4.1%	19.5%	0.0%	48.2%	45831	65.7%
46.2%	36.8%	17.0%	0.0%	0.0%	9.4%	80626	80.2%
43.6%	36.2%	19.9%	0.0%	0.4%	7.4%	80054	83.8%
37.0%	11.3%	37.4%	14.3%	0.0%	0.5%	79672	74.3%
58.1%	13.6%	27.6%	0.0%	0.6%	30.5%	69817	76.6%
35.1%	50.1%	9.9%	3.5%	1.4%	15.0%	57229	81.9%
56.2%	26.6%	14.9%	0.0%	2.3%	29.6%	83535	79.2%
49.7%	40.4%	8.9%	0.0%	1.1%	9.3%	70790	83.4%
36.2%	51.0%	12.8%	0.0%	0.0%	14.8%	67427	75.3%
47.9%	38.0%	13.6%	0.0%	0.5%	10.0%	68263	77.9%
11.7%	58.0%	11.4%	19.0%	0.0%	39.0%	52062	73.7%
19.5%	41.0%	0.0%	0.0%	39.5%	3.8%	47790	74.6%
55.3%	11.2%	33.2%	0.0%	0.4%	22.1%	77265	78.5%
26.9%	57.8%	11.5%	0.0%	3.7%	30.9%	56768	61.2%
29.0%	53.4%	15.0%	0.0%	2.7%	24.4%	60220	61.4%
50.6%	35.6%	12.4%	0.0%	1.4%	15.0%	77644	82.3%
42.7%	43.5%	12.7%	0.0%	1.1%	0.8%	73402	78.7%
28.7%	59.7%	10.4%	0.0%	1.3%	31.0%	74909	78.3%
17.6%	55.2%	7.5%	19.7%	0.0%	35.4%	61572	76.1%
37.0%	51.0%	10.0%	0.0%	2.0%	14.0%	47504	71.5%
64.2%	9.2%	24.8%	0.0%	1.7%	39.4%	93393	79.3%
58.1%	12.6%	27.9%	0.0%	1.4%	30.2%	73036	80.8%
41.8%	45.1%	11.2%	0.0%	1.9%	3.4%	58452	72.7%
54.6%	11.9%	33.0%	0.0%	0.5%	21.6%	76514	82.1%
47.0%	41.8%	11.3%	0.0%	0.0%	5.2%	69467	81.6%
53.9%	12.2%	32.7%	0.0%	1.3%	21.2%	76250	78.0%
52.9%	33.8%	10.9%	0.0%	2.4%	19.1%	74837	77.7%
55.2%	22.5%	20.2%	0.0%	2.1%	32.7%	69675	78.6%
34.9%	51.9%	13.3%	0.0%	0.0%	17.0%	67969	76.1%
51.9%	23.3%	24.4%	0.0%	0.4%	27.5%	80261	77.7%
47.6%	15.7%	35.2%	0.0%	1.5%	12.3%	71839	74.9%
55.0%	18.7%	25.0%	0.0%	1.4%	30.0%	74245	79.0%
44.9%	44.8%	10.3%	0.0%	0.0%	0.1%	55024	78.9%
44.8%	11.7%	43.1%	0.0%	0.4%	1.7%	64300	85.0%

Constituency	Con	Lab	LDem	Nat	Other	Votes	maj
Hemsworth	7867	29942	4459			42268	22075
Hendon N	20569	13447	4136		525	38677	7122
Hendon S	20593	8546	5609		289	35037	12047
Henley	30835	7676	12443		705	51659	18392
Hereford	26727	6005	23314		596	56642	3413
Hertford	35716	10125	15506		780	62127	20210
Herts N	33679	16449	17148		339	67615	16531
Herts SW	33825	11512	13718		281	59336	20107
Herts W	33340	19400	10464		1514	64718	13940
Hertsmere	32133	13398	10681		373	56585	18735
Hexham	24967	11529	10344		781	47621	13438
Heywood	14306	22380	5252		891	42829	8074
High Peak	27538	22719	8861		794	59912	4819
Holborn	11419	22243	5476		1479	40617	10824
Holland	29159	15328	8434			52921	13831
Honiton	33533	8142	17022		5272	63969	16511
Hornchurch	25817	16652	5366		453	48288	9165
Hornsey	21843	27020	5547		1337	55747	5177
Horsham	42210	6745	17138		2305	68398	25072
Houghton	13925	34733	7346			56004	20808
Hove	24525	12257	9709		3598	50089	12268

JNP Furness, Ind Con, took 2,658 votes (5.3%)

Constituency	Con	Lab	LDem	Nat	Other	Votes	maj
Huddersfield	16574	23832	7777		711	48894	7258
Hull E	11373	30096	6050		323	47842	18723
Hull N	11235	26619	9504		253	47611	15384
Hull W	10554	21139	4867		308	36868	10585
Huntingdon	48662	12432	9386		3074	73554	36230
Hyndburn	21082	23042	4886		150	49160	1960
Ilford N	24678	15627	5430			45735	9051
Ilford S	19016	19418	4126		269	42829	402
Inverness,	11517	12800	13258	12562	766	50903	458
Ipswich	23415	23680	6159		772	54026	265
Isle of Wight	38163	4784	36336		350	79633	1827
Islington N	8958	21742	5732		1420	37852	12784
Islington	9934	20586	9387		374	40281	10652
Islwyn	6180	30908	2352	1606	547	41593	24728
Jarrow	11049	28956	6608			46613	17907

Con	Lab	LDem	Nat	Other	% maj	Electors	Turnout
18.6%	70.8%	10.5%	0.0%	0.0%	52.2%	55696	75.9%
53.2%	34.8%	10.7%	0.0%	1.4%	18.4%	51514	75.1%
58.8%	24.4%	16.0%	0.0%	0.8%	34.4%	48401	72.4%
59.7%	14.9%	24.1%	0.0%	1.4%	35.6%	64698	79.8%
47.2%	10.6%	41.2%	0.0%	1.1%	6.0%	69686	81.3%
57.5%	16.3%	25.0%	0.0%	1.3%	32.5%	76655	81.0%
49.8%	24.3%	25.4%	0.0%	0.5%	24.4%	80086	84.4%
57.0%	19.4%	23.1%	0.0%	0.5%	33.9%	70913	83.7%
51.5%	30.0%	16.2%	0.0%	2.3%	21.5%	78554	82.4%
56.8%	23.7%	18.9%	0.0%	0.7%	33.1%	69952	80.9%
52.4%	24.2%	21.7%	0.0%	1.6%	28.2%	57812	82.4%
33.4%	52.2%	12.3%	0.0%	2.1%	18.8%	57177	74.9%
46.0%	37.9%	14.8%	0.0%	1.3%	8.0%	70793	84.6%
28.1%	54.8%	13.5%	0.0%	3.6%	26.6%	64794	62.7%
55.1%	29.0%	15.9%	0.0%	0.0%	26.1%	67900	77.9%
52.4%	12.7%	26.6%	0.0%	8.2%	25.8%	79224	80.7%
53.5%	34.5%	11.1%	0.0%	0.9%	19.0%	60484	79.8%
39.2%	48.5%	10.0%	0.0%	2.4%	9.3%	73668	75.7%
61.7%	9.9%	25.1%	0.0%	3.4%	36.7%	84159	81.3%
24.9%	62.0%	13.1%	0.0%	0.0%	37.2%	79326	70.6%
49.0%	24.5%	19.4%	0.0%	7.2%	24.5%	67566	74.1%
33.9%	48.7%	15.9%	0.0%	1.5%	14.8%	67574	72.4%
23.8%	62.9%	12.6%	0.0%	0.7%	39.1%	69078	69.3%
23.6%	55.9%	20.0%	0.0%	0.5%	32.3%	71395	66.7%
28.6%	57.3%	13.2%	0.0%	0.8%	28.7%	56136	65.7%
66.2%	16.9%	12.8%	0.0%	4.1%	49.3%	92914	79.2%
42.9%	46.9%	9.9%	0.0%	0.3%	4.0%	58560	83.9%
54.0%	34.2%	11.9%	0.0%	0.0%	19.8%	58695	77.9%
44.4%	45.3%	9.6%	0.0%	0.6%	0.9%	55857	76.7%
22.6%	25.1%	26.0%	24.7%	1.5%	0.9%	69151	73.6%
43.3%	43.8%	11.4%	0.0%	1.4%	0.5%	67289	80.3%
47.9%	6.0%	45.6%	0.0%	0.4%	2.3%	99839	79.8%
23.7%	57.4%	15.1%	0.0%	3.8%	33.8%	56814	66.6%
24.7%	51.1%	23.3%	0.0%	0.9%	26.4%	57060	70.6%
14.8%	74.3%	5.7%	3.9%	1.3%	59.4%	51082	81.4%
23.7%	62.1%	14.2%	0.0%	0.0%	38.4%	62612	74.4%

Constituency	Con	Lab	LDem	Nat	Other	Votes	maj
Keighley	25983	22387	5793		642	54805	3596
Kensington	15540	11992	2770		576	30878	3548
Kent Mid	33633	13984	11476		224	59317	19649
Kettering	29115	17961	8962			56038	11154
Kilmarnock	9438	22210	2722	15231		49601	6979
Kincardine	22924	4795	18429	5927	381	52456	4495
Kingston	20675	7748	10522		1106	40051	10153
Kingswood	24404	26774	8967			60145	2370
Kirkcaldy	8476	17887	3729	8761		38853	9126
Knowsley N	5114	27517	1515		1359	35505	22403
Knowsley S	9922	31933	4480		217	46552	22011
Lancs W	28051	30120	4884		882	63937	2069
Lancaster	21084	18131	6524		516	46255	2953
Langbaurgh	30018	28454	7615			66087	1564
Leeds C	8653	23673	5713			38039	15020
Leeds E	12232	24929	6040			43201	12697
Leeds NE	22462	18218	8274		546	49500	4244
Leeds NW	21750	13782	14079		946	50557	7671
Leeds S & Morley	16524	23896	5062		327	45809	7372
Leeds W	12482	26310	4252		4681	47725	13828

M. Meadowcroft Lib, took 3.980 votes (8.3%)

Constituency	Con	Lab	LDem	Nat	Other	Votes	maj
Leicester E	16807	28123	4043		947	49920	11316
Leicester S	18494	27934	6271		708	53407	9440
Leicester W	18596	22574	6402		688	48260	3978
Leics NW	28379	27400	6353		229	62361	979
Leigh	13398	32225	6621		320	52564	18827
Leominster	32783	6874	16103		2143	57903	16680
Lewes	33042	5758	20867		806	60473	12175
Lewisham E	18481	19576	4877		196	43130	1095
Lewisham W	18569	20378	4295		125	43367	1809
Leyton	8882	20334	8180		1229	38625	11452
Lincoln	28792	26743	6316		603	62454	2049
Lindsey E	31916	9477	20070		1018	62481	11846
Linlithgow	8424	21603	3446	14577		48050	7026
Littleborough	23682	10649	19188			53519	4494
Lpl Broadgreen	5405	18062	11035		7312	41814	7027

T. Fields, Former Labour MP, took 5,952 votes (14.2%)

Con	Lab	LDem	Nat	Other	% maj	Electors	Turnout
47.4%	40.8%	10.6%	0.0%	1.2%	6.6%	66379	82.6%
50.3%	38.8%	9.0%	0.0%	1.9%	11.5%	42129	73.3%
56.7%	23.6%	19.3%	0.0%	0.4%	33.1%	74460	79.7%
52.0%	32.1%	16.0%	0.0%	0.0%	19.9%	67854	82.6%
19.0%	44.8%	5.5%	30.7%	0.0%	14.1%	62043	79.9%
43.7%	9.1%	35.1%	11.3%	0.7%	8.6%	66169	79.3%
51.6%	19.3%	26.3%	0.0%	2.8%	25.4%	51078	78.4%
40.6%	44.5%	14.9%	0.0%	0.0%	3.9%	71740	83.8%
21.8%	46.0%	9.6%	22.5%	0.0%	23.5%	51955	74.8%
14.4%	77.5%	4.3%	0.0%	3.8%	63.1%	48783	72.8%
21.3%	68.6%	9.6%	0.0%	0.5%	47.3%	62295	74.7%
43.9%	47.1%	7.6%	0.0%	1.4%	3.2%	77463	82.5%
45.6%	39.2%	14.1%	0.0%	1.1%	6.4%	58616	78.9%
45.4%	43.1%	11.5%	0.0%	0.0%	2.4%	79563	83.1%
22.7%	62.2%	15.0%	0.0%	0.0%	39.5%	62059	61.3%
28.3%	57.7%	14.0%	0.0%	0.0%	29.4%	61720	70.0%
45.4%	36.8%	16.7%	0.0%	1.1%	8.6%	64607	76.6%
43.0%	27.3%	27.8%	0.0%	1.9%	15.2%	69733	72.5%
36.1%	52.2%	11.1%	0.0%	0.7%	16.1%	63155	72.5%
26.2%	55.1%	8.9%	0.0%	9.8%	29.0%	67074	71.2%
33.8%	56.5%	8.1%	0.0%	1.5%	22.8%	63435	78.7%
34.6%	52.3%	11.7%	0.0%	1.3%	17.7%	71120	75.1%
38.5%	46.8%	13.3%	0.0%	1.4%	8.2%	65511	73.7%
45.5%	43.9%	10.2%	0.0%	0.4%	1.6%	72419	86.1%
25.5%	61.3%	12.6%	0.0%	0.6%	35.8%	70065	75.0%
56.6%	11.9%	27.8%	0.0%	3.7%	28.8%	70874	81.7%
54.6%	9.5%	34.5%	0.0%	1.3%	20.1%	73918	81.8%
42.8%	45.4%	11.3%	0.0%	0.5%	2.5%	57725	74.7%
42.8%	47.0%	9.9%	0.0%	0.3%	4.2%	59372	73.0%
23.0%	52.6%	21.2%	0.0%	3.2%	29.7%	57272	67.4%
46.1%	42.8%	10.1%	0.0%	1.0%	3.3%	78944	79.1%
51.1%	15.2%	32.1%	0.0%	1.6%	19.0%	80027	78.1%
17.5%	45.0%	7.2%	30.3%	0.0%	14.6%	61082	78.7%
44.2%	19.9%	35.9%	0.0%	0.0%	8.4%	65577	81.6%
12.9%	43.2%	26.4%	0.0%	17.5%	16.8%	60080	69.6%

Constituency	Con	Lab	LDem	Nat	Other	Votes	maj
Lpl Garston	10933	23212	5398		1081	40624	12279
Lpl Mossley Hill	4269	17203	19809		114	41395	2606
Lpl Riverside	3113	20550	2498		907	27068	17437
Lpl Walton	5915	34214	5672		1454	47255	28299
Lpl W Derby	6589	27014	4838		1175	39616	20425
Livingston	8824	20245	3911	12140	469	45589	8105
Llanelli	8532	27802	6404	7878		50616	19270
Loughborough	30064	19181	8953		1050	59248	10883
Ludlow	28719	11709	14567		758	55753	14152
Luton N	33777	20683	7570		925	62955	13094
Luton S	25900	25101	6020		741	57762	799
Macclesfield	36447	13680	12600		268	62995	22767
Maidstone	31611	10517	15325		879	58332	16286
Makerfield	14714	32832	5097		1706	54349	18118
M/c Blackley	10642	23031	4324		288	38285	12389
M/c Central	5299	23336	3151		334	32120	18037
M/c Gorton	7392	23671	5327		1584	37974	16279
M/c Withington	14227	23962	6457		853	45499	9735
M/c W'shawe	10595	22591	3633		495	37314	11996
Mansfield	18208	29932	6925			55065	11724
Medway	25924	17138	4751		1714	49527	8786
Meirionnydd	6995	4978	2358	11608	471	26410	4613
Meriden	33462	18763	8489			60714	14699
Merthyr Tydfil	4904	31710	4997	2704		44315	26713
Middlesbrough	10559	26343	4201			41103	15784
Midlothian	9443	20588	6164	10254	476	46925	10334
Milton Keynes NE	26212	12036	11693		857	50798	14176
Milton Keynes SW	23840	19153	7429		727	51149	4687
Mitcham	23789	22055	4687		655	51186	1734
Mole Valley	32549	5291	16599		442	54881	15950
Monklands E	5830	22266	1679	6554		36329	15712
Monklands W	6074	23384	2382	6319		38159	17065
Monmouth	24059	20855	5562	431		50907	3204

Joint PC-Green party candidate took 431 votes (0.8%)

Constituency	Con	Lab	LDem	Nat	Other	Votes	maj
Montgomery	10822	4115	16031	1581	508	33057	5209
Moray	17455	5448	2634	20299		45836	2844
Morecambe	22507	10998	9584		1121	44210	11509

Con	Lab	LDem	Nat	Other	% maj	Electors	Turnout
26.9%	57.1%	13.3%	0.0%	2.7%	30.2%	57539	70.6%
10.3%	41.6%	47.9%	0.0%	0.3%	6.3%	60409	68.5%
11.5%	75.9%	9.2%	0.0%	3.4%	64.4%	49595	54.6%
12.5%	72.4%	12.0%	0.0%	3.1%	59.9%	70118	67.4%
16.6%	68.2%	12.2%	0.0%	3.0%	51.6%	56724	69.8%
19.4%	44.4%	8.6%	26.6%	1.0%	17.8%	61093	74.6%
16.9%	54.9%	12.7%	15.6%	0.0%	38.1%	65057	77.8%
50.7%	32.4%	15.1%	0.0%	1.8%	18.4%	75451	78.5%
51.5%	21.0%	26.1%	0.0%	1.4%	25.4%	68937	80.9%
53.7%	32.9%	12.0%	0.0%	1.5%	20.8%	76940	81.8%
44.8%	43.5%	10.4%	0.0%	1.3%	1.4%	73016	79.1%
57.9%	21.7%	20.0%	0.0%	0.4%	36.1%	76549	82.3%
54.2%	18.0%	26.3%	0.0%	1.5%	27.9%	72862	80.1%
27.1%	60.4%	9.4%	0.0%	3.1%	33.3%	71426	76.1%
27.8%	60.2%	11.3%	0.0%	0.8%	32.4%	55235	69.3%
16.5%	72.7%	9.8%	0.0%	1.0%	56.2%	56447	56.9%
19.5%	62.3%	14.0%	0.0%	4.2%	42.9%	62410	60.8%
31.3%	52.7%	14.2%	0.0%	1.9%	21.4%	63838	71.3%
28.4%	60.5%	9.7%	0.0%	1.3%	32.1%	53549	69.7%
33.1%	54.4%	12.6%	0.0%	0.0%	21.3%	66965	82.2%
52.3%	34.6%	9.6%	0.0%	3.5%	17.7%	61737	80.2%
26.5%	18.8%	8.9%	44.0%	1.8%	17.5%	32413	81.5%
55.1%	30.9%	14.0%	0.0%	0.0%	24.2%	77009	78.8%
11.1%	71.6%	11.3%	6.1%	0.0%	60.3%	58430	75.8%
25.7%	64.1%	10.2%	0.0%	0.0%	38.4%	58852	69.8%
20.1%	43.9%	13.1%	21.9%	1.0%	22.0%	60311	77.8%
51.6%	23.7%	23.0%	0.0%	1.7%	27.9%	63545	79.9%
46.6%	37.4%	14.5%	0.0%	1.4%	9.2%	67365	76.0%
46.5%	43.1%	9.2%	0.0%	1.3%	3.4%	63752	80.3%
59.3%	9.6%	30.2%	0.0%	0.8%	29.1%	66963	82.0%
16.0%	61.3%	4.6%	18.0%	0.0%	43.2%	48430	75.0%
15.9%	61.3%	6.2%	16.6%	0.0%	44.7%	49300	77.4%
47.3%	41.0%	10.9%	0.8%	0.0%	6.3%	59148	86.1%
32.7%	12.4%	48.5%	4.8%	1.5%	15.8%	41386	79.9%
38.1%	11.9%	5.7%	44.3%	0.0%	6.2%	62605	73.2%
50.9%	24.9%	21.7%	0.0%	2.5%	26.0%	56432	78.3%

Constituency	Con	Lab	LDem	Nat	Other	Votes	maj
Motherwell N	5011	27852	2145	8942		43950	18910
Motherwell S	6097	21771	2349	7758	146	38121	14013
Neath	6928	30903	2467	5145		45443	23975
New Forest	37986	4989	17581		350	60906	20405
Newark	28494	20265	7342		435	56536	8229
Newbury	37135	3962	24778		539	66414	12357
Newcastle C	15835	21123	5816			42774	5288
Newcastle E	10465	24342	4883		744	40434	13877
Newcastle N	16175	25121	9542			50838	8946
N'castle-u-L	15813	25652	11727		314	53506	9839
Newham NE	10966	20952	4020			35938	9986
Newham NW	6740	15911	2445		939	26035	9171
Newham S	11856	14358	4572			30786	2502
Newport E	13151	23050	4991	716		41908	9899
Joint PC-Green party candidate took 716 votes (1.7%)							
Newport W	16360	24139	4296	653		45448	7779
Joint PC-Green Party candidate took 653 votes (1.4%)							
Norfolk Mid	35620	16672	13072		226	65590	18948
Norfolk N	28810	13850	16365		726	59751	12445
Norfolk NW	32554	20990	8599		330	62473	11564
Norfolk S	36081	12422	18516		1594	68613	17565
Norfolk SW	33637	16706	11237			61580	16931
Normanton	16986	25936	7137			50059	8950
Northampton N	24865	20957	8236		232	54290	3908
Northampton S	36882	19909	9912			66703	16973
Northavon	35338	10290	23477		1169	70274	11861
Norwich N	22419	22153	6706		526	51804	266
Norwich S	18784	24965	6609		907	51265	6181
Norwood	11175	18391	4087		928	34581	7216
Nottingham E	17346	25026	3695		1548	47615	7680
Nottingham N	18309	29052	4477		274	52112	10743
Nottingham S	22590	25771	5408		263	54032	3181
Nuneaton	25526	27157	6671			59354	1631
Ogmore	6359	30186	2868	2667		42080	23827
Old Bexley	24450	8751	6438		881	40520	15699
Oldham C	14640	23246	7224		403	45513	8606
Oldham W	13247	21580	5525		551	40903	8333
Orkney	4542	4093	9575	2301	115	20626	5033

Con	Lab	LDem	Nat	Other	% maj	Electors	Turnout
11.4%	63.4%	4.9%	20.3%	0.0%	43.0%	57140	76.9%
16.0%	57.1%	6.2%	20.4%	0.4%	36.8%	50086	76.1%
15.2%	68.0%	5.4%	11.3%	0.0%	52.8%	56355	80.6%
62.4%	8.2%	28.9%	0.0%	0.6%	33.5%	75413	80.8%
50.4%	35.8%	13.0%	0.0%	0.8%	14.6%	68802	82.2%
55.9%	6.0%	37.3%	0.0%	0.8%	18.6%	80254	82.8%
37.0%	49.4%	13.6%	0.0%	0.0%	12.4%	59973	71.3%
25.9%	60.2%	12.1%	0.0%	1.8%	34.3%	57165	70.7%
31.8%	49.4%	18.8%	0.0%	0.0%	17.6%	66187	76.8%
29.6%	47.9%	21.9%	0.0%	0.6%	18.4%	66595	80.3%
30.5%	58.3%	11.2%	0.0%	0.0%	27.8%	59610	60.3%
25.9%	61.1%	9.4%	0.0%	3.6%	35.2%	46475	56.0%
38.5%	46.6%	14.9%	0.0%	0.0%	8.1%	51110	60.2%
31.4%	55.0%	11.9%	1.7%	0.0%	23.6%	51602	81.2%
36.0%	53.1%	9.5%	1.4%	0.0%	17.1%	54872	82.8%
54.3%	25.4%	19.9%	0.0%	0.3%	28.9%	80525	81.5%
48.3%	23.2%	27.3%	0.0%	1.2%	21.0%	73780	81.0%
52.1%	33.6%	13.8%	0.0%	0.5%	18.5%	77439	80.7%
52.6%	18.1%	27.0%	0.0%	2.3%	25.6%	81647	84.0%
54.6%	27.1%	18.2%	0.0%	0.0%	27.5%	77652	79.3%
33.9%	51.8%	14.3%	0.0%	0.0%	17.9%	65587	76.3%
45.8%	38.6%	15.2%	0.0%	0.4%	7.2%	69140	78.5%
55.3%	29.8%	14.9%	0.0%	0.0%	25.4%	83476	79.9%
50.3%	14.6%	33.4%	0.0%	1.7%	16.9%	83348	84.3%
43.3%	42.8%	12.9%	0.0%	1.0%	0.5%	63309	81.8%
36.6%	48.7%	12.9%	0.0%	1.8%	12.1%	63604	80.6%
32.3%	53.2%	11.8%	0.0%	2.7%	20.9%	52290	66.1%
36.4%	52.6%	7.8%	0.0%	3.3%	16.1%	67939	70.1%
35.1%	55.7%	8.6%	0.0%	0.5%	20.6%	69495	75.0%
41.8%	47.7%	10.0%	0.0%	0.5%	5.9%	72796	74.2%
43.0%	45.8%	11.2%	0.0%	0.0%	2.7%	70907	83.7%
15.1%	71.7%	6.8%	6.3%	0.0%	56.6%	52196	80.6%
60.3%	21.6%	15.9%	0.0%	2.2%	38.7%	49449	81.9%
32.2%	51.1%	15.9%	0.0%	0.9%	18.9%	61360	74.2%
32.4%	52.8%	13.5%	0.0%	1.3%	20.4%	54075	75.6%
22.0%	19.8%	46.4%	11.2%	0.6%	24.4%	31472	65.5%

Constituency	Con	Lab	LDem	Nat	Other	Votes	maj
Orpington	27421	5512	14486		539	47958	12935
Oxford E	16164	23702	6105		1082	47053	7538
Oxford W	25163	7652	21624		1027	55466	3539
Paisley N	5576	17269	2779	7948	493	34065	9321
Paisley S	5703	18202	3271	8653	93	35922	9549
Peckham	7386	19391	4331		286	31394	12005
Pembroke	25498	26253	6625	1627	642	60645	755
Pendle	21384	23497	7976		263	53120	2113
Penrith & Border	33808	8871	15359		739	58777	18449
Perth & Kinross	20195	6267	5714	18101		50277	2094
Peterborough	31827	26451	5208		2354	65840	5376
Plym Devonport	17541	24953	6315		2407	51216	7412
Plym Drake	17075	15062	5893		1012	39042	2013
Plym Sutton	27070	15120	12291		256	54737	11950
Pontefract	10051	33546	4410			48007	23495
Pontypridd	9925	29722	4180	4448	615	48890	19797
Poole	33445	6912	20614		1923	62894	12831
Portsmouth N	32240	18359	10101		628	61328	13881
Portsmouth S	22798	7857	22556		440	53651	242
Preston	12808	24983	7897		341	46029	12175
Pudsey	25067	16695	15153		466	57381	8372
Putney	25188	17662	4636		757	48243	7526
Ravensbourne	29506	6182	9792		1040	46520	19714
Reading E	29148	14593	9528		861	54130	14555
Reading W	28048	14750	9572		613	52983	13298
Redcar	15607	27184	5789			48580	11577
Reigate	32220	9150	14566		513	56449	17654
Renfrew W	15341	17085	4668	9448	149	46691	1744
Rhondda	3588	34243	2431	5427	245	45934	28816
Ribble Valley	29178	3649	22636		264	55727	6542
Richmond	22894	2632	19025		574	45125	3869
Richmond, Yorks	40202	7523	16698		570	64993	23504
Rochdale	8626	20937	22776		831	53170	1839
Rochford	38967	10537	12931		1362	63797	26036
Romford	23834	12414	5329		546	42123	11420
Romsey	37375	8688	22071		577	68711	15304
Ross, C & S	9436	6275	17066	7618	642	41037	7630

Con	Lab	LDem	Nat	Other	% maj	Electors	Turnout
57.2%	11.5%	30.2%	0.0%	1.1%	27.0%	57352	83.6%
34.4%	50.4%	13.0%	0.0%	2.3%	16.0%	63078	74.6%
45.4%	13.8%	39.0%	0.0%	1.9%	6.4%	72328	76.7%
16.4%	50.7%	8.2%	23.3%	1.4%	27.4%	46424	73.4%
15.9%	50.7%	9.1%	24.1%	0.3%	26.6%	47919	75.0%
23.5%	61.8%	13.8%	0.0%	0.9%	38.2%	58320	53.8%
42.0%	43.3%	10.9%	2.7%	1.1%	1.2%	73187	82.9%
40.3%	44.2%	15.0%	0.0%	0.5%	4.0%	64066	82.9%
57.5%	15.1%	26.1%	0.0%	1.3%	31.4%	73770	79.7%
40.2%	12.5%	11.4%	36.0%	0.0%	4.2%	65410	76.9%
48.3%	40.2%	7.9%	0.0%	3.6%	8.2%	87639	75.1%
34.2%	48.7%	12.3%	0.0%	4.7%	14.5%	65800	77.8%
43.7%	38.6%	15.1%	0.0%	2.6%	5.2%	51667	75.6%
49.5%	27.6%	22.5%	0.0%	0.5%	21.8%	67430	81.2%
20.9%	69.9%	9.2%	0.0%	0.0%	48.9%	64655	74.3%
20.3%	60.8%	8.5%	9.1%	1.3%	40.5%	61685	79.3%
53.2%	11.0%	32.8%	0.0%	3.1%	20.4%	79223	79.4%
52.6%	29.9%	16.5%	0.0%	1.0%	22.6%	79592	77.1%
42.5%	14.6%	42.0%	0.0%	0.8%	0.5%	77648	69.1%
27.8%	54.3%	17.2%	0.0%	0.7%	26.5%	64159	71.7%
44.1%	28.3%	26.7%	0.0%	0.8%	14.6%	70996	80.8%
52.2%	36.6%	9.6%	0.0%	1.6%	15.6%	61915	77.9%
63.4%	13.3%	21.0%	0.0%	2.2%	42.4%	57285	81.2%
53.8%	27.0%	17.6%	0.0%	1.6%	26.9%	72152	75.0%
52.9%	27.8%	18.1%	0.0%	1.2%	25.1%	67938	78.0%
32.1%	56.0%	11.9%	0.0%	0.0%	23.8%	62494	77.7%
57.1%	16.2%	25.8%	0.0%	0.9%	31.3%	71876	78.5%
32.9%	36.6%	10.0%	20.2%	0.3%	3.7%	58164	80.3%
7.8%	74.5%	5.3%	11.8%	0.5%	62.7%	59955	76.6%
52.4%	6.5%	40.6%	0.0%	0.5%	11.7%	65552	85.7%
50.7%	5.8%	42.2%	0.0%	1.3%	8.6%	53138	84.9%
61.9%	11.6%	25.7%	0.0%	0.9%	36.2%	82880	78.4%
16.2%	39.4%	42.8%	0.0%	1.6%	3.5%	69522	76.5%
61.1%	16.5%	20.3%	0.0%	2.1%	40.8%	76869	83.0%
56.6%	29.5%	12.7%	0.0%	1.3%	27.1%	53981	78.0%
54.4%	12.6%	32.1%	0.0%	0.8%	22.3%	82628	83.2%
23.0%	15.3%	41.6%	18.6%	1.6%	18.6%	55771	73.6%

Constituency	Con	Lab	LDem	Nat	Other	Votes	maj
Rossendale	27908	28028	7226		721	63883	120
Rother Valley	13755	30977	6483			51215	17222
Rotherham	10372	27933	5375			43680	17561
Roxburgh	11595	2909	15852	3437		33793	4257
Rugby	34110	20862	9934		202	65108	13248
Ruislip	28097	8306	7739		214	44356	19791
Rushcliffe	34448	14682	12660		1536	63326	19766
Rutland	38603	13068	12682		1098	65451	25535
Ryedale	39888	9812	21449			71149	18439
Saffron Walden	35272	8933	17848		260	62313	17424
St Albans	32709	12016	16305		895	61925	16404
St Helens N	15686	31930	7224		287	55127	16244
St Helens S	12182	30391	6933		295	49801	18209
St Ives	24528	9144	22883		577	57132	1645
Salford E	9092	20327	3836		613	33868	11235
Salisbury	31546	5483	22573		1052	60654	8973
Scarborough	29334	17600	11133		876	58943	11734
Sedgefield	13594	28453	4982			47029	14859
Selby	31067	21559	9244			61870	9508
Sevenoaks	33245	9470	14091		996	57802	19154
Sheff Attercliffe	13083	28563	7283		751	49680	15480
Sheff Brightside	7090	29771	5273		150	42284	22681
Sheff Central	5470	22764	3856		1054	33144	17294
Sheff Hallam	24693	10930	17952		673	54248	6741
Sheff Heeley	13051	28005	9247			50303	14954
Sheff Hillsborough	11640	27563	20500			59703	7063
Sherwood	26878	29788	6039			62705	2910
Shipley	28463	16081	11288		680	56512	12382
Shoreham	32670	6123	18384		659	57836	14286
Shrewsbury	26681	15157	15716		677	58231	10965
Shropshire N	32443	15550	16232			64225	16211
Skipton & Ripon	35937	8978	16607			61522	19330
Slough	25793	25279	4041		2702	57815	514
Solihull	38385	10544	13239		925	63093	25146
Somerton	28052	6154	23711		1130	59047	4341
Southall	16610	23476	3790		5629	49505	6866

S. Bidwell, former Labour MP, took 4,665 votes (9.4%)

Con	Lab	LDem	Nat	Other	% maj	Electors	Turnout
43.7%	43.9%	11.3%	0.0%	1.1%	0.2%	76926	83.0%
26.9%	60.5%	12.7%	0.0%	0.0%	33.6%	68304	75.0%
23.7%	63.9%	12.3%	0.0%	0.0%	40.2%	60937	71.7%
34.3%	8.6%	46.9%	10.2%	0.0%	12.6%	43572	77.6%
52.4%	32.0%	15.3%	0.0%	0.3%	20.3%	77767	83.7%
63.3%	18.7%	17.4%	0.0%	0.5%	44.6%	54033	82.1%
54.4%	23.2%	20.0%	0.0%	2.4%	31.2%	76284	83.0%
59.0%	20.0%	19.4%	0.0%	1.7%	39.0%	80975	80.8%
56.1%	13.8%	30.1%	0.0%	0.0%	25.9%	87063	81.7%
56.6%	14.3%	28.6%	0.0%	0.4%	28.0%	74940	83.2%
52.8%	19.4%	26.3%	0.0%	1.4%	26.5%	74189	83.5%
28.5%	57.9%	13.1%	0.0%	0.5%	29.5%	71262	77.4%
24.5%	61.0%	13.9%	0.0%	0.6%	36.6%	67521	73.8%
42.9%	16.0%	40.1%	0.0%	1.0%	2.9%	71154	80.3%
26.8%	60.0%	11.3%	0.0%	1.8%	33.2%	52616	64.4%
52.0%	9.0%	37.2%	0.0%	1.7%	14.8%	75917	79.9%
49.8%	29.9%	18.9%	0.0%	1.5%	19.9%	76364	77.2%
28.9%	60.5%	10.6%	0.0%	0.0%	31.6%	61029	77.1%
50.2%	34.8%	14.9%	0.0%	0.0%	15.4%	77180	80.2%
57.5%	16.4%	24.4%	0.0%	1.7%	33.1%	71092	81.3%
26.3%	57.5%	14.7%	0.0%	1.5%	31.2%	69177	71.8%
16.8%	70.4%	12.5%	0.0%	0.4%	53.6%	63810	66.3%
16.5%	68.7%	11.6%	0.0%	3.2%	52.2%	59060	56.1%
45.5%	20.1%	33.1%	0.0%	1.2%	12.4%	76585	70.8%
25.9%	55.7%	18.4%	0.0%	0.0%	29.7%	70953	70.9%
19.5%	46.2%	34.3%	0.0%	0.0%	11.8%	77343	77.2%
42.9%	47.5%	9.6%	0.0%	0.0%	4.6%	73355	85.5%
50.4%	28.5%	20.0%	0.0%	1.2%	21.9%	68827	82.1%
56.5%	10.6%	31.8%	0.0%	1.1%	24.7%	71252	81.2%
45.8%	26.0%	27.0%	0.0%	1.2%	18.8%	70636	82.4%
50.5%	24.2%	25.3%	0.0%	0.0%	25.2%	82676	77.7%
58.4%	14.6%	27.0%	0.0%	0.0%	31.4%	75629	81.3%
44.6%	43.7%	7.0%	0.0%	4.7%	0.9%	74103	78.0%
60.8%	16.7%	21.0%	0.0%	1.5%	39.9%	77332	81.6%
47.5%	10.4%	40.2%	0.0%	1.9%	7.4%	71358	82.7%
33.6%	47.4%	7.7%	0.0%	11.4%	13.9%	65574	75.5%

Constituency	Con	Lab	LDem	Nat	Other	Votes	maj
Southgate	28422	12859	7080		696	49057	15563
South Hams	35951	8091	22240		1073	67355	13711
South Ribble	30828	24855	8928		269	64880	5973
South Shields	11399	24876	5344			41619	13477
So'ton Itchen	23851	24402	7221			55474	551
So'ton Test	24504	23919	7391		636	56450	585
Southend E	24591	11480	5107		673	41851	13111
Southend W	27319	6139	15417		1073	49948	11902
Southport	26081	5637	23018		704	55440	3063
Southwark	3794	11614	21459		867	37734	9845
Spelthorne	32627	12784	9202		1113	55726	19843
Stafford	30876	19976	10702		354	61908	10900
Staffs Mid	31227	24991	6402		239	62859	6236
Staffs Moorlands	29240	21830	9326		2382	62778	7410
Staffs S	40266	17633	9584			67483	22633
Staffs SE	29180	21988	5540		895	57603	7192
Stalybridge	17376	26207	4740		1774	50097	8831
Stamford	35965	13096	11939			61000	22869
Stevenage	26652	21764	9668		233	58317	4888
Stirling	19174	18471	3337	6558	410	47950	703
Stockport	19674	21096	6539		486	47795	1422
Stockton N	17444	27918	7454		550	53366	10474
Stockton S	28418	25049	9410			62877	3369
Stoke C	12477	25897	6073		196	44643	13420
Stoke N	15687	30464	7167		387	53705	14777
Stoke S	19471	26380	6870		291	53012	6909
Stratford-on-Avon	40251	8932	17359		1432	67974	22892
Strathkelvin	18105	21267	4585	6275	90	50322	3162
Streatham	16608	18925	3858		839	40230	2317
Stretford	11163	22300	3722		268	37453	11137
Stroud	32201	18796	16751		2005	69753	13405
Suffolk Central	32917	15615	16886		990	66408	16031
Suffolk Coastal	34680	13508	15395		1175	64758	19285
Suffolk S	34773	16623	17504		420	69320	17269
Sunderland N	13477	30481	5389		841	50188	17004
Sunderland S	14898	29399	5844		596	50737	14501
Surbiton	19033	6384	9394		161	34972	9639

Con	Lab	LDem	Nat	Other	% maj	Electors	Turnout
57.9%	26.2%	14.4%	0.0%	1.4%	31.7%	64312	76.3%
53.4%	12.0%	33.0%	0.0%	1.6%	20.4%	83140	81.0%
47.5%	38.3%	13.8%	0.0%	0.4%	9.2%	78171	83.0%
27.4%	59.8%	12.8%	0.0%	0.0%	32.4%	59392	70.1%
43.0%	44.0%	13.0%	0.0%	0.0%	1.0%	72105	76.9%
43.4%	42.4%	13.1%	0.0%	1.1%	1.0%	72932	77.4%
58.8%	27.4%	12.2%	0.0%	1.6%	31.3%	56709	73.8%
54.7%	12.3%	30.9%	0.0%	2.1%	23.8%	64199	77.8%
47.0%	10.2%	41.5%	0.0%	1.3%	5.5%	71444	77.6%
10.1%	30.8%	56.9%	0.0%	2.3%	26.1%	60564	62.3%
58.5%	22.9%	16.5%	0.0%	2.0%	35.6%	69344	80.4%
49.9%	32.3%	17.3%	0.0%	0.6%	17.6%	74668	82.9%
49.7%	39.7%	10.2%	0.0%	0.4%	9.9%	73435	85.6%
46.6%	34.8%	14.9%	0.0%	3.8%	11.8%	75037	83.7%
59.7%	26.1%	14.2%	0.0%	0.0%	33.5%	82759	81.5%
50.7%	38.2%	9.6%	0.0%	1.6%	12.5%	70207	82.0%
34.7%	52.3%	9.5%	0.0%	3.5%	17.6%	68192	73.5%
59.0%	21.5%	19.6%	0.0%	0.0%	37.5%	75154	81.2%
45.7%	37.3%	16.6%	0.0%	0.4%	8.4%	70229	83.0%
40.0%	38.5%	7.0%	13.7%	0.9%	1.5%	58267	82.3%
41.2%	44.1%	13.7%	0.0%	1.0%	3.0%	58096	82.3%
32.7%	52.3%	14.0%	0.0%	1.0%	19.6%	69458	76.8%
45.2%	39.8%	15.0%	0.0%	0.0%	5.4%	75959	82.8%
27.9%	58.0%	13.6%	0.0%	0.4%	30.1%	65528	68.1%
29.2%	56.7%	13.3%	0.0%	0.7%	27.5%	73141	73.4%
36.7%	49.8%	13.0%	0.0%	0.5%	13.0%	71317	74.3%
59.2%	13.1%	25.5%	0.0%	2.1%	33.7%	82818	82.1%
36.0%	42.3%	9.1%	12.5%	0.2%	6.3%	61210	82.2%
41.3%	47.0%	9.6%	0.0%	2.1%	5.8%	57212	70.3%
29.8%	59.5%	9.9%	0.0%	0.7%	29.7%	54468	68.8%
46.2%	26.9%	24.0%	0.0%	2.9%	19.2%	82553	84.5%
49.6%	23.5%	25.4%	0.0%	1.5%	24.1%	82735	80.3%
53.6%	20.9%	23.8%	0.0%	1.8%	29.8%	79334	81.6%
50.2%	24.0%	25.2%	0.0%	0.6%	24.9%	84835	81.7%
26.9%	60.7%	10.7%	0.0%	1.7%	33.9%	72874	68.9%
29.4%	57.9%	11.5%	0.0%	1.2%	28.6%	72608	69.9%
54.4%	18.3%	26.9%	0.0%	0.5%	27.6%	42422	82.4%

Constituency	Con	Lab	LDem	Nat	Other	Votes	maj
Surrey E	29767	5075	12111		819	47772	17656
Surrey NW	41772	8886	13378		1441	65477	28394
Surrey SW	35008	3840	20033		955	59836	14975
Sussex Mid	39524	6951	18996		1499	66970	20528
Sutton & Cheam	27710	4980	16954		577	50221	10756
Sutton Coldfield	37001	8490	10965		324	56780	26036
Swansea E	7697	31179	4248	1607		44731	23482
Swansea W	13760	23238	4620	1668	564	43850	9478
Swindon	31749	28923	11737		961	73370	2826
Tatton	31658	15798	9597		410	57463	15860
Taunton	29576	8151	26240		279	64246	3336
Tayside N	20283	3094	3791	16288		43456	3995
Teignbridge	31274	8128	22416		671	62489	8858
Thanet N	30867	12657	9563		873	53960	18210
Thanet S	25253	13740	8948		871	48812	11513
Thurrock	23619	24791	5145		508	54063	1172
Tiverton	30376	5950	19287		3328	58941	11089
Tonbridge	36542	11533	14984		833	63892	21558
Tooting	20494	24601	3776		2217	51088	4107
Torbay	28624	5503	22837		425	57389	5787
Torfaen	9598	30352	6178	1210		47338	20754

Joint PC-Green party Candidate took 1,210 votes (2.6%)

Constituency	Con	Lab	LDem	Nat	Other	Votes	maj
Tottenham	13341	25309	5120		1053	44823	11968
Truro	23660	6078	31230		885	61853	7570
Tunbridge Wells	34162	8300	17030		503	59995	17132
Tweeddale	9776	3328	12296	5244	177	30821	2520
Twickenham	26804	4919	21093		340	53156	5711
Tyne Bridge	7118	22328	3804			33250	15210
Tynemouth	27731	27134	4855		543	60263	597
Upminster	28791	14970	7848			51609	13821
Uxbridge	27487	14308	5900		1008	48703	13179
Vale of Glam	24220	24201	5045		1160	54626	19
Vauxhall	10840	21328	5678		1111	38957	10488
Wakefield	20374	26964	5900			53238	6590
Wallasey	22722	26531	4177		785	54215	3809
Wallsend	13969	33439	10369			57777	19470

Con	Lab	LDem	Nat	Other	% maj	Electors	Turnout
62.3%	10.6%	25.4%	0.0%	1.7%	37.0%	58014	82.3%
63.8%	13.6%	20.4%	0.0%	2.2%	43.4%	83577	78.3%
58.5%	6.4%	33.5%	0.0%	1.6%	25.0%	72312	82.7%
59.0%	10.4%	28.4%	0.0%	2.2%	30.7%	80828	82.9%
55.2%	9.9%	33.8%	0.0%	1.1%	21.4%	60995	82.3%
65.2%	15.0%	19.3%	0.0%	0.6%	45.9%	71444	79.5%
17.2%	69.7%	9.5%	3.6%	0.0%	52.5%	59187	75.6%
31.4%	53.0%	10.5%	3.8%	1.3%	21.6%	59791	73.3%
43.3%	39.4%	16.0%	0.0%	1.3%	3.9%	90068	81.5%
55.1%	27.5%	16.7%	0.0%	0.7%	27.6%	71085	80.8%
46.0%	12.7%	40.8%	0.0%	0.4%	5.2%	78037	82.3%
46.7%	7.1%	8.7%	37.5%	0.0%	9.2%	55970	77.6%
50.0%	13.0%	35.9%	0.0%	1.1%	14.2%	75798	82.4%
57.2%	23.5%	17.7%	0.0%	1.6%	33.7%	70977	76.0%
51.7%	28.1%	18.3%	0.0%	1.8%	23.6%	62440	78.2%
43.7%	45.9%	9.5%	0.0%	0.9%	2.2%	69211	78.1%
51.5%	10.1%	32.7%	0.0%	5.6%	18.8%	70742	83.3%
57.2%	18.1%	23.5%	0.0%	1.3%	33.7%	77257	82.7%
40.1%	48.2%	7.4%	0.0%	4.3%	8.0%	68307	74.8%
49.9%	9.6%	39.8%	0.0%	0.7%	10.1%	71184	80.6%
20.3%	64.1%	13.1%	2.6%	0.0%	43.8%	61103	77.5%
29.8%	56.5%	11.4%	0.0%	2.3%	26.7%	68404	65.5%
38.3%	9.8%	50.5%	0.0%	1.4%	12.2%	75119	82.3%
56.9%	13.8%	28.4%	0.0%	0.8%	28.6%	76807	78.1%
31.7%	10.8%	39.9%	17.0%	0.6%	8.2%	39478	78.1%
50.4%	9.3%	39.7%	0.0%	0.6%	10.7%	63152	84.2%
21.4%	67.2%	11.4%	0.0%	0.0%	45.7%	53080	62.6%
46.0%	45.0%	8.1%	0.0%	0.9%	1.0%	74956	80.4%
55.8%	29.0%	15.2%	0.0%	0.0%	26.8%	64125	80.5%
56.4%	29.4%	12.1%	0.0%	2.1%	27.1%	61604	79.1%
44.3%	44.3%	9.2%	0.0%	2.1%	0.0%	66673	81.9%
27.8%	54.7%	14.6%	0.0%	2.9%	26.9%	62595	62.2%
38.3%	50.6%	11.1%	0.0%	0.0%	12.4%	69825	76.2%
41.9%	49.0%	7.7%	0.0%	1.4%	7.0%	65670	82.6%
24.2%	57.9%	17.9%	0.0%	0.0%	33.7%	77941	74.1%

Constituency	Con	Lab	LDem	Nat	Other	Votes	maj
Walsall N	20563	24387	6629		614	52193	3824
Walsall S	20955	24133	4132		840	50060	3178
Walthamstow	13229	16251	5142		929	35551	3022
Wansbeck	11872	30046	7691		710	50319	18174
Wansdyke	31389	18048	14834		800	65071	13341
Wanstead	26204	9319	7362		815	43700	16885
Wantage	30575	10955	14102		867	56499	16473
Warley E	12097	19891	4547		561	37096	7794
Warley W	15914	21386	4945			42245	5472
Warrington N	20397	33019	6965		400	60781	12622
Warrington S	27628	27819	7978		321	63746	191
Warwick	28093	19158	9645		1210	58106	8935
Warwickshire N	26145	27599	6167			59911	1454
Watford	29072	19482	10231		742	59527	9590
Waveney	33174	26472	8925		302	68873	6702
Wealden	37263	5579	16332		1184	60358	20931
Wellingborough	32302	20486	7714			60502	11816
Wells	28620	6126	21971		1042	57759	6649
Welwyn Hatfield	29447	20982	10196		264	60889	8465
Wentworth	10490	32939	4629			48058	22449
W Bromwich E	17100	19913	5630		477	43120	2813
W Bromwich W	14421	22251	3925			40597	7830
Westbury	36568	9642	23950		2328	72488	12618
Western Isles	1362	7664	552	5961	491	16030	1703
Westminster N	21828	18095	3349		1313	44585	3733
Westmorland	31798	8436	15362		287	55883	16436
Weston-s-M	30022	6913	24680		1262	62877	5342
Wigan	13068	34910	6111		1313	55402	21842
Wiltshire N	39028	6945	22640		1538	70151	16388
Wimbledon	26331	11570	10569		1211	49681	14761
Winchester	33113	4917	24992		3095	66117	8121
Windsor	35075	4975	22147		964	63161	12928
Wirral S	25590	17407	6581		766	50344	8183
Wirral W	26852	15788	7420		888	50948	11064
Witney	36256	13688	13393		969	64306	22568
Woking	37744	8080	17902		302	64028	19842

Con	Lab	LDem	Nat	Other	% maj	Electors	Turnout
39.4%	46.7%	12.7%	0.0%	1.2%	7.3%	69605	75.0%
41.9%	48.2%	8.3%	0.0%	1.7%	6.3%	65643	76.3%
37.2%	45.7%	14.5%	0.0%	2.6%	8.5%	49347	72.0%
23.6%	59.7%	15.3%	0.0%	1.4%	36.1%	63502	79.2%
48.2%	27.7%	22.8%	0.0%	1.2%	20.5%	77245	84.2%
60.0%	21.3%	16.8%	0.0%	1.9%	38.6%	55867	78.2%
54.1%	19.4%	25.0%	0.0%	1.5%	29.2%	68329	82.7%
32.6%	53.6%	12.3%	0.0%	1.5%	21.0%	5175	71.7%
37.7%	50.6%	11.7%	0.0%	0.0%	13.0%	57158	73.9%
33.6%	54.3%	11.5%	0.0%	0.7%	20.8%	78654	77.3%
43.3%	43.6%	12.5%	0.0%	0.5%	0.3%	77693	82.0%
48.3%	33.0%	16.6%	0.0%	2.1%	15.4%	71260	81.5%
43.6%	46.1%	10.3%	0.0%	0.0%	2.4%	71473	83.8%
48.8%	32.7%	17.2%	0.0%	1.2%	16.1%	72291	82.3%
48.2%	38.4%	13.0%	0.0%	0.4%	9.7%	84181	81.8%
61.7%	9.2%	27.1%	0.0%	2.0%	34.7%	74558	81.0%
53.4%	33.9%	12.7%	0.0%	0.0%	19.5%	73876	81.9%
49.6%	10.6%	38.0%	0.0%	1.8%	11.5%	69833	82.7%
48.4%	34.5%	16.7%	0.0%	0.4%	13.9%	72236	84.3%
21.8%	68.5%	9.6%	0.0%	0.0%	46.7%	64915	74.0%
39.9%	46.5%	12.5%	0.0%	1.1%	6.6%	56945	75.7%
35.5%	54.8%	9.7%	0.0%	0.0%	19.3%	57666	70.4%
50.4%	13.3%	33.1%	0.0%	3.2%	17.4%	87537	82.8%
8.5%	47.8%	3.4%	37.2%	3.1%	10.6%	22785	70.4%
49.0%	40.6%	7.5%	0.0%	2.9%	8.4%	59405	75.1%
56.9%	15.1%	27.5%	0.0%	0.5%	29.4%	71864	77.8%
47.7%	11.0%	39.3%	0.0%	2.0%	8.5%	78843	79.7%
23.6%	63.0%	11.0%	0.0%	2.4%	39.4%	72741	76.2%
55.6%	9.9%	32.3%	0.0%	2.2%	23.4%	85852	81.7%
53.0%	23.3%	21.3%	0.0%	2.4%	29.7%	61966	80.2%
50.1%	7.4%	37.8%	0.0%	4.7%	12.3%	79432	83.2%
55.5%	7.9%	35.1%	0.0%	1.5%	20.5%	77427	81.6%
50.8%	34.6%	13.1%	0.0%	1.5%	16.3%	61135	82.3%
52.7%	31.0%	14.6%	0.0%	1.7%	21.7%	62471	81.6%
56.4%	21.3%	20.8%	0.0%	1.5%	35.1%	78541	81.9%
58.9%	12.6%	28.0%	0.0%	0.5%	31.0%	80814	79.2%

Constituency	Con	Lab	LDem	Nat	Other	Votes	maj
Wokingham	43497	8846	17788		679	70810	25709
W'hampton NE	20167	24106	3546		1087	48906	3939
W'hampton SE	12975	23215	3881		850	40921	10240
W'hampton SW	25969	21003	4470		1237	52679	4966
Woodspring	35175	9942	17666		1737	64520	17509
Woolwich	6598	17551			15546	39695	2225

J. Cartwright, former SDP MP, took 15,326 votes (38.6%)

Constituency	Con	Lab	LDem	Nat	Other	Votes	maj
Worcester	27883	21731	9561		935	60110	6152
Worcs Mid	33964	24094	9745		520	68323	9870
Worcs S	34792	9727	18641		1178	64338	16151
Workington	16270	26719	3028		938	46955	10449
Worsley	19406	29418	6490		853	56167	10012
Worthing	34198	6679	17665		1485	60027	16533
Wrekin	27217	33865	8032		1008	70122	6648
Wrexham	18114	24830	7074		1415	51433	6716
Wycombe	30081	12222	13005		1303	56611	17076
Wyre	29449	17785	6420		260	53914	11664
Wyre Forest	28983	18642	12958			60583	10341
Yeovil	22125	5765	30958		1047	59895	8833
Ynys Mon	14878	10126	1891	15984	182	43061	1106
York	25183	31525	6811		648	64167	6342

Con	Lab	LDem	Nat	Other	% maj	Electors	Turnout
61.4%	12.5%	25.1%	0.0%	1.0%	36.3%	86545	81.8%
41.2%	49.3%	7.3%	0.0%	2.2%	8.1%	62701	78.0%
31.7%	56.7%	9.5%	0.0%	2.1%	25.0%	56170	72.9%
49.3%	39.9%	8.5%	0.0%	2.3%	9.4%	67368	78.2%
54.5%	15.4%	27.4%	0.0%	2.7%	27.1%	77532	83.2%
16.6%	44.2%	0.0%	0.0%	39.2%	5.6%	55977	70.9%
46.4%	36.2%	15.9%	0.0%	1.6%	10.2%	74201	81.0%
49.7%	35.3%	14.3%	0.0%	0.8%	14.4%	84290	81.1%
54.1%	15.1%	29.0%	0.0%	1.8%	25.1%	80157	80.3%
34.7%	56.9%	6.4%	0.0%	2.0%	22.3%	57608	81.5%
34.6%	52.4%	11.6%	0.0%	1.5%	17.8%	72244	77.7%
57.0%	11.1%	29.4%	0.0%	2.5%	27.5%	77550	77.4%
38.8%	48.3%	11.5%	0.0%	1.4%	9.5%	90893	77.1%
35.2%	48.3%	13.8%	0.0%	2.8%	13.1%	63729	80.7%
53.1%	21.6%	23.0%	0.0%	2.3%	30.2%	72565	78.0%
54.6%	33.0%	11.9%	0.0%	0.5%	21.6%	67778	79.5%
47.8%	30.8%	21.4%	0.0%	0.0%	17.1%	73602	82.3%
36.9%	9.6%	51.7%	0.0%	1.7%	14.7%	73060	82.0%
34.6%	23.5%	4.4%	37.1%	0.4%	2.6%	53412	80.6%
39.2%	49.1%	10.6%	0.0%	1.0%	9.9%	79242	81.0%

Constituency	UUP	DUP	Con	APNI	SDLP	SF	others	maj
Antrim E	16966	9544	3359	9132			250	7422
Antrim N	8216	23152	2263	3442	6512	1916		14936
Antrim S	29956			5224	5397	1220	442	24559
Belfast E		18437	3314	10650		679	2711	7787
Belfast N	17240		2107	2246	7615	4693	2013	9625
Belfast S	16336		3356	5054	6266	1123	1449	10070
Belfast W	4766				17415	16826	963	589
Down N		4414	14371	6611			19560	4934

J Kilfedder, UPUP, took 19305 votes (42.9%) and was elected

Constituency	UUP	DUP	Con	APNI	SDLP	SF	others	maj
Down S	25181		1488	1542	31523	1843		6342
Fermanagh	26923			950	12810	12604	1841	14113
Foyle		13705		1390	26710	9149	936	13005
Lagan Vall	29772		4423	6207	4626	3346	582	23565
L'Derry E	30370		1589	3613	11843	5320		18527
Newry	18982			972	26073	6547		7091
Strangford	19517	10606	6782	7585			295	8911
Ulster Mid		23181		1506	16994	10248	2834	6187
Upper Bann	26824		1556	2541	10661	2777	1120	16163

UUP%	DUP%	Con%	APNI%	SDLP%	SF%	others%	maj%	electors	turnout%
43.2	24.3	8.6	23.3			0.6	18.9	62864	62.4
18.1	50.9	5.0	7.6	14.3	4.2		32.8	69114	65.8
70.9			12.4	12.8	2.9	1.0	58.1	67192	62.9
	51.5	9.3	29.8		1.9	7.6	21.8	52869	67.7
48.0		5.9	6.3	21.2	13.1	5.6	26.8	55068	65.2
48.6		10.0	15.0	18.7	3.3	4.3	30.0	52050	64.5
11.9				43.6	42.1	2.4	1.5	54644	73.1
	9.8	32.0	14.7			43.5	11.0	68662	65.5
40.9		2.4	2.5	51.2	3.0		10.3	76186	80.8
48.8			1.7	23.2	22.9	3.3	25.6	70253	78.5
	26.4		2.7	51.5	17.6	1.8	25.1	74673	69.5
60.8		9.0	12.7	9.4	6.8	1.2	48.1	72708	67.3
57.6		3.0	6.9	22.5	10.1		35.1	75587	69.8
36.1			1.8	49.6	12.5		13.5	67531	77.9
43.6	23.7	15.1	16.9			0.7	19.9	68901	65.0
	42.3		2.8	31.0	18.7	5.2	11.3	69138	79.2
59.0		3.4	5.6	23.4	6.1	2.5	35.5	67460	67.4

MARGINALS SINCE THE 1992 ELECTION

The list shows the seats with the smallest majorities after the 1992 election. Constituency boundaries are being reviewed. If the next election comes before the changes are complete, the election will be fought on existing boundaries and these will be the most marginal seats. If the changes are made before the election, some of the seats listed here will no longer exist. Others now safe will become marginal, while others now marginal will become safe.

CONSERVATIVE SEATS VULNERABLE TO LABOUR

Constituency	% maj	Constituency	% maj
Vale of Glamorgan	0.0%	Plymouth Drake	5.2%
Bristol NW	0.1%	Harlow	5.2%
Hayes & Harlington	0.1%	Stockton S	5.4%
Ayr	0.2%	Elmet	5.6%
Bolton NE	0.4%	Cardiff N	6.2%
Norwich N	0.5%	Monmouth	6.3%
Corby	0.6%	Lancaster	6.4%
Slough	0.9%	Chorley	6.5%
Tynemouth	1.0%	Keighley	6.6%
Southampton Test	1.0%	Derbyshire S	6.6%
Amber Valley	1.2%	Blackpool N	6.7%
Edmonton	1.2%	Brighton Kemptown	7.0%
Luton S	1.4%	Northampton N	7.2%
Dover	1.4%	Gloucs W	7.4%
Bury S	1.5%	Derby N	7.5%
Stirling	1.5%	B'hm Hall Gn	7.8%
Leics NW	1.6%	Calder Valley	8.0%
Bolton W	1.8%	High Peak	8.0%
Chester	2.1%	Bury N	8.1%
Batley & Spen	2.3%	Dudley W	8.1%
Langbaurgh	2.4%	Peterborough	8.2%
Basildon	2.8%	Brighton Pavilion	8.3%
Coventry SW	2.8%	Westminster N	8.4%
Lincoln	3.3%	Stevenage	8.4%
Mitcham & Morden	3.4%	Leeds NE	8.6%
Aberdeen S	3.7%	Davyhulme	8.8%
Blackpool S	3.8%	Erewash	9.0%
Swindon	3.9%	Milton Keynes SW	9.2%
Brentford & Isleworth	3.9%	South Ribble	9.2%
Eltham	4.1%	Battersea	9.3%
Exeter	4.9%	Gravesham	9.3%
Erith & Crayford	5.0%	Gloucester	9.4%

W'hampton SW	9.4%		Newark	14.6%
Edinbgh Pentlands	9.6%		Pudsey	14.6%
Burton	9.7%		Halesowen & S'bridge	15.0%
Waveney	9.7%		Selby	15.4%
Staffs Mid	9.9%		Warwick & Leamington	15.4%
Gt Yarmouth	10.0%		Finchley	15.5%
Worcester	10.2%		Putney	15.6%
B'hm Edgbaston	11.4%		Acton	15.7%
Clwyd NW	11.4%		Croydon NE	16.1%
Kensington	11.5%		Watford	16.1%
Staffs Moorlands	11.8%		Broxtowe	16.2%
Ealing N	11.9%		Wirral S	16.3%
Colne Valley	12.2%		Fulham	16.4%
Staffs SE	12.5%		Wyre Forest	17.1%
Crawley	12.5%		Dartford	17.1%
Dumfries	13.1%		Stafford	17.6%
Welwyn Hatfield	13.9%		Medway	17.7%
Brigg & C'thorpes	14.4%		Enfield N	18.0%
Worcs Mid	14.5%			

CONSERVATIVE SEATS VULNERABLE TO LIBERAL DEMOCRATS

Constituency	% maj			
Brecon & Radnor	0.3%		Kincardine & Deeside	8.6%
Portsmouth S	0.5%		Richmond & Barnes	8.6%
Hazel Grove	1.7%		Eastbourne	8.9%
Edinburgh W	1.8%		Torbay	10.1%
Isle of Wight	2.3%		Twickenham	10.7%
Conwy	2.4%		Wells	11.5%
St Ives	2.9%		Bristol W	11.6%
Taunton	5.2%		Ribble Valley	11.7%
Southport	5.5%		Winchester	12.3%
Falmouth & Camborne	5.7%		Hastings & Rye	12.3%
Devon W & Torridge	5.8%		Sheff Hallam	12.4%
Hereford	6.0%		Cornwall SE	12.8%
Oxford W & Abingdon	6.4%		Teignbridge	14.2%
Somerton & Frome	7.4%		Dorset W	14.7%
Littleborough	8.4%		Salisbury	14.8%
Weston-super-Mare	8.5%		Leeds NW	15.2%

Dorset N	16.1%	Newbury	18.6%
Northavon	16.9%	Congleton	18.7%
Folkestone & Hythe	17.0%	Tiverton	11.8%
Bridgwater	17.1%	Shrewsbury & Atcham	18.8%
Westbury	17.4%	Carshalton	18.8%
Canterbury	18.4%	Lindsey E	19.0%

LABOUR SEATS VULNERABLE TO CONSERVATIVES

Constituency	% maj		
		Crewe & Nantwich	4.4%
		Sherwood	4.6%
Rossendale & Darwen	0.2%	Darlington	5.1%
Warrington S	0.3%	Copeland	5.3%
Birmingham Yardley	0.4%	Bristol E	5.4%
Ipswich	0.5%	Edinburgh C	5.4%
Halifax	0.8%	Dulwich	5.5%
Ilford S	0.9%	Streatham	5.7%
Southampton Itchen	1.0%	Nottingham S	5.9%
Dewsbury	1.1%	Strathkelvin & Bearsden	6.3%
Cambridge	1.1%	Walsall S	6.3%
Birmingham Northfield	1.2%	Barrow	6.4%
Pembroke	1.2%	W Bromwich E	6.6%
Thurrock	2.2%	Cunninghame N	6.9%
Warwickshire N	2.4%	Wallasey	7.0%
Cannock & Burntwood	2.5%	Carlisle	7.1%
Lewisham E	2.5%	Walsall N	7.3%
Nuneaton	2.7%	Tooting	8.0%
Stockport	3.0%	Wolverhampton NE	8.1%
Lancashire W	3.2%	Cardiff C	8.1%
Ellesmere Port & Neston	3.3%	Newham S	8.1%
Feltham & Heston	3.3%	Leicester W	8.2%
Hampstead & Highgate	3.4%	Walthamstow	8.5%
Coventry SE	3.6%	Bradford S	9.3%
Delyn	3.7%	Hornsey & Wood Green	9.3%
Birmingham Selly Oak	3.7%	Edinburgh S	9.4%
Renfrew W & Inverclyde	3.7%	Wrekin	9.5%
Croydon NW	3.8%	York	9.9%
Kingswood	3.9%	Clwyd SW	10.0%
Pendle	4.0%	Derbyshire NE	10.6%
Hyndburn	4.0%	Blackburn	11.0%
Lewisham W	4.2%	Norwich S	12.1%

Newcastle C	12.4%
Wakefield	12.4%
Birmingham Erdington	12.9%
Warley W	13.0%
Stoke S	13.0%
Wrexham	13.1%
Derby S	13.8%
Southall	13.9%

Dumbarton	13.9%
Hammersmith	14.0%
Plymouth Devonport	14.5%
Glanford & Scunthorpe	14.5%
Gt Grimsby	14.8%
Huddersfield	14.8%
Gower	15.0%

LIBERAL DEMOCRAT SEATS VULNERABLE TO:

CONSERVATIVE

Constituency	% maj
Gordon	0.5
Devon N	1.4%
Cheltenham	2.6%
Cornwall N	3.1%
Bath	7.2%
Argyll	7.2%
Fife NE	7.9%
Tweeddale Ettrick & L'dale	8.2%
Berwick	11.6%
Truro	12.2%
Roxburgh & Berwickshire	12.6%
Yeovil	14.7%

LABOUR

Inverness, Nairn & Lochaber	0.5%
Rochdale	3.5%
Liverpool Mossley Hill	6.3%

OTHER MARGINALS

Constituency	% maj
LAB OVER LD	
Greenwich	3.8%
Woolwich	5.6%
Chesterfield	11.5%
Sheff Hillsborough	11.8%
Glasgow Hillhead	12.3%
CON OVER NAT	
Perth & Kinross	4.2%
Galloway & U.Nithsdale	5.5%
Tayside N	9.2
LAB OVER NAT	
Carmarthen	5.1%
Western Isles	10.6%
Dundee E	10.7%
Glasgow Govan	11.8%
Edinbgh Leith	12.4%
Kilmarnock	14.1%
Linlithgow	14.6

NAT OVER CON	
Angus East	2.0%
Ynys Mon	2.6%
Moray	6.2%
Banff	8.9%
NAT OVER LD	
Ceredigion & P'broke N	6.2%
DUP OVER SDLP	
Ulster Mid	11.3
SDLP OVER SF	
Belfast W	1.5
SDLP OVER UU	
Down S	10.3
UPUP OVER CON	
Down N	11.0

BY-ELECTIONS 1992-93

There were no by-elections in 1992, the only year this century when this has occurred.

May 6 1993

NEWBURY (death of Judith Chaplin, February 19)

	vote	%vote	%vote GE
David Rendel *Lib Dem*	37,590	65.1	37.3
Julian Davidson *Con*	15,535	26.9	55.9
Steve Bilcliffe *Lab*	1,151	2.0	6.0
Alan Sked *Anti-Federalist*	601	1.0	
Andrew Bannon *Con candidate*	561	1.0	
Stephen Martin *Commoners Party*	435	0.8	
Lord David Sutch *Monster Raving Loony*	432	0.7	
Jim Wallis *Green*	341	0.6	0.8
Robin Marlar *Referendum Party*	338	0.6	
John Browne *Con Party Rebel*	267	0.5	
Lindi St Clair *Corrective*	170	0.3	
William Board *Maastricht Referendum*	84	0.1	
Michael Grenville *Natural Law*	60	0.1	
Johnathan Day *People and Pensioners*	49	0.1	
Colin Palmer *21st Century*	40	0.1	
Mladen Grbin *Defend Children in Bosnia*	33	0.1	
Alan Page *SDP*	33	0.1	
Anne Murphy *CPGB*	32	0.1	
Michael Stone *Royal billions for Schools*	21	0.0	

LibDem majority B/E:	22,055	38.2	
Con majority 1992 GE:			18.6
Swing from Con to LibDem:		28.4%	
Electorate B/E:	81,081		
Percentage poll:		71.3	82.8

All candidates except Rendel and Davidson lost their deposits

July 29 1993

CHRISTCHURCH (death of Robert Adley, May 13)

	vote	%vote	GE
Diana Maddock *Liberal Democrat*	33,164	62.2	23.6
Robert Hayward *Conservative*	16,737	31.4	63.5
Nigel Lickley *Labour*	1,453	2.7	12.1
Alan Sked *Anti-Federalist*	878	1.6	
Lord D.Sutch *Monster Raving Loony*	404	0.8	
A.Bannon *Con candidate*	357	0.7	
P.Newman *Sack Graham Taylor*	80	0.1	
Ms T.B.Jackson *Daily Sport*	67	0.1	
P.Hollyman *Save the NHS*	60	0.1	
J.Crockard *Highlander IV*	48	0.1	
M.Griffiths *Natural Law*	45	0.1	0.4
M.Belcher *Ian for King*	23	0.0	
K.Fitzhugh *Alfred Chicken*	18	0.0	
J.Walley *Rainbow Alliance*	16	0.0	

LibDem majority B/E:	16,427	30.8	
Con majority 1992 GE:			39.9
Swing from Con to LibDem:	35.8		
Electorate B/E:	71,868		
Percentage poll:		74.2	80.7

All candidates except Maddock and Hayward lost their deposits

JOHN MAJOR'S CABINETS

	28.11.90	11.4.92	25.9.92	27.5.93
PRIME MINISTER:	J.Major	J.Major	J.Major	J.Major
LORD CHANCELLOR:	Ld Mackay	Ld Mackay	Ld Mackay	Ld Mackay
HOME SECRETARY:	K.Baker	K.Clarke	K.Clarke	M.Howard
FOREIGN SECRETARY:	D.Hurd	D.Hurd	D.Hurd	D.Hurd
CHANCELLOR:	N.Lamont	N.Lamont	N.Lamont	K.Clarke
CHIEF SECRETARY:	D.Mellor	M.Portillo	M.Portillo	M.Portillo
TRADE & INDUSTRY:	P.Lilley	M.Heseltine	M.Heseltine	M.Heseltine
EMPLOYMENT:	M.Howard	G.Shephard	G.Shephard	D.Hunt
DEFENCE:	T.King	M.Rifkind	M.Rifkind	M.Rifkind
LORD PRESIDENT OF THE COUNCIL:	J.MacGregor	T.Newton	T.Newton	T.Newton
CHANCELLOR OF THE DUCHY/PUBLIC SERVICE	C.Patten*	W.Waldegrave	W.Waldegrave	W.Waldegrave
LORD PRIVY SEAL:	Ld Waddington	Ld Wakeham	Ld Wakeham	Ld Wakeham
EDUCATION:	K.Clarke	J.Patten	J.Patten	J.Patten
HEALTH:	W.Waldegrave	V.Bottomley	V.Bottomley	V.Bottomley
SOCIAL SECURITY:	T.Newton	P.Lilley	P.Lilley	P.Lilley
ENVIRONMENT:	M.Heseltine	M.Howard	M.Howard	J.Gummer
TRANSPORT:	M.Rifkind	J.MacGregor	J.MacGregor	J.MacGregor
ENERGY:	J.Wakeham	DEPARTMENT DISCONTINUED		
AGRICULTURE:	J.Gummer	J.Gummer	J.Gummer	G.Shephard
HERITAGE:	(no appointment)	D.Mellor	P.Brooke	P.Brooke
SCOTLAND:	I.Lang	I.Lang	I.Lang	I.Lang
WALES:	D.Hunt	D.Hunt	D.Hunt	J.Redwood
N IRELAND:	P.Brooke	Sir P.Mayhew	Sir P.Mayhew	Sir P.Mayhew

Outside Cabinet--

ATTORNEY-GENERAL:	Sir P. Mayhew	Sir N. Lyell	Sir N. Lyell	Sir N. Lyell
CHIEF WHIP:	R.Ryder	R.Ryder	R.Ryder	R.Ryder

* Patten was chairman of Conservative party; Waldegrave was first secretary of state for Public Service and Science

DEPARTMENTS AND THEIR MINISTERS: CHANGES SINCE THE ELECTION

	April 11 1992	May 27 1993
AGRICULTURE, FISHERIES AND FOOD		
MINISTER:	**JOHN GUMMER**	**GILLIAN SHEPHARD**
Ministers of state:	David Curry	Michael Jack
Parly secretary:	Earl Howe	Earl Howe
	Nicholas Soames	Nicholas Soames
DEFENCE		
SEC. OF STATE:	**MALCOLM RIFKIND**	**MALCOLM RIFKIND**
Ministers of state:	Archie Hamilton	Jeremy Hanley
	Jonathan Aitken	Jonathan Aitken
Under secretary:	Viscount Cranborne	Viscount Cranborne
EDUCATION		
SEC. OF STATE:	**JOHN PATTEN**	**JOHN PATTEN**
Ministers of state:	Baroness Blatch	Baroness Blatch
Under secretaries:	Eric Forth	Eric Forth
	Nigel Forman*	Tim Boswell
		Robin Squire

Forman left Government on December 11, 1992, replaced by Timothy Boswell

EMPLOYMENT		
SEC. OF STATE:	**GILLIAN SHEPHARD**	**DAVID HUNT**
Ministers of state:	Michael Forsyth	Michael Forsyth
Under secretaries:	Patrick McLoughlin	Ann Widdecombe
	Viscount Ullswater	Viscount Ullswater
ENVIRONMENT		
SEC. OF STATE:	**MICHAEL HOWARD**	**JOHN GUMMER**
Ministers of state:	John Redwood	David Curry
	David Maclean	Timothy Yeo
Minister for Housing and Planning:	Sir George Young	Sir George Young
Under secretaries:	Tony Baldry	Tony Baldry
	Robin Squire	Lord Strathclyde
	Lord Strathclyde	
FOREIGN AND COMMONWEALTH AFFAIRS		
SEC. OF STATE:	**DOUGLAS HURD**	**DOUGLAS HURD**
Minister for Overseas Development:	Baroness Chalker	Baroness Chalker
Ministers of state:	Alastair Goodlad	Alastair Goodlad
	Douglas Hogg	Douglas Hogg
	Tristan Garel-Jones	David Heathcoat-Amory
Under secretary:	Mark Lennox-Boyd	Mark Lennox-Boyd

	April 11 1992	May 27 1993
HEALTH		
SEC. OF STATE:	**VIRGINIA BOTTOMLEY**	**VIRGINIA BOTTOMLEY**
Minister of state:	Brian Mawhinney	Brian Mawhinney
Under secretaries:	Tim Yeo	John Bowis
	Tom Sackville	Tom Sackville
	Baroness Cumberledge	Baroness Cumberledge
HOME OFFICE		
SEC. OF STATE:	**KENNETH CLARKE**	**MICHAEL HOWARD**
Ministers of state:	Peter Lloyd	Peter Lloyd
	Michael Jack	David Maclean
	Earl Ferrers	Earl Ferrers
Under secretary:	Charles Wardle	Charles Wardle
LAW OFFICERS		
ATTORNEY-GENERAL:	Sir Nicholas Lyell	Sir Nicholas Lyell
SOLICITOR-GENERAL:	Sir Derek Spencer	Sir Derek Spencer
LORD ADVOCATE:	Lord Rodger	Lord Rodger
SOL.-GENERAL, SCOTLAND:	Thomas Dawson	Thomas Dawson
LORD CHANCELLOR'S DEPARTMENT		
LORD CHANCELLOR:	**LORD MACKAY**	**LORD MACKAY**
Parly secretary:	John M.Taylor	John M.Taylor
NATIONAL HERITAGE:	**DAVID MELLOR***	**PETER BROOKE**
Under secretary:	Robert Key	Iain Sproat

Mellor left Government on September 24, 1992 replaced by Peter Brooke

NORTHERN IRELAND OFFICE:		
SECRETARY OF STATE:	**SIR PATRICK MAYHEW**	**SIR PATRICK MAYHEW**
Ministers of state:	Michael Mates	Michael Mates*
	Robert Atkins	Robert Atkins
Under secretaries:	Jeremy Hanley	Michael Ancram
	The Earl of Arran	The Earl of Arran

Mates left Government on June 24, 1993 replaced by John Wheeler June 25

PAYMASTER GENERAL'S DEPARTMENT:		
Paymaster General:	Sir John Cope	Sir John Cope
PRIVY COUNCIL OFFICE:		
Lord President of the Council,		
Leader of Commons:	Tony Newton	Tony Newton
Lord Privy Seal, Leader of the Lords:	Lord Wakeham	Lord Wakeham
PUBLIC SERVICE AND SCIENCE		
SEC. OF STATE:	**WILLIAM WALDEGRAVE**	**WILLIAM WALDEGRAVE**
Ministers of state:		
Under secretary:	Robert Jackson	David Davis

SCOTTISH OFFICE

SEC. OF STATE:	IAN LANG	IAN LANG
Ministers of state:	Lord Fraser	Lord Fraser
Under secretaries:	Lord J.Douglas-Hamilton	Lord J.Douglas-Hamilton
	Allan Stewart	Allan Stewart
	Sir Hector Monro	Sir Hector Monro

SOCIAL SECURITY

SEC. OF STATE	PETER LILLEY	PETER LILLEY
Minister for Social Security		
& Disabled People:	Nicholas Scott	Nicholas Scott
Under secretaries:	Alistair Burt	Alistair Burt
	Ann Widdecombe	William Hague
	Lord Henley	Lord Henley

TRADE & INDUSTRY

SEC. OF STATE:	MICHAEL HESELTINE	MICHAEL HESELTINE
Ministers of state:	Tim Eggar	Tim Eggar
	Richard Needham	Richard Needham
Under secretaries:	Baroness Denton	Baroness Denton
	Neil Hamilton	Neil Hamilton
	Edward Leigh	Patrick McLoughlin

TRANSPORT SEC. OF STATE:	JOHN MACGREGOR	JOHN MACGREGOR
Ministers of state:	Earl of Caithness	Earl of Caithness
Minister for Public Transport:	Roger Freeman	Roger Freeman
Under secretaries:	Kenneth Carlisle	Robert Key
	Stephen Norris	Stephen Norris

TREASURY

CHANCELLOR:	NORMAN LAMONT	KENNETH CLARKE
CHIEF SECRETARY:	MICHAEL PORTILLO	MICHAEL PORTILLO
Financial Secretary:	Stephen Dorrell	Stephen Dorrell
Paymaster General	Sir John Cope	Sir John Cope
Economic Secretary:	Anthony Nelson	Anthony Nelson

WELSH OFFICE

SEC. OF STATE:	DAVID HUNT	JOHN REDWOOD
Ministers of state:	Sir Wyn Roberts	Sir Wyn Roberts
Under secretaries:	Gwilym Jones	Gwilym Jones

GOVERNMENT WHIPS

CHIEF WHIP:	Richard Ryder	Richard Ryder
Deputy Chief Whip:	David Heathcoat-Amory	Greg Knight
Whips:	David Lightbown	David Lightbown
	Sydney Chapman	Sydney Chapman
	Irvine Patnick	Irvine Patnick

	Timothy Wood	Timothy Wood
	Timothy Boswell*	Timothy Kirkhope
		(from December 15 1992)
		Andrew Mackay

transferred to Education December 11, 1992, replaced by Timothy Kirkhope

Assistant Whips:	Timothy Kirkhope	Michael Brown
	David Davis	Derek Conway
	Robert G.Hughes	Robert G.Hughes
	James Arbuthnot	James Arbuthnot
	Andrew Mackay	Andrew Mitchell
	Andrew Mitchell	

LORDS WHIPS

CHIEF WHIP:	Lord Hesketh	Lord Hesketh
Deputy Chief Whip:	Earl of Strathmore	Earl of Strathmore
Whips:	Viscount Long	Viscount Long
	Baroness Trumpington	Baroness Trumpington
	Viscount Astor	Viscount Astor
	Viscount St Davids	Viscount St Davids
	Viscount Goschen	Viscount Goschen
	Lord Cavendish	

EXECUTIVE OF THE CONSERVATIVE
1922 COMMITTEE OF BACKBENCH MPS
(as at June 30 1993):

Chairman-	Sir M.Fox (Shipley)
Vice-chairs-	Sir G.Johnson-Smith (Wealden)
	Dame J.Knight (Birmingham Edgbaston)
Treasurer-	Sir G.Shaw (Pudsey)
Hon secretaries	Sir J.Hannam (Exeter)
	Sir P.Hordern (Horsham)
Officers:	Sir R.Boyson (Brent N), R.Dunn (Dartford), Sir A.Durant, (Reading W), Sir G.Gardiner (Reigate), Sir A.Grant (Cambs SW), Sir T.Higgins (Worthing), Sir I.Lawrence (Burton), Sir M.Neubert (Romford), J.Pawsey (Rugby), Mrs M.Roe (Broxbourne), Sir D.Thompson (Calder Valley), J.Townend (Bridlington)

THE LABOUR FRONT BENCH
Showing changes since appointments in July 1992

Leader	John Smith
Leader of House, Campaigns Co-ordinator	Margaret Beckett
	Nick Brown*
Treasury, economic affairs	Gordon Brown
	Harriet Harman
	Alistair Darling
	Andrew Smith
	Nick Brown*
Home affairs	Tony Blair
	Joan Ruddock
	Alun Michael
	Graham Allen
Trade & Industry	Robin Cook
	Martin O'Neill (Energy)
	Derek Fatchett
	Nigel Griffiths
	Stuart Bell
	Jim Cousins
Employment	Frank Dobson
	Tony Lloyd*
	Joyce Quin
	Sam Galbraith
Transport	John Prescott
	Peter Snape
	Joan Walley
	Tony Banks*
	Brian Wilson (transferred from Citizen's Charter)
National Heritage (from DATE)	Bryan Gould (resigned DATE)
	Ann Clwyd (replaced Bryan Gould, resigned)
	Robin Corbett
	Tom Pendry
Citizen's Charter, Women	Mo Mowlam
	Brian Wilson (transferred to Transport)
	Lewis Moonie
	Kate Hoey (sacked for defying whip)
	Mark Fisher

Environmental Protection	Chris Smith
	Clare Short
Wales	Ann Clwyd (transferred to Heritage)
	Ron Davies (transferred from Agriculture)
	Paul Murphy
	Rhodri Morgan
Education	Ann Taylor
	Jeff Rooker
	Win Griffiths
	Tony Lloyd*
Foreign	Jack Cunningham
	George Robertson
	Allan Rogers
	Bruce Grocott
Development & Co-operation	Michael Meacher
	Tony Worthington
Social Security	Donald Dewar
	Keith Bradley
	Llin Golding
Health	David Blunkett
	Dawn Primarolo
	David Hinchcliffe
	Ian McCartney
Local Government	Jack Straw
	John Battle
	Doug Henderson
	Keith Vaz
	Peter Pike
	Tony Banks*
Scotland	Tom Clarke
	Henry McLeish
	John McFall
	Maria Fyfe
Defence, disarmament, arms control	David Clark
	George Foulkes
	John Reid
	Eric Martlew

Food, agriculture, rural affairs	Ron Davies (transferred to Wales, replaced by Gavin Strang)
	Elliot Morley
	Dale Campbell-Savours
Northern Ireland	Kevin McNamara
	Roger Stott
	Bill O'Brien
Law Officers	John Morris
	John Fraser
Lord Chancellor's department	Paul Boateng
Disabled people's rights	Barry Sheerman

denotes spokesman with responsibilities in more than one department

CONTEST FOR LABOUR LEADERSHIP
AND DEPUTY LEADERSHIP 1992

Results announced July 18:

Figures show % of vote taken, section by section. Unions have 40% of the vote, CLPs (constituency Labour parties) and the PLP (Parliamentary Labour Party) each have 30%.

LEADER:	CLPs	PLP	unions	%total
John Smith	29.311	23.187	38.518	91.016
Bryan Gould	0.689	6.813	1.482	8.984

DEPUTY LEADER:				
Margaret Beckett	19.038	12.871	25.394	57.303
John Prescott	7.096	9.406	11.627	28.129
Bryan Gould	3.866	7.723	2.979	14.568

SHADOW CABINET ELECTIONS
July 23 1993

	1993	1992*
1. Gordon Brown	165	150 (1)
2. Tony Blair	150	132 (8)
3. Robin Cook	149	149 (2)
4. Frank Dobson	140	134 (6=)
5. John Prescott	137	118 (15=)
6. Bryan Gould	135	136 (5)
Harriet Harman	135	45
Mo Mowlam	135	dns
Chris Smith	135	32
10. Ann Clwyd	133	137 (4)
11. Ann Taylor	129	126 (9)
12. Jack Cunningham	124	121 (12=)
13. Michael Meacher	122	118 (15=)
14. Donald Dewar	121	122 (10)
15. David Blunkett	112	dns
16. Jack Straw	111	119 (14)
17. Tom Clarke	105	dns
18. David Clark	104	122 (10)

Not elected

Ron Davies	89	83
George Robertson	82	48
Barry Jones	80	113 (17)
Clare Short	73	45
Dawn Primarolo	71	dns
Joyce Quin	71	dns
Hilary Armstrong	70	dns
Martin O'Neill	63	86
Jo Richardson	62	107 (18)
Kevin McNamara	61	59
Stuart Bell	60	dns
Chris Mullin	58	dns
George Foulkes	57	dns
Derek Fatchett	54	dns
Henry McLeish	53	dns
Clive Soley	53	31
Llin Golding	51	61
Tony Benn	47	39

	1993	1992
Mildred Gordon	47	40
Jeff Rooker	44	dns
Tony Banks	42	41
Bruce Grocott	42	dns
Mark Fisher	41	dns
Alun Michael	39	dns
Gavin Strang	39	50
John Marek	38	dns
Alf Morris	37	dns
Tony Lloyd	33	dns
Barry Sheerman	31	32
Graham Allen	29	dns
Bernie Grant	29	30
Dennis Canavan	26	35
John Garrett	26	dns
Austin Mitchell	20	dns
Stuart Randall	19	dns

dns indicates candidate who did not stand in 1992

Candidates who were defeated in 1991 and did not stand in 1992:

Joan Lestor	72
Bob Cryer	29
Tam Dalyell	26
Keith Vaz	22

Three candidates elected in 1991 did not stand in 1992. John Smith was 3rd in 1991 with 141 votes; as leader, did not stand in 1992. Margaret Beckett was equal 6th in 1991 with 134 votes; as deputy leader, did not stand in 1992. Gerald Kaufman was equal 12th in 1991 with 121 votes; did not stand in 1992.

After the resignation of Bryan Gould, Ron Davies was elected on November 4 to fill the vacancy, defeating George Robertson

	first round	second round
Ron Davies	78	125
George Robertson	77	88
Tony Banks	34	
Clare Short	27	

LABOUR NEC ELECTIONS 1993

Those elected were:

Trade union section (12 seats):

Dan Duffy	(Transport and General Workers Union)	4,812,000
Bill Connor	(shop workers' union Usdaw)	4,780,000
Charles Kelly	(Builders' union Ucatt)	4,771,000
Tom Sawyer	(National Union of Public Employees)	4,769,000
Gordon Colling	(Graphical Paper and Media Union)	4,745,000
Vernon Hince	(Rail, Maritime and Transport workers union)	4,745,000
Judith Church	(Manufacturing, Science and Finance union)	4,743,000
Tony Clarke	(Union of Communication Workers)	4,730,000
David Ward	(National Communications Union)	4,706,000
Nigel Harris	(Amalgamated Engineering and Electrical Union)	4,651,000
Richard Rosser	(Transport Salaried Staff Association)	3,972,000
Colm O'Kane	(Confederation of Health Service Employees)	3,333,000

Socialist Co-operative and other organisations section (one seat):

John Evans	(NULSC)	52,000

Constituency Labour parties section (seven seats):

Neil Kinnock	(Islwyn)	533,000
David Blunkett	(Sheffield Brightside)	531,000
Gordon Brown	(Dunfermline)	523,000
John Prescott	(Hull East)	446,000
Robin Cook	(Livingston)	426,000
Tony Blair	(Sedgefield)	387,000
Tony Benn	(Chesterfield)	354,000

Women members section (Five seats):

Joan Lestor	(Eccles)	5,152,000
Clare Short	(Birmingham Ladywood)	5,062,000
Diana Jeuda	(Usdaw)	5,049,000
Hilary Armstrong	(MSF)	4,986,000
Brenda Etchells	(AEEU)	3,695,000

Treasurer:

Tom Burlison	(GMB general union)	3,307,000

LIBERAL DEMOCRAT FRONT BENCH
May 5 1992

Leader	Paddy Ashdown
Deputy Leader, Treasury & Civil Service	Alan Beith
Trade & Industry	Malcolm Bruce
Environment & natural resources	Simon Hughes
Employment	Alex Carlile
Agriculture & rural affairs	Paul Tyler
Transport	Nick Harvey
Home affairs, Heritage	Robert Maclennan
England, Local Government, Housing	Nigel Jones
Charters, Youth	Matthew Taylor
Women	Ray Michie
Defence, Disarmament, Sport	Menzies Campbell
Social security, older people, disabled	Archy Kirkwood*
Health, Community Care	Liz Lynne
Education & training	Don Foster
Foreign Affairs	David Steel
Europe, East-West	Charles Kennedy, Russell Johnston
Overseas Development	Lord Bonham-Carter
Scotland	Jim Wallace
Northern Ireland	Lord Holme
Wales	Alex Carlile

* Kirkwood succeeded Wallace as Chief Whip

THE YEAR IN EUROPE

Dan Bindman

April '92

26 Three weeks after the Italian general election, President Francesco Cossiga resigned 10 weeks before his mandate ended, saying he lacked sufficient power and authority.

May

21 EC agriculture ministers agreed to reform the Common Agricultural Policy with a shift from price support to income support for farmers.
22 At a summit in La Rochelle, France's President Mitterrand and Germany's Helmut Kohl announced the creation of a "Eurocorps" Franco-German defence force.
June 2 Danish voters rejected the Maastricht treaty on European Union by 50.7% to 49.3% — a margin of just 46,269 votes — in a referendum result which severely undermined the wider movement towards European integration. The turnout was 82.3%
10 The European Parliament passed a resolution, by 238 votes to 55 with 10 abstentions, insisting that European union should "proceed without delay" and expressing hope that "Denmark will be in a position to return to the fold as soon as possible".
18 Socialist Unity party leader Guiliano Amato, 54, became Italian prime minister, heading a coalition composed of the same four parties as the outgoing government. He appointed a 25-member government 10 days later — Italy's 51st administration since 1945.
18 In a referendum, two-thirds (68.7%) of Irish voters endorsed ratification of the Maastricht treaty after the four main political parties made a joint call for a Yes vote. The turnout was 57.3%.
26 The European Council met in Lisbon for a two-day summit. On the Maastricht treaty, leaders of the 12 states declared their "determination to press ahead with European construction". On future funding, a decision on the financing of the "Delors II" package was postponed until December 1992. A proposal to extend the package's 30% increase in spending for another two years (to 1999) was rejected. On Community enlargement, it was decided that negotiations with Efta countries applying for membership should not begin on an official level before the Maastricht treaty was ratified or EC financing was resolved. In a move designed to aid ratification of Maastricht, the Council agreed that dialogue with European citizens on the treaty should be strengthened, and openness in EC decision-making should be increased. The mandate of President of the Commission Jacques Delors was renewed for a further two years.

July

1 Britain took over the EC presidency from Portugal.
2 Luxembourg's parliament approved the Maastricht treaty by 51 votes to six with three abstentions.
6-8 The Group of Seven (G7) leaders met in Munich. Acknowledging economic gloom among the industrialised countries, they pledged to pursue confidence-building and job-creating economic policies. They expressed hope that agreement on the Uruguay Round of trade talks would

be made by December 1992. They met with Russian President Boris Yeltsin and formally approved the payment of a the first tranche of an aid package worth $24 million. They also set up a $100 million multilateral fund to ensure nuclear safety in eastern Europe.

17 The 212-member lower house of Belgium's parliament voted 146 to 33 with three abstentions to ratify the Maastricht treaty, with the major parties all voting in favour. The treaty still required approval by Belgium's senate and the Flemish and Walloon parliaments.

26-7 John Major opened an international conference in London on the Yugoslav crisis. Resolutions made included tighter sanctions on Serbia, recognition of borders and humanitarian aid. Lord Owen replaced Lord Carrington as EC mediator.

27 EC finance ministers agreed in principle to a minimum standard Vat rate of 15% until the end of 1996.

31 The 300-seat Greek parliament, the Vouli, voted by 286 to eight to ratify Maastricht treaty.

September

9 Italian president Oscar Scalfero vetoed a request from prime minister Amato for three-year emergency economic powers.

13 The Italian lira was devalued by 7%. In Britain, the chancellor of the exchequer Norman Lamont repeated his government's commitment to maintaining the current DM2.95 central parity of the pound.

16 After a chaotic day in which interest rates were raised from 10 to 12% and then 15%, millions were spent defending the pound, Britain withdrew from the ERM, leading to a 10 % loss in the pound's value. Italy also left the ERM and the Spanish peseta was devalued by 5% within the ERM.

17 The Italian senate approved by 176 votes to 16 with one abstention the ratification of the Maastricht treaty.

2 By a margin of less than 1%, French voters said Yes to the Maastricht treaty in a referendum.

October

16 EC heads of state and government met in Birmingham for a special summit following the Danish and French referendums on Maastricht and the European currency crisis of the previous month. The European Council restated the urgency of ratifying the Maastricht treaty without it being renegotiated. It expressed concern at lower growth and rising unemployment and stressed the importance of economic convergence within the EC. The ERM was described as "a key factor of economic stability in Europe". The EC leaders also reiterated their Lisbon summit pledge to improve openness in EC decision-making. The history, culture and traditions of individual nations should be respected and citizens should be made aware that EC membership brought additional rights and protection. To placate fears of over-centralisation, the Council reaffirmed its commitment to activating the principle of "subsidiarity" or "nearness".

29 By 403 votes to 46 with 18 abstentions, the Italian chamber of deputies approved ratification of the Maastricht treaty. On the same day, the Spanish congress of deputies also approved the treaty's ratification by 314 votes to three with eight abstentions.

November

4 Britain's House of Commons voted by 319 to 316 with seven abstentions to resume parliamentary consideration of a Bill to ratify the Maastricht treaty, which was suspended after Denmark's No vote on the treaty in June.

5 Belgium's senate approved ratification of the Maastricht treaty by 115 votes to 26.

12 In the Netherlands, the second chamber approved by 137 votes to 13 a Bill to ratify the Maastricht treaty on condition that parliament be consulted before the introduction of a single European currency.

25 In the Irish general election, Dick Spring's Labour party made sweeping gains, largely at the expense of the ruling Fianna Fail (Republican party). The final results were Fianna Fail 67 seats (previously 77), Fine Gael (United Ireland party) 45 (55), Labour party 33 (15), Progressive Democrats 10 (6), Democratic Left 5 (6). The outgoing government of prime minister Albert Reynolds remained in office in a caretaker capacity.

25 The Spanish senate voted 222 to nil with three abstentions to ratify the Maastricht treaty. The congress of deputies had given its approval in October.

December

2 The Greek prime minister Constantine Mitsotakis sacked his entire cabinet. A new cabinet was appointed the next day, including Tzannis Tzannetakis, deputy prime minister, Michalis Papaconstantinou, foreign affairs, and Stefanos Manos, national economy, finance.

2 On condition that it be allowed a vote in 1996 on the introduction of a single European currency, the German Bundestag (lower house) voted by 543 to 17 with eight abstentions to ratify the Maastricht treaty.

6 In a Swiss referendum, 16 out of 23 cantons voted against joining the European Economic Area, which was to link the seven Efta countries with the EC 12 in an enlarged common market. However, the popular vote was finely balanced, with 50.3% (1,786,121) voting No to 49.7% (1,763,016) voting Yes, in an impressive turnout of 78.3%.

10 The Portuguese parliament approved ratification of Maastricht treaty by 200 to 21 votes.

11-12 At the Edinburgh Summit, EC heads of state and government did much to regain the momentum towards European integration lost in the wake of the Danish No vote in June. Crucially, an opt-out package was agreed and declarations made specifically designed to appeal to Danish voters in a second referendum on Maastricht. Denmark was to be excluded from key treaty provisions including those relating to defence, monetary union, and citizenship. Also, to please the Danes, a clarified definition of "subsidiarity" was agreed and minor concessions to greater openness in EC deliberations pledged. On EC funding, a compromise was struck which would increase available resources from 1.2% in 1992 to 1.27% by 1999 of Community GDP, significantly less than the 1.37% increase by 1995 proposed by the commission 10 months earlier. However, under pressure from Spain's Felipe Gonzalez, new "cohesion" cash available to the poorer "southern" EC states (Spain, Portugal, Ireland and Greece) was set at £12.1 billion over seven years. A growth initiative was approved with a projected £24 billion available for infrastructure development through the European Investment Bank and a new European Investment Fund. On expanding EC membership, it was announced that negotiations would begin with Austria, Sweden and Finland at the beginning of 1993. The number of seats in the European Parliament was increased from 518 to 567 to take account of German unification.

14-15 In local elections, Italy's major parties suffered heavy defeats, making the federalist Northern League the largest party in northern Italy.

15 In the Netherlands the First Chamber approved ratification of the Maastricht treaty.

18 The German Bundesrat (upper house) unanimously approved the Maastricht treaty

January '93

1 The single European market was established, implementing the Single European Act and allowing the free movement of certain goods, services, capital and persons throughout the EC.

1 Denmark took over the EC presidency from the United Kingdom.

12 In Ireland, the largest party Fianna Fail (Republican party) and the Labour party for the first time formed a coalition government together. Albert Reynolds (FF) was elected prime minister (Taoiseach) and Dick Spring (Lab) became deputy prime minister and foreign minister. Bertie Ahern (FF) was appointed finance minister.

13 Germany's ruling coalition parties agreed on draft amendments to the constitution to allow German soldiers to participate in international peacekeeping operations outside the Nato area.

14 Danish prime minister and leader of the Conservative People's party, Poul Shluter, resigned after the publication of a 6,000-word report claiming that he had misled parliament over the so-called "Tamilgate" scandal. The affair concerned a banning order — later rescinded — preventing Sri Lankan relatives of Tamil refugees in Denmark from being allowed to join them.

25 Social Democrat Poul Nyrup Rasmussen, aged 49, became Denmark's prime minister after forming a governing coalition with three small centrist parties, the Centre Democrats (CD), the Radical Liberals (RV), and the Christian People's party (KrF). With 90 seats in the 179-strong parliament, the coalition was Denmark's first majority administration since 1971. Niels Helvig Petersen (RV) became foreign minister and Marianne Jelved (RV) economics minister.

30 The Irish punt was devalued by 10% within the ERM, the fourth realignment in less than five months, after key interest rate reductions in EC and non-EC countries in the preceding few weeks.

February

1 The EC formally opened negotiations with Austria, Sweden and Finland on their applications for membership, with a view to their joining the Community by January 1 1995.

3 German defence minister Volker Ruhe announced savage cuts in arms spending, saving DM860 million in the current year and DM700 million in each of the next three years, to fund increased spending in eastern Germany. Official figures showed that in January unemployment had increased to 3.45 million; 7.4% of the workforce in western Germany and 14.7% in the east.

12 By majority vote, EC agriculture ministers formally adopted measures regulating EC banana imports despite opposition from Germany and Benelux countries.

15-16 The interior or justice ministers of 35 European countries and others met in Budapest to draw up a common policy on illegal immigration. Measures adopted included: criminal offences for smuggling illegal immigrants, penalties for airlines carrying them and the adoption of advanced technology to co-ordinate border checks and information.

24 Irish finance minister Ahern delivered a budget with a net deficit of Ir£760 million, equal to 2.9% of GDP. He announced job creation was top priority, unemployment having topped 300,000 (16.8% of the workforce) for the first time in January.

25 The Italian government won a vote of confidence, tabled by prime minister Amato, by 310 votes to 265 after the Milan corruption scandal led to three government ministers resigning.

March

8 In the British government's first House of Commons defeat since John Major took office in November 1990, an opposition amendment to the Bill to ratify the Maastricht treaty was approved by 314 votes to 292, despite a Conservative majority of 20. Twenty six Conservatives reportedly voted with the Opposition and 22 abstained.

9 As a growing number of politicians were implicated in corruption scandals, Italian prime minister Amato withdrew a controversial decree decriminalising the illicit financing of political parties. President

Scalfaro had declined to sign the decree the day before.

23 Belgium's prime minister Jean-Luc Dehaene tendered his resignation to King Baudouin after his centre-left coalition reached deadlock over measures to reduce the budget deficit. The King refused to accept the resignation and on March 30 the coalition reached an agreement on austerity measures, approved by Parliament two days later.

28 In the second round run-off of the French National Assembly elections, prime minister Pierre Beregovoy's Socialist party was routed by the Gaullist RPR and the centre-right UDF parties. Of the total 577 seats the RPR won 247 (126 previously), the UDF 213 (131), and other right-wing groups 24. The Socialists were stripped of all but 54 of the 252 seats they had held previously, the Communists won 23 (25), the Left Radicals six, and other left groups 10. Overall, the left parties won 36.18% of the popular vote, the right parties 63.33%.

29 France's President Mitterrand appointed Edouard Balladur (RPR), 63, as prime minister and head of a new RPR-UDF coalition government. The following day Balladur announced his cabinet appointments. Ministers of state included Simone Veil at social affairs, health and urban reform; Charles Pasqua at interior and administrative reform; and Francois Leotard at defence. Ministers included Alain Juppe at foreign affairs and Edmond Alphandery at economy.

April

18-19 In a referendum, Italians voted on eight questions including several proposals for constitutional change. A large majority (82.7%) approved an increase in the number of senate seats elected by majority vote; 90.3% approved the ending of state funding of political parties; 70.1% and 82.2% approved abolition of agriculture and tourism ministries respectively.

22 Amato resigned as Italian prime minis-

ter. He was replaced by Bank of Italy governor Carlo Azeglio Campo, who became Italy's first non-parliamentarian PM this century.

May

1 French former prime minister Pierre Beregovoy committed suicide, apparently deeply hurt by allegations of financial impropriety.

3 Social Democrat (SPD) chair Bjorn Engholm became the first of a number of leading German politicians to resign over corruption scandals. Among the others were federal transport minister Gunther Krause (CDU) and the Bavarian minister president Max Streibl (CSU).

13 Within the Exchange Rate Mechanism, the Spanish peseta was devalued by 8 %, its third devaluation since September 1992, and Portugal's escudo was devalued by 6.5 %.

18 In the second referendum on European union in less than a year, Denmark voted for the Maastricht treaty by 56.7% to 43.3% in an 86.2% turnout. Riots took place in Copenhagen after the result was announced. Police shot and wounded 11 demonstrators.

20 The European Communities (Amendment) Bill passed its third reading in the British House of Commons by 292 votes to 112. Forty one Conservative MPs broke ranks to oppose the Bill and five abstained, including former cabinet minister Kenneth Baker. Sixty six Labour MPs ignored the party line to abstain, voting against to demonstrate their opposition to Britain's exclusion from Maastricht's social chapter, and five voted with the government.

20 Giorgio Benvenuto, leader of the Italian Socialist party (PSI), resigned along with its president, Gino Giugni, and five members of the PSI executive, having failed to re-launch the party after more than a year of corruption scandals.

23 The president of Bosnia-Herzegovina, Alija Izetbegovic, angrily rejected a pro-

posed international operation to create
and protect safe havens for Muslims, in a
move widely viewed as spelling the end of
the Vance-Owen joint UN-EC peace plan.
27 In a Cabinet reshuffle, chancellor Lamont
was sacked and replaced by Kenneth
Clarke, the former home secretary. Environment
secretary, Michael Howard, was
promoted to home secretary and replaced
by John Gummer.

June
6 Spain's Socialist party (PSOE), led by
prime minister Gonzalez, won an unexpected
general election victory, defeating
its main rival, Jose Maria Aznar's centre-right
People's party (PP), by a margin of
18 seats. But the PSOE fell short of winning
the requisite 176 seats for a majority
in the 350-seat congress of deputies.
13 In an American-style primary election,
Germany's Social Democrats (SPD) voted
Rudolf Scharping, premier of Rhineland-Palatinate,
to the party leadership.
20 In a humiliating retreat from the
Vance-Owen peace plan for Bosnia, EC
foreign ministers instructed Owen to
negotiate a settlement based more closely
on territorial gains.
21-22 At the European summit in Copenhagen,
security issues and unemployment
dominated the agenda. EC leaders finally
complied with a UN request for troops and
cash to finance Security Council-designated
Moslem "safe havens" in Bosnia, pledging
7,500 soldiers. The heads of state and
government expressed "deep concern"
over unemployment in the member states,
although they failed to resolve long-running
disagreements on how far welfare
state benefits should be sacrificed at the
altar of European competitiveness in
world markets. They stressed the
importance of lowering interest rates and
approved a recovery package which
included a new £2.35 billion lending
facility for the European Investment Bank
and a £4 billion bridging facility to speed
up planned regional development
schemes. Delors was given the go-ahead

to prepare a White Paper on economic
renewal, for presentation at the December
summit. Admission to the European
Community of Austria, Finland, Sweden
and Norway was timetabled for January 1
1995. On relations with the central and
eastern European states, it was agreed
that associated countries that wished to
join the EC should become members as
soon as they could meet the obligations
of Community membership.
25 Jacques Attali, president of the London-based
European Bank for Reconstruction
and Development, resigned from the
£150,000-a-year post after criticism of the
bank's estimated £200 million running
costs since it was set up in 1991.

July
1 Belgium took over the EC presidency
from Denmark.
2 The Italian senate approved an electoral
reform Bill amendment that would prevent
politicians from holding parliamentary
seats for more than 15 years. If passed
by the chamber of deputies (lower house),
it would mean that about 160 MPs would
be unable to stand in the next general
election.
4 The German interior minister, Rudolf
Seiters, resigned after a bungled police
ambush and killing of a suspected terrorist
two weeks earlier.
7 At a G7 summit in Tokyo, the US, Canada,
Japan and the EC agreed sweeping tariff
cuts for a range of imports
13 Spanish prime minister Gonzalez
announced his 18-member cabinet,
approved by his Basque and Catalan
nationalist coalition partners. Economy
and finance went to Pedro Solbes, formerly
agriculture minister. The deputy prime
minister Narcis Serra and foreign minister
Javier Solana retained their posts.
14 The House of Lords rejected pleas by
Eurosceptic politicians for a referendum
on Maastricht by 445 to 176 — the largest
turnout this century. Noble rebels included
90 Conservatives and 25 Labour peers,

all of whom defied their whips.

15 Italy's senate approved a law providing for three-quarters of the lower house of parliament to be elected by a straight majority, the remainder by the existing system of proportional representation.

19 EC foreign ministers meeting in Brussels declined to implement economic sanctions against Croatia after objections from Germany.

20 After its third reading, The House of Lords approved the Maastricht treaty Bill by 141 to 29, a government majority of 112.

22-3 Prime minister Major raised the prospect of a general election after losing a House of Commons vote on the Maastricht treaty. A Labour amendment calling for the social chapter to be adopted was defeated by 318 to 317 (due to a miscount, initially with the casting vote of the Speaker), but the main government motion was lost by 324 to 316. In a second day of parliamentary drama, Major's gamble paid off when he won a vote of confidence on the Government's handling of the Maastricht treaty ratification by 339 votes to 299 — a majority of 40. A Labour amendment similar to the previous night's was defeated by 399 to 301 votes.

26 Following an Anglo-French summit in London, president Mitterrand predicted that the EC would have a single currency within a few years.

27 In an apparent return to the "strategy of tension" in Italy, three car bombs exploded in Rome and Milan, killing five people and damaging churches and a museum. Fifty thousand people demonstrated against the attacks in Milan.

29 After a week-long barrage of speculation against the system, the ERM was thrown into chaos when the Bundesbank announced it was lowering its Lombard rate by half a per cent but leaving its discount rate unchanged.●

THE EUROPEAN COMMISSION
Headquarters: Rue de la Loi 200, 1049 Brussels (Tel: 235 11 11)
London: Jean Monnet House, 8 Storey's Gate, London SW1P 3 AT (071 793 1992)

MEMBERS OF THE COMMISSION AND THEIR RESPONSIBILITIES

President:	Jacques Delors (F)
	Secretariat-General and Legal Services, Monetary Affairs, Spokesman's Service Forecast Group, Joint Interpreting and Conference Service Security Office
Vice-Presidents:	Martin Bangemann (Ge)
	Industrial affairs and information technology
	Henning Christopherson (D)
	Economic and financial affairs
	Manuel Marin (S)
	Co-operation and development, EC humanitarian aid
	Sir Leon Brittan (UK)
	External economic affairs and trade
Commissioners:	Rene Steichen (L)
	Agriculture
	Karel van Miert (B)
	Competition and personnel
	Padraig Flynn (Ir)
	Social affairs, employment, immigration and judicial affairs
	Joao Deus de Pinheiro (P)
	Communications, information and culture
	Bruce Millan (UK)
	Regional policy
	Christiane Scrivener (F)
	Taxation, customs union and consumer policy
	Peter M.Schmidhuber (Ge)
	Budget and fraud prevention
	Abel Matutes (S)
	Energy and transport
	Antonio Ruberti (It)
	Science, research and development
	Ioannis Paleokrassas (Gr)
	Environment and fisheries
	Raniero Vanni d'Archirafi (It)
	Internal market and financial institutions

B-Belgium D-Denmark F-France Ge -Germany Gr-Greece Ir-Ireland It-Italy

L-Luxembourg N-Netherlands P-Portugal S-Spain UK-United Kingdom

EUROPEAN PARLIAMENT ELECTIONS
June 1994

ENGLAND, SCOTLAND, WALES
% shares of vote

CONSERVATIVES DEFENDING

	MAJ	CON	LAB	LD	GRN	NAT	OTHER	%poll
Dorset E & Hampshire W	27.9 over Grn	50.4	17.2	9.9	22.4	—	—	36.3
Surrey W	27.4 over Grn	49.8	15.7	10.0	22.4	—	2.0	34.9
Sussex E	26.6 over Lab	48.2	21.6	8.4	21.2	—	0.6	36.1
Devon	24.1 over Grn	46.4	17.1	9.8	22.3	—	4.4	39.9
Oxford & Buckinghamshire	24.1 over Lab	46.8	22.8	7.3	21.3	—	1.9	35.2
Hertfordshire	23.3 over Lab	46.6	23.4	7.2	20.0	—	2.7	36.0
Sussex W	22.9 over Grn	47.4	15.8	12.3	24.5	—	—	36.5
Wiltshire	22.1 over Lab	44.4	22.3	8.7	22.3	—	2.3	36.9
Somerset & Dorset W	22.0 over Grn	45.0	19.5	12.1	23.0	—	—	40.7
Cotswolds	21.7 over Grn	45.1	22.9	8.6	23.4	—	—	37.7
Wight & Hampshire E	19.6 over Lab	44.9	25.3	9.7	20.1	—	—	35.2
Essex NE	18.9 over Lab	44.5	25.6	8.1	21.7	—	—	34.8
London S & Surrey E	17.9 over Lab	45.4	27.5	8.7	18.5	—	—	34.8
Cambridge & BedfordshireN	17.1 over Lab	44.5	27.4	8.0	20.1	—	—	33.6
Thames Valley	15.5 over Lab	42.7	27.2	8.5	21.5	—	—	31.6
Hampshire C	15.3 over Lab	43.4	28.1	10.2	18.3	—	—	33.2
Kent E	14.9 over Lab	44.0	29.1	7.9	19.0	—	—	34.2
Suffolk	13.6 over Lab	43.6	30.0	6.7	19.7	—	—	34.4
Kent W	12.7 over Lab	43.4	30.7	8.5	17.4	—	—	33.4
Hereford and Worcester	12.1 over Lab	41.3	29.2	6.4	23.1	—	—	35.8
Lincolnshire	10.2 over Lab	45.4	35.2	7.1	12.3	—	—	34.6
Northamptonshire	9.9 over Lab	41.8	31.9	5.6	20.7	—	—	35.3
Norfolk	9.6 over Lab	42.3	32.7	4.1	18.6	—	2.3	37.8
Cornwall & Plymouth	8.7 over LD	38.9	18.3	30.2	10.8	—	1.9	41.9
York	8.1 over Lab	43.4	35.3	6.7	14.7	—	—	34.6
Essex SW	5.0 over Lab	41.1	36.1	5.6	17.1	—	—	33.1

London NW	4.1 over Lab	41.3	37.2	5.8	15.6	—	—	35.8
London SE	3.6 over Lab	38.2	34.6	4.3	17.8	—	5.0	37.8
Lancashire C	3.0 over Lab	42.1	39.1	3.8	14.9	—	—	35.8
Bedfordshire S	1.6 over Lab	38.6	37.0	4.6	18.1	—	1.6	33.8
Shropshire & Stafford	1.2 over Lab	41.0	39.8	5.0	14.1	—	—	35.0
Cumbria & Lancashire N	1.1 over Lab	41.2	40.1	6.2	10.4	—	2.1	36.3

LABOUR DEFENDING

	MAJ	CON	LAB	LD	GRN	NAT	OTHER	%poll
Yorkshire S	52.6 over Con	16.8	69.4	2.9	10.9	—	—	33.5
Tyne & Wear	52.4 over Con	16.9	69.3	3.3	9.9	—	0.5	34.4
Wales SE	50.2 over Con	14.1	64.3	2.2	12.9	6.6	—	38.3
Merseyside E	47.1 over Con	18.6	65.7	3.5	12.3	—	—	31.4
Durham	45.9 over Con	19.9	65.8	4.4	9.9	—	—	35.7
Sheffield	36.8 over Con	21.4	58.2	5.8	14.2	—	0.3	33.7
Yorkshire SW	35.3 over Con	22.7	58.0	5.5	13.7	—	—	35.7
London NE	33.8 over Con	20.1	53.9	6.8	18.4	—	0.8	27.6
Wales S	31.5 over Con	23.2	54.7	2.0	13.1	5.4	1.6	38.1
Strathclyde E	31.1 over SNP	11.4	56.2	2.2	5.0	25.1	—	39.3
Northumbria	30.4 over Con	25.7	56.1	5.6	12.6	—	—	38.4
Glasgow	30.4 over SNP	10.7	55.4	2.0	6.3	25.0	0.7	39.9
Merseyside W	27.8 over Con	24.6	52.4	9.1	12.9	—	1.0	35.1
Birmingham E	26.1 over Con	27.6	53.7	2.2	12.6	—	3.8	33.8
London S Inner	25.9 over Con	26.1	52.0	5.9	15.1	—	0.9	32.9
Greater Manchester W	26.6 over Con	28.1	54.7	3.5	11.4	—	2.3	38.2
Scotland Mid & Fife	23.5 over SNP	21.0	46.1	4.0	6.4	22.6	—	41.5
Greater Manchester C	23.1 over Con	28.6	51.7	5.6	11.8	—	2.2	34.9
Wales Mid & West	23.0 over Con	23.9	46.9	4.5	13.2	11.6	—	41.2
Leeds	22.8 over Con	29.4	52.2	6.3	12.1	—	—	37.1
Midlands W	21.4 over Con	32.0	53.4	3.5	11.0	—	—	37.3
Lancashire E	20.8 over Con	30.7	51.5	6.7	11.0	—	—	35.5
Strathclyde W	18.9 over SNP	21.8	42.7	3.9	7.8	23.8	—	42.6

	MAJ	CON	LAB	LD	GRN	NAT	OTHER	%poll
Greater Manchester E	18.4 over Con	31.3	49.7	8.9	10.2	—	—	37.0
Birmingham W	18.0 over Con	32.5	50.5	4.5	12.5	—	—	33.2
Lothians	17.7 over Con	23.6	41.3	4.2	10.4	20.4	—	42.0
Yorkshire W	17.5 over Con	32.5	50.0	4.5	13.0	—	—	38.5
Staffordshire E	16.9 over Con	33.5	50.3	3.7	12.4	—	—	32.4
Derbyshire	16.1 over Con	34.9	51.0	2.2	10.0	—	1.9	36.8
London E	14.6 over Con	34.9	49.5	3.9	11.4	—	0.4	35.4
Cleveland & Yorkshire N	12.1 over Con	35.5	47.6	4.2	8.6	—	4.0	34.9
Cheshire W	10.6 over Con	36.6	47.2	4.3	11.9	—	—	40.1
Humberside	10.0 over Con	35.4	45.4	2.4	14.6	—	2.1	32.2
Scotland S	7.6 over Con	32.2	39.8	5.1	5.7	17.2	—	41.5
Leicester	7.2 over Con	35.4	42.6	3.2	15.5	—	3.3	36.8
Nottingham	6.9 over Con	36.8	43.8	3.2	16.2	—	—	37.3
London W	6.8 over Con	36.2	43.0	4.3	15.1	—	1.3	41.9
London C	6.2 over Con	36.0	42.2	4.2	15.1	—	2.7	38.0
Bristol	4.5 over Con	35.0	39.5	7.3	17.7	—	0.5	39.6
London N	2.9 over Con	38.3	41.2	4.3	14.8	—	1.4	36.3
Midlands C	2.6 over Con	35.9	38.5	4.2	21.4	—	—	37.0
Wales N	1.8 over Con	31.3	33.1	4.0	6.3	25.4	—	46.8
Scotland NE	1.3 over SNP	26.7	30.7	6.0	7.3	29.4	—	38.4
Cheshire E	1.0 over Con	40.2	41.2	6.8	11.8	—	—	35.0
London SW	0.3 over Con	38.0	38.3	5.4	18.3	—	—	39.9

SCOTTISH NATIONALISTS DEFENDING

	MAJ	CON	LAB	LD	GRN	NAT	OTHER	%poll
Highlands & Islands	34.8 over Con	16.8	13.9	8.3	9.5	51.6	—	41.0

NORTHERN IRISH SEATS
(by proportional representation)

	proportion of first preference
DUP	29.6
SDUP	25.2
OUP	22.0

COUNTY COUNCIL ELECTIONS May 6 1993

ENGLAND
change of

council	Con	Lab	LDem PC	Oth	Vacant	Control
Avon	25	33	18			
Bedfordshire	28	31	13	1		
Berkshire	16	24	33	3		
Buckinghamshire	39	13	1	6	3	
Cambridgeshire	33	21	21	2		CON to NOC
Cheshire	22	35	14			
Cleveland	14	51	12			
Cornwall	6	8	42	23		NOC to L DEM
Cumbria	27	39	14	3		
Derbyshire	21	55	7	1		
Devon	19	21	40	5		CON to NOC
Dorset	29	6	38	4		CON to NOC
Durham	6	56	6	4		
East Sussex	22	18	30			CON to NOC
Essex	32	33	32	1		CON to NOC
Gloucestershire	10	20	30	3		
Hampshire	29	24	48	1		CON to NOC
Herefd & Worcs	25	24	23	4		
Hertfordshire	27	30	19	1		CON to NOC
Humberside	22	43	10			
Isle of Wight	9	28		6		
Kent	41	30	28			CON to NOC
Lancashire	35	53	10		1	
Leicestershire	31	37	17			
Lincolnshire	32	25	15	4		CON to NOC
Norfolk	34	32	16	2		CON to NOC
N Yorkshire	29	23	35	9		
Northamptonshire	27	36	5			NOC to LAB
Northumberland	13	40	11	2		
Nottinghamshire	23	58	6		1	
Oxfordshire	25	24	20	1		
Shropshire	26	23	13	4		
Somerset	13	2	41	1		CON to LDEM
Staffordshire	22	53	4	3		
Suffolk	26	31	19	4		CON to NOC
Surrey	34	8	29	5		CON to NOC
Warwickshire	19	30	10	3		CON to NOC

ENGLAND
change of

council	Con	Lab	LDem	PC	Oth	Vacant	Control
West Sussex	26	10	34		1		CON to NOC
Wiltshire	18	17	33				

WALES

	Con	Lab	LDem	PC	Oth	Vacant	Control
Clwyd	8	32	3	3	17	1	
Dyfed	1	22	8	7	32		
Gwent	6	55	1	1			
Gwynedd	1	9	7	18	27		
Mid Glamorgan	1	60		10	3		
Powys		6	4		36		
South Glamorgan	12	40	8	1	1		
West Glamorgan	3	46	3	1	7	1	

Total England/Wales   **967**   **1,387**   **874**   **41**   **227**   **4**
Total seats E & W (inc vacant) 3,500

GAINS AND LOSSES, ENGLAND AND WALES
excluding Wiltshire and Clwyd, affected by boundary changes

FROM TO:	Con	Lab	LDem	PC	Ind/Other	Total
CON		11	7		9	27
LAB	136		8	2	17	163
L DEM	339	44		1	21	405
PC		9			6	15
OTH/IND	24	9	7		3	43
TOTALS	499	73	22	3	56	

Net change: CON down 472, LAB up 90, LIB DEM up 383, PC up 12, OTHER/IND down 13.

DISTRICT COUNCIL ELECTIONS TO BE HELD MAY 5 1994

NON-METROPOLITAN
(ONE THIRD OF COUNCIL ONLY)

Adur, Amber Valley,

Barrow, Basildon, Basingstoke & Deane, Bassetlaw, Bath, Blackburn, Brentwood, Brighton, Bristol, Broadland, Broxbourne, Burnley

Cambridge, Cannock Chase, Carlisle, Cheltenham, Cherwell, Chester, Chorley, Colchester, Congleton, Craven, Crawley, Crewe & Nantwich

Daventry, Derby

Eastbourne, Eastleigh, Ellesmere Port & Neston, Elmbridge, Epping Forest, Exeter

Fareham

Gillingham, Gloucester, Gosport, Great Grimsby, Great Yarmouth

Halton, Harlow, Harrogate, Hart, Hartlepool, Hastings, Havant, Hereford, Hertsmere, Hull, Huntingdonshire, Hyndburn

Ipswich

Leominster, Lincoln

Macclesfield, Maidstone, Mid Sussex, Milton Keynes, Mole Valley

Newcastle under Lyme, N. Bedfordshire, N. Hertfordshire, Norwich, Nuneaton & Bedworth

Oadby & Wigston, Oxford

Pendle, Penwith, Peterborough, Portsmouth, Preston, Purbeck

Reading, Redditch, Reigate, Rochford, Rossendale, Rugby, Runnymede, Rushmoor

St Albans, Scunthorpe, Shrewsbury & Atcham, Slough, Southampton, S. Bedfordshire, S. Cambridgeshire, Southend-on-Sea, S. Herefordshire, S.Lakeland, Stevenage, Stoke-on-Trent, Stratford-upon-Avon, Stroud, Swale

Tamworth, Tandridge, Thamesdown, Three Rivers, Thurrock, Tonbridge & Malling, Torbay, Tunbridge Wells

Watford, Waveney, Welwyn Hatfield

W. Lancashire, W. Lindsey, W. Oxfordshire, Weymouth & Portland, Winchester, Woking, Wokingham, Worcester, Worthing, Wyre Forest

York

METROPOLITAN
(ONE THIRD OF COUNCIL ONLY)

Barnsley, Birmingham, Bolton, Bradford,Bury

Calderdale, Coventry

Doncaster, Dudley

Gateshead

Kirklees, Knowsley

Leeds, Liverpool

Manchester

Newcastle upon Tyne, N. Tyneside

Oldham

Rochdale, Rotherham

St Helens, Salford, Sandwell, Sefton, Sheffield, Solihull, S.Tyneside, Stockport, Sunderland

Tameside, Trafford

Wakefield, Walsall, Wigan, Wirral, Wolverhampton

LONDON BOROUGHS
(WHOLE COUNCIL)

Barking, Barnet, Bexley, Brent, Bromley,

Camden,Croydon

Ealing, Enfield

Greenwich

Hackney, Hammersmith & Fulham, Haringey, Harrow, Havering, Hillingdon, Hounslow

Islington

Kensington & Chelsea, Kingston upon Thames

Lambeth, Lewisham

Merton

Newham

Redbridge , Richmond upon Thames

Southwark, Sutton

Tower Hamlets

Waltham Forest, Wandsworth, Westminster

CHAIRS OF COMMONS SELECT COMMITTEES
(as at June 1993)

(Subject committees which shadow government departments in capitals)

Accommodation & Works R. Powell (Lab)

Administration M. Martin (Lab)

AGRICULTURE Sir J.Wiggin (Con)

Catering C.Shepherd (Con)

Court of Referees M.Morris (deputy Speaker)

DEFENCE Sir N.Bonsor (Con)

EDUCATION Sir M.Thornton(Con)

EMPLOYMENT G.Janner (Lab)

ENVIRONMENT R.B.Jones (Con)

European legislation J.Hood (Lab)

Finance & services P.Channon (Con)

FOREIGN AFFAIRS D.Howell (Con)

HEALTH Mrs M.Roe (Con)

HOME AFFAIRS Sir I.Lawrence

Information G.Waller (Con)

Liaison (includes the chairs of select committees)

Sir T.Higgins (Con)

Members' interests Sir G.Johnson-Smith (Con)

NATIONAL HERITAGE G.Kaufman (Lab)

Parliamentary commissioner for administration

J.Pawsey (Con)

Procedure Sir P.Emery (Con)

Public accounts R.Sheldon (Lab)

Selection Sir F.Montgomery (Con)

SOCIAL SECURITY F.Field (Lab)

Standing orders M.Morris (deputy Speaker)

Statutory Instruments (joint committee with House of Lords)

B.Cryer (Lab)

Science & technology Sir G.Shaw (Con)

SCOTTISH AFFAIRS W.McKelvey (Lab)

TRADE & INDUSTRY R.Caborn (Lab)

TRANSPORT (vacant on death of R.Adley (Con)

TREASURY & CIVIL SERVICE J.Watts (Con)

WELSH AFFAIRS G.Wardell (Lab)

MAJOR HONOURS

DISSOLUTION HONOURS JUNE 5 1992

Con	Lab	Other

Life peerages awarded to former MPs:

Con	Lab	Other
J.Amery	P.Archer	G.Howells (Lib Dem)
I.Gilmour	J.Ashley	D.Owen (SDP)
G.Howe	H.Ewing	D.E.Thomas (PC)
N.Lawson	D.Healey	B.Weatherill (Spkr)
J.Moore	D.Howell	
C.Parkinson	M.Rees	
N.Ridley		
N.Tebbit		
Mrs M.Thatcher		
P.Walker		
G.Younger		

Knighthoods for defeated Conservative MPs

A.Beaumont-Dark

N.Thorne

D.Trippier

Knighthood for former deputy speaker (still in Commons)

H.Walker

BIRTHDAY HONOURS JULY 12 1992

New "working peers"

Con	Lab	Other
J.Archer*	J.Eatwell	V.Cooke (UU)
Sir D.Barber	Margaret Jay	
Sir B.Braine*	R. Plant	
Sir W.Clark*	Gareth W. Williams	
Sir G.Finsberg*		
Sir B.Hayhoe*		
I.Stewart*		

* denotes a former Conservative MP
(Sir D.Barber was chairman of the Countryside Commission 1981-91. Victor Cooke is chairman and managing director of Springvale EPS. John Eatwell was economic adviser to Neil Kinnock. Margaret Jay, daughter of the former prime minister James Callaghan, is director of the National Aids Trust. Gareth Wyn Williams was formerly chairman of the Bar Council.)

Con	Lab	Other

Knighthoods for sitting MPs

Con	Lab	Other
I.Lawrence J.Kilfedder		(UPUP)
K.Speed		
M.Thornton		

NEW YEAR HONOURS 1993

Peerages for former MPs:

Con	Lab	Other
		Shirley Williams(LD)

Knighthoods for sitting MPs

R.Moate

T.Higgins

J.Wiggin

Knighthoods for former MPs

M.Latham

BIRTHDAY HONOURS JUNE 12 1993

Knighthoods for sitting MPs

Ralph Howell

David Knox

THE YEAR IN POLITICS

April '92

9 Conservatives win general election with majority of 21 seats: Conservatives 336, Labour 271, Liberal Democrats 20, SDP eliminated from Commons. Conservative chairman Chris Patten loses his seat.

10 TUC Congress votes in favour of read-mitting EETPU expelled in 1988. Union has merged with AEU. IRA bomb explodes in City killing 3, injuring many more and causing extensive damage to property. Another IRA bomb damages a North Circular Road flyover.

12 Major completes Cabinet reshuffle. Kenneth Baker (home secretary) dropped, replaced by Kenneth Clarke; Clarke's place at education is taken by John Patten. David Mellor to run new heritage department, Michael Portillo replaces him as chief secretary to the Treasury. Other switches: Michael Heseltine environment to trade and industry; Peter Lilley, trade and industry to social security; Malcolm Rifkind transport to defence; Tony Newton, social security to Leader of House; Michael Howard, employment to environment; William Waldegrave, health to new department running citizen's charter. Virginia Bottomley (health) and Gillian Shephard (employment) join the Cabinet; Peter Brooke and Tom King drop out. Department of Energy abolished.
Norman Fowler becomes party chairman.

13 Kinnock says he is resigning as Labour leader. Roy Hattersley, deputy leader, says he will quit too.

23 Former Conservative PM Ted Heath named Knight of the Garter.

24 Chris Patten named Governor of Hong Kong.

27 Commons elects its first woman Speaker, Betty Boothroyd.

29 Resumption of inter-party talks in N Ireland.

30 Interest rates cut from 10.5 to 10%.

May

6 Parliament resumes. Queen's speech promises Bills to extend privatisation and set up a national lottery. PM says MI5 is to be placed on a statutory basis.

7 Local elections: best Conservative results for 13 years — net gain of 308 seats.

8 Home secretary says MI5 will take over responsibility for intelligence operations against IRA from Special Branch of Metropolitan police.

9 In a speech at Chard Liberal Democrat. leader Paddy Ashdown calls for co-operation on the centre left to prevent continuing Conservative hegemony. Labour response is unenthusiastic.

11 Judith Ward, jailed in 1974 for IRA bombing, freed by Appeal Court.

19 PM publishes details of 26 Cabinet committees or sub-committees. Previously Governments had not acknowledged that such committees existed.

20 New home secretary Kenneth Clarke announces an inquiry into the working practices of the police.

28 Administrators appointed to Olympia & York, developers of Canary Wharf in London Docklands

June

2 Virginia Bottomley, health secretary, says there will be a 7% cut in dentists' fees to adjust for earlier overpayments.

3 After Danish referendum rejects Maastricht terms John Major says progress on the European Communities (Amendment) Bill will be suspended. More than 100 Conservative MPs sign a Commons motion calling for a fresh start in Europe and warning against creation of a European super state.

5 Dissolution Honours. Thatcher, Howe, Lawson, Parkinson, Tebbit, Ridley, Healey, Owen, go to Lords.
12 Queen's Birthday honours. Additionally new "working peers" are announced — five Conservative, four Labour, one Ulster Unionist.
15 Defence secretary Rifkind says Navy is to scrap seaborne nuclear weapons. IRA forces taxi driver to be "human bomb" in London.
23 GDP for first quarter show 0.5% drop.
24/25 Skirmishes off Scilly Isles between Cornish and French fishermen; Cornishmen's nets cut.
26 EC summit, Lisbon: deals mainly with EC budget, events in former Yugoslavia, enlargement of Community.

July

1 Britain takes over presidency of EC for six months.
6 In continuing dispute with Government, dentists vote not to admit new NHS patients. Ulster Unionist MPs take part in talks in Dublin with Irish ministers. Defence secretary Rifkind meets his German counterpart in bid to reverse German decision to pull out of European fighter aircraft project.
9 Major rejects report on top people's pay which calls for rises of up to 24%; sets limit of 4%.
14 MPs vote themselves a 38% increase in their expense allowances. Transport secretary MacGregor says British Rail will be split in two. A track authority, remaining in public sector; a second authority in charge of running the trains, with operations progressively franchised to private operators. Freight services will be privatised.
18 John Smith elected leader of Labour party with huge majority over Bryan Gould. Margaret Beckett is deputy leader.
22 Government announces new system for determining levels of public spending. Cabinet to set a total figure; ministers then to decide between them how this is to be allocated.

23 Gordon Brown tops Labour shadow Cabinet ballot. In changes announced the next day, Jack Cunningham succeeds Gerald Kaufman as Labour spokesman on foreign affairs. Gordon Brown replaces John Smith as shadow chancellor, Tony Blair replaces Roy Hattersley as shadow home secretary; Robin Cook, formerly health, takes on trade and industry.
27 Chancellor agrees to plans, previously resisted, for minimum rate of Vat across EC.

August

10 Emergency Cabinet meeting agrees that RAF should join international force to protect Iraq Shias and should send 1,800 troops to protect UN convoys in Bosnia.
26 Amid turbulence on foreign exchanges Lamont says Britain will stay in the ERM and will not devalue. Bank of England mounts big operation to defend pound.
27 Lord Carrington resigns as EC peacemaker in Yugoslavia, succeeded by Lord Owen. 3,000th killing in Northern Ireland since IRA activity resumed in 1969.

September

1 Details appear of strong condemnation by schools inspectors of GCSE standards.
3 Chancellor announces he is borrowing £7.3 billion to defend pound.
4-6 Economic and finance ministers of EC meet at Bath.
9 Patten announces review of English teaching in schools.
13 Liberal Democrat conference opens, Harrogate. Pacts with Labour ruled out, but co-operation with people in other parties can be explored. A leading Green party figure, Sara Parkin, resigns, telling conference: the party must change or die.
16 Black Wednesday (or for opponents of ERM, White Wednesday). Unable to halt run on pound, chancellor says British membership of ERM is suspended. Interest rates fall from 12% to 10% the following day.
22 Interest rates cut from 10 to 9%.

24 David Mellor, heritage secretary resigns. He has been in trouble over affair with actress Antonia de Sancha and evidence in a libel case that he and his family accepted a free holiday from a friend whose father was a PLO member. Replaced by Peter Brooke.

27 Labour conference opens, Blackpool. Bryan Gould resigns from shadow Cabinet because of disagreement with leadership policies, especially support for Maastricht.

28 Bryan Gould and Dennis Skinner voted off Labour NEC. Tony Blair and Gordon Brown are elected.

30 Conference agrees to reduce weight of unions' conference vote from 87% to 70%.

October

1 New Criminal Justice Act comes into force.

6 Conservative conference opens, Brighton. Serious ructions over European policy and ERM, with Norman Tebbit denouncing the policy from the floor. Thatcher does not speak but in article for the European opposes European policy.

7 Speech by Governor Patten on democratic reform in Hong Kong brings bitter criticism from Chinese government.

8 Lamont announces new direction for economic policy after departure from ERM.

12 IRA bomb kills man in Covent Garden pub; part of renewed bout of activity on the mainland.

13 British Coal announces plans to shut 31 pits, putting 30,000 miners out of work.

16 One-day EC summit at Birmingham, called by Major after September's currency debacle.

20 Interest rates cut to 8%.In television interviews, Major talks of a new economic strategy, giving priority to growth. Government is to retain Sir Leon Brittan and Bruce Millan as EC commissioners. Expected appointment of Neil Kinnock will not now take place.

21 Tory backbenchers revolt in division on Government plans for severe reduction

in number of pits and jobs in coal industry.

23 Tomlinson Report on London's hospitals recommends cuts and closures.

30 IRA bomb explodes outside Cabinet Office in Whitehall

30 British Coal issues notices of closure on 10 pits.

November

4 Government majority cut to three in division on "paving motion" to reopen debate on the European Communities (Amendment) Bill; 26 Conservatives vote against the Government.

9 Three executives of Matrix Churchill acquitted on charges of illegally supplying arms-related equipment to Iraq after evidence that a government minister, Alan Clark, had known of the deal.

10 Inquiry into Matrix Churchill affair announced: to be headed by a High Court judge, Lord Justice Scott.

12 Lamont announces further cut in base rate to 7%.

18 First league tables of examination results at GCSE and advanced level published.

24 Queen speaks of her "annus horribilis".

25 Commons agrees to freeze on MPs pay for a year.

26 Major tells Commons that Queen and Prince of Wales have agreed to pay tax on their private incomes; Civil List is to be restricted to Queen, Duke of Edinburgh and Queen Mother.

27 Clarke publishes possible options for change in Sunday trading laws.

28 Revealed that £4,700 bill towards cost incurred by the chancellor in attempting to evict a tenant from his London home has been passed to the taxpayer.

December

1 Labour Social Justice Commission to be chaired by Sir Gordon Borrie.

9 Major announces that the Prince and Princess of Wales are to separate.

11-12 Edinburgh summit. Agreement on

concessions to Denmark on Maastricht.
16 European Court of Justice says UK
legislation restricting Sunday trading does
not contravene EC law.
21 High Court says British Coal acted
unlawfully in proceeding with closure
plans without consultation.
22 Tristan Garel-Jones, Foreign Office
minister, says he will leave Government
for personal reasons once Maastricht Bill is
through.
31 New Year honours. Peerage for Shirley
Williams.

January '93

1 Single European market comes into
force.
5 Oil tanker Braer runs aground off Shet-
land; extensive pollution feared.
13 Air strikes against Iraq by US British
and French planes after Iraqi violations of
UN Security Council resolutions. First
British death in Bosnia-Herzegovina.
14 Sir David Calcutt, who in 1990 published report on privacy, issues further
report on press behaviour and regulation;
advocates statutory body to replace Press
Complaints Commission.
20 In wake of controversy over money
paid to Norman Lamont from public funds
in connection with the eviction of a tenant, new guidelines are promised.
21 House of Commons select committee
on employment publishes its report on
planned pit closures: strong criticism of
Government.
26 Interest rates cut to 6%.
28 After reports in New Statesman and
Scallywag about alleged relationship
between prime minister and Clare Latimer,
a caterer, Major issues writs for libel.
29 House of Commons select committee
on industry reports on pit closures,
making a series of counter proposals for
the industry.

February

3 Defence secretary Malcolm Rifkind
revises plans for defence cuts: four

infantry regiments threatened with merger
are reprieved. A speech by John Major at
the Carlton Club is seen as the first step
towards introducing "workfare".
16 Virginia Bottomley announces partial
acceptance of Tomlinson Report on London hospitals: some famous hospitals,
including Bart's, are threatened with
merger or closure.
17 House of Commons Public Accounts
committee issues critical report on
payment of public money to Norman
Lamont to help him meet legal costs.
19 Death of Judith Chaplin, Conservative
MP for Newbury.
22 Foreign secretary Douglas Hurd tells
Commons that British opt-out on social
chapter of Maastricht treaty will continue
even if Commons votes against it.
23 Major holds talks with President
Clinton, Washington.
24 Smith proposes reduced role for
unions in selection of candidates and
election of party leader.

March

1 Welsh secretary David Hunt publishes
White Paper proposing 21 unitary authorities for Wales.
2 Home secretary announces a network of
detention centres to curb juvenile crime.
3 DPP says Alan Clark, former defence
minister alleged to have given inconsistent
evidence in Matrix Churchill case, will not
be prosecuted.
4 Major announces reform of honours
system to reflect merit rather than class.
8 Government defeated in division on
Maastricht Bill. Commons carried Labour
amendment to have elected councillors
rather than appointees on EC committee
of the regions. Twenty six Conservatives
vote with Labour.
11 Education secretary tells Commons
select committee that one-third of 14 year
olds have the reading age of children
under 11.
15 Chinese prime minister Li Peng
accuses Hong Kong Governor Chris Patten

of "treachery" and threatens reprisals over his plans for democratic reform.

17 Budget. Vat on domestic fuel, previously zero rated — at 8% from 1994, 17.5% the following year. Personal tax allowances and thresholds frozen; lower-rate band extended to cover incomes up to £2,500. Mortgage interest tax relief to be limited.

18 After back-bench complaints, Major announces 10 million poorer people will be helped to meet the cost of Vat on fuel.

19 February jobless figures show a 22,000 fall on previous month, the first reduction for 34 months.

20. IRA bombs in Warrington, Cheshire, kill Johnathan Ball aged three and fatally injure Tim Parry, 12. IRA statement "profoundly regrets" deaths and injuries.

23 At end of five-day debate on Budget, Government has majority of 27. In vote on extension of Vat to fuel, majority is 25, two Conservative MPs abstaining.

Home secretary announces plans to cut number of police forces and to reduce local government representation on police committees.

25 Heseltine announces £500m pit rescue deal.

29 Government has majority of 22 on plans for pit closures after Heseltine offers further concessions, including extension of subsidies and possibly three new enterprise zones. Four Conservative MPs voted with Labour, three abstained.

French and Guernsey fishermen agree to four-week cooling off period after further clashes in dispute over fishing rights off Channel Islands.

31 Labour Party's Plant committee on electoral system votes for abandonment of first-past-the-post. By nine votes to seven, favours Supplementary Vote system, a variant of the Alternative Vote.

April

5 Law Society says it will sue Lord Chancellor over cuts in legal aid.

7 Gordon Wilson, whose daughter was killed by IRA bombs at Enniskillen in 1987, meets IRA representatives. Says later that meeting was a failure.

12 NUT votes against taking part in concerted public sector union action against government policy; but on April 13 votes for strike over pay and a ballot on appraisal of schools

13 After months of tension, Britain and China agree to resume talks on future of Hong Kong. Peking drops insistence that governor Patten must withdraw his democratic reform programme first.

Lady Thatcher condemns Western inaction on Bosnia: says EC countries have been "accomplices to massacre".

15 Deputy Speaker rules that there cannot be a vote on Labour amendment to Maastricht Bill dealing with British opt-out on social chapter. Government had feared defeat in this vote

16 Labour leader John Smith says Labour would support air strikes against Bosnian Serbs if they fail to agree to a ceasefire.

20. The DPP, Barbara Mills, calls for scrapping of defendant's right to demand trial by jury.

21. Emergency three-hour debate on motion censuring Deputy Speaker for refusing vote on social chapter during committee stage of Maastricht Bill ends in rejection of motion by 450 to 81.

In the absence of two Conservative members, Commons select committee on Treasury carries Labour amendment saying the chancellor should quit.

23 Defence secretary Rifkind says in Washington that air strikes would be preferable to lifting the arms embargo on Bosnian Muslims

24 Huge bomb blast in Bishopsgate, City of London. Early estimates say cost may be £1 billion — later scaled down. A News of the World photographer is killed; 44 people injured.

26 After Bosnian Serbs reject Vance-Owen peace plan, there are reports from US that President Clinton is ready to authorise air strikes, despite objections from British and other allies.

The recession is officially declared to be at an end: gross domestic product is growing at 0.2% a quarter.

Norman Willis announces he will take early retirement as general-secretary of TUC, leaving at end of TUC congress in September.

29 Commons debate on Bosnia produces sharp differences over case for intervention. Debate ends without a vote. Finance ministers from G7 leading industrial nations, meeting in Washington, urge Europe and Japan to take further steps to boost their economies.

May

6 Conservatives lose Newbury by-election to Liberal Democrats on a swing of 29%, the highest since Sutton and Cheam by-election of 1972. In local elections, Liberal Democrats and Labour make big advances at Conservatives' expense. Conservatives left in control of only one county, Buckinghamshire.

11 Education secretary John Patten says tests for 14 year olds must go ahead this summer despite union opposition, but there will be sweeping changes next year, easing teachers' workloads.

12 ICM poll in Guardian puts Conservative support at 29%, lowest for seven years.

13 Home secretary tells Commons that sections of new Criminal Justice Act dealing with computation of fines and the right of courts to consider offenders' criminal records are to be scrapped after only eight months in operation.

18 Danes vote yes in second Maastricht referendum.

19 Four detectives accused of conspiracy to pervert course of justice in Guildford 4 case are cleared by Old Bailey jury.

20 Commons gives third reading to Maastricht treaty Bill by 292 votes to 112. Forty one Conservatives vote against it, as do 66 Labour MPs (whipped to abstain), 4 Ulster Unionists and 1 Liberal Democrat. Five

Labour MPs vote with the Government.

21 Inflation falls to 1.3%, lowest figure for 29 years.

23 IRA detonates fourth large bomb in Northern Ireland in four days — in Magherafelt, Co Londonderry.

24 Sir Patrick Mayhew, the former attorney-general, denies trying to prevent crucial evidence about the Iraqi supergun affair from reaching court, after former Tory MP Sir Hal Miller accuses Mayhew of urging him to effect a cover-up.

25 In a major policy U-turn, transport secretary John MacGregor forestalls a Tory rebellion of up to 15 MPs by guaranteeing discount rail fares for millions of pensioners, students and commuters after privatisation.

27 In John Major's first top-level Cabinet reshuffle, chancellor Norman Lamont is sacked and replaced by Kenneth Clarke, the former home secretary. Environment secretary Michael Howard promoted to home secretary; John Gummer moves from agriculture to environment; Gillian Shephard from employment to agriculture; David Hunt from the Welsh Office to employment; and John Redwood, a right-winger, becomes Welsh secretary

28 Winston Churchill, Conservative MP for Davyhulme, provokes an outcry by calling for immediate end to the "relentless flow" of immigrants into Britain and by stating that the population of many northern cities is "well over 50% immigrant". He later concedes this figure was incorrect.

30 Fugitive tycoon Asil Nadir's lawyers confirm he received a gift of a watch inscribed "Don't let the buggers get you down" from Northern Ireland minister Michael Mates.

June

1 Britain mounts legal challenge to the EC over a controversial directive imposing a maximum 48-hour working week.

2 Education secretary John Patten heckled and booed by headteachers while addressing their conference in Newcastle.

4 John Major shown by Gallup to be the least popular prime minister since opinion polling began.

9 In resignation statement to the Commons, former chancellor Norman Lamont accuses the Government of "too much reacting to events, not enough shaping of events" and reveals Major had rejected his proposal to withdraw sterling temporarily from the ERM.

10 Through an intermediary, Norman Lamont warns John Major of further unspecified damage unless he ends the series of personal attacks being made on him by senior Tories.

15 Chancellor Kenneth Clarke, foreshadows tax increases as an option for his November Budget.

16 Following the admission that the Tories had received £440,000 from Asil Nadir, party chairman Sir Norman Fowler denies that political gifts can buy influence or honours and promises to repay any money that proved to be stolen.

20 One in 12 households reported in arrears with their mortgages, an increase of 27,000 over the past year.

21 Michael Heseltine suffers a heart attack.

24 Michael Mates resigns as Northern Ireland minister, after 25-day barrage of criticism over his links with Asil Nadir.

25 John Wheeler, 53, replaces Michael Mates as Northern Ireland minister.

28 In a White Paper, the Government pledges to begin judging the police against national and local performance

29 In a 30-minute resignation statement, Michael Mates accuses Serious Fraud Office of exerting improper pressure on a judge in the Asil Nadir case. Attorney-general Sir Nicholas Lyell rejects Mates's call for independent inquiry into SFO.

July

5 In a defence White Paper, the Government announces further reductions on top of the Options for Change review, which cut the armed services by 25%.

6 Royal Commission on Criminal Justice, chaired by Lord Runciman of Doxford, recommends 352 reforms designed to restore public confidence in the criminal justice system. Lord Chief Justice, Lord Taylor of Gosforth, and civil libertarians express misgivings over recommended scrapping of right to elect jury trial.

7 Major claims that a breakthrough in the deadlocked Gatt talks — reached in a G7 summit in Tokyo — will result in the creation of at least 250,000 extra British jobs over the next decade and add £10 billion to annual UK exports.

13 Manufacturing production hits best level for nearly three years.

14 Lords votes down referendum on Maastricht by 445 to 176: highest turnout in chamber this century.

16 MI5 goes public with director-general taking photo-call.

19 Lord Rees-Mogg successfully applies for judicial review before Maastricht treaty is ratified.

21 Speaker of Commons warns courts not to infringe rights of House when dealing with Maastricht treaty.

22 Commons debate on social chapter opt-out ends in Government defeat by 324 to 316 after tie in vote on Labour amendment (Speaker's casting vote given to Government).

23 Government wins confidence vote clearing way for ratification of Maastricht. Only one Conservative MP, Rupert Allason, fails to vote with Government.

25 Major reported to have spoken of "bastards" opposing his European policy — including three unnamed Cabinet ministers.

29 Christchurch by-election: Conservatives lose seat to Liberal Democrats on biggest swing against a Conservative government this century.

August

2 ERM in virtual collapse. Rees-Mogg application fails. Government ratifies Maastricht treaty.●

QUOTE, UNQUOTE

The sun is out and so are the Tories
*Neil Kinnock, before Labour's general election
defeat was announced, April 9 1992*

Mr John Patten attributes the rise in crime
to the decline of religion. Why, then, is
Italy the home of Catholicism, also the
home of the Mafia, and why has the
renaissance of religion in Russia been
accompanied by a rise in crime?
Letter, Daily Telegraph, April 22 1992

I shall certainly wear the robe and the
buckle shoes and other things associated
with the Speaker. But a wig — no.
*Betty Boothroyd, newly elected Speaker.
April 29 1992*

The prime minister's social conscience
will shape everything from privatisation
to tax reform.
Daily Mail, May 8 1992

There is no obvious reason why Labour
cannot adapt to the new individualist
values. We are, after all, the party of
dissent and individual free speech.
Robin Cook in the Observer, May 11 1992

I am not an intellectual.
*John Prescott, Daily Telegraph,
May 13 1992*

A practical joker included my pet
Australian frog on the voters' list . . . under
his scientific name of Mr Hyla Caerulea.
Things suddenly got nasty when
the Daily Mail were tipped off that
an exotic foreign rent boy had moved in
with me.
Ken Livingstone, the Sun, May 14 1992

It's frightening to think that they will be
voting on something they do not
understand.

*Sir Teddy Taylor on the Maastricht treaty
debate, the Times, May 22 1992*

I personally pledge to ensure that the
bottles from Downing Street are put in the
bottle bank.
*John Major at the Earth Summit, Rio, June 13
1992*

We have become atomised, seeking fulfil-
ment simply as individuals. It is not just
that this is, in the end, spiritually deficient
— although I think it is — but that it
doesn't work.
Tony Blair, Mail on Sunday, June 29 1992

The prime minister tells us that
referendums are a "device of demagogues
and dictators". In which category does he
place his Danish, Irish and
French colleagues?
Letter to the Times, July 3 1992

I can understand David Mellor's interest in
actresses a lot more than I can understand
John Major's interest in cricket.
*Caller to Radio 4's Call Nick Ross,
July 22 1992*

He has simply been exposed as an
adulterer and a fool in his private life.
Sunday Telegraph leader, July 27 1992

Every prime minister says how hard it is to
wield the axe — which could explain why
so often it is replaced by a knife between
the shoulder blades.
David Seymour, Today, July 29 1992

At last, something to cheer about. The
revolution in education plotted by
Margaret Thatcher has gained irreversible
momentum under John Major.
Daily Mail leader, July 30 1992

I admire Norman Tebbit. But his elevation

to the peerage has unhinged me.
Woodrow Wyatt, August 3 1992

Unless we see a change of emphasis and a statement expressing understanding of the real problems that British industry is facing, and some solutions, including a drop in interest rates, then I see little future for the chancellor.
John Carlisle, Conservative MP,
August 4 1992

This is another example of the Tory government rounding on the victims of its own incompetence.
Frank Dobson, on the Government's plans to slash benefits, August 12 1992

The election of John Smith as leader of the Labour party underlines the fact that the Opposition is poised to present a vigorous challenge to the Government.
John Biffen, August 15 1992

Anyone who thinks this country is turning the corner is round the bend.
TUC general secretary Norman Willis,
August 5 1992

I'm not an expert on the economy.
Norman Lamont, Today, September 8 1992

As we have seen in Scandinavia this week, it is a cold world outside the ERM.
John Major after the Swedish central bank's short-term interest rate rose to 75%, the Independent, September 12 1992

I should be very surprised if we didn't see a fall in interest rates reasonably soon.
Tim Smith, Conservative party vice-chairman,
September 18 1992

My wife says she's never heard me singing in the bath until last week
Norman Lamont, September 21 1992

This is a prime minister who watches football on Saturday, watches cricket on

Sunday, watches the pound on Wednesday. Under his captaincy, England collapse before lunch. Gnomes of Zurich three, gnomes of Downing Street nil.
Gordon Brown, September 29 1992

We were promised a New Statesman, and what have we got instead? The Spectator.
John Smith on John Major,
September 30 1992

After the simultaneous collapse of both his foreign and his economic policies, Mr Major could have chosen to resign. He has not. Now he needs to make other choices: first, he should ask for Norman Lamont's resignation; second, he should demand a new economic policy from Mr Lamont's successor; third, he should pass the Maastricht treaty through the House of Commons.
Leader, Financial Times, October 2 1992

John Major, Norman Lamont. I wouldn't spit in their mouths if their teeth were on fire.
Rodney Bickerstaffe, NUPE general secretary,
October 1 1992

No wonder they call Mrs Bottomley Golden Virginia.
David Blunkett, health spokesman, on Imperial Tobacco's donation of poster sites to the Tories during the, election

Norman Lamont is proving to be King Midas in reverse: everything he touches turns to dross.
Sunday Times leader, October 5 1992

Essex man did not vote for a president of Europe, he voted for a prime minister of the UK. If John Major wants to remain in Downing Street, it is high time he started acting like one.
Richard Littlejohn, the Sun, October 6 1992

I remember when she used to talk

about loyalty. It is about time that she showed some.
Edwina Currie on Baroness Thatcher, October 8 1992

At the heart of our policy lies one objective — a cold, clear-eyed calculation of the British national interest.
John Major, October 9 1992

John Major may think he's been badly treated by the press and broadcasters over the past few weeks, but he's had it soft compared to what they used to say about Labour's most successful leader, Harold Wilson.
Joe Haines in the Daily Mirror, October 27 1992

Not while I'm still alive she bloody won't.
Sir Denis Thatcher asked about a possible return to power of his wife, November 1 1992

The Government is giving my party a bad name. I am ready if the country needs me.
Lord Sutch, leader of the Official Monster Raving Loony party, November 4 1992

It's just occurred to me, I've been up to my neck in this stuff all month.
John Major as he shovelled compost around the base of a newly planted tree at Sawtry Village College, November 14 1992

We still go to our bank managers for loans and advice, comfort and succour, but to whom do bank managers go when they need a bit of comfort and succour? To head office? Oh, come on. Going to a bank's head office for tenderness is rather like going to the Devil for moral guidance, or the Home Office for a visa to get you out of Bosnia.
Miles Kington, the Times, November 19 1992

This little old lady's home was wrecked by fire. She was not insured. So taxpayers are going to pay £60 million to fix it again. This old man is 84, lives in a cottage which floods, is riddled with damp and eats up

his pension in heating bills. The royals want to put his rent up 50%.
Daily Mirror, after Windsor Castle fire, November 25 1992

Mr Major has only a short time . . . to move Mr Lamont from a post in which he is neither use nor ornament. He should not delay beyond Christmas, nor wait until the first cuckoo of spring.
Sunday Times, December 7 1992

Brilliant though the conduct of our operations in support of the UN in Bosnia is, I am still unclear as to what its aim is.
Paddy Ashdown, December 16 1992

Mr Major has issued a citizen's charter. It is as worthless as the scrap of paper Neville Chamberlain brought back from Munich.
Paul Johnson, Sunday Times, December 21 1992

This is the thanks I get for being a good British businessman.
Margaret Thatcher responding to MPs' allegations about arms dealing, January 4 1993

Churchill made blunders in his life. As chancellor he made Norman Lamont look like an economic maestro.
Peter Hitchens, Daily Express, January 5 1993

What is really sleazy is the number of Tories sticking their snouts in a trough of their own making.
Richard Littlejohn on leading Conservatives on the payrolls of former nationalised industries, the Sun, January 19 1993

He is brighter and sharper than most of his Cabinet colleagues. But then so is Trigger.
Richard Littlejohn on Kenneth Clarke, the Sun, February 5 1993

What the hell's the point of electing MPs to represent us if the Government cheats and changes the rules? To tell MPs that their votes in parliament are worthless

reduces democracy to farce.
Sun editorial on the Government's handling
of the Maastricht treaty vote, February 18 1993

Society needs to condemn a little more and
understand a little less.
John Major on crime, in an interview with the
Mail on Sunday, February 21 1993

He is the man who has turned sloth into an
art form, indolence into a political
philosophy, inaction into a declaration of
intent. He is a man whose family coat of
arms ought to be a snail rampant, with
crossed pillows and a couple of aspirins
below.
Sir Norman Fowler on John Smith,
March 2 1993

Mr Clark: Well, it's our old friend, being
economical, isn't it?
Mr Robertson: With the truth?
Mr Clark: With the actualité.
Courtroom exchange between Alan Clark, for-
mer minister, and Geoffrey Robertson QC about
a minute in which Clark was alleged to have
said that machine tools destined for military
use in Iraq were for "general engineering
purposes", March 3 1993

Nobody wants a tax on knowledge. But
who could argue convincingly against a
tax on tripe?
Richard Ingrams on the possibility of Vat on
books, the Observer, March 8 1993

John Major has the great political luck of

not possessing on obvious successor.
Leader in the Times, April 9 1993

I am ashamed of the European Community
that this is happening in the heart of
Europe and they have not done anything
about it. There is no conscience. We have
been like accomplices to massacre.
Lady Thatcher on Bosnia, April 13 1993

The political left in Britain has become
about as dry as a Chippendales' condom.
Elsie Owusu, editor of Body Politic,
April 24 1993

The Government are beginning to
resemble Eldorado — rotten actors, lousy
script and no popularity
Tony Banks, House of Commons, May 18 1993

I am afraid most Tory money is raised by
the selling of jam, more often than not sold
for less than it will cost the donor to make
the stuff.
Alistair McAlpine, June 25 1993

Ideally, a chief secretary to the Treasury
should be flinty-eyed, stone-hearted and
odious. I believe that I fit the bill.
Michael Portillo, Hansard, July 15 1993

The problem is that while there may be
only three in the Cabinet, there are a lot
more among the lower echelons of
Government who could have their parent-
age questioned.
Gordon Greig, the Daily Mail, July 27 1993

POLITICAL DIARY
(OCTOBER '93 - OCTOBER '94)

1993

October 5-8	Conservative party conference in Blackpool

October 13-14 and December 2 Extra sessions of the European Parliament to take place in Brussels

October 28-30	Plaid Cymru conference in Cardiff
November 14-16	CBI conference in Harrogate

November 11   Budget Statement — the first unified Budget in which public expenditure and revenue raising measures will be announced together.

December 10-11	European heads of state and government summit in Brussels.
December 15	Final Gatt talks in Geneva

1994

1994 -   German Bundestag elections (last elected for maximum four-year term on Dec 2 1990)

1994	Danish elections must take place before December 12
1994	Greek parliament (300-member Vouli) to be re-elected by April/May
January 1	Greece takes over EC presidency from Belgium

February 4-6   Labour party European conference running concurrently with Local Government Conference in Glasgow

March 9-11	TUC Women's conference in Scarborough
May 3	Netherlands parliamentary elections (both chambers)

May 6   The Channel Tunnel (or Chunnel) rail link is expected to be officially opened by the Queen and French president Francois Mitterrand. They plan to travel in high-speed Eurostar trains from London and Paris respectively and meet in mid-tunnel for the formal ceremony. The Anglo-French tunnel operator, Eurotunnel, expects to be operating freight — and possibly passenger — trains before the opening date. For the first time in 10,000 years Britain will be physically joined to the European continent. The twin tunnels are 31.03 miles (49.94km) long, the world's second longest vehicular tunnels. The total cost was estimated in mid-1993 to be £9.9 billion, more than double its original 1987 estimate of £4.7 billion. Planned opening dates included June 15 1993. Chunnel builders Transmanche Link, a consortium of five British and five French contractors, were frequently in dispute with Eurotunnel over the mounting costs of the project, including in late 1991 a High Court action to prevent work being halted

June	European Parliament elections (probably week ending June 9)

June 6   Fiftieth anniversary of D-Day, when Allied forces landed in Normandy in the largest seaborne invasion in history, code-named Operation Overlord

June 12	Luxembourg national parliamentary (Chamber of Deputies) elections
June 24-5	European heads of state and government summit in Corfu.

September 5-9	TUC conference in Blackpool
September 17-22	Liberal Democrats conference in Brighton
September 21-24	Scottish National Party conference in Inverness
October	Plaid Cymru conference in Llandudno
October 3-7	Labour party conference in Blackpool
October 4-7	Conservative party conference in Bournemouth

APPOINTMENTS

1992

April 13 Lord WADDINGTON (62): former Conservative home secretary, appointed Governor of Bermuda

April 24 PATTEN, Chris (47): former Conservative environment secretary and party chairman, defeated at Bath in the election, named Governor of Hong Kong

May 6 Lord WALKER (Peter Walker (60): former Conservative Cabinet minister, to head new Urban Regeneration Agency

May 12. SUTHERLAND, Stewart (51), Vice Chancellor of London University: to be HM Chief Inspector of Schools, initially part-time

September 9: MIDDLETON, Peter (52): chief executive Thomas Cook, once a monk, to be chief executive of Lloyd's

August 12. Lord Justice BINGHAM (58): to succeed Lord Donaldson as Master of the Rolls from September 30

September 10 Lord WOOLF (60) Lord of Appeal in Ordinary

October 20. BRITTAN, Sir Leon (52) and MILLAN, Bruce (65): to continue as EC Commissioners

October 23. CONDON, Paul (45): appointed Metropolitan Police Commissioner to succeed Sir Peter Imbert (retiring) from January 1 1993

November 5 Lord RICHARD (60): former Labour minister, EC commissioner, UK permanent representative at the UN, succeeds Lord Cledwyn as leader of Labour peers

November 17 OUSELEY, Herman (46): to head Commission for Racial Equality

December 3 ODGERS, Graeme (58): to succeed Sir Sidney Lipworth as chairman of Monopolies and Mergers Commission. Formerly head of Alfred McAlpine, construction company

December 16 JINKINSON, Alan (57), former general secretary of Nalgo, general secretary of the new merged union UNISON from July 1 1993

December 21 LEWIS, Derek (46), chairman of a satellite TV company, to be director-general of the Prison Service from April 1 1993

1993

January 2 STRACHAN, Valerie (52): promoted from deputy chairman to chairman, Board of Customs and Excise

January 14. HOUGHAM, John:(55): chairman of ACAS

January 22. GEORGE, Eddie (54): deputy Governor of Bank of England, promoted to Governor; PENNANT-REA, Rupert (44): editor of Economist, becomes Deputy Governor

March 2. DEARING, Sir Ron (62): former head of the Post Office, to be head of new School Curriculum and Assessment Authority — preferred to David Pascall (contract not renewed)

April 28 BAHL, Kamlesh (36): Ugandan-born woman lawyer to head Equal Opportunities Commission.

June 4 Lady HOWE (Elspeth Howe) (61) former chair of the EOC, chair of the Broadcasting Standards Council from June 16 1993

June 9 SUTHERLAND, Peter (47), Irish lawyer, former EC Commissioner, to be director-general, GATT, from July 1 1993

June 23 ROWE-BEDDOE, David (55), chair of Cavendish Service Group to head Welsh Development Agency

DIS-APPOINTMENTS

MELLOR, David, heritage secretary: on account of an actress and the gift of a holiday

LAMONT, Norman, chancellor: he regretted nothing at Newbury

ATTALI, Jacques, President of the European Bank for Reconstruction and Development, after spending too lavishly closer to home

MATES, Michael, N.Ireland minister: connections with a fugitive financier